THE FUTURE OF THE INTERNATIONAL LABOUR ORGANIZATION IN THE GLOBAL ECONOMY

The International Labour Organization was created in 1919, as part of the Treaty of Versailles that ended the First World War, to reflect the belief that universal and lasting peace can be accomplished only if it is based on social justice. As the oldest organisation in the UN system, approaching its 100th anniversary in 2019, the ILO faces unprecedented strains and challenges. Since before the financial crisis, the global economy has tested the limits of a regulatory regime which was conceived in 1919. The organisation's founders only entrusted it with balancing social progress with the constraints of an interconnected open economy, but gambled almost entirely on tools of persuasion to ensure that this would happen. Whether that gamble is still capable of paying-off is the subject of this book, by a former ILO insider with an unrivalled knowledge of its work.

The book forms part of a broader inquiry into the relevance of founding institutional principles to today's context, and strives to show that the bet made on persuasion may yet pay off. In part, the text argues that there may be little alternative anyway, showing that the pathways to more binding solutions are fraught with difficulty. It also shows the ILO's considerable future potential for promoting effective, universal regulations by extending its tools of persuasion in as yet insufficiently explored directions. Starting with an examination of how the organisation's institutional context differs from 93 years ago, the author goes on to evaluate the prospects of numerous proposals put forward today, including the trade/labour linkage, but going beyond this.

As a case study in how strategic choices can be made under legal, social and institutional constraints, the book should be valuable not only to those with an interest in the ILO, but to anyone who studies international organisation, labour law, law and society or political economy.

The Future of the International Labour Organization in the Global Economy

Francis Maupain

•HART•
PUBLISHING
OXFORD AND PORTLAND, OREGON
2013

Published in the United Kingdom by Hart Publishing Ltd
16C Worcester Place, Oxford, OX1 2JW
Telephone: +44 (0)1865 517530
Fax: +44 (0)1865 510710
E-mail: mail@hartpub.co.uk
Website: http://www.hartpub.co.uk

Published in North America (US and Canada) by
Hart Publishing
c/o International Specialized Book Services
920 NE 58th Avenue, Suite 300
Portland, OR 97213-3786
USA
Tel: +1 503 287 3093 or toll-free: (1) 800 944 6190
Fax: +1 503 280 8832
E-mail: orders@isbs.com
Website: http://www.isbs.com

British Library Cataloguing in Publication Data
Data Available

ISBN: 978-1-84946-502-1

Typeset by Hope Services, Abingdon
Printed and bound in Great Britain by
TJ International Ltd, Padstow, Cornwall

FOREWORD

It is a privilege and a pleasure to introduce the English version of Francis Maupain's very important book on the future of the International Labour Organization and international labour regulation. Dr Maupain is an 'inside' expert. He spent most of his professional life as an international lawyer and civil servant working in the ILO serving directly five successive Directors-General. No one is better placed than him to understand the objectives and working methods of the organisation, and to offer valuable insights into its possible future.

The mission of the ILO is of great relevance in the modern globalised economy. Workers in many countries still suffer from degrading and dangerous conditions of work, as recent tragic incidents in Bangladesh and China demonstrate. Because of non-ratification of fundamental conventions by large countries such as the United States and China, the ILO-guaranteed right to form and join trade unions and engage in collective bargaining covers less than 50 per cent of the world's workers. Women and other disadvantaged groups still suffer from widespread discrimination and harassment at work. Forced labour and child labour continue to exist. In 1818, Robert Owen, a British mill owner, appealed to the European powers who were signing the Treaty of Aix-la-Chapelle to protect the new working classes emerging from the industrial revolution from 'the causes which perpetually generate misery in human society', and 170 years ago Daniel Legrand, an Alsatian manufacturer, argued that international regulation of labour was the only way to protect industrialising countries from unfair competition by countries that do not adopt humanitarian labour standards. Yet, despite a century of effort and achievement by the ILO, including 189 Conventions and 202 Recommendations, the 1998 Declaration of Fundamental Principles and Rights at Work and the Decent Work programme, the ideals of Owen, Legrand and the founders of the ILO are still far from being been universally realised.

There are many voices that say that the ILO has outlived its usefulness. In particular, there are serious doubts about its standard-setting activities, most recently evidenced in strong criticism by the Employers group of longstanding interpretations adopted by the Committee on Freedom of Association. The ILO's principle of tripartism or 'social dialogue', based on the free balancing of worker and employer interests under the mediation of governments, has also been attacked. There are some who would like to see the ILO reduced to a kind of international development agency focusing on a few Third World countries. The core issue which the author magisterially examines is whether the ILO has the institutional capacity to fulfil its mandate in the circumstances of the twenty-first century. He offers carefully argued proposals for the 'institutional reinvention' of the organisation: ensuring universal and effective diffusion of international labour standards and social dialogue; using the opportunities offered by globalisation, such as education and training, to develop social protection systems that facilitate adjustment and labour market regulation that ensures an equitable redistribution of the benefits of growth; and the promotion of greater policy coherence among sister organisations such as the WTO and IMF. He shows that these objectives can be reached without sacrificing tripartism; indeed, success depends on the active participation of all the ILO's constituents.

We are fortunate that Dr Maupain is making his thought-provoking work available to a wider audience. It is essential reading for those who work in or advise international organisations, the governments of Member States and multinational corporations and trade unions. This book should be on the reading lists of all students of international organisations and of international labour regulation.

Professor Sir Bob Hepple, QC FBA
Emeritus Professor Law, University of Cambridge
4 June 2013

ACKNOWLEDGMENTS

The reflections to be found in this book are the fruit of a long experience in the service of the International Labour Organization (ILO), and of the no doubt unique privilege I had of working in succession directly with five of its Directors-General.

That privilege, together with the wealth of professional experience it earned me (almost in spite of myself) created a kind of moral debt to draw out whatever lessons might be valuable for the future of the institution that had offered them to me, and that will soon see the dawning of its second century. That debt is owed, in fact, not only to the institution but equally to the quartet of mentors who after guiding me through my years of apprenticeship, later became true friends: Nicolas Valticos, Francis Wolf, Felice Morgenstern and Jacques Lemoine.

Despite their foundation in my own experience, it will be seen that the resulting reflections do not cling to anecdote. Rather, they aim at finding a common thread in developments that day-to-day concerns often left undetectable, and at finding coherence which some will no doubt find excessive. To that end, they are as-of-yet incomplete reflections, addressing only part of a subject too vast to be covered in a single volume.

These reflections, it should still be emphasised, are personal ones. As much as they are intended to aid the ILO by stimulating debate on the edge of its centenary, they are not intended to commit the organisation; nor could they, given that I ended my service there several years ago.

I must in this regard express first and foremost my gratitude to the International Institute of Labour Studies, and to its Director Raymond Torres. In offering me a place as a 'Fellow' once I left active service, and in agreeing to publish these reflections, he submitted me to a yoke as imperceptible as it was merciless.

Imperceptible, inasmuch as, while sparing neither criticism nor advice when it was requested, he offered me full freedom to pursue my reflections where they took me, sometimes leading quite far from the well-marked path of orthodoxy. Such freedom, I must say, is among the keys to the ILO's future. Indeed, only such freedom is capable of stimulating the free and informed debate on the main institutional issues which will shape the ILO's capacity to respond in a credible and sustainable manner to the challenges of the financialised global economy.

Merciless, because the hospitality of the Institute nonetheless left me with an inescapable responsibility to produce something. It thus abandoned me to a discipline which, left to my own devices, I would likely have been incapable of mustering. Without that discipline, I would probably have abandoned the intellectual and material investment required by an undertaking whose magnitude, by naïvely convincing myself I knew the topic, I grossly underestimated at the outset.

I must also give my thanks to everyone within the International Labour Office who interested themselves in the project and agreed to contribute to it in one form or another; contributions all the more valuable given that they do not necessarily share, it is needless to say, the overall theme or its specific analyses: to the current and former executive directors of sector 1, Kari Tapiola and Guy Ryder, who agreed to provide logistical support at a critical moment; to Emmanuel Reynaud, Tomi Kohiyama and Jordi Agusti-Panareda, for their careful reading of the preliminary draft and the useful comments they contributed toward its revision; to Xavier Beaudonnet, to whom I am indebted for the comments on both substance and form, many of which subsequently made their way into the French version; to Mathieu Charpe for some aspects of Part I, and Franz Ebert and Konstantinos Papadakis for their very important contributions to Parts III and IV; and finally, to Ariel Golan at the ILO Library, whose knowledge of ILO sources seemed at times as inexhaustible as his helpfulness.

Outside the Office, I want especially to thank Pieter Jan Kuijper, Ludivine Tamiotti and Pieter Leeknegt for everything touching on the WTO, as well as Alain Supiot, Brian Langille, Bruce Jenks, Niels Blokker and Luis Hinojosa for the overall interest and support they provided to this project, and for valuable suggestions they each provided me on one specific aspect or another. Needless to say, none of this assistance makes these individuals in any way responsible for my ideas, nor for any of those parts of the remaining text still sure to generate controversy.

Thanks to the International Institute for Labour Studies, I also benefitted from the substantial support of successive generations of interns, including Dieudonné Somda, Roberto Recalde, Marie Walter and Marieke Louis (whose research on decent work, along with proofreading and development of the French version, aided me immensely in bringing the text to completion).

My gratitude must however extend in a very particular sense to Liam McHugh-Russell, whose knowledge of the literature, intellectual rigor, patience and attention to detail in the finalisation of the text and references proved to be literally irreplaceable. Without him and his assistance, this undertaking – and especially in its English form – could not have come together, nor contributed to this decisive point in the ILO's decisions about its destiny.

CONTENTS

ABBREVIATIONS

ACP	Africa, the Caribbean and the Pacific
CSR	corporate social responsibility
DSB	WTO Dispute Settlement Body
DSU	WTO Dispute Settlement Understanding
DWCP	Decent Work Country Programme
ECJ	European Court of Justice
FDI	foreign direct investment
GATS	General Agreement on Trade in Services
GATT	General Agreement on Tariffs and Trade
GSP	Generalised System of Preferences
ICJ	International Court of Justice
IFA	International Framework Agreement
IFC	International Finance Corporation
IFI	international financial institution
ILO	International Labour Organization
IOE	International Organization of Employers
ISO	International Organization for Standardization
ITUC	International Trade Union Confederation
MIGA	Multilateral Investment Guarantee Agency
NAALC	North American Agreement on Labour Cooperation
OTCA	Omnibus Foreign Trade and Competitiveness Act (US)
PPM	process and production method
RBSA	Regular Budget Supplementary Account
TBT	Technical Barriers to Trade
TC	technical cooperation
USTR	United States Trade Representative
WTO	World Trade Organization

TABLE OF CASES

European Court of Human Rights

European Court of Justice

GATT

PCIJ

WTO

TABLE OF INTERNATIONAL MATERIALS

Primary Texts

International materials

Introduction: Whither the ILO's Second Century? Persuasion at its Limits in the Global Economy

Just seven years remain before the International Labour Organization (ILO) celebrates its centenary. Such longevity makes the organisation unique among its peers.[1] Born out of the Treaty of Versailles, it remains one of the rare chapters not to have been subsequently disavowed by history.

This looming anniversary will no doubt spark ruminations on the fate of the organisation and draw keen attention to its remarkable resilience across the convulsions and upheavals of the twentieth century. In that vein, the International Labour Office ('the Office') has already launched a 'Century Project' to address various aspects and episodes of its history; these efforts can only be warmly welcomed. The reflections collected here are, however, conducted completely independently of this enterprise. They have a perspective that is neither hagiographic nor retrospective, but deliberately prospective and assiduously institutional.

At the heart of this book is a daunting question: how can an organisation whose structure, mandate and resources were developed almost a century ago pretend to retain relevance and effectiveness in the face of realities that have virtually nothing in common with those of its origins?

The issue, of course, is not whether the ILO, already fondly regarded as the 'older sister' in the United Nations family at the celebration of its *fiftieth* anniversary, will survive the pomp of its hundredth birthday.[2] Indeed, just as 'each thing, as far as it can by its own power, strives to persevere in its being'[3], the tendency of things to go on existing is certainly no less pronounced in an international bureaucracy than it is for a national one. Indeed, given the extraordinary resilience it

[1] It is precisely this longevity that led Ernst B Haas half a century ago, at the approach of the organisation's 50th anniversary, to take the ILO as a case study to develop and test his functionalist thesis in *Beyond the Nation-State: Functionalism and International Organization* (Stanford, CA, Stanford University Press, 1964). See also the recent edition of the same title (ECPR Press, 2008), which included a new introduction from Peter M Haas, John Ruggie and others. Jasmien van Daele had good reason, in her introduction to Jasmien van Daele and others, *ILO Histories: Essays on the International Labour Organization and Its Impact on the World During the Twentieth Century* (Bern, Peter Lang, 2010) to express surprise at the lack of interest in both Haas' work and that of the ILO's own Robert Cox. But this simply confirms that we may well do with functionalism what Molière's M. Jourdain did with prose . . .

[2] Including, presumably, the award of a second Nobel Peace Prize . . .

[3] Baruch Spinoza in Edwin Curley, *A Spinoza Reader, Ethics and other works* (Princeton, Princeton University Press 1994), Part III Prop. 6, 159

demonstrated across the turbulence and tragedies of the twentieth century, there are good reasons to believe that this tendency is particularly pronounced in the case of the ILO.

Nor does the problem lie in the concern expressed in some quarters that the organisation must choose between survival and loyalty to its founding purposes. As will be seen, this claim sets up an artificial dilemma based on questionable premises.

Indeed, the issue is best cast in terms of the continuing validity of institutional choices (one might even venture to call them gambles) made at its founding, now that the organisation confronts a globalised and financialised economy whose true colours were revealed during the 2007 crisis and its aftermath.

This book is dedicated to addressing exactly this question. Before getting into the thick of it, however, it is worth clearly stating the two tensions which will ultimately structure the ILO's institutional future.

I. The (False) Dilemma: Survival or Integrity

During the last century's political convulsions, through 90 years of radical transformations in the international system, from the multipolar world of the early twentieth century, through the bipolar world of the Cold War, past the beginnings of fleeting unipolar globalisation, and into today's possibly apolar system,[4] the ILO has been subjected to a series of 'stress tests' more taxing than any bank will probably ever have to face. Just a few benchmarks will likely suffice to prove the point. And that is why concerns expressed about the organisation's future are not a matter of its ability to survive as such, but more a question of its ability to stay true to its purpose.

A. Resilient Elder Sister of the UN Family

Almost as soon as it had found its footing, the ILO was forced to face its first ordeal. Only a decade after its founding, the Great Depression seized the greater part of a generation with the 'injustice, hardship and privation' that the organisation had been created to alleviate, and the world would only be rescued from the scourge of economic collapse by the eruption of a new world war that starkly rebuked the Constitution's promise of a 'universal and lasting peace' based on social justice.

Under the weight of these setbacks, logic would have seen the ILO swallowed up by the sinking of the League of Nations, on board which it had originally set sail.

[4] *cf* Bertrand Badie, *La diplomatie de connivence: Les dérives oligarchiques du système international* (Paris, La Découverte, 2011).

It would not have survived if it had not set up camp with the Allies early on, first emigrating to Montreal and then lending its support, from 1941 onward, to the economic and social principles of the Atlantic Charter. There was no exaggeration in its boast at the time that it possessed 'the confidence of the free peoples'.[5]

Even the victory of the 'free peoples' however, was not enough to secure the organisation's future. The Allies had intended to replace the League of Nations complex with a completely new structure under the banner of the United Nations. There was some reason to believe – or, for the ILO, to fear – that the United Nations would be called upon to perform the ILO's functions in a more integrated way.[6] With the support of the International Labour Conference (ILC), however, those remaining in charge of the Office (reduced to a rump-secretariat in Montreal)[7] succeeded in mobilising the energies of tripartite constituents to break the legal ties between the ILO and the League, and to vindicate the ILO as the competent body 'for the accomplishment of the purposes set forth [in its Constitution]'.[8] Obviously, the organisation's tripartite structure was also instrumental in this reprieve. Given the urgency of reconstruction efforts and the risk of social unrest rising to epidemic proportions in countries devastated by war, this structure provided an important guarantee to workers and employers that they would continue to be formally represented, and to have their voices heard in the new system.

Just as this major challenge was subsiding, the onset of the Cold War and the rise of the decolonisation movement put the ILO in a completely new context: these changes not only meant an influx of new Members and a brisk stride toward true universality, but participation in ILO governance by states and regimes each staunchly proclaiming their commitment to the organisation's goals of progress and social justice, but nonetheless radically divergent in their understanding of those goals. These differences, along with even greater disagreements about how to *achieve* those goals, not only disrupted the organisation's normal operations, but threatened its very existence.

In this context, two phenomena combined to put the organisation's governance institutions out of sync with the logic of tripartism: on the one hand, the de facto alliance on numerous issues between the Eastern bloc countries and the

[5] See ILO, *Record of Proceedings* (New York and Washington DC, ILC, 27 October–6 November 1941) 168.

[6] Louis B Sohn, 'The Contribution of the International Labour Organization to the Concept of Economic, Social and Cultural Rights' in René-Jean Dupuy and Linos-Alexandre Sicilianos (eds), *Mélanges en l'honneur de Nicolas Valticos : droit et justice* (Paris, Pedone, 1999) 603.

[7] *cf* Wilfred Jenks, 'L'OIT en temps de guerre' (brochure edited by the Canadian Department of Labour on the occasion of the ILO's Fiftieth Anniversary, 1969), who concluded from the experience, 'La seule conclusion que l'on en puisse tirer, est que l'avenir comme le passé, sera déterminé par la mesure dans laquelle on saura choisir, dans le flux et reflux des affaires humaines, le moment opportun pour mettre les voiles' ['The only conclusion that can be drawn, is that future as the past, will be determined by the extent within which we will know how to choose, in the flow and ebb of human affairs, the appropriate time to set sail', trans].

[8] Agreement between the United Nations and the International Labour Organization (signed 30 May 1946, entered into force 14 December 1946) 29(4) *Official Bulletin of the ILO*, art 1.

developing country 'Group of 77'; and, on the other hand, the discrepancy between the demands of 'internal' tripartism, focused on the representativity and absolute autonomy of the groups, and the realities of what could be called 'external' tripartism[9] in some of its Members in which this independence was a fiction. These two phenomena frequently led to the formation of 'automatic' majorities on the most sensitive of political issues. Indeed, this situation was ultimately behind the US withdrawal from the organisation in 1977.[10] Under the light shed by the letter giving notice of withdrawal (sent by none other than Henry Kissinger)[11] the US departure brought to a critical point the existential challenge the Cold War posed to the ILO. Not only did the departure substantially hollow out its financial resources, but (and we will return to this dimension) it also seemed likely to deliver a *coup de grace* to the pretence that the organisation could be *universal* while remaining true to its *tripartite* structure and philosophy.

As the Solidarnosc struggles intensified in Poland, however, the United States quickly realised that the ILO could be a key actor in confronting a Soviet model now clearly on the defensive. Hence their very rapid return[12] to the fold in 1980.

Just as they were inaugurated by the happy return of the United States, the 1980s also came to a close with a certain degree of triumph for the ILO. Indeed, marked as it was by the fall of the Berlin Wall, it would be hard to deny that the decade represented a ringing victory for the organisation. In the face of the collapse of the totalitarian alternative, the period stood out as a vindication (however temporary) of the organisation's model of social progress, based on pluralism and the free conciliation of interests.

This celebration was followed by two decades of considerable effort to modernise the organisation and its work. While only the warp and weave of those efforts is provided in what follows, suffice it to say that the threads running through the period are epitomised in the 1998 Declaration on Fundamental Principles and Rights at Work, the launch of the Decent Work strategy and the adoption of the Declaration on Social Justice for a Fair Globalization in 2008.[13]

[9] See Francis Maupain, 'L'OIT, la justice sociale et la mondialisation' (1999) 278 *Recueil des Cours de l'Académie de Droit International* 331.

[10] The withdrawal was announced in response to the vote of the ILC admitting the Palestinian Liberation Organisation as an observer, though it also followed on the heels of a series of other incidents, ranging from the appointment of a Soviet citizen as a deputy Director-General to statements at the ILC condemning the policy of racial discrimination and trade union rights violations committed by Israel. See Yves Beigbeder, 'The United States' Withdrawal from the International Labor Organization' (1979) 34 *Industrial Relations* 226.

[11] Kissinger's letter suggested that the withdrawal was motivated by the erosion of tripartism, the politicisation of the representative bodies and a tendency to apply a 'double standard' vis-à-vis breaches of obligations undertaken by bloc countries.

[12] Especially compared to their long absence from UNESCO.

[13] For more details of these initiatives, see Chapter 3.

B. Facing Existential Angst

If these innovative recipes have provided an undoubted boon to the ILO's public reputation, the new menu has not been to everyone's taste. Indeed, the partial focusing of normative efforts on workers' fundamental rights has given rise to reservations, and even some harsh criticisms,[14] some of which have been levelled against the Decent Work strategy as well, though perhaps on a reduced scale.[15] While informed by a diversity of legal, economic and sociological perspectives, these criticisms have drawn from a common concern that the pursuit of these changes entails a departure from, or even a betrayal of, the ILO's basic regulatory function.

Indeed, some see a future where the organisation's constitutional functions, and its distinguishing normative activities in particular, are put in stasis,[16] allowing the ILO to follow the example set by the United Nations Industrial Development Organization and embrace full membership in the club of international development agencies, though perhaps with a special expertise in the social dimensions of development.

These warnings seem to have aroused little alarm within the Office or among the organisation's constituents. Indeed, they could easily be waved off as insignificant in light of the highly successful public relations impact of the slogans being criticised. In the circumstances, those questioning these adjustments in reverence of an essentially fixed identity could themselves be faulted for nostalgic overindulgence, or even for practising full-blown institutional fetishism. After all, would it really be so problematic for the ILO to shed some of its historical practices, if it ended up better positioned to meet the challenges of today's profoundly changed world of work?

Unfortunately, the underlying concerns cannot be so easily brushed off.

First of all, these changes are not solely a matter of abstract principle: they could easily entail very tangible implications for the ILO, an impact on its financial resources being far from least among them. The choice under consideration – unmooring the organisation from its original foundations and staking its future on social and economic development functions just as easily served by other entities – is not without certain risks in the context of a financial crisis which has placed major contributors under an extremely rigorous weight-loss regime. Obviously, the ILO's institutional functions have an important symbolic dimension, and it is not unreasonable to imagine that the erosion of the ILO's

[14] To get an idea of the extensive literature on this subject, see in particular the debate among Philip Alston, Brian Langille and the author in June 2005, 16(3) *European Journal of International Law*, 467–480. This literature is addressed more closely in Part III.

[15] See, eg Guy Standing, 'The ILO: An Agency for Globalization?' (2008) 39 *Development and Change* 355, 370–71.

[16] This proposal for the ILO's future gave rise to the harsh criticisms of Guy Standing and his resistance to the Decent Work strategy in particular, ibid.

distinctiveness might tempt Members into, as it were, putting the organisation on its own diet.[17]

Beyond the instrumental risks of change, however, moving in this direction may also be an intrinsic mistake. After all, the social impacts of the crisis have highlighted that the ILO's constitutional functions not only set it apart, but also make it highly relevant in the current context. The specific nature of these functions however begs to be clarified. If criticisms of alleged ILO drift have the merit of connecting the ILO's future not only to its survival, but to its institutional identity, their inherent weakness is that they reduce that identity to its principal means of action, rather than seeking to identify the integral functions those means are meant to serve.

C. A *Raison d'être* that Rests on Two Key Functions

Though not always made explicit, criticisms of reform have to date taken it as a given that the ILO's identity is founded on standards or, put differently, on its so-called normative 'function'. Leaving aside for the moment the complexities of the concept of 'function', the 'normative function' can more straightforwardly be defined as the process whereby the objectives and principles enshrined in the Preamble to the ILO Constitution are translated into standards taking the form of either Conventions[18] or Recommendations.[19]

As widespread as it may be, the view that this 'normative function' is at the heart of the ILO's raison d'être nevertheless reflects a conflation of the ILO's overall mandate with its particular means of action.[20] No doubt, normative activities are the backbone of ILO efforts to serve its constitutional objectives. And, as will be shown later, it is indisputably through this mechanism that the organisation plays a 'magisterial' role for its Members, giving precise content to the goals of progress and social justice enshrined in its constitution;[21] undeniably, it thereby provides

[17] This risk is far from academic: the decision by the British government to withdraw non-mandatory funding from ILO programs was no doubt influenced by the particularly hard impact of the financial crisis on the country's finances. If the British unions argued that the methodology of the government's review of this funding 'did not adequately take into account the actual nature and mandate of the ILO', the UK government could hardly take the full brunt of the blame for treating the ILO as if it were an aid organisation. See Brendan Barber, 'TUC response to DFID Multilateral Aid Review and the ILO' (Trades Union Congress, 9 May 2011), available at www.tuc.org.uk/international/tuc-19553-f0.cfm.

[18] Conventions are treaties, which are therefore binding on Members once they have been ratified.

[19] Recommendations cannot be ratified. Members are encouraged to apply them, but they create no legal effect except to the degree that they are incorporated into domestic law.

[20] This point was underlined by the Director-General in his 1997 annual report: 'ILO standards are not an end in themselves; they are one of the means – undeniably the most important – that the Organization has at its disposal to attain its objectives and ensure that the values enshrined in its Constitution and the Declaration of Philadelphia are put into practice.' ILO, *Report of the Director-General* (ILC, 85th Session, Geneva, June 1997) 3. In the same sense, see ILO, *Report V: Strengthening the Capacity of the ILO to Assist its Members' Efforts to Promote its Objectives in the Context of Globalization* (ILC, 96th Session, Geneva, 30 May–15 June 2007) para 23.

[21] 'Magisterial' is used here according to the positive sense of its etymological roots, of carrying some degree of moral authority and providing edification and guidance. It is not meant to carry the negative

the benchmark against which the reality of such progress can be measured amongst its Members.

However, it must be seen at the same time that this activity has no intrinsic relevance and importance in its own right. The ILO's true raison d'être cannot be delimited by reference to its 'normative function'; after all, its standards hardly makes it exceptional among international organisations. Rather, the ILO's unique ability to impact on living standards and working conditions is entirely dependent on two factors: the *legitimacy* conferred by universal, tripartite debate, and its *institutional capacity* to ensure that those standards are actually translated into national legislation and practice. These factors in turn help to identify the two specific functions which its founders intended the ILO to perform in the international system and which give its standards their relevance and impact.

The first, what might be called the 'social dialogue' function, is political: to promote a model of social progress whose legitimacy is based on the free balancing of worker and employer interests under the careful mediation of governments. The second, 'regulating interdependence' function is economic: to reconcile the goal of social progress outlined in the Constitution with the constraints posed by the openness and interdependence of economies understood as necessary to fuel that progress.

It probably goes without saying that neither of these functions has lost its currency or relevance under the realities of the global, financialised economy – quite the contrary! The real question, and the real dilemma faced by the ILO, concerns its capacity to fulfil these goals effectively in this new context, using institutional choices (or gambles) originally made by its founders in 1919 – choices which have remained fundamentally unchanged ever since.

II. The Real Challenge: Are 100-Year-Old Institutional Choices Still Valid in the Twenty-first Century?

When the ILO was founded, the realities of the historical moment demanded particular forms of compromise between the ideal and the possible, forcing the ILO's founders to lay all their chips on a set of unproven institutional structures. In the case of the social dialogue function, focused on the universal promotion of the tripartite model of social progress, they were forced to stake its success on formal institutional *universality*. When it came to the matter of reconciling social progress

connotations of presumptuousness or arrogance implied by some modern usage. The point is that the standards function, even without universal ratification, and can give substance to particular claims for justice at work, especially for certain groups of workers. Indeed, this 'magisterial' function not only provides moral clout that may be useful in particular political struggles, but also has a very tangible impact, particularly by providing a regulatory model to countries which do not have legislation in certain areas, or which hope to revise existing legislation, or who lack a history of legislating on a particular subject matter.

with economic interdependence, however, they made an even more audacious gamble: trying to achieve that reconciliation through standards measures whose effectiveness, when push comes to shove, relies only on the ILO's capacity to *persuade*. As will be seen, both bets were up against tough odds.

A. Tripartism and the Wager on Universalism

The social dialogue function finds its genesis not only in the founders' partiality for a model of social progress based on a free meeting of workers' and employers' interests under the neutral mediation of governments, but also in the degree to which that model's effectiveness depends on wide diffusion. This 'reformist' option is given expression in the tripartite structure of the ILO's representative bodies, a structure that is (somewhat ironically) revolutionary, in the sense that it places the representatives of employers and workers on an equal footing with government representatives in decision-making. In this regard, the ILO remains unique in the UN landscape.

The reformist option was directly opposed to a model of 'democratic centralism' proposed (or rather imposed) at the same time by the Bolshevik revolution. It is difficult today to appreciate the virulence of the attacks it faced at the time. The Third International swore to wage war without mercy against the International Labour Office, and against the International Federation of Trade Unions (IFTU), which it considered 'a rallying point for the international bourgeoisie'.[22] Not that there was any love lost on the ILO side: not to be outdone, the first director of the ILO, Albert Thomas, denounced 'the powerful fascination' Bolshevism exerted on the masses, and questioned its ability to do anything other than 'organise a Jacobin dictatorship on the one hand, and . . . cause discontent and poverty on the other'.[23]

The vehemence of this mutual animosity makes it all the more remarkable that the founders staked the organisation's prospects on the promise of universality, opening the organisation to any state, whether it stood among the victors or the defeated at war's end, and no matter the stripe of its political or social regime.

(i) From the Winning Gamble on Universal Composition

Of course, this bet was entirely consistent with the values of dignity, freedom and non-discrimination enshrined in the Constitution; and clearly so, insomuch as these values would be meaningless if they were not projected and practised at the level of organisational membership. The underlying logic was beautifully summed up at the height of the Cold War by a British government delegate to the International Labour Conference:

[22] Antony Alcock, *The History of the International Labour Organization* (London, Macmillan, 1971) 128.

[23] Albert Thomas, 'The International Labour Organization: Its Origins, Development and Future' (1921) 1 *International Labour Review* 5, 20–21.

> I know there are varying views about the definition of universality, but surely on one thing we can all agree and that is that all people everywhere are entitled to the benefits of the objectives of the ILO, not only the people living in states which are mainly free-enterprise states.[24]

Nonetheless, as coherent and upright as this choice may have been, it was at the same time an extraordinarily bold gamble. Indeed, at the founding of the ILO, tripartism was an ideal that corresponded with realities in only a handful of (principally European) countries. Moreover, following the Second World War, many European countries, and numerous others besides, fell into the orbit of the USSR and its model of democratic centralism. With the withdrawal of the United States in 1977, for a short moment it became more than reasonable to believe the founders had made a losing bet. As recalled by Francis Blanchard, there were ideas at the time developed in American Federation of Labor and Congress of Industrial Organizations (AFL-CIO) quarters to graft tripartism onto regional organisations such as the Organization of American States (OAS) and the Organisation for Economic Co-operation and Development (OECD),[25] so that countries practising a genuine tripartism could gather together in mutual recognition. Needless to say, the temptation to retreat behind the walls of an exclusive, if genuinely tripartite, stronghold stood at odds with the universalist ideas of the founders, whose philosophy was eloquently summarised by Jenks' quip that '[t]he world community is not a club of the mutually congenial but an experiment in the organised government of all mankind'.[26]

At least for the time being, history has accorded that philosophy its due. Far from being a losing gambit, the end of the Cold War sounded the apparent rout of the rival model, revealing universality as a strategy with a substantial pay-off indeed. While nobody claims that the ILO brought down the Berlin Wall, there is no doubt that the organisation's support for Solidarnosc in Poland helped land the first blows. In any case, the model of social progress based on pluralism and the free conciliation of interests emerged victorious in its long confrontation with its totalitarian rival. Yet, with the benefit of two decades of hindsight, it becomes easier to see the celebrated success as somewhat of a Pyrrhic victory.

(ii) To the Challenge of Universal Competence

First, though the collapse of the rival model provided undeniable but ultimately passing prestige for the ILO, it simultaneously had the unfortunate effect of

[24] ILO, *Provisional Record* (ILC, 39th Session, Geneva, 1956) 191. As noted later in the Report of the Credentials Committee submitted to the Conference, 'Paramount in that concept [of universality] is the idea that the aims and purposes of the ILO and the action that it takes must correspond with the needs of all the people throughout the world, whatever social or economic regime exists in their countries', ibid 586.

[25] Francis Blanchard, *L'organisation internationale du travail : De la guerre froide à un nouvel ordre mondial* (Paris, Seuil, 2004) 139–40.

[26] Wilfred C Jenks, 'Universality and Ideology in the ILO' (Address at the Institute of International Studies, Geneva, 27 October 1969) reproduced in (1970) 1 *Annals of International Studies* 45, 51.

deflating the persuasive capacity which had supported the organisation's 'regulating interdependence' function – the function focused on reconciling the requirements of social progress with the constraints imposed by economic interdependence under trade liberalisation.

Second, this victory has not definitively closed the debate on the ability of the tripartite model to deliver on the promise of social justice. Leaving aside philosophical questions that might be raised against the model, from a Rawlsian perspective[27] or otherwise,[28] a new tension has emerged between the principles of tripartism and the modern realities of production. The ILO's successful claim to embrace all forms of work, and all categories of workers,[29] means the organisation has had to respond to a growing diversity of situations, which threatens to explode the tripartite categories. Thus, while the category of 'employer' once largely overlapped with that of 'entrepreneur', this is much less the case under the terms of a financial capitalism which shifted power into the hands of bankers and financiers, essentially if not exclusively concerned with the interests and benefits of anonymous shareholders.[30] As for workers, work now takes forms so varied that the traditional model of a formal job and stable employment can almost be described as atypical. Not to mention that the boundary between the category of 'employer' and that of 'worker' has itself become blurred in some cases, with the emergence of the 'self-employed' as an increasingly pressing example.

Rather than universal *membership*, the new threat to the ILO's governance model is what might be described as the tension between tripartism and the organisation's claim to a universal *competence* covering all types of work and every kind

[27] To the extent that the tripartite model claims not only to further 'social progress' but to actually ensure 'social justice' the question arises whether Rawls' account of social justice is compatible with a de facto compromise between interests, or whether such a compromise would fail to meet the definition of principles agreed upon behind the 'veil of ignorance'.

[28] There has been a surge of literature of late trying to re-found labour law on the 'capabilities' approach of Amartya Sen. In one example, Bob Hepple has argued that 'a central task of international labour law in the era of modern globalisation must be to facilitate equality of capabilities' (Bob Hepple, *Labour Laws and Global Trade* (Oxford, Hart, 2005) 19). By this light, one might ask whether the results of tripartite negotiations will necessarily provide broad access to market capabilities. On the other hand, Sen himself has argued, 'it is not clear that there is any royal road to evaluation of economic and social policies' (Amartya Sen, *Development as Freedom* (New York, Knopf, 1999)). This suggests a primarily procedural view of Sen's framework, which means that the important question can instead be phrased as a matter of what kind of tripartism can broadly empower individual capabilities. Judy Fudge has provided a critical review of divergent approaches (Judy Fudge, 'The New Discourse of Labor Rights: From Social to Fundamental Rights?' (2007) 29 *Comparative Labor Law & Policy Journal* 29). Sen's most recent work, *The Idea of Justice* (Cambride MA, Belknap Press 2009), seems to endorse a more procedural approach that explicitly rejects approaches, like those of Rawls, that are founded in particular, idealised arrangements of resources or particular institutions.

[29] This competence followed specifically from rulings Nos 2 and 13 of the Permanent Court of International Justice (PCIJ) and the practice developed as a result of the Declaration of Philadelphia. On the impact of the PCIJ decisions, see Maupain, 'L'OIT, la justice sociale et la mondialisation' (n 8) 318 ff. It hardly helped matters in this regard that the 'workers group' was known in French as the 'labourers group' ('*groupe ouvrier*') during the post-war years (and indeed, retains that name today).

[30] For a fascinating review of the connections linking changes in the world of work to correlated changes in the structure of global capitalism, see Peer Zumbansen, 'The Parallel Worlds of Corporate Governance and Labor Law' (2006) 13 *Indiana Journal of Global Legal Studies* 261.

of worker. But understanding that problem and its potential solutions is a task large enough to deserve its own book.

Suffice it here, then, to emphasise how this new challenge to universalism relates back to the issue at the centre of this book, ie the ILO's capacity to reconcile its objectives with the opening of markets, on the basis of a collection of means of action that, in the final account, depend on persuasion alone. There is, in fact, an important connection: the ILO's persuasiveness is not only a function of external factors like the existence of the 'Bolshevik menace' (or more recently, the threat of a global economic implosion), but also depends on the legitimacy of its claim to represent what has nowadays come to be called the 'real economy'.

B. Gambling on Persuasion: Pursuing Social Progress under Economic Interdependence

In the penultimate paragraph of its Preamble, the ILO Constitution bears the clear mark of the so-called 'first globalisation',[31] where under the influence of the United Kingdom, the interdependence of economies through open markets and free trade were largely taken for granted.

If there are some who doubt that social justice can be founded only on the free conciliation of interests, the belief that social justice depends on relatively open markets is sure to raise even more eyebrows. Indeed, it is easy to construct the argument that social justice is only truly possible in a relatively closed, if not primitive, society. This ideal of equality in frugality was most notably promoted by Rousseau, who thought the affairs of the city should not depend on trade with other nations, leaving autarky as the sole system capable of protecting the public from the corrupting influences, rivalries and permanent conflict ultimately inseparable from state interdependence.[32] It must, however, be noted that, with the exception perhaps of Bhutan (and even that country is relatively open to tourism), there is no example of a country making such a basic social choice in circumstances which could not be described as despotic.

(i) 'Sweet Trade' Might Fuel Social Progress

However, one comes down in this debate, it would be hard to read the ILO Constitution so as to endorse an ideal for social progress based on an equal

[31] Dani Rodrik provides a useful overview of the early twentieth century's 'first globalisation' (and its collapse) in the second chapter of his most recent book, *The Globalization Paradox: Democracy and the Future of the World Economy* (New York, WW Norton & Company, 2011) 24–46.

[32] Stanley Hoffmann and David P Fidler (eds), *Rousseau on International Relations* (Oxford, Clarendon Press, 1991) xxxi. See also ch IV of Bk III of Rousseau's *On The Social Contract* (quoted here in the 1782 translation of GDH Cole), in which Rousseau warns against excessive luxury, which 'corrupts at once rich and poor; the rich by possession, the poor by covetousness'. According to Pierre Hassner, Rousseau's allegiances in the contemporary debate on globalisation would clearly have lain with the anti-globalisers. See Pierre Hassner, 'Rousseau et les relations internationales' (2012) 140 *Commentaire* 1089, 1109.

distribution of privation. Rather, as expressly put in the Declaration of Philadelphia,[33] the organisation aims explicitly at 'the raising of living standards'. Moreover, the Declaration affirms that the accomplishment of the objectives set out in the Constitution requires 'a fuller and broader utilization of the world's productive resources'.[34] In other words, the ILO legal framework gives little quarter to pursuing a static or Spartan vision of social justice, but rather endorses a progressive vision that provides workers access to 'material progress' while ensuring their 'spiritual development',[35] even if it does not go as far as promising universal affluence.[36] And the question raised by this proposition is how might increasing prosperity and wellbeing be promoted, if not precisely by the 'sweet trade' (or, in the original French, '*doux commerce*') which Montesquieu imagined would bring about peaceful relations and prosperity among both nations and people?[37]

(ii) But Locks States into a 'Prisoner's Dilemma'

The problem is, however, that if 'sweet trade' can provide for social progress by supporting economic prosperity, it may also conceal precisely the type of subtle poison dreaded by Rousseau. Indeed, the interdependence implied by trade goes hand in hand with economic competition, and with that competition comes a desire to safeguard competitiveness. According to the traditional game theory model, the *poison* becomes a *prison*: under interdependence and competition, states thereby find themselves in the well known 'prisoner's dilemma'.

It was fear of this outcome that led the ILO's founders to insert the last paragraph into the Constitution's Preamble, stating that 'the failure of any nation to adopt humane conditions of labour[38] is an obstacle in the way of other nations which desire to improve the conditions in their own countries'.[39]

In today's world, the decisive tone of this rationale may seem excessively simplistic, or at least dated.[40] For one, the overlap and interaction between economies

[33] Declaration concerning the Aims and Purposes of the International Labour Organisation (adopted 10 May 1944, annexed to the ILO Constitution, below (n 38), in 1946) Pt III(a) (Declaration of Philadelphia).

[34] ibid Pt IV.

[35] As put in the Declaration of Philadelphia (n 32) Pt II(a).

[36] The ILO's commitment to material progress is well represented in a fresco in the original ILO headquarters, which by an irony of history is now the seat of the World Trade Organization.

[37] According to his well-known formulation in *The Spirit of Laws* (1758), 'Peace is the natural effect of trade. Two nations who traffic with each other become reciprocally dependent; for if one has an interest in buying, the other has an interest in selling: and thus their union is founded in their mutual necessities' (Charles Louis de Secondat de Montesquieu, *The Spirit of Laws* (trans. Thomas Nugent, London, G Bell & Sons, 1914)).

[38] Today we might say 'decent work', leaving each to measure its own progress!

[39] Constitution of the International Labour Organization (1 April 1919) Preamble, para 3 ('ILO Constitution').

[40] Such a concern might seem dated given that Rousseau's fear is based on an implicit assumption that a country can be treated more or less as would a company competing against others, based in turn to some degree on a model in which products are manufactured within a single country's borders. This rationale has echoes of very old thinking (see discussion in Christophe Bezou, *La clause sociale: la*

reduces the utility of arguing about state motivations and behaviour by analogy with individual firms.[41] The same phenomenon makes the relationship between comparative advantage and social legislation seem less of a binary opposition than apparently suggested by the original formulation.[42] Given the changes the world has seen since the rationale was formulated, it is perfectly understandable that this approach should be cast as inadequate to modern purposes.

Given these critiques, some clarifications of the underlying claim seem called for.

First off, the rationale is not intended to *prescribe* dependence on international trade in pursuit of social progress, but is only predicated on it; it is clear that it does not fall within the ILO's mandate to push its Members onto the path of trade liberalization – even to the degree that the underlying intent is the cultivation of social progress.[43]

Furthermore, what is most important about the provision (for our purposes) is not so much *how* it highlights the significance of this function, as that it does identify it, and that the Constitution attributes it to the ILO and its organs: under

négociation internationale menée par l'OIT (Paris, ESKA, 2008)) and may be particularly strong in the Colbertist tradition which sees the nation as a firm. Some have strongly argued that this model has no correspondence at all with the realities of internationalised production (see Brian A Langille, 'Imagining Post-"Geneva Consensus" Labor Law for Post-"Washington Consensus" Development' (2010) 31 *Comparative Labor Law and Policy Journal* 523). Yet, while production may now be disintegrated, working conditions remain territorial, as does the principle of non-discrimination, which expects equal pay for work of equal value. Therefore, it is no longer the products, but the working conditions themselves that are in competition (see Hepple (n 27) 251).

[41] Leaving off from the deconstruction of the phenomenon proposed by Élie Cohen (in *La tentation hexagonale: la souveraineté à l'épreuve de la mondialisation* (Paris, Fayard, 1996)), Christian Chavagneux summarises their respective strategies as follows: 'States seek to maximize the portion of global demand served from their territory, no matter the nationality of the firm involved; on the other side, firms hope to maximize their control of production processes serving global markets, no matter the territory where production takes place. These two objectives can give rise just as easily to clashing or cooperative relationships' (Christian Chavagneux, 'L'instabilité du monde : inégalités, finance, environnement' in *Esprit* (Paris, December 2011) 49, 55 (author's translation)). The fact that states cannot be treated as firms does not, however, prevent them from continuing to be tempted to attract investment by way of a 'lowest bidder' social policy, which means that the logic of the objective and the mission conferred on the ILO to combat that temptation remain totally relevant.

[42] Hepple (n 27) especially at 252–53.

[43] Evidence for this limitation may be taken from the fact that while free trade was taken as a given when the ILO was conceived, the situation quickly gave way to widespread protectionism. One could even argue that there was a time during the Cold War where the proponents of an open economy represented only a minority of Members against supporters of a planned economy sheltered from vagaries of difficult-to-cross customs borders. Yet no one has suggested that this prevented the ILO from continuing its work in service of social progress!

One could even argue that on the basis of its 'trade-neutral' mandate, it might have an important role in mediating an emergent debate about the merits of 'deglobalisation' and a certain amount of protectionism from the social point of view. Obviously, to provide an objective basis for such a debate, the ILO's ability to conduct independent research and analysis would need not only to be guaranteed, but strengthened – an important dimension for institutional reform addressed in Part II. It is worth noting that the concept of 'deglobalisation', which originated in the writings of Filipino writer and politician Walden Bello (see, eg *Deglobalization: Ideas for a New World Economy*, 2nd edn (London, Zed Books, 2004), has recently been taken up by a number of French authors, including Jacques Sapir in *La démondialisation* (Paris, Seuil, 2011).

Article 1(1) of its Constitution, this 'permanent organization' 'is established for "the promotion of the objects set forth in the Preamble to this Constitution"'.[44] Just how important this function was in the minds of the founders is illustrated by two subsequent developments. The first example is provided by a 1922 action brought by France before the Permanent Court of International Justice (PCIJ), challenging the ILO's competence to regulate agricultural working conditions. Among France's arguments against ILO competence, (particularly ironic in retrospect) was the claim that agricultural working conditions *had no impact on competitiveness*![45] Secondly, one can consider the words of Albert Thomas who, despite standing firm against the position put forward by France, in that case, nevertheless expressed in the Paris Review the equally significant view that: 'if the International Labour Office harmonises and raises labour conditions, if it tends to substitute humane, collegial competition for an inequitable form based on the exploitation of workers, it will effectively aid the peace. This was the contention of the founders'.[46]

Given this historical perspective, it appears that the true question (and real dilemma) for the ILO is whether the means it was given at birth to achieve this function remain relevant and adequate to do so.

(iii) Escaping the Prisoner's Dilemma: The Risky but Unavoidable Gamble on Persuasion

It is worth noting from the outset that the choice (or simple acceptance) of market liberalisation is perfectly consistent both with open societies and with the institutional commitment to universal membership. More precisely, ensuring progress towards the ILO's goals while bound by the constraints of economic interdependence is perfectly consistent with the ILO's social dialogue function aimed at promoting a model for social progress based on balancing worker and employer interests.

[44] Specifically, the ILO is responsible 'for the promotion of the objects set forth in the Preamble to this Constitution and in the Declaration concerning the aims and purposes of the International Labour Organization adopted at Philadelphia on 10 May 1944, the text of which is annexed to this Constitution'.

[45] In areas which affect competitiveness, France argued in its written memorial, 'Nous sommes en présence, ne l'oublions pas, d'un texte [la Constitution de l'OIT] apportant une restriction à la souveraineté interne autant qu'externe' ['We shall not forget that we are in presence of a text [the ILO Constitution], bringing restrictions to the internal sovereignty as well as to the external one', trans]. See Francis Maupain, 'Mondialisation de l'économie et universalité de la protection des droits des travailleurs' in Institut René Cassin (ed), *Commerce mondial et protection des droits de l'homme: les droits de l'homme à l'épreuve de la globalisation des échanges économiques* (Brusells, Bruylant, 2001) 121–22. On the question of the ILO's competence in agriculture, see Georges Fischer, 'Les rapports entre l'Organisation internationale du travail et la Cour permanente de justice internationale' (DPhil thesis, University of Geneva, 1946) 319–31.

[46] Author's translation. Original: 'si le Bureau International du Travail uniformise et relève les conditions de travail, s'il tend à substituer une émulation loyale et humaine à la concurrence déloyale fondée sur une exploitation des forces ouvrières, il aidera efficacement la paix. Voilà ce qu'ont voulu affirmer les négociateurs.' Albert Thomas, 'Justice sociale et paix universelle' *Revue de Paris* (Paris, 15 March 1924) 5.

Again, however, the pursuit of this reconciliation depends on a rather risky institutional approach: no matter how effective they have been in some circumstances,[47] when push comes to shove, the collection of measures and methods which the ILO can activate to free Members from the 'prisoner's dilemma' rests solely on its capacity to *persuade* the membership to take action. Though the founders may have admittedly had little choice in this regard, the current realities of financial globalisation have made the disproportion between the magnitude of the organisation's regulatory burden and its seemingly limited powers seem insurmountable.

Those responsible for putting the organisation's foundations in place, or at least some of them, were well aware that, if it applied to anything less than the whole membership, 'international labour legislation' would provide no easy escape from the prisoner's dilemma; to the contrary, such voluntary legislation was liable to embolden 'free riders'. This was why some had in mind a more radical formula: the International Labour Conference would be given the competence to adopt a genuine international labour code, through agreements binding on all Members, subject only to temporary 'opt out' clauses.[48] With great realism, however, they quickly realised that a binding solution of this sort could lead to results in direct conflict with the intended goals of universal progress.[49] Indeed, it would easily lead to one of two outcomes:

(1) if an ILC majority coalesced, committed to creating a truly progressive international regime, in all likelihood the resulting regime would deter the less developed countries from becoming or remaining Members;
(2) on the other hand, if the whole cohort of states were to join, they might conspire to simply craft legislation conforming to the lowest common denominator of existing legislation.

The sole remaining option was a constitutional structure that, notwithstanding its highly original and progressive developments,[50] nevertheless cleaves to the classical principle of international agreements, with a collection of Conventions and Recommendations that must be ratified or accepted by states to produce any effect within their domestic legal order.

Broadly speaking, this book is devoted to addressing the sustainability of this gambit in the context of economic globalisation, and in the world of the ILO's second century more generally.

[47] A topic deserving broad attention which will have to be canvassed another time.

[48] These provisions were contained in section 18 of the British proposal on which the Commission drafting the international labour legislation had worked. See James Thomson Shotwell, *The Origins of the International Labour Organization* (New York, Columbia University Press, 1934) vol 1, 145–63.

[49] Maurice Guerreau, *Une nouvelle institution du droit des gens: l'Organisation permanente du travail* (Paris, Rousseau, 1923) 266 ff.

[50] In particular, Members who have not ratified a Convention are subject under Art 19(5)(e) of the Constitution to a residual obligation to report on the follow-up they have given to the Convention's requirements. It is this provision that justified, among other things, the monitoring established under the 1998 Declaration.

III. The Core Issue

Expressed in the starkest terms, addressing the continued merits of the 'persuasion gambit' inevitably puts in question the ILO's institutional capacity to fulfil its mandate in the circumstances of the twenty-first century. Put so bluntly, it should not be too surprising that it remains an awkward issue for ILO insiders. Yet, it is neither a question that can be evaded nor, given that the search for plausible alternatives still seems to come up empty, one that offers a short-cut to an easy answer.

A. An Almost Taboo Subject Within the ILO

The heated debates (whose content will be canvassed more fully later on)[51] surrounding the introduction of a 'social clause' into the WTO agreements once again called into question, if indirectly, the 'voluntarist' approach of the ILO Constitution. For obvious reasons, however, raising that question directly remains relatively taboo within the ILO. It is symptomatic in this regard that the ILC discussions eventually leading to the 2008 Declaration took place under the agenda heading of 'Strengthening ILO's capacity to support the efforts of its Members to achieve its objectives in the context of globalization'. This less-than-straightforward title betrayed a clear intention not to depart from the blueprint set down in the ILO Constitution, and to leave unquestioned the limits it imposed: of essentially doing no more than providing voluntary 'assistance' to Members.

Given the scars left by the late-1990s conflicts around the social clause, the ILO could hardly have been expected to go out on a limb. The alleged inadequacy of the ILO's purely voluntary means of action as 'false debate' by the 2007 report intended to serve as the basis of these debates was thus predictably dismissed.[52] Instead, making a virtue of necessity, it suggested that it is counter to the very nature of social progress objectives to impose them from the outside.[53] To be sustainable, improvements to the ILO's capacity to promote its objectives does not therefore require new constitutional means, but are simply a matter of better governance; real improvement demands only the amelioration of its persuasive capacity, by way of a more integrated implementation of its objectives, and a more judicious use of the means available to pursue them.

Faced with growing frustration with 'deficits' in the 'social dimension' of globalisation (in the modestly rigorous terminology of ILO documents) the

[51] See especially Part III, Introduction.

[52] See ILO, *Report V* (n 19) paras 6–7.

[53] ibid para 12. Indeed, attention to historical experience (including the dislocation of the social model of the Soviet bloc) readily suggests that, while being based on ILO standards, the implementation of these goals must be anchored in the realities and choices of the tripartite constituents in each country.

question is whether the ILO can avoid losing – or at least avoid the impression of having lost – the bet on persuasion, just as it nearly lost its bet on universality. It would be hard for anyone to miss the irony were the advent of globalisation, after providing an apparent pay-out to the bet made on the universality of the tripartite model, to reveal the flaws in the other key gamble, the reliance on persuasion.

B. That Demands Re-examination in Light of Key Changes to Global Context

Clearly, the advisability of choosing persuasion to reconcile social progress objectives with relatively open markets cannot be judged in the present on the same terms as it might have been in 1919. Many changes have intervened to modify the strength of the hand dealt to the organisation by its founders. A judicious evaluation of the options requires prior identification of the developments which may have had an impact on the appropriateness of this choice, either by strengthening or weakening: (i) the need for 'regulation' itself; (ii) the capacity of the ILO to meet that need by deploying its persuasive powers in particular ways; or (iii) the plausibility of any alternative to persuasion. Four factors may be isolated which have contributed to shifts in one or more of these dimensions: first, of course, changes in the international system, and the transition from the Cold War to globalisation in particular; secondly, the emergence of new inter- or supra-state actors since the end of the Second World War; thirdly, the more recent emergence of a consensus on the 'rules of the game' that must guide all actors with a hand in social protection and labour rights; and finally, the emerging embrace by individual members of civil society, acting in their role as consumers, of engagement in environmental and social activism. Before getting into the thick of it, let us briefly take up each of these phenomena to understand the nature of their sometimes contradictory impacts on the core issues.

First, the changes in the international system and especially the transition from the Cold War to globalisation. The end of the Cold War and the advent of globalisation played out in two opposing directions on the 'demand' for regulation and on the ILO's ability to respond effectively through persuasion. First, by exacerbating competition between states, the advent of globalisation increased the need for coordinated 'regulation' at the international level, while restoring a political raison d'être which had at least partially been stolen from the ILO by the end of the Cold War and the demise of the rival totalitarian model of social justice. But, pulling in the opposite direction, both these changes also had quite a negative impact on the ILO's capacity to persuade and, by extension, on the credibility of using normative activities to meet this new regulatory need.

Secondly, the diversification of actors. The ILO no longer finds itself in an almost exclusive[54] one-on-one with its Members in supporting and guiding their social progress efforts. According to Pieter Jan Kuijper, the establishment of the United Nations at the end of the 1940s represented the 'Big Bang' in a quickly expanding universe of international organisations and agreements.[55] Today, the ILO must deal with the existence of a host of organisations influencing national social policy choices, each according to its own objectives and perspectives. Even if these objectives (economic, commercial or financial) are oblique to the ILO's own social goals, there is simply no escaping from the interdependence of the economic, financial and social spheres. Clearly unable to impose the pre-eminence of its own objectives against those of these other organisations, nor empowered to force them to apply its own normative instruments, the ILO has no choice but to act upon them by persuasion, promoting greater consistency in the name of greater overall effectiveness.[56] The question is, in other words, whether the tools of persuasion can help displace the current reality of competition between mandates and objectives, in favour of coherence and consistency.

Thirdly, the emergence of an agreement on universal 'rules of the game' regarding workers' rights, which states are expected to observe regardless of their level of development. The irony here is that, after having played a key role in the successful identification of these critical rules by dialogue and persuasion, the ILO finds itself by way of a kind of boomerang effect left to address the equally crucial issue of how to ensure universal compliance with them. Is it possible to achieve universal effectiveness without giving these rules the same mandatory status enjoyed by the 'rules of the game' (ie the legal framework) of world trade, if necessary by linking their fates? This logic would seem all the more cogent, even inevitable, given that trade rules are the precise source of the interdependence and interpenetration of economies giving rise to the prisoner's dilemma in the first place. Yet, if nothing stands in the way of such a link as a matter of coherent principles, a broader consideration that includes both a closer analysis to the potential practical consequences entailed by such a link, and especially heightened attention to questions of political acceptability, reveals a path still littered with obstacles. Moreover, attempts to 'decentralise' the relationship through preferential agreements at the bilateral or multilateral level (efforts resulting largely from the failure to reach agreement at the universal level) remain relatively inconclusive as well.

Lastly, the appearance of a form of social and environmental awareness among the public and among consumers. Just like the emergence of new super-state actors in the post-war period, this phenomenon is likely to impact on the interaction

[54] The ILO never had a wholly exclusive role in social regulation, given the important role of the League of Nations in the economic field, to be discussed in Chapter 4.

[55] Pieter Jan Kuijper, *Conflicting Rules and Clashing Courts: The Case of Environmental Agreements, Free Trade Agreements and the WTO*, Issue Paper No 10 (International Centre for Trade and Sustainable Development, September 2010) 64.

[56] As already stated in the 2008 Declaration. With all the nuances and all the compromises inherent in a negotiated text, the 2008 Declaration clearly highlights the need for coherence between economic and social policies, without which globalisation could implode.

between the states and the ILO as originally envisaged, but in a very different way. Indeed, the question is whether the persuasive force represented by this new activism is capable of taking over from the ILO's own ability (or inability) to persuade and thereby leverage a 'market for social justice' to ensure much more effective enforcement of the 'rules of the game' mentioned above.

Part I
Ninety Years of Transformations in the International System: Challenges Posed to ILO Persuasiveness

Introduction

According to the International Labour Office report to the 2007 International Labour Conference introducing the debate on what would become the Declaration on Social Justice for a Fair Globalization, 'for the first time since its creation, the context makes it possible . . . for the ILO to do exactly what it was established to do'.[1]

Beyond those most intimate with the ILO and its history, this remark likely baffled readers (as rare as they might have been): was this language meant to imply that the ILO had done so little in its first 90 years?

Of course, the intention was simply to underline that the globalised economy, framed during the prior decade primarily as a threat to ILO objectives, had in fact forced the organisation to return to one of its original core functions. After all, the organisation had been founded precisely to reconcile the social progress objectives listed in the Constitution with the constraints created by the global market forces unleashed by the advent of deepening economic interdependence.

In this regard, we shall see without a doubt that this function, of balancing the demands of progress with the constraints of interdependence and economic competition, found itself sidelined for much of the organisation's history. As explored in the Introduction, the *political competition* of the Cold War was pushed to the fore by the antagonism of two blocs, each engaged in an unrelenting effort to simultaneously keep in the workers' good graces and win the support of the 'Third World'. There was, however, another side of the coin: those years may have lulled some into an overestimation of the organisation's capacity to maintain a virtuous circle between economic development and social progress, whether by its 'traditional' normative activities or any of the other voluntary means at its disposal, including technical cooperation and research. Thus, while there is no doubt that the end of the Cold War and the post-war boom restored the ILO's underlying 'economic' raison d'être its priority of place, it also put an abrupt end to a

[1] ILO, *Report VI: Strengthening the ILO's Capacity to Assist its Members' Efforts to Reach its Objectives in the Context of Globalization* (ILC, 97th Session, Geneva, 28 May–13 June 2008) para 3.

(somewhat contrived) 'golden age' for the ILO itself. No doubt, the ILO strove to respond by 'inventing' new ways to maximise its persuasiveness, through new forms of regulation. These efforts will be examined in the second chapter. Since 2008, however, it has become fair to wonder whether these efforts at diversification and renewal had already been overtaken by the successive developments of the financial crisis, which seem to strengthen the demand for new, perhaps even *binding* regulations, in the social sphere no less than any other. That claim will be examined in its turn; but understanding the demands of the present requires turning first to a look at history.

1

The Cold War and the *trente glorieuses*, a Not-Quite Golden Age for the ILO and its Persuasiveness

Just 10 years into the normative projects launched through the ILO in 1919, the Great Depression intervened to dampen the enthusiasm they had generated. The experience of those years immediately confirmed that progress toward ILO objectives had nothing to gain from a retreat into protectionism.[1] In addition to its highly negative impact on employment and living standards, the beggar-thy-neighbour trade policies adopted following the 1929 crisis doomed ILO efforts to ensure a 'level playing field' of working conditions which had to that point been pursued primarily by way of promoting the ratification of Conventions of general scope.

These events led the organisation to moderate its ambitions of pursuing a level playing field in working conditions by way of standards of (potentially) universal application; it turned instead toward the path of least resistance, ie the adoption of standards of 'sectorial' application, pinning hopes on the stronger functional relationships and greater solidarity likely to exist in specific industries.[2] Unfortunately, in terms of ratifications earned, this change in strategy was less than an unmitigated success. As a matter of ILO credibility, moreover, it contributed to the image of its normative instruments as simultaneously fragmented in purpose and excessively detailed in execution.

Following on the heels of the Second World War, the Cold War years allowed partial restoration of economic interdependence attached to international trade, but in a world profoundly transformed by its division into two rival, hostile political blocs. A third bloc, the Group of 77, hardly made the challenge any easier; in large part, it turned out to be a stake in the rivalry between the other two. In this context, the demands of social progress may have been less limited by the constraints of economic interdependence, but it was subject to numerous other complicating factors.

[1] See ILO, Resolution concerning action to be taken to remedy the present crisis, reproduced in *Record of Proceedings* (ILC, 16th Session, Geneva 12–30 April 1932) 589. The resolution was proposed by Mr Jouhaux, French Workers' delegate, Mr Mertens, Belgian Workers' delegate, and Mr Schürch, Swiss Workers' delegate.

[2] Ernst B Haas, *Beyond the Nation-State: Functionalism and International Organization* (Stanford, CA, Stanford University Press, 1964) 156.

Economically, the period was no doubt coloured in OECD countries by the triumph of *industrial capitalism* or, as labelled by Robert Reich, 'democratic capitalism'.[3] This group of countries enjoyed nearly three decades of growth leading to unprecedented prosperity – well known in France as the *trente glorieuses.* The period was marked by considerable improvements in the status and working conditions of industrial workers, providing access to middle class comforts for a substantial portion of the population.

Politically, *ideological competition* took precedence over issues of economic interdependence and the economic competition it would have entailed. The three blocs into which members were divided each claimed 'social justice' as their own motto, but were sharply divided over the contents of the concept – and how to achieve it. Though its value as a rhetorical touchstone thereby increased during the period, which of the wildly divergent visions was concealed behind the 'social justice' banner ultimately depended on who was waving it.

According to the prevailing pluralistic view of the industrialised countries of the OECD, the concept referred mainly to finding a balance between the competing but supposedly equally legitimate interests of workers and employers.

This pluralistic vision[4] was radically opposed to the monolithic conception which prevailed in the primarily eastern-European Soviet Bloc countries, for whom social justice was to be exercised in favour of the sole legitimate interest: that of the proletariat. Needless to say, the proletariat was not invited actually to give their view on the subject. Rather, according to the logic of 'democratic centralism', monopoly on the interpretation of their interests lay with the Party alone, with unions serving only as a kind of political conveyer belt of the Party's decisions. After using the creation of the Economic and Social Council (ECOSOC) to try and marginalise, if not destroy, the ILO, the decision taken by the USSR in the early 1950s to become an active participant, followed in due course by its entire cohort of Eastern Europe satellites, relied on its own policy of entryism. In short, it sought to insert itself into procedures and internal dynamics in such a way as to advance its own monolithic vision and its particular political interests.[5]

[3] Robert B Reich, *Supercapitalism: The Transformation of Business, Democracy and Everyday Life* (New York, Knopf, 2007) 6–7.

[4] Unabashedly defined as 'corporatist' by some analysts. See, Lucio Baccaro, *Orchestration for the "Social Partners Only: Internal Constraints on the ILO,* unpublished manuscript; Université de Genève, 2013

[5] This strategy included trying to impose equal participation by 'socialist enterprise directors' (as designated by the states themselves) in the employers group (see Francis Maupain, 'La réforme de l'Organisation internationale du Travail' (1987) 33(33) *Annuaire Français de Droit International* 478). These criticisms notwithstanding, the contribution of these countries to standards production (especially in occupational health and safety) was far from negligible, and probably deserves more extensive study. Neither, given their drive to be viable contenders in the competition between models for social justice, did they achieve a trivial score on standards ratification. They could moreover rely in the overall competition on their relatively low official unemployment rate. Of course, the salience of their employment claims was disputed by their opponents on the ground that such employment neither met the conditions of 'as productive as possible' and 'freely chosen' laid down in Convention No 122; nor of 'full and productive employment' called for in the language of GATT Art XII(3)(d). The picture was further darkened when the view was widened to include application of the Conventions on

As for the developing countries, the appeal to social justice, at least as expressed by their governments, was not so much connected to their domestic political situations as it was used to back claims vis-à-vis the international system itself. Those claims were made particularly through the recognition of a 'right to development',[6] with corresponding duties for developed countries and especially the former colonial powers. In this context, the developing countries looked to the ILO first and foremost to provide a better platform for their demands – whence their efforts to change the balance of power in the representative bodies to their benefit including, inter alia, the demand to eliminate the non-elected seats at the Governing Body reserved for 'States of chief industrial importance'.[7] Further and more practically, they hoped to be provided with technical assistance to help them catch up in social infrastructure, while at the same time bringing in foreign currency as rare as it was precious.[8]

There should be no mistake, either: ideological competition over the meaning of social justice had real benefits for workers, at least in the OECD countries. Daniel Cohen puts his finger on this dimension when he observes that industrial capitalism was able not only to survive but prosper, whether in the shadow of the

discrimination, and especially those regarding freedom of association. The belief, as naive as it was cynical, that their control over society was sufficiently complete to maintain the appearance of compliance may explain their decision (somewhat foolhardy in retrospect) nonetheless to ratify the Conventions in the first place (Krzysztof Drzewicki, 'Freedom of Association in One-Party Systems' (1990) *Nordic Journal of Human Rights* 28). Indeed, their gamble overestimated their ability to manage long-term social change, while underestimating the tenacity both of their own constituents and of the ILO's supervisory bodies. This double miscalculation led to a confrontation that, by way of the Solidarnosc affair, became a precipitating factor in an outcome which in the final account was likely inevitable, given their model's inability to compete with Western production levels (Louis Emmerij, Richard Jolly and Thomas George Weiss, *Ahead of the Curve? UN Ideas and Global Challenges* (Blomington, IN, Indiana University Press, 2001) 149). This outcome may be claimed, as it were, to prove Rousseau's case, but by counterexample. Even where interdependence was limited to the arms race and the conquest of space, an imposed commitment to an economic model of relative scarcity could only be maintained by force alone. And yet, if authoritarianism and a relative lack of freedom can be maintained while living standards are on the rise (as evidenced not only by the Bismarckian model, but also perhaps by the Chinese model of 'market Leninism'), they are unlikely to have much staying power in combination with a frugality that exposes a vast portion of the population to relative deprivation.

[6] For a contemporary analysis of the merits and weaknesses of the 'right to development' discourse, see Philip Alston, 'Making Space for New Human Rights: The Case of the Right to Development' (1988) 1 *Harvard Human Rights Yearbook* 3. See also Karin Mickelson, 'Rhetoric and Rage: Third World Voices in International Legal Discourse' (1997–1998) 16(2) *Wisconsin International Law Journal* 353, 374–86, who points to objections from some quarters based on the apparent contradiction between the external claims being made by some of the most militant proponents of the concept, and their internal practices (ibid 377).

[7] Maupain, 'La réforme' (n 5).

[8] Hence their apparently paradoxical reaction to the 'basic needs' strategy put in place by the ILO especially for their benefit in the years 1970–1980. As explained by a collective work published under the auspices of the United Nations, though the pursuit for international redistribution of income had been the crux of the project, these countries were thrown off by a strategy which they suspected of championing universal support for *internal* income redistribution. Their suspicions, right or wrong, were only made worse by the subsequent support it received from the international financial institutions (Emmerij, Jolly and Weiss, *Ahead of the Curve?* (n 5) 75–79).

crisis of the 1930s, among the strife of the Second World War, or (especially) under the pressures of the Cold War.[9]

This combination of ideological and economic circumstances gives the Cold War a retrospective sheen of a 'not-quite Golden Age' for workers in industrialised countries, a label also fairly applied to expanding normative production at the ILO.[10] Indeed, year after year, the adoption, and regular update, of Conventions and Recommendations was the core of the ILO's work and the focus of the International Labour Conference.[11]

Given such a context, the choice made by the ILO's founders to stake the success of its objectives on voluntary standards activities no longer seemed such a long shot. Rather, it was legitimate to imagine that the gamble had already paid off, especially in view of the remarkable success of the doctrine of automatic succession that subjected newly independent states to obligations under Conventions which had been ratified by their respective colonial rulers![12] Ideological competition and rising living standards in industrialised countries, in summary, helped create and maintain the optimistic perception of a virtuous circle between economic development and social progress, as if state practice had suddenly found itself imbued with 'the Spirit of Philadelphia' dear to Alain Supiot.[13]

The subsequent course of events has unfortunately revealed that perceptions at the time were subject to somewhat of an optical illusion. Indeed, the dynamics of the era rested on a pair of circumstances whose contingency was never fully grasped at the time.

First off, developed countries were relatively sheltered from competition with the rest of the world, primarily due to their overwhelming productive and technological superiority. Beyond this economic imbalance, they benefitted more generally from an asymmetric power relationship with the developing and former colonial countries, a dimension emphasised by many economists, perhaps most famously by Raul Prebisch.[14]

[9] Quoting Peter Sloterdijk, Cohen rightly notes from this perspective that the Cold War was an ally of Western employees to whom it 'suffisait de diriger discrètement leur regard sur les réalités du deuxième monde pour faire comprendre à leurs employeurs qu'ici aussi, la paix sociale avait son prix' ['it was sufficient to discreetly direct their gaze on the realities of the Communist bloc to make their employers conscious that here too, social peace had its price', trans] (Daniel Cohen, *La prospérité du vice* (Paris, Albin Michel, 2009) 247).

[10] On 'the not-quite Golden Age' of capitalist development, see Reich, *Supercapitalism* (n 3) 15–49. On the concurrent 'not-quite Golden Age' of standards production supported by these conditions, see Francis Maupain, 'New Foundation or New Façade? The ILO and the 2008 Declaration on Social Justice for a Fair Globalization' (2009) 20(3) *European Journal of International Law* 823, 826.

[11] Within the ILO, a department's ability to secure a spot on the ILC's agenda for the adoption of a new instrument became a litmus test of its influence, and an essential precondition of obtaining a larger share of the regular budget.

[12] This success was particularly impressive given the more general principle of *tabula rasa* prevailing elsewhere in matters treaty succession. On the ILO doctrine, see Francis Maupain, 'La succession à l'OIT' in Geneviève Burdeau and Brigitte Stern (eds), *Dissolution, continuation et succession en Europe de l'Est: succession d'États et relations économiques internationales* (Paris, Montchrestien, 1994).

[13] Alain Supiot, *L'esprit de Philadelphie: La justice sociale face au marché total* (Paris, Seuil, 2010).

[14] See Pierre de Senarclens, *Mondialisation, souveraineté et théories des relations internationales* (Paris, Armand Colin, 1998).

Furthermore, notwithstanding the 'captive demand' of these still-dependent countries, the relative weakness of external demand from the developed countries meant that their growth in output called for sustained domestic consumption (and vice versa).[15] In other words, the triumph of industrial capitalism was closely linked to the development of the so-called 'Fordist model', coupling demand for industrial products with the compensation package offered to industrial workers.[16]

To draw out one dimension of these observations explicitly: the optimistic view neglected the fact that the phenomenon was confined to a limited group of countries, roughly corresponding to the OECD's membership. During the same period, most other countries (leaving aside Eastern Europe) seemed doomed, despite the successive 'development decades' declared at the United Nations, to stagnate or worse, to sink deeper into poverty under the combined weight of demographic change, declining terms of trade and weak governance.[17]

Even if it was not realised immediately, the fact is that the abrupt end of the Cold War quickly burst the 'bubble' buoying the biggest beneficiaries of the period.

[15] Even more, there is some argument that the economic success of the period in the industrialised countries may have depended on a history of resource extraction and labour commodification in the Global South connected to the legacy of colonialism, a reality that stretched well into the post-Second World War 'golden age' and whose legacy in the form of relative poverty continued even after the victory of decolonisation in the early 1960s. Adelle Blackett and Christian Lévesque, 'Introduction: Social Regionalism in the Global Economy' in Adelle Blackett and Christian Lévesque (eds), *Social Regionalism in the Global Economy* (London, Routledge, 2011) 8.

[16] To which we now oppose a model that Peer Zumbansen associates with the 'Dell effect,' which facilitates production 'freed' from a connection to a particular place, from responsibilities to any community, and from the dictates of a vertically integrated assembly line. See Peer Zumbansen, 'The Parallel Worlds of Corporate Governance and Labor Law' (2006) 13 *Indiana Journal of Global Legal Studies* 261, 263–64. Of course, Apple, a current contender for world's largest company, has generated most of the recent headlines regarding the ethical and legal questions connected to globally disintegrated production, though ironically, Apple may actually be a leader in raising labour standards in the electronics industry. See, eg Keith Bradsher, 'Signs of changes taking hold in electronics factories in China', *New York Times*, 26 December 2012.

[17] To move from this observation to the perspective adopted by Prebisch and some of his peers casting the divide as a more-or-less zero sum game (so that improving the situation of some would always contribute to the reduction or stagnation of living standards for others) is a leap a non-economist would be wary of making. Even without adopting his view wholesale, appreciating the reversal of perspectives, from a Third World which had felt 'enough was enough', to those 'once-developed' countries in Europe and elsewhere which now feel on the defensive, has much to gain from a reference to Mohammed Bedjaoui's 1979 tract on the 'new international economic order' (Mohammed Bedjaoui, *Pour un nouvel ordre économique international: Nouveaux défis au droit international* (Paris, UNESCO, 1979)).

2

Globalisation Ascendant: The ILO's *raison d'être* Restored – But the Gamble on Persuasion Nearly Lost

Taking advantage of the liberalisation of capital movements in the last quarter of the twentieth century, financial capitalism wrested control from an industrial capitalism whose dynamism had already foundered on increasing oil prices, falling productivity, and inflation among the OECD countries, placing dominion of the global economy in the guiding hand of shareholders and their proxies.[1] The result is a degree of interdependence and economic integration which would have been almost inconceivable during the Cold War.

These developments had a counterpart on the ideological level: when the fall of the Berlin Wall cleared the path toward a truly global market,[2] it also fostered a near-religious millennial fervour. Combined with the breakthrough of new technologies, some saw in these events a playing out of the 'end of history', and the promise of a bounty which might feed a worldwide expansion in overall wellbeing – consigning the ILO, its procedures and its corpus of standards from another age, to history's recycling bin, if not the trash heap.[3]

Thus, as much as the fall of the Berlin Wall seemed to have hailed the triumph of the ILO's reformist social model, it also opened the floodgates to a truly global economy that represented a formidable challenge to the organisation's

[1] John Peters provides an excellent synthesis of the phenomenon in 'The Rise of Finance and the Decline of Organized Labour in the Advanced Capitalist Countries' (2011) 16(1) *New Political Economy* 73, 75–84.

[2] See the genealogy of the phenomenon as explained by Nicolas Baverez, who distinguishes successive 'ages' in this process: from 1979 to 1989 (including the arrival of Margaret Thatcher to power and the election of Pope John Paul II); from 1989 to 2001 (its golden age with the collapse of the Soviet empire); and, since 2001, an ongoing turbulence including a chain of economic 'bubbles' (Nicolas Baverez, 'L'Europe à l'âge de l'histoire universelle' (2011) 135 *Commentaire* 640, 641).

[3] Of course, in his report to the 85th Session of the ILC, Michel Hansenne indirectly pointed out the parallels between this frame of mind and the doctrinaire Marxist vision of the approaching end of history: 'By a strange irony of history, the "dawning of a new age" is no longer expected to occur with the end of the class struggle, which finally reaches its fulfilment in the withering away of the State; this time will only come now once the State has been stripped of its social and economic prerogatives and a global civil society emerges which is answerable only to the laws of economic rationality, itself the sole guarantee of a future so full of prosperity and promises that people forget the harshness of their present circumstances.' (ILO, *The ILO, Standard Setting and Globalization: Report of the Director-General* (ILC, 85th Session, Geneva, 3–19 June 1997) 6).

constitutional capacity to pursue its endeavours. It was perhaps insufficiently appreciated at the time that the collapse of the ILO's rival model would deprive the organisation of an ideological counterweight that had proven to be an essential element of its persuasive powers not only vis-à-vis employers, but with a number of governments as well. Moreover, given that the effective implementation of its standards depended on declining powers of persuasion, much of the credibility it had enjoyed in the eyes of workers as an agency for effective regulation of the global economy also quickly drained away.

Tracing the line of these developments, Michel Hansenne reported the depth of his bewilderment on attending a dinner shortly after the fall of the Wall (having only taken office a few months earlier) in honour of the departing US Employers' representative to the Governing Body, Charles Smith. In his farewell speech, Smith expressed his satisfaction at leaving the ILO with a sense of accomplishment, having contributed to the victory of both democracy and the market economy over communism, leading Hansenne to wonder whether 'most people, like Charles Smith, saw the ILO as a machine to combat communism within the context of the Cold War? And if that was the case, what would become of the organisation once that period of history ended?'[4]

The course of events would respond to this question with an answer both clear and disturbing: clear, insofar as it rapidly became obvious that the 'second' globalisation, far from being a panacea, has instead generated new imbalances that threatened the sustainability of the system and gave rise to new regulatory imperatives; but disturbing, as well, in that the ILO's natural tendency to respond through its normative activities was considerably weakened in the eyes of many,[5] albeit for diametrically opposed reasons.

I. Two Decades of Recurrent Social Disappointments and the Corresponding Demand for Greater Social Regulation

Two decades later, many of the millenarian prophets have changed their tune. The end of the 'end of history', brought on by the rise in the obvious shortcomings in 'the social dimension' of globalisation, has by now been the object of countless analyses. Within the ILO, the most striking is that found in the 2004 report of the

[4] Michel Hansenne, *Un garde-fou pour la mondialisation: Le BIT dans l'après-guerre froide* (Geneva, Zoe, 1999) 84 (author's translation).

[5] See, eg the statements of the German Employers' representative to the Governing Body during the discussion of the Director-General's report at the 1994 ILC (coinciding with the ILO's 75th anniversary), suggesting that the organisation's constitutional mission concerns neither trade nor competition, and thereby directly challenging the idea that the ILO can be considered 'as an instrument of regulation in international trade' (ILO, *Record of Proceedings* (ILC, 81st Session, Geneva, 7–24 June 1994) 18/39, quoted in Hansenne, *Un garde-fou* (n 4) 98).

World Commission on the Social Dimension of Globalisation (which will merit another look later on in the text), ideally read in light of a recent report of the Director-General to the ILC.[6] Some findings drawn from this abundant body of literature may shed light on the situation and the evolving demand it creates for social regulation.

A. An Overall Balance in Deficit

If realities have more or less silenced those prophets who had foreseen globalisation as a painless process, drawing up a fair account of the social 'deficits' probably demands that the recent record be compared with that of the prior decades. Setting aside the OECD countries, it might be asked: at the end of the day, have the rapid changes driven by globalisation not resulted in outcomes for workers around the world rather less disappointing than the two strained and chaotic 'development decades' that preceded them?

Although this precise comparison does not seem to have been carried out, the response gleaned from official reports seems to lean toward the affirmative. Thus, the UNDP's *2010 Human Development Report*,[7] despite a few exceptions and the persistence of inequalities,[8] reported a marked improvement in the HDI of most developing countries and concluded that 'over the last twenty years, many people around the world have experienced dramatic improvements in key aspects of their lives'.[9] The report puts forward the conclusion that '[o]verall, poor countries are catching up with rich countries in the HDI. This convergence paints a far more optimistic picture than a perspective limited to trends in income, where divergence has continued'.[10]

The significant development of the middle class in a number of emerging countries in both Asia (notably India) and Latin America (notably Brazil) appears in this respect as a particularly sharp break with the previous decades. The case of China as a 'former' but re-emergent global power undoubtedly provides a case

[6] ILO, *A New Era of Social Justice: Report of the Director-General* (ILC, 100th Session, Geneva, 1–17 June 2011).

[7] UN Development Programme, *Human Development Report 2010 – The Real Wealth of Nations: Pathways to Human Development* (New York, UNDP, 2010).

[8] ILO, *A New Era of Social Justice* (n 6) paras 10–38.

[9] UNDP, *Human Development Report 2010* (n 7) 3.

[10] ibid. Note that, for its part, the *Human Development Report 2011 – Sustainability and Equity: A Better Future for All* does voice a number of caveats, including the deterioration of key environmental indicators and widening income disparities at the national level. Despite the progressive reduction of poverty and the improvements of the past two decades, the Director-General's 2011 report to the ILC was more explicit, reminding constituents that 'these last decades have been difficult for us. Dominant economic policy basically disregarded the founding values of the ILO and built an unequal and unbalanced globalization' (ILO, *A New Era of Social Justice* (n 6) para 14). Furthermore, Jacques Sapir, citing Ha-Joon Chang, proceeds to argue that, far from promoting 'l'intérêt général ou l'intérêt des plus pauvres', globalisation has instead been 'un moyen pour "tirer l'échelle" sur laquelle voulaient monter les pays en développement' ['the general interest or the interest of the poorest' (. . .) 'a way to pull the ladder upon which developing countries wanted to climb'. trans] (Jacques Sapir, *La démondialisation* (Paris, Seuil, 2011) 66.

apart. The bounding strides (if not to say great leaps) of industrial growth in China have bolstered a growing middle class and maintained a climate of optimism and dynamism, unfortunately accompanied by rising inequality and insecurity among the masses of workers drawn from the countryside to fuel the expansion of exports, construction and public works.[11]

It thus seems fair to say that, if the period as a whole represented undeniable material progress for a large number of individuals, it has left large pockets of stagnation and resulted in growing inequalities both between countries and within them.[12] But it is especially marked by twin scourges which stand in the way of ILO efficacy on the two poles of its 'decent work' strategy: 'work' itself is challenged by the persistence (and growth since the financial crisis) of unemployment, and 'decency' by the phenomenon of casualisation.

Far from retreating, unemployment is in fact increasing in all regions of the world, especially after the crisis: ILO data shows that the global unemployment rate in 2012 (of 5.9 per cent) still remains above the level from 2007 (5.6 per cent),[13] and the increase is uneven across regions. Whereas the most recent developments of the crisis show unemployment has declined in many developing countries, the continued impact of the crisis in the advanced economies can be seen in the dramatic increase in long-term unemployment (from 28.6 per cent in the third quarter 2008 to 40 per cent in the third quarter of 2010).[14] As noted in the ILO-published *Global Employment Trends 2013*, 'there is a great deal of heterogeneity among the regions of the world with regard to trends in unemployment, and there is also a general divide between developed and developing regions'.[15] In the developed economies and European Union, which saw the largest regional increase in the unemployment rate between 2007 and 2009 (2.7 percentage points),

[11] However, in a context where the demographic pyramid is upended, and where the level of education has increased, the need to address the increasingly assertive claims and demands for improved working conditions, reasonable wages, social protection and retirement security, and to manage those claims without abrupt eruptions of unrest, seems to require an eventual inquiry into the inevitable problem of effectively (that is to say, legitimately) representing the interests of all stakeholders.

[12] The situation in the former Group of 77 member states appears to be particularly mixed. The vast majority have moved away from the rhetoric of self-reliant development under which they had rallied during the post-colonial period, becoming fervent converts to the virtues of the market, increased economic interdependence by way of trade liberalisation, and the promise these policies make of providing a short-cut to growth and prosperity for all, through foreign investment and access to new markets. Understandably, having paid for these policies with years of social disruption, they could hardly appreciate being handed an invoice including a slew of unplanned costs, in the form of social conditionalities. Their resistance is especially easy to understand, given that the new deal is being proposed by many of the same people who had not only pushed them toward conversion but had, according to the 'right to development' discourse, originally been those with a debt to pay! In this respect, it is interesting to note that by adopting a strategy focused on so-called 'basic needs', the ILO kept itself out of the debate surrounding the right to development, enshrined in the UN Declaration on the Right to Development (adopted 4 December 1986) UNGA Res 41/128, at the time a theme dear to developing countries. On the right to development see above (Chapter 1, n 6).

[13] ILO, *Global Employment Trends 2013: Recovering from a Second Jobs Dip* (Geneva, ILO, 2013) 165.

[14] ILO (Working Party on the Social Dimension of Globalization), *Recovering from Global Crisis – Addressing the Global Crisis: Findings of Country Experiences* (Governing Body, 310th Session, Geneva, March 2011) GB.310/WP/SDG/2/1, 2.

[15] ILO, *Global Employment Trends 2013* (n 13) 13.

the unemployment rate has remained high, near 8.6 per cent. On the other hand, unemployment has significantly declined in Latin America, Central and South-Eastern Europe (non-EU) and CIS and South-East Asia (see Tables 2.1, 2.2).

Table 2.1 Unemployment rate by region (%)

Region	2000	2005	2006	2007	2008	2009	2010	2011	2012 CI Lower Bound	2012 Prelim Estimate	2012 CI Upper Bound
World	6.3	6.1	5.7	5.4	5.6	6.2	6.0	5.9	5.8	5.9	6.1
Developed economies and European Union	6.7	6.9	6.3	5.8	6.1	8.4	8.8	8.4	8.4	8.6	8.6
Central and South-Eastern Europe (non-EU) and CIS	10.7	9.1	9.0	8.3	8.3	10.1	9.4	8.7	8.1	8.2	8.4
East Asia	4.5	4.2	4.0	3.8	4.3	4.4	4.2	4.3	4.3	4.4	4.6
South-East Asia and the Pacific	5.0	6.4	6.1	5.5	5.3	5.2	4.7	4.4	4.3	4.4	4.5
South Asia	4.5	4.7	4.1	3.9	3.9	4.1	3.9	3.8	3.7	3.8	3.9
Latin America and the Caribbean	8.6	8.1	7.5	7.0	6.6	7.8	6.8	6.5	6.4	6.6	6.7
Middle East	11.5	11.2	10.9	10.3	10.5	10.7	11.2	11.1	10.5	11.1	11.8
North Africa	13.2	11.0	10.0	9.6	9.1	9.1	8.9	10.0	9.9	10.3	10.6
Sub-Saharan Africa	8.5	7.5	7.5	7.4	7.5	7.6	7.6	7.6	7.4	7.5	7.6

Source: ILO, *Global Employment Trends 2013: Recovering from a Second Jobs Dip* (Geneva, ILO, 2013) 165.
Estimates for 2012 are preliminary. 'CI' are the confidence intervals at 95 per cent

Regarding the impact of liberalisation on employment and unemployment in the G20, reference can be made to a joint analysis commissioned by the G20 in 2010 from the World Bank, the ILO, the WTO and the OECD.[16] The analysis submitted in Seoul is not without its ambiguities, which may reflect the tension between the approaches and philosophies of the various organisations involved.[17] Nonetheless, the account it offers has the merit of being agreed to on all sides. The general conclusion is that while globalisation has created many jobs[18] it has

[16] OECD, ILO, World Bank and WTO, *Seizing the Benefits of Trade for Employment and Growth: Final Report* (G20 Summit, Seoul, 11–12 November 2010).
[17] Centre d'études sur l'intégration et la mondialisation (CEIM), 'Lien commerce-emploi: les organisations internationales se prononcent' (December 2010) 1(2) *Chronique Humaniser le commerce* 3.
[18] *cf* 'The International Labour Organization has estimated that between 1995 and 2005, thanks to this global expansion, 40 million additional jobs have been created every year in its member countries' (ILO and WTO, *Globalization and Informal Jobs in Developing Countries* (Geneva, WTO, 2009) 23).

destroyed many others in declining sectors.[19] It would be interesting for historians to compare this nuanced picture to the press kits prepared by the Press Office of the GATT at the Marrakesh Conference in 1994, touting to developing and developed countries alike the millions of new jobs to be created following the creation of the WTO.[20]

Table 2.2 Rates of unemployment in different regions of the world

	Unemployment rates			*Percentage growth in numbers unemployed*	
Region	*1987*	*1993*	*1997*	*1987–97*	*1993–97*
Developed countries	7.6	8	7.3	0.7	−1.6
Europe	10.4	10.6	10.5	1.1	0.01
Japan	2.8	2.5	3.4	2.9	8.5
United States	6.2	6.9	4.9	−1	−6.8
Other developed countries	8.3	11	8.8	2	−4.1
Latin America and the Caribbean	5.7 (1990)	–	7.4	7.3(1990–97)	–
China	2	2.6	3.0(1996)	–	–
India	3.4	2.3	–	–	–
Other countries in Asia	4.3(1990)	4.4	4.2(1996)	1.6(1990–96)	0.8(1993–96)
Central and Eastern Europe	–	7.2	9.6(1996)	–	9.1(1993–96)

Source: ILO, *World Employment Report 1998–99: Employability in the Global Economy – How Training Matters* (Geneva, ILO, 1998) 10.

Qualitatively, or as a matter of 'decency', the dominant phenomenon is the growth of 'precarity.'[21] The only type of work that seems to be reliably available is in the informal economy,[22] a phenomenon that reached massive proportions in the poorest countries.[23] The unabashed cynicism of Nicholas Kristof, according to whom '[t]he central challenge in the poor countries is not that sweatshops exploit too many people but that they don't exploit enough'[24] would likely be meagre consolation for those concerned, assuming they had any way of hearing it. Indeed, informal work often means a very low level of wages, non-existent job security, the

[19] For the G7 countries alone, Peters has calculated a significant drop in employment in the industrial sector (from 89.3 to 79 million between 1980 and 2005), a continuing trend since the 1970s (Peters, 'The Rise of Finance' (n 1) 85–86).

[20] Without dwelling too much on the fraught relationship between jobs destroyed by new technological developments that made worker qualifications redundant and those jobs made redundant more directly through the new realities of global production.

[21] On precarity, see generally Judy Fudge and Rosemary J Owens (eds), *Precarious Work, Women, and the New Economy: The Challenge to Legal Norms* (Oxford, Hart Publishing, 2006).

[22] ILO and WTO, *Globalization and Informal Jobs* (n 18) 75.

[23] According to the joint report of the ILO and WTO on employment and trade, the share of informal work in the non-agricultural sector of developing countries in Asia would reach 78 per cent, 52 per cent in Latin America, and 56 per cent in Africa (ILO and WTO, *Globalization and Informal Jobs* (n 18) 27).

[24] Nicholas Kristof, 'Dreaming of sweatshops', *International Herald Tribune* (Paris), 5 January 2009.

absence of any social protection and extremely limited access to further education or training.[25] The ILO/WTO report estimates in this regard that 'the existence of a large informal economy largely explains why developing countries do not fully benefit from their integration into the global economy'.[26] The estimate by the ILO of the huge proportion of workers who are in vulnerable employment (that is to say, own-account and contributing family workers, a category that still covers only a portion of informal workers) gives a striking example: 'On the basis of available data, the current estimate of the number of workers in vulnerable employment in 2009 is 1.53 billion, which corresponds to a global vulnerable employment rate of 50.1 per cent'.[27]

B. A Mixed Record of Progress which Puts the ILO Model on the Defensive

Even many of the staunchest supporters of globalisation have ended up recognising its ambivalent impact, admitting in the end that globalisation has had its 'winners' and 'losers'. The problem is that the winners have ended up mostly in the East and the losers among the West's previously sizeable industrial workforce.

It seems in this regard that it is less-skilled and traditional industrial workers in the 'old developed countries' who have suffered the worst from the displacement of investment and competition from emerging countries.[28] Without a doubt, the most emblematic manifestation of this trend is the unceremonious eviction of blue-collar workers from the middle class comfort they had managed to win during the post-war period[29] and the resulting emergence of what Rana Foroobar describes as the 'boomerang generation'.[30] More generally, the prospect of a better outcome for future generations which had comforted worker endurance through

[25] Eric Gravel, Tomi Kohiyama and Katerina Tsotroudi, 'The Role of International Labour Standards in Rebalancing Globalization: A Legal Perspective' in ILO (ed), *The Global Crisis, Causes, Responses and Challenges* (Geneva, ILO, 2011) 7.

[26] ILO and WTO, *Globalization and Informal Jobs* (n 18) 25.

[27] ILO, *Global Employment Trends 2011: The Challenges of a Jobs Recovery* (Geneva, ILO, 2011) ix.

[28] Peters provides data showing that, in OECD countries, financial capitalism had a very negative impact on the quality of employment: 'the maturation and spread of shareholder capitalism has led to changes in labour management and industrial relations that have lowered wages and created poor jobs. Finance-driven corporate restructuring has also meant layoffs and systematic pressure to worsen collective bargaining and weaken Union power' (Peters, 'The Rise of Finance' (n 1) 12).

[29] One important result of this outcome has been a fracture between an old guard of industrial workers who buy into the soft protectionism of the earlier era, and those working in services who generally favour further liberalisation in this sector – a gap which helps explain the split of the AFL/CIO in the United States (see Bill Moyers, 'Shades of Howard Zinn: It's OK if it's Impossible' in *Common Dreams* (2 November 2010), available at www.commondreams.org/view/2010/11/02-2).

[30] Rana Foroobar, 'The truth about the US poverty crisis', *Time*, 26 September 2011, at 20. The author notes in particular that the average wage of a blue-collar worker is lower in real terms than it was in 1964, though it remains true that 'the fastest way to poverty is job loss'. This is likely why the 'boomerang generation' is fighting for investment in education, while the former are fighting to protect social security benefits.

hard times after the second industrial revolution now seems upended,[31] arousing a climate of gloom and distrust of globalisation among the affected populations.

No doubt it is objectively true that everywhere, even in these countries, globalisation offers many opportunities. But at what cost? Is the amount of effort, initiative and skill required to make good on these opportunities in countries abandoned by 'old' industry really in the end very different from that required for the creation of a business? And what level of compensation can be expected by comparison? This last question inevitably evokes another age-old tension: the re-emergent issue of the division of returns to capital and to labour, a concern ultimately going to the heart of the ILO's mandate to promote social justice.

Over the last few decades, it is easy to trace the rise in the returns to capital at the expense of labour (even through the recent convulsions in the financial sector). On top of that trend, the prevalence of working poor in both developed *and* developing countries[32] and long-term unemployment have both assumed alarming proportions in many countries working to adjust to new realities.[33] The causes of this discrepancy are the subject of some debate among economists.[34] Besides technological innovation, the transition from industrial capitalism to financial capitalism is undoubtedly a significant factor.[35] From the point of view that concerns us here, another possible explanation deserves special attention: the likely relationship between this growing discrepancy and the persistent 'deficit' in the implementation of fundamental rights – especially collective rights. As we will have the opportunity to examine in greater detail below, the specific 'enabling' function of these rights as it was proclaimed by the 1998 Declaration on Fundamental Principles and Rights at Work is in fact to allow workers to receive a fair share of the wealth they have helped to generate. And this link has been confirmed in practice, as shown in the 2011 *World of Work Report*.[36]

[31] Indeed, it is being replaced in countries such as France with an explicit 'fear of status loss' (Éric Maurin, *La peur du déclassement: Une sociologie des récessions* (Paris, Seuil, 2009)). It should be kept in mind that falling social status played an important role in the disorders of the first half of the twentieth century. The problem seems to take on an even more acute dimension in Italy.

[32] Nomaan Majid, 'The Working Poor in Developing Countries' (2001) 140(3) *International Labour Review* 271.

[33] The case of the restructuring in post-communist countries is from this point of view particularly telling. The existence of a 'lost generation' is generally acknowledged: those now arriving at retirement who failed to find a stable or profitable position after the 'shock therapy' of the early 1990s therefore face a particularly difficult old age.

[34] For some recent contributions to the debate, see Samuel Bentolila and Gilles Saint-Paul, 'Explaining Movements in the Labor Share' (2003) 3(1) *The BE Journal of Macroeconomics* 9; Arjun Jayadev, 'Capital Account Openness and the Labour Share of Income' (2007) 31(3) *Cambridge Journal of Economics* 423.

[35] For a very strong analysis of the impact of financial capitalism on employment, business strategies, regulation strategies of states and union organisation, see Peters, 'The Rise of Finance' (n 1). See also ILO and International Institute for Labour Studies (IILS), *World of Work Report 2008: Income Inequalities in the Age of Financial Globalization* (Geneva, ILO, 2008); ILO and IILS, *World of Work Report 2011: Making Markets Work for Jobs* (Geneva, ILO, 2011) 55–67. Jayadev, 'Capital Account Openness' (n 34) provides a higher-level account, which focuses on the enabling conditions of global financial liberalisation.

[36] ILO and IILS, *World of Work Report 2011* (n 35) 62–63.

More than a tidal phenomenon lifting all ships (large and small) toward greater prosperity and wellbeing, in line with the millenarian vision of a globalisation without (too much) pain, it is therefore fair to see instead the realities of globalisation as an illustration of the principle of communicating vessels.[37]

Assuming for a moment that things do line up in this way, does this state of affairs, though being far from satisfactory, really represent a clear regression in comparison to the situation that prevailed over prior decades?[38] Which makes the next question inevitable: why is it so imperative in the current context for the ILO to find more effective forms of regulation? There are two arguable answers to this question.

The first amounts to saying that, in the absence of new forms of regulation capable of ensuring globalisation of the economy takes a more socially equitable form, current trends are simply not sustainable. The hypothesised implosion of the global order as a result of inadequate 'social equity' under globalisation has already been alluded to in various quarters, including in the 2004 Report of the World Commission on the Social Dimension of Globalization established under ILO auspices.[39] By a further irony of history, the threat of such an implosion would thus conveniently fill the gap left by the disappearance of the Bolshevik menace which the ILO relied on both for its persuasiveness and for the development of its normative activities throughout the period of the Cold War.[40] The onset of the financial crisis three years after the completion of the World Commission's work, however, abruptly took the issue away from the field of rhetoric, and confronted the world with realities which certainly vindicated the ILO's warnings. Unfortunately, it also presented an organisation hamstrung actually to prevent or curb such incidents through appropriate regulation.

The second argument is that the ILO's inability to fulfil its function of mediating between interdependence and global social progress at the universal level could, in turn, undermine its ability to fulfil its other key function concerning the diffusion of the pluralistic, tripartite model that was supposed to have triumphed at the end of the Cold War. Instead, the model might be forced once again to

[37] Such a conclusion could hardly be drawn without putting into question elements of ILO orthodoxy, including some drawn from the Declaration of Philadelphia. As Charnovitz has already done (Steve Charnovitz, 'Promoting Higher Labor Standards,' (1995) 18(3) *Washington Quarterly* 167, 169) it might be worth asking if there is not some need to reverse the famous dictum that poverty anywhere is a threat to prosperity everywhere. Indeed, one might fairly conclude that prosperity feeds on poverty, with the only consolation being that it changes sides from time to time.

[38] It is convenient in this regard to suspend judgement regarding the as-of-yet unpredictable social consequences of the continued economic troubles brought about by the crisis.

[39] World Commission on the Social Dimension of Globalization, *A Fair Globalization: Creating Opportunities for All* (Geneva, ILO, 2004).

[40] Drawing from this perspective, prominent Austrian professor of international law, Friedl Weiss, did not hesitate to ask in all seriousness whether, having saved capitalism the first time during the Cold War, the ILO should not intervene again to save it from a self-made crisis which could easily prove fatal! Friedl Weiss, 'Coherence in International Law and Organization' (Presentation to the ILO, Geneva, 27 November 2011).

defend itself,[41] this time against the 'Beijing Consensus', combining hyper-growth and centralisation of power in a new form of neo-Bismarckian 'market Leninism'.[42] With the sovereign debt crisis in developed countries, the ILO seemed to become even less able to prevent the unravelling of the progressive social model whose promotion it had championed and which prevailed among its main (primarily Western) financial backers. Recent statements on Al-Jazeera from the President of the Chinese sovereign wealth fund (the CIC) brutally summarise the new situation. He claimed, in effect, 'The root cause of the trouble is the over-burdened welfare system, built up since the Second World War in Europe – the sloth-inducing, indolence-inducing labour laws' that, in short, 'are outdated'.[43] There is good news resulting from the string of changes the Chinese economy has had to adopt to confront recent challenges: the drying up of European markets because of the apparent 'laziness' of its people; the bursting of the housing bubble and the resumption of growth. In particular, these adaptations have meant that Chinese leaders seem increasingly to realise that, for better or for worse, the sustainability of their own model must make some room for pluralism and provide increasing autonomy to social actors acting in defence of their interests[44] – not to mention pursuing a more equitable sharing of wealth.

II. Which Puts into Question its Capacity to Meet the Demand Through the 'Traditional' Normative Strategy

Even before the outbreak of the financial crisis, the social deficits of globalisation provided affirmation of at least one of the ILO's fundamental assumptions, namely, that social progress is unlikely to be spontaneous but rather requires voluntary and coordinated action on the part of states. From this point of view, the function of reconciling social progress with market integration assigned to the ILO from the very beginning was painted with a patina of necessity and usefulness which had become somewhat hazy in the post-war years. However, the persistence and possible worsening of the situation, added to the endless twists and

[41] Although it might only be momentary, as seems suggested by the Arab Spring movements and their claims for greater civil society autonomy.

[42] *cf* Michael Bernhard, 'The Leadership Secrets of Bismarck and Imperial Germany, and Competitive Authoritarianism' (2011) 90(6) *Foreign Affairs* 150 (reviewing the book by Jonathan Steinberg, *Bismarck: A Life*), providing an interesting parallel between Bismarckian policies and those of contemporary China. The first use of the term 'market Leninism' to describe China's model is attributed to Nicholas Kristof, 'China sees "Market-Leninism" as way to future', *New York Times* (New York), 6 September 1993.

[43] Sarah Rainey, 'Britons are "lazy" and "addicted to benefits", China claims', *The Telegraph* (London), 20 October 2011; 'Jin Liqun: Europe induces "sloth, indolence"', *Al Jazeera*, 27 December 2011, available at www.aljazeera.com/programmes/talktojazeera/2011/11/2011114434664695.html.

[44] See, eg, the supplement to the *Herald Tribune* in July 2011, funded by the Central Committee of Chinese Communist Party, in which its secretary emphasised the need for autonomy of trade unions in defending their interests.

aftershocks of the financial crisis, give renewed intensity to the parallel question of whether the gamble made – to carry out this function through standards activities relying on persuasion – might be facing losing odds.[45]

When it comes to pursuing gradual and universal progress towards the ILO's constitutional objectives within the constraints of a globalised economy, what is primarily at issue is the continued utility of what might be described as the ILO's traditional *normative technique*. By contrast, the *normative tools* provided by the ILO Constitution might still be perfectly suited to that purpose, so long as they are focused on 'the rules of the game' and on a dynamic process of 'levelling up' rather than on meeting pre-established levels, and effectively combined with other modes of persuasion available to the ILO.[46] It should be recognised at the same time that along with the effectiveness of this normative tool comes a limit, or rather a genetic defect: in principle, it operates solely on traditional state actors, who are themselves influenced in many key areas by policy prescriptions from other inter- or supra-state actors.

A. A Lost Cause: The Ability of the Traditional 'Normative Grid' to Provide a Universal Level Playing Field

To understand the difficulty, we must return to the double gambit chosen by the ILO's founders. On the one hand, they intended to reconcile the constitutional objectives of social progress with international economic interdependence, using collectively agreed standards to help states overcome the 'prisoner's dilemma' inherent to the choice of open trade. On the other hand, these standards could be made binding only through the formal consent expressed through ratification (of Conventions; Recommendations would require only transposition into domestic legislation).

With the benefit of hindsight, it may seem obvious that this double bet was lost as soon as it was made. From the perspective of the time in question, however, it was not an unreasonable choice. The founders could have been confident that the ILO's persuasive capacities would prove hard to resist, and might have even been cocky about its ability to bring about at least a partial levelling of working conditions between countries, given its possession of three powerful levers: an unquestionable legitimacy linked to a unique tripartite structure and its universal membership; the reasonable accommodation of every country's capabilities through the so-called flexibility provisions; and, finally, the residual capacity

[45] Hansenne, *Un garde-fou* (n 4) 84.

[46] There is some resonance here with Simon Deakin's idea of a model of international economic competition he calls 'reflexive harmonisation', in which the interaction between jurisdictions is valued 'not for the end state or equilibrium which it brings about, but for the process which it engenders'. He contrasts this model with 'competitive federalism' where central rules are used to reproduce an ideal equilibrium of laws. Simon Deakin, 'Social Rights in a Globalized Economy' in Philip Alston (ed), *Labour Rights as Human Rights* (Oxford, Oxford University Press, 2005) 40–41.

conferred by Article 19.5 of the Constitution to pester (or even harass) countries that were slow to put them into action.[47]

The inclusion of country-specific clauses in the first Conventions adopted by the ILO[48] is particularly significant from this perspective. Such named exceptions do seem particularly incongruous today. They have, of course, been overtaken by the long-standing practice, greatly expanded since 1946, of using the so-called flexibility clauses, couched in general terms and appealing to a wide variety of methods for varying obligations.[49] Yet the former practice actually had a double significance: it was, of course, aimed at adapting the requirements of the Convention to the conditions of specified countries (as do the flexibility clauses found in later instruments), but adopting the relevant instruments with these tailor-made adjustments to their predilections was also, and perhaps above all, intended to cement the moral commitment of the countries thus identified to ratify it.

This expectation, however, was quickly disappointed not only by the countries, thus single out, but also by the founders themselves, who failed in their responsibility to lead by example.[50] And, of course, the eventual context of beggar thy neighbour protectionism that arose during the inter-war years only exacerbated a shared reluctance to comply with common rules.

Such inauspicious beginnings were hardly determinative, however. Almost as soon as the Second World War ended, the rhythm of normative production came close to matching the impressive pace seen in the organisation's earliest years.[51]

[47] A country's freedom to ratify (or not) was supposed to have been constrained by several devices intended to make subsequent refusal of the extensively negotiated text (intended to be adapted to the realities of each country) very difficult. In practice, it would also mean breaking a tacit code of conduct among Members of what started out as a relatively exclusive 'club'. Particularly notable among these devices are the obligation to submit the adopted Conventions to the competent authority for ratification in Art 19(5)(b), and the obligation to report on the 'follow-up' to these Conventions even when they have not been ratified, provided for in Art 19(5)(e) (see Francis Maupain, 'International Labour Organization Recommendations and Similar Instruments' in Dinah Shelton, *Commitment and Compliance: The Role of Non-Binding Norms in the International Legal System* (Oxford, Oxford University Press, 2000); see generally, ibid Pt II).

[48] Thus, Art 10 of ILO Convention No 1 On the Hours of Work in Industry (adopted 28 November 1919, entered into force 13 June 1921) authorises British India to implement a working week of 60 hours (rather than 48). Similarly, Art 5 of Convention No 4 On the Night Work of Women (adopted 28 November 1919, entered into force 13 June 1921) provides that India and Siam may suspend the application of Art 3 providing that women cannot work in industrial undertakings.

[49] See Jean-Michel Servais, 'Flexibility and Rigidity in International Labour Standards' (1986) 125(2) *International Labour Review* 193; Wilfred Jenks, 'ILO Standards: Are They Obsolete, Premature, Marginal or Important' in ILO, *Social Policy in a Changing World: The ILO Response: Selected Speeches by Wilfred Jenks* (Geneva, ILO, 1976).

[50] In this regard, to avoid subjecting themselves even more stringently to a moral suasion for which Albert Thomas had been the tireless salesman, some of the founders were driven to devise innovative formulas, including the 'conditional ratification' by which the State undertakes to ratify as long as others, and particularly direct industrial competitors, do the same. There were 13 assorted ratifications subject to such a condition (Nicolas Valticos, 'The Nature and Scope of the Legal Ratification of International Labour Conventions' in Yoram Dinstein (ed), *International Law at a Time of Perplexity: Essays in Honour of Shabtai Rosenne* (Dordrect, Martinus Nijhoff, 1989) 993 ff).

[51] And not without some criticism. See Efrén Cordova, 'Some Reflections on the Overproduction of International Labour Standards' (1993) 14 *Comparative Labor Law and Policy Journal* 138.

Unfortunately, the record of ratifications failed to enjoy such a drastic recovery. While the rate of ratification during the late 1960s and the 1970s showed incontestable progress, the recovery was relatively short-lived and to some extent misleading. Specifically, it was inflated by the success of the 'automatic succession' doctrine during the decolonisation period, under which the obligations of former colonial powers were automatically adopted by the numerous newly independent states.

To avoid throwing out the baby with the bathwater, it is nevertheless important to discern whether this bleak state of affairs is inherent to the nature of the normative tools available, or is more a result of the particular form that normative production has taken during the ILO's first near-century. Such a question in turn requires distinguishing between two dimensions of standard setting which put into play the ILO's persuasive powers. There is, first of all, the *content of the standards.* If the dawdling pace of ratification reveals the ILO's limited persuasiveness, we will see that in reality this pace largely reflects the more or less deliberate bias of standards policy in favour of overall international 'clout' at the expense of attention to national-level 'ratifiability' that would evidence an aim actually to create a level playing field. There is, as well, the question of the pace of normative production itself. We will see here that the 'breakdown' of normative production is closely linked to the ebbing persuasiveness of an ILO no longer buoyed by ideological competition.

(i) General Trend of Normative Production Toward the 'Magisterial'

The highpoint of standards production resulted from a development that seemed to suit everyone's purposes – though, ironically, for sometimes diametrically opposed reasons. On the workers' side, the dream of pursuing a level playing field by ensuring that the text of the Conventions could be ratified by as many members as possible was dispelled early on by the persistent difficulty of obtaining ratifications beyond a limited circle of 'star pupils'. The ideal thus logically gave way to texts which could represent a measurable, if only symbolic, improvement in working conditions for the majority of those concerned. This trend suited employers perfectly: it had the twin advantage of evincing their commitment to social progress in the face of the Bolshevik threat, while having limited practical consequences (or even perverse consequences, insofar as the higher the standards demanded, the lower the chance the instruments would be ratified). Finally, the governments of the industrialised countries, both East and West, were not to be outdone in the ideological competition in which their underlying models were engaged. And rather than a positive rule forcing governments to be consistent with their votes in favour of adoption, the Constitution's obligation on members to submit every newly-adopted instrument to the competent authority for implementation, was for the most part treated as a simple formality, providing further validation of the rule of customary international law separating a country's ratification of a treaty from its support for the text at the time of a treaty's adoption.[52]

As understandable as it may have been to favour symbolic value over practical contribution to a level playing field, the net result of this practice was a paucity of ratifications,[53] undermining both the practical significance and the very credibility of Conventions. It is important to keep in mind in this respect that, in its Conventional form, the normative tool is invaluable not so much because it entails an advance in national legislation[54] but for two specific reasons: first, it exerts a 'ratcheting' effect, preventing the backsliding of that legislation because of the difficulty and stigma attached to denunciation of Conventions; and second, it ensures supervision of the effective application of implementing legislation, thereby making up for any gap or failure in national supervision institutions. Sacrificing 'ratifiability' in favour of clout alone undermined this double advantage and the credibility of the Conventions themselves.

That is why successive post-war Directors-General, and most notably Francis Blanchard and Michael Hansenne, were so consistent in their warnings against practices that could 'demonetise' the ILO's main normative tool, and why they kept proposing possible alternatives. It is worth touching on the outcomes of two of these proposed alternatives, because they quite starkly reveal the challenges posed by the complexity of the underlying dynamics.

The first trial balloon was the attempt to shift standards policy toward the adoption of Recommendations in cases where the subject was insufficiently ripe, or where there was good reason to fear that proceeding by way of Convention might result in a rate of ratifications so low as to further dull the edge of the most effective weapon in the ILO's arsenal. The workers recurrently opposed the idea, invoking the argument that even non-ratified Conventions remain a reference-point for legislation and collective bargaining.[55] This was, of course, pure sophistry (a non-ratified Convention has *exactly* the same legal effect as a Recommendation)[56] intended to hide the real reason: the idea that progressive symbolism of a text is

[52] That is, countries focused on the plain text of Art 19(5)(e) that suggested that 'no further obligation' lay on non-ratifying countries, rather than on the principle expressed in the remainder of the article, creating an obligation to seek ratification and to provide positive reasons where ratification was not forthcoming.

[53] In 2006, for the eight fundamental Conventions, the ratification rate exceeded 90 per cent for Europe, Africa and the Americas. It was almost 75 per cent for the Arab States and 65 per cent for Asia. However, for the Conventions that are neither fundamental nor designated as priority or 'governance' Conventions (81, 122, 129, 144), the rate has stagnated since the 1980s: it is about 35 per cent for Europe, 25 per cent for the Americas, 15 per cent for Africa and just over 10 per cent for the Arab States and Asia (ILO, 'Improvements in the Standards-related Activities of the ILO: A Progress Report' (2006) GB.295/LILS/5, Tables A1 and A4).

[54] To the extent that ratification in many cases marks pre-existing compliance of the Convention with existing legislation, rather than vice versa. Unfortunately, no study appears to have been conducted on this dynamic.

[55] See ILO, *Record of Proceedings* (ILC, 85th Session, Geneva, 1997).

[56] That is, a Recommendation is no harder to use as a reference point in legislation, nor any more binding on members, than is an unratified Convention (Maupain, 'Recommendations and Similar Instruments' (n 47) 373 ff).

greater when it is capable (even only theoretically!) of becoming binding through ratification.

The same fate met a proposal in the report of the Director-General to the Conference of 1997,[57] which drew from the same logic to offer up one way of addressing the confrontation of normative activities with the challenges of globalisation. The proposal aimed to increase the pressure to ratify on states that had supported the adoption of a draft Convention at the ILC, by asking them, in accordance with Article 19 of the Constitution, to provide specific reasons for their non-ratification given their original vote in favour. In strongly opposing the proposal, the Workers' spokesman relied on a surprising grab-bag of reasons: it would undermine the sovereignty of governments; it would interfere with policy changes inherent in any democracy; it would amount to exercising a form of blackmail on the civil servants representing governments in Geneva. He also felt it would be unfair to subject the government to such a requirement, given that neither the employers nor the workers could be so compelled.[58] Such unexpected arguments from a Workers' representative could hardly conceal the real reason for their hostility: by encouraging governments that participated in the drafting of a Convention to be more consistent with themselves, such a reform would almost certainly encourage them to pay more attention to how 'ratifiable' a text was, at the expense of the overall progressive symbolism of its content.

At the same time, once one takes into account the difficulty of obtaining ratification beyond a small circle of star pupils, prioritising the symbolic value of the texts over their ability to ensure an effective alignment of (minimum) working conditions among Members seems far from absurd. Moreover, the strategy was pursued not only in the context of the Cold War, where economic competition was partly overshadowed by political competition between systems, but also during the *trente glorieuses*, where economic prosperity in the developed countries fed an upward trend in domestic legislation, whether or not the relevant Conventions were ratified. The problem is that the end of the Cold War, the advent of globalisation, and the triumph of financial capitalism combined to deflate political competition and put economic competition back on the front burner, thereby undermining the assumptions underlying this logic. In this new context, the priority given to 'clout' lost out in two ways: as a matter of levelling the field, given that the more demanding standards in the Conventions (and the related case law) now stand in the way of their universal ratification;[59] and as a matter of soft power as

[57] ILO, 'Standard Setting and Globalization' (n 3) 54.

[58] ILO, Minutes of the 273rd Session (Governing Body, 273rd Session, Geneva, 27 October–6 November 1998) V/9.

[59] Given that it is otherwise treated as rather emblematic (including from the perspective of 'levelling the playing field'), one example seems particularly revealing from the perspective of ratifications. Though its technical sophistication and flexibility have meant that ILO Convention 102 on Social Security (Minimum Standards) (adopted 28 June 1952, entered into force 27 April 1955) has been hailed as an unsurpassable model for standard setting, it continues to struggle to find uptake beyond the borders of Europe and Latin America. Even within those regions, it recently seems to have fallen somewhat out of favour. The popularity, even among some European countries bound by the Convention , of the Social Protection Floor initiative, entrusted to a working group chaired by former

well, since further normative production has to a large extent dried up in this new environment, with the employers, supported by a number of governments, determined to focus future standards activity mostly on the relaxation of existing instruments. The paradoxical result of this strategy is that the workers found themselves led by its very logic to look beyond traditional normative production, and indeed outside the ILO itself, for a regime capable of effectively balancing the ILO's social progress objectives with the constraints of a global market created by the open economy: whence the social clause debate. We will have ample opportunity to canvass the issues surrounding those debates in Part III.

(ii) Normative Production Orphaned by the End of the Cold War

The fact that the Cold War's conclusion preceded a marked slowdown in standards production was far from coincidence. The new situation has broken down inhibitions and unmasked true intentions. During the Cold War, of course, employers had to confront pressure from Eastern Bloc countries to allow representation for 'social enterprise directors' at the Governing Body. They thus, at least on the key issue of safeguarding the autonomy of the groups, had to maintain a common front with workers, and the value of that alliance may to some extent explain their cooperation in normative activities. Yet, the need for that alliance, the cost to be paid and the cooperation on normative activities – each disappeared along with the Bloc itself. From that point forward, continued normative production, even reduced to its symbolic value and logic of international 'clout', seemed a bridge too far. Except in exceptional cases where there was a clear need or demand from all sides, normative activity was in the employers' view to be limited to the revision of existing instruments adopted during the prior period to make them more realistic (if not ratifiable). As for governments, the desire to slow

Chilean president, Michelle Bachelet, which was the subject of a report published in October 2011 (Social Protection Floor Advisory Group, *Social Protection Floor for a Fair and Inclusive Globalization* (Geneva, ILO, 2011)), cannot fail to provoke some reflection in this regard. If the intermittent use of the term 'universal' in connection with these efforts highlights the shared obligation of all States to implement policies guaranteeing minimum coverage to workers (hence the use of the term 'floor'), it is precisely the establishment of nationally-determined 'floors' (in the plural) which is, in light of Convention 102, the real issue. When the project earned the support of the G20 summit in Cannes on 3 and 4 November 2011, its final declaration was clear that 'employment must be at the heart of the actions and policies to restore growth and confidence that we undertake under the Framework for strong, sustainable and balanced growth', expressing the determination of the G20 countries 'to combat unemployment and promote decent jobs' and yet it stressed, in the end the importance 'of investing in *nationally determined social protection floors* in each of our countries' (emphasis added). See also the B20-L20 Joint Statement in which workers and employers together expressed support for the principle of social protection *floors* and recall the centrality of the ILO and the social partners in the implementation of the social objectives *set by the G20.* These efforts led to the adoption of ILO Recommendation 202: Social Protection Floors Recommendation (Recommendation concerning National Floors of Social Protection) (101st Session, Geneva, 14 June 2012), which provides guidance to ILO Members on 'establishing and maintaining national social protection floors as a fundamental element of their national social security systems' and 'implementing their floors with strategies for the extension of social security that progressively ensure higher levels of social security to as many people as possible, guided by ILO social security standards'.

normative production usually reflected more down-to-earth considerations: the need to contain the proliferation of treaties and procedures across the entire system, the overall burden of which (even though that burden might be limited to marginal obligation of reporting on existing practice) ended up putting them in a state sometimes diagnosed as 'normative fatigue'. The rejection by new Members of automatic succession to Conventions which had previously been applicable to their territory, in Europe or elsewhere, can be understood as indicative of this overall trend.[60]

The fact, at the end of the day, is that the compromise laboriously developed in Washington[61] to establish a rhythm of standards production which would include a larger role for the revision of existing instruments, did not survive long given the reluctance of the majority of the Governing Body.[62] While standards production has far from completely dried up (see Table 2.3) it has proceeded more or less ad hoc[63] and without any real strategy, despite laudable attempts at the turn of the millennium to introduce an 'integrated approach'.[64]

(iii) Uncharted Potential of the Normative Tool

The conclusion that emerges from all these remarks is not the one at which they might appear to drive. It would be quite wrong to infer that the standards-making power is itself inherently incapable either of ensuring effective social regulation of

[60] Notable here is that the Committee of Experts itself did not dare subsequently intervene to rescue the doctrine (Francis Maupain, 'La succession à l'OIT' in Geneviève Burdeau and Brigitte Stern (eds), *Dissolution, continuation et succession en Europe de l'Est: succession d'États et relations économiques internationales* (Paris, Montchrestien, 1994)).

[61] On this agreement, see Francis Maupain, 'Le renouveau du débat normatif à l'OIT de la fin de la guerre froide à la mondialisation' (2001) *Bulletin de droit comparé du travail et de la sécurité sociale* 3, n 24.

[62] This reluctance becomes quite clear when one compares the pace of adoption of binding instruments in the decade between 1987 and 1996 to that running 1997–2006. Indeed, the score is 21 to 10! In the reverse sense, however, the new realist concern can no doubt explain the pace of ratifications: given only five of the 21 adopted instruments adopted in the earlier period have obtained 20 or more ratifications, it is remarkable that six of the 10 Conventions adopted in the latter period have passed that benchmark. Notable as well in that regard is that certain Conventions seem to have been 'rediscovered', perhaps under the influence of decentralised ILO structures: ILO Convention No 81 on Labour Inspection (adopted 11 July 1947, entered into force 7 April 1950) and ILO Convention No 155 on Occupational Health and Safety (adopted 22 June 1981, entered into force 11 August 1983) have received, respectively, 18 and 28 ratifications since 2000.

[63] And sometimes with very commendable results, as was the case in the 2011 adoption of ILO Convention No 189 concerning Decent Work for Domestic Workers (adopted 16 June 2011, entry into force 5 September 2013), intended to finally offer a framework of protection to a considerable body of workers (estimated at 100 million) whose conditions of work have until now been very precarious in both developed and developing countries.

[64] The phenomenon is particularly striking given that there is no shortage of topics touching the heart of the ILO's mandate so directly, such as the boundaries of the employment relationship, or the development of labour courts that can offer real guarantees of independence and objectivity to workers and employers. The system of recurring reports under the Declaration on Social Justice for a Fair Globalization (adopted 10 June 2008), intended to allow the International Labour Conference to annually review progress to date and ongoing needs in each of the four strategic objectives, including standard-setting, is supposed to remedy this lack of strategy. It is perhaps too early to say whether its impact will live up to expectations.

Table 2.3 Conventions adopted since the early 1990s

Year	*ILO Conventions*	*Ratifications*	*Entry into force*
1990	C170 Chemicals Convention	17	4 November 1993
1990	C171 Night Work Convention	11	1 April 1995
1991	C172 Working Conditions (Hotels and Restaurants) Convention	15	7 July 1994
1992	C173 Protection of Workers' Claims (Employer's Insolvency) Convention	20	6 August 1995
1993	C174 Prevention of Major Industrial Accidents Convention	17	1 March 1997
1994	C175 Part-Time Work Convention	14	28 February 1998
1995	C176 Safety and Health in Mines Convention	26	5 June 1998
1996	C177 Home Work Convention	10	22 April 2000
1996	C178 Labour Inspection (Seafarers) Convention	15	22 April 2000
1996	C179 Recruitment and Placement of Seafarers Convention	10	22 April 2000
1996	C180 Seafarers' Hours of Work and the Manning of Ships Convention	21	8 August 2002
1997	C181 Private Employment Agencies Convention	26	10 May 2000
1999	C182 Worst Forms of Child Labour Convention	177	19 November 2000
2000	C183 Maternity Protection Convention	26	7 February 2002
2001	C184 Safety and Health in Agriculture Convention	15	20 September 2003
2003	C185 Seafarers' Identity Documents Convention (Revised)	24	2 September 2005
2006	MLC Maritime Labour Convention	35	20 August 2013
2006	C187 Promotional Framework for Occupational Safety and Health Convention	25	20 February 2009
2007	C188 Work in Fishing Convention	2	Not in force
2011	C189 Domestic Workers Convention	4	5 September 2013

the global economy, or of effectively tying improvements in the livelihoods of all workers to advances in economic integration and prosperity.

What *is* at issue in this regard is not the utility of the normative (or standards-making) *tool* so much as the specific legislative or normative *technique* it has traditionally employed in practice. That practice, from which it has rightly taken some pride, has involved the creation of a tight normative 'grid' drawn from the all relevant aspects of the ILO's constitutional objectives, but expressed through a number of specific instruments which the Members are supposed to implement individually. Indeed, as rightly pointed out by Klaus Samson,[65] this approach radically distinguishes ILO practice from that followed by the United Nations and the regional human rights bodies.

If this technique is suitable to the exercise of the 'magisterial' approach discussed above,[66] experience shows it to be ill-suited to promoting the sort of dynamic interrelationship between increasing economic prosperity and gradual progress towards the ILO's assorted constitutional objectives, as ultimately called for by the ILO's 'regulating interdependence' function. Two factors make the approach a poor fit: first, Conventions tend to focus on the results Members should achieve in the specific subject-area covered; secondly, the way the result is defined makes universal ratification virtually impossible (despite flexibility clauses attempting to account for each country's individual capabilities).

These considerations likely provided inspiration when the ILO Director-General (then Hansenne) laid out potential paths forward in his 1997 report to the ILC.[67] Those ideas provided the background for the eventual passage of the 1998 Declaration, but also tried unsuccessfully to open a path 'toward a model based on a consolidation of existing standards into a smaller number of framework instruments, supplemented where necessary by more specific and more easily-amended protocols'.[68] Over the last 15 years, the urgency of the situation has only increased. In light of these ideas and the experience gained since, there is good reason to believe that the effectiveness of the normative tool could be restored if it is deployed in a way that draws on two key aspects of building a level playing field:

- First, by emphasising a handful of fundamental 'rules of the game' recognised as a necessary precondition for workers to receive a fair return on their contribution to collective prosperity. While it is true that the universal application of the relevant Conventions also stumbles on the voluntary nature of their ratification, as we shall see, the ILO has still been able to put in place a transitory solution based on the obligations of membership implicit in the ILO Constitution itself, in the form of the 1998 and 2008 Declarations.
- More innovatively, by focusing broadly on the dynamics tying global economic integration to social progress, rather than more narrowly targeting the desired level to be met in each of the areas covered by an existing instrument. Put in another way, the proper conduct expected from Members could be defined in

[65] Klaus Samson, 'The Protection of Economic and Social Rights Within the Framework of the International Labour Organization' in Franz Matscher, *Implementation of Economic and Social Rights: National, International and Comparative Aspects* (Kehl Am Rhein, Engel Verlag, 1991).

[66] And if it remains indispensable, symbolically as much as practically, in the amelioration of the conditions of workers whose situation falls outside the traditional twentieth-century categories, as it was applied to the plight of domestic workers by the ILC in 2011.

[67] ILO, 'Standard Setting and Globalization' (n 3).

[68] If the latter path has in fact been followed (for reasons that are largely specific to the maritime industry) in the form of the Maritime Labour Convention, pursuing it demands, as recognized by the rest of his report, a great deal of time and effort.

> terms of their ongoing efforts (in consultation with the participation of the interested groups) to balance economic progress against the equitable distribution of benefits (and costs) of that progress, rather than in terms of specific and (more or less pre-established) results[69] set out in the various subject matters covered by existing instruments. Of course, these instruments would continue to provide models the Members would be invited to follow or apply in their domestic legislation.[70]

As we shall see, the ILO has made great strides to revive or renew normative action in both of these directions. Such efforts, however, have so far left unanswered what may appear as the genetic defect of standard setting, ie the fact that it is not operative in respect of non-state actors.

B. Limited Influence Over Non-State Actors

When it was founded, the ILO's promotion of its social objectives took place in a relatively exclusive dialogue with States (leaving aside momentarily the important role played by the League of Nations in economic issues), and the normative tools provided to support that interaction were also intended to have States as their sole subject.[71] This is especially true of Conventions, which can be ratified only by States. Today, however, States have increasingly ceded at least some part of their competence in relevant matters to supra-national bodies like the European Union. This simple example, however, shows how radically the situation has changed since those simple beginnings: de jure and de facto, in certain areas and for certain objectives, the reality is that States possess only limited control.

The implications of this change may be concretely illustrated in connection with one of the ILO's top priorities (to be described in greater detail in Part II): employment. It was the priority accorded to this goal that naturally led the ILO to put its preferred policy instrument into action. The resulting standards were intended not only to recognise employment's place in social policy, but its importance in the economic policy of its Members, as well. Convention No 122 on employment policy was adopted in 1964 precisely according to this vein of thinking.[72]

[69] Which are admittedly, thanks to the flexibility clauses, intended to be adapted to each country's individual level of development.

[70] In many ways, this combination of a focus on gradual progress, with encouragement to use the existing models, is precisely the approach taken by ILO Recommendation 202 (n 59).

[71] The Tripartite Declaration of Principles concerning Multinational Enterprises and Social Policy (adopted 1977) which caters at the same time to multinational corporations, governments, employers and workers, is a sui generis case that has the distinction of having been adopted by the ILO's Governing Body, unlike classic normative instruments, Conventions and Recommendations, which only the ILC is empowered to adopt.

[72] As put by Guy Standing, 'The ILO . . . over-reached itself – when in 1964 it created Convention No 122' (Guy Standing, 'The ILO: An Agency for Globalization?' (2008) 39 *Development and Change* 355, 359).

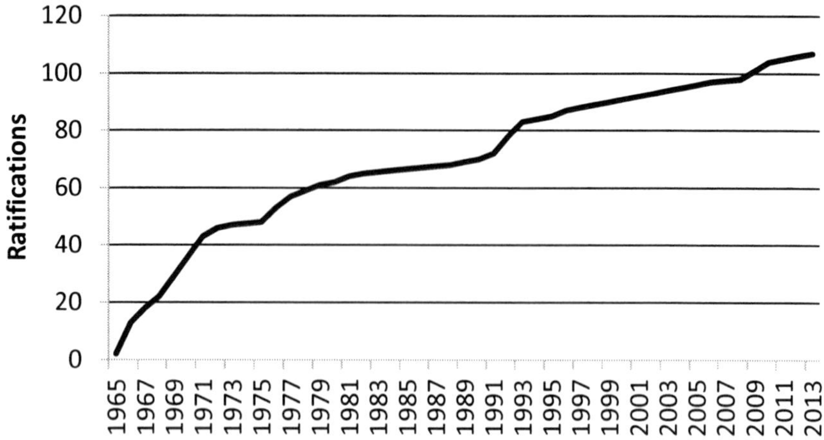

Figure 1 Ratifications of Convention 122 on Employment Policy
Source: Author's Calculations

The obligation the instrument places on ratifying states is *not* to ensure full employment, but merely to pursue an 'active policy' to promote employment. The fact that this Convention can boast a decent score of ratifications (as can be seen in Table 2.3) and was identified as a 'governance standard' in the 2008 Declaration does not exhaust the question of its usefulness[73] (to be carefully distinguished from *the effectiveness* of its implementation)[74] in a vastly different context from the time of its adoption. Comparing the performance of states that have ratified to those that have not is in this respect a rather sobering experience.[75]

[73] It is significant that Peter Auer does not even mention it when talking about the internationalisation of labour standards in his article on the internationalisation of employment, preferring minimum standards to avoid totally free competition in labour markets (Peter Auer, 'The Internationalization of Employment: A Challenge to Fair Globalization?' (2006) 145 *International Labour Review* 119).

[74] In fact, this Convention provides a good illustration of the difference between the question of effectiveness of implementation (how easy it is to implement) and efficacy (relative success) in achieving the underlying objective (Maupain, 'Recommendations and Similar Instruments' (n 47) 383). This distinction can also be made in terms of 'intrinsic' and 'extrinsic' efficacy (Francis Maupain, 'Mondialisation de l'économie et universalité de la protection des droits des travailleurs' in Institut René Cassin (ed), *Commerce mondial et protection des droits de l'homme: les droits de l'homme à l'épreuve de la globalisation des échanges économiques* (Brussels, Bruylant, 2001) 140–44).

[75] Limiting the inquiry to Europe, it is striking to find both the worst and best performing countries among those who have ratified Convention No 122: thus one finds Austria and Denmark, who have managed to keep the unemployment rate impressively low, shoulder to shoulder with countries suffering from rampant unemployment, such as Spain or Portugal. The same is true of countries that have not ratified, among whom are a number of countries whose performance arouses widespread envy, including Luxembourg and Switzerland (which for its own part is one of the few examples where social and economic policy are integrated through a single ministry, the SECO). The fact that Switzerland recently announced its intention to ratify Convention No 122 nearly half a century after its adoption suggests that it intends to draw the moral benefit attached to such a decision, without actually changing anything about its policy. The United States, also a non-ratifying country, has long enjoyed a record and reputation for its remarkable dynamism in employment. On the reasons for the apparent passivity of current victims of unemployment in the United States, see Catherine Rampell, 'US jobless stay silent despite bleak prospects', *International Herald Tribune* (Paris), 11 July 2011.

It is perhaps tempting to lay the blame for this inconclusive result solely on the inadequacy of the normative tool, given that employment is an issue as eminently *economic* as it is *social*. The fact is, whether read alone or together with instruments grouped into the same 'family',[76] the Convention provides no recipe for the content of this 'active policy'[77] which might help the states concerned achieve full employment, except insofar as it calls on them to 'mobilise all efforts' in view of their level of development and their economic capacity, and invites them to create certain institutions (eg to ensure no explicit legal barriers exist for any individual to freely choose a job).[78]

Yet, all this misses the more likely explanation for the situation – or at least the primary one.[79] Rather than searching in the Convention itself, the cause may be sought in the fact, already noted in the Introduction, that the Convention's subjects (as for all Conventions) are states. Any country which ratifies the Convention is as a consequence expected to give due priority to employment, by way of some appropriate policy. However, the independence of most states over economic and social policies has proven to be somewhat illusory, given the growing influence of other sources, particularly the international financial institutions (IFIs) (and the OECD). To the extent that, for reasons well known, the beginning of the 1980s saw the victory of the neoliberal Washington Consensus over the Keynesian vision, the very meaning of employment policy has been profoundly transformed, not only within the IFIs but in the countries under their influence. Indeed, that influence may stretch even further; according to some, the consensus has also strongly shaped the United Nations' approach.[80]

[76] ILO, *General Survey Concerning Employment Instruments in Light of the 2008 Declaration on Social Justice for a Fair Globalization* (Geneva, ILO, 2010) paras 511–19.

[77] As noted by one of the fathers of the Convention, John Mainwaring, full employment (or at least, low unemployment) likely stands for any population among the most widely shared of social goals, and the ratification of the text provides public authorities an opportunity to demonstrate their commitment to that goal. As Mainwaring notes, no matter how high a country's unemployment rate in practice, no government is willing to admit that it is neglecting employment, nor to exclude full, productive and freely chosen employment from its stated priorities. Ratification is intended to show precisely how seriously a government takes this goal. In addition, in an era steeped in Keynesianism, there was still confidence that states had sufficient knowledge of economic dynamics for an active employment policy to consistently lead to that objective. It is from this perspective that a federal state like his, normally reticent to rush into ratification for fear of stepping into provincial jurisdiction, found itself able to make an exception. It is clear that such countries hardly expected the supervisory bodies to call upon them years later, seeking evidence that rising unemployment resulted not from an erosion of their underlying resolve, but from an inherent limitation of economic policies to deal with a profoundly transformed context, impacted not least of all by relatively open borders (John Mainwaring, *The International Labour Organization: A Canadian View* (Ottawa, Canadian Government Publishing Centre, 1986) 127, 162).

[78] ILO, *General Survey Concerning Employment Instruments* (n 76) para 516.

[79] It is common in this regard to have recourse to 'best efforts' obligations in international instruments, and they are not all doomed to inefficacy. As Mainwaring suggests, and as reiterated in the 2010 General Survey (ILO, *General Survey Concerning Employment Instruments* (n 76) para 127), there was at the time a good reason for the Convention to provide no guidance on the types of macroeconomic policy instrument to be used in achieving the goal. For the designers, the matter was clear: it was enough to refer to the Keynesian manual!

[80] Emmerij, Jolly and Weiss complain of the 1995 Copenhagen Summit, that it 'never fundamentally challenged structural adjustment . . . Poverty and employment policies looked like second-order

Thus, we see that, along with a general need to reinvigorate its activities and more specifically to renew its normative techniques, the ILO must look for ways to exercise its powers of persuasion in new forms and, where possible, on other institutional actors.[81] Among these solutions, we shall consider the possibility of developing a 'coherence instrument' – to be developed and possibly even implemented with the involvement of the relevant organisations – on the basis of precedent established, or at least outlined, by ILO Convention No 117 on Social Policy in 1962.

objectives after economic priorities were determined. The challenge became not to curb the emerging global economy but to adopt social policies to mitigate the human costs of the economic transformation associated with globalization' (Louis Emmerij, Richard Jolly and Thomas George Weiss, *Ahead of the Curve? UN Ideas and Global Challenges* (Blomington, IN, Indiana University Press, 2001) 115). It is interesting to note that Kerry Rittich has raised very similar concerns regarding the conclusions of the World Commission on the Social Dimension of Globalization: 'There is great stress on the imperative of growth and many references to growth as the best route to full employment. However, *A Fair Globalization* contains relatively little analysis of the specific demands of pro-employment growth.' As Rittich notes further: 'This issue should be much more central to a global labour or social justice analysis; whether growth without employment is desirable in itself raises some of the issues discussed' (Kerry Rittich, 'Rights, Risk, and Reward: Governance Norms in the International Order and the Problem of Precarious Work' in Judy Fudge and Rosemary J Owens (eds), *Precarious Work, Women, and the New Economy: The Challenge to Legal Norms* (Oxford, Hart Publishing, 2006) 42).

[81] To understand how much space there is for the ILO to develop in these directions, consider the content of the 2010 General Survey on employment. Despite the OECD's considerable role in research, and the significant influence of the guidance it has provided through peer review of economic and social policies, the report gave it only passing mention in one paragraph (ILO, *General Survey Concerning Employment Instruments* (n 76) para 551).

3

Have Recent Efforts at Institutional Renewal Already Fallen Behind the Pace of Change in the Economic Environment?

The ILO has not stood still as global realities shifted away from their historical configuration. Quite to the contrary, it has shown a remarkable capacity for innovation. In the decade between the 1998 and 2008 Declarations, it committed itself under the successive leadership of Michel Hansenne and Juan Somavia to a series of very large-scale initiatives, each corresponding approximately to a different stage of the ILO's (renewed) attempts to influence the dynamics of globalisation. This huge and commendable effort, however, seems to have already been overwhelmed by the pace of economic and social change, which has only accelerated since the onset of the financial crisis.

I. A Renewal in Four Stages

A. 1998 Declaration on Fundamental Principles and Rights at Work

This initiative remains the centrepiece of ILO efforts to circumvent the limitations of traditional standard-setting in the current context. By focusing on the fundamental rights of workers, it aimed to provide an institutional response – even if only a partial one – to the question of the organisation's capacity to bring about a universally applicable 'level playing field'. And this response settles both the procedural question, namely, the legal basis for the universal promotion of these rights, and the substantial problem of how to delimit the workers' rights whose respect can be universally required.

Thus, the text first sets out a universal obligation, applicable to all Members by virtue of their acceptance of the Constitution, ie that links the obligation to the very fact of membership. It thereby skirts the obstacle presented by the requirement that the ratification of international labour Conventions is left to the fickle goodwill of each Member.

Some delegations expressed suspicion that the initiative constituted 'mandate creep', the possible ramifications of which were particularly alarming in view of the freedom of association precedent and the extension made by freedom of association complaints.[1]

In the early years of globalisation, the International Labour Office did indeed turn to the freedom of association precedent to find a way to develop a 'level playing field', notwithstanding the obstacle based in the voluntary nature of ratification, and considered the possibility to extend this formula to other basic rights, including non-discrimination and the prohibition on forced labour.[2] This extrapolation would offer a response to the request of workers and some governments, including the United States shortly after their return to the fold,[3] to establish a floor of rights which would be universally applicable in the context of trade liberalisation. The objections raised against a solution of this kind were for the most part predictable and, according to Hansenne,[4] were in some sense deliberately provoked to clear the way for the formula which would eventually be at the centre of the 1998 Declaration on Fundamental Principles and Rights at Work. Supervision under the Declaration differs from the freedom of association procedures in one essential way: it does not rely on a complaint mechanism, but on a combination of annual reports targeting states that have not ratified the Conventions, and periodic reports covering the situation in all states, whether they have ratified or not. We will have the opportunity to consider the limitations and weaknesses peculiar to this formula a bit further on. Suffice it to point out for the time being that, like existing standards activities, it has in principle no hold on the non-state actors whose role has become essential to achieving the ILO's objectives.

[1] And it should be noted that this precedent had a notable relationship with the ILO's social dialogue function. Once the ILO's membership became meaningfully universal in the post-war period, this precondition for its work was almost completely absent in many countries, and its diffusion was hampered by the voluntary character of ratification of Conventions Nos 87 and 98, adopted in the same period. The ILO, as we know, was able to at least partially overcome this barrier by establishing a procedure for freedom of association complaints, applicable even against countries that had not ratified the relevant Conventions. As in 1998, the procedure was considered applicable based on the minimum obligations inherent in membership and on the principles and values of the Constitution (Nicolas Valticos, *Droit international du travail*, 2nd edn (Paris, Dalloz, 1983) para 783). See Francis Maupain, 'The Settlement of Disputes Within the International Labour Organization' (1999) 2(2) *Journal of International Economic Law* 273.

[2] Note that at the end of the 1960s, the ILO did try to set up a pale replica of the freedom of association procedure for discrimination (Valticos, *Droit international du travail* (n 1) paras 800 and 801).

[3] See the speech by Ray Marshall, Secretary of Labor, asking the ILO to establish a floor of 'MILS' (Minimum International Labour Standards) in ILO, *Provisional Record* (ILC, 66th Session, Geneva, 1980) 7–8.

[4] Hansenne said that he deliberately agreed to this proposal, ignoring the warnings of some of his colleagues, because he felt it had to be done it to clear the way for the proposal which was to become the 1998 Declaration (Michel Hansenne, *Un garde-fou pour la mondialisation: Le BIT dans l'après-guerre froide* (Geneva, Zoe, 1999) 120 ff).

The second major contribution of the 1998 Declaration was to focus that universal obligation on a handful of fundamental rights whose character shared both an *underlying nature* as basic human rights and a *functional role* in the realisation of other rights. The task to be addressed by the Declaration in this regard was essentially (though more remains to be said) to determine those rights which, by virtue of their intrinsic importance and the 'function' they performed in achieving other rights, should be treated as the 'rules of the game' when it came to workers' rights in the globalised economy. Located at the intersection of the ILO's two functions, these rights merit the qualification of 'fundamental' twice over: as a matter of policy, the diffusion of a model of social progress based on the balancing of interests requires an environment which ensures the free expression of those interests through the recognition of fundamental rights; as a matter of political justice, the dynamic hunt for a 'level playing field' for workers presupposes that they will, at the very least, have rights which empower them to claim – and if possible receive – a fair return for their contribution to the common-weal.

In this regard, it is arguable that the 1998 Declaration had a greater impact from the viewpoint of principles, by helping to crystallise a consensus on the 'rules of the game', than it did as a practical matter, notwithstanding the role it may have played in significantly increasing ratifications of the relevant Conventions. As discussed further in Part III, this nonetheless leaves open the question of whether, and more importantly *how*, it might be possible to encourage greater compliance with those principles.

B. 'Decent Work' Strategy

The second stage in the ILO's response was the introduction of the concept of 'decent work' by Juan Somavia, the Director-General first elected in 1999. This concept gained traction quickly, both within and outside the ILO, assisted no doubt by the challenge anyone would face in aligning themselves against it.[5] This public relations initiative aimed at revamping the ILO's image by offering a synthetic, more meaningful frame for its objectives in place of the kaleidoscopic and in some places archaic enumeration provided by the Constitution and the Declaration of Philadelphia. Furthermore, and more significantly, it helped restore a facade of political consensus and common vision on two key issues, ostensibly bridging the divergences among workers, employers and governments which had been opened up by the termination of the Cold War.

In particular, the decent work 'strategy' not only allowed the ILO to take its leave from the recurrent, highly contentious debate on a possible 'social clause' but also and perhaps above all, allowed the debate on slowing, stalling or continuing standards production to fade into a hazy ether of diffuse, pervasive normativity.

[5] As highlighted in the report headed up by Christine Boutin, *De la mondialisation à l'universalisation: une ambition sociale,* Rapport intermédiaire au Président de la République (Paris, La Documentation française, 2010).

In parallel, the broad uptake of the concept in United Nations discourse,[6] as much as it was intended to ward off the spectre of the social clause, nevertheless had the merit of vindicating the importance of the social dimension of globalisation, while offering at least the *appearance* of consensus on the necessity of reconciling economic and social objectives, not only within the UN system but also within the international financial institutions (IFIs).[7] Below the veneer of consensus, however, clear differences and misunderstandings persist. As per the closer review conducted in Part II, even employment, ostensibly central to each institution's vision of such a reconciliation, nonetheless fails to achieve anything close to common treatment.

For all these reasons, as long as this strategy remained essentially a matter of public relations spin, neither employers nor the majority of governments could help but warmly welcome it. Given their traditional attachment to standards activities (not to mention the social clause) the wholehearted support it received from workers is somewhat more intriguing. The explanation may lay in part in the erosion of their influence, discussed further below,[8] but also in the malleability of a concept that, like a kind of normative potluck, allows everyone to take away whatever they themselves bring to the table. Such plasticity made it possible for workers to read into the concept a sort of coded resistance to the 'race to the bottom' allegedly brought about by the free movement of capital.[9] Many probably also wanted to be convinced that, guarded by the concept's multivalence, the normative dimension could advance surreptitiously, before finding an opportunity to reassert itself.

Indeed, the concept was in no way doomed to remain promotional at best, or a 'feel good' device at worst. At an early stage the Office did consider how it might be 'operationalised',[10] and many ideas were subsequently tested in this regard, including not only decent work country programmes,[11] but also a proposal for a consistent set of 'decent work indicators'.[12] Unfortunately, these diverse proposals very quickly came up against the will of certain constituents, and in particular the employers, to leave as large a discretion as possible to national authorities to specify the content of the concepts according to each country's inclination.

[6] See Marieke Louis, *L'organisation internationale du travail et le travail décent: Un agenda social pour le multilatéralisme* (Paris, L'Harmattan, 2011).

[7] It is striking in this regard that the generally sympathetic inclusion of references to 'decent work' in a number of UN texts is supposed to provide the Governing Body with probative evidence of the concept's impact and its ability to rally other organisations: yet it could just as easily be taken as proof of the expertise of the ILO's own representatives during the development of these texts, buttressed by the underlying ambiguity of the idea's content.

[8] According to Peters, developments in finance and corporate governance in recent decades mark a fundamental break with the post-war situation. This break is due to the reaffirmation by capital of its pre-eminence vis-à-vis labour markets and labour organisations (John Peters, 'The Rise of Finance and the Decline of Organized Labour in the Advanced Capitalist Countries' (2011) 16(1) *New Political Economy* 73).

[9] Of the type that has been observed in the 1990s in the context of post-communist transition in Eastern Europe.

[10] Louis, *Travail décent* (n 6) 70.

[11] ibid 77–81.

[12] These efforts went as far as holding a joint conference of statisticians on the issue.

In the end, and to the workers' chagrin,[13] the country programmes provided little of the expected opportunity to sift through national laws in search of any 'gaps' in national legislation compared to relevant ILO standards. Instead, it allowed participating countries to secure a more flattering social image, while obtaining assistance from the ILO for their often-disparate priorities[14] at a generally minimum normative cost. Indeed, the idea of 'decency' seemed at times to come at so low a cost as to make fundamental rights seem a sort of deluxe option by comparison![15] A similar fate met the idea formulated by the working group on social security, chaired by Professor Supiot, of putting a country's commitments to promote decent work in the form of a 'compact' with the ILO, for which they would in return receive certain funding.[16]

As for the project of defining decent work indicators, neither the large magnitude of documents and discussions[17] nor a conference of expert statisticians[18] could overcome the similar difficulties it faced.

All this suggests that decent work would remain a highly malleable notion as long as no attempt was made to give it some form of authoritative definition. This is why the employers were so careful during preliminary discussions on the 2008 Declaration to 'red line' any attempt to do so.[19] The almost paradoxical result was

[13] See the statement of the workers' representative reproduced in ILO, *Report of the Committee for Technical Cooperation* (Governing Body, 297th Session, Geneva, 2006) para 18.

[14] ILO, *Report V: Strengthening the Capacity of the ILO to Assist its Members' Efforts to Promote its Objectives in the Context of Globalization* (ILC, 96th Session, Geneva, 30 May–15 June 2007) para 67 ff.

[15] Within the context of the Decent Work Country Programmes, it appeared that waving the 'decent work' flag could allow a country to show its loyalty to (and obtain technical assistance from) the ILO, even though the flag itself could be raised above highly variable realities, in some cases leaving fundamental rights aside. Such a conclusion is easily drawn from the recurrent report on Fundamental Principles and Rights at Work submitted to the 101st Session of the ILC (ILO, *Report VI: Fundamental Principles and Rights at Work: From Commitment to Action* (ILC, 101st Session, Geneva, 30 May–15 June 2012). Its conclusions indicate that the inclusion of fundamental rights in country programmes is far from consistent, and that this is doubly so for freedom of association and collective bargaining which are, if not exactly ignored, at least treated as poor relations in the overall decent work framework (ibid 18, Table 2.3).

[16] The idea was originally advanced by Prof Goldin (Adrian Goldin, 'Extending Social Security Coverage: The Normative Route' (2006), 27(2), Social Protection and Decent Work: New Prospects for International Labor Standards, *Comparative Labor Law and Policy Journal*, 257–72). Although included among the proposals contained in a report provided to the ILC (ILO, *Report V: Strengthening the Capacity* (n 14) para 71), it unfortunately received little further attention. Nonetheless, the 2008 Declaration left the door open to further exploration of the idea.

[17] See Louis, *Travail décent* (n 6) 72–74.

[18] See International Labour Office, *Measurement of Decent Work: Discussion Paper* (Tripartite Meeting of Experts on the Measurement of Decent Work, TMEMDW/2008, Geneva, 8–10 September 2008).

[19] This also explains an irony revealed by the *travaux préparatoires* of the text. While the 2008 Declaration was originally intended, inter alia, to give the decent work concept a clearer legal status, reaching consensus on the final document required a painstakingly elaborated undertaking that it was not intended and could not be understood to revisit ILO constitutional objectives; rather, negotiations made clear that it was intended only to define a new integrated *approach* to their implementation which would still recognise the discretion of each Member to give each of these objectives (except fundamental rights) a priority corresponding to its idiosyncrasies. Or to put it differently, the concept was not designed to provide a predefined product so much as framing a shared process. On this dimension of the negotiation, see Francis Maupain, 'New Foundation or New Façade? The ILO and the 2008

that the only real effort to operationalise decent work by giving it a clear legal status inside an institutional tripartite framework ended up, as we will see later, omitting the concept from its title!

C. World Commission on the Social Dimension of Globalization

The third stage of the ILO's response came in the form of two nested initiatives to operationalise the decent work concept, and support engagement in the institutional renewal needed to realise a meaningful regulatory regime based only on the sheer force of persuasion: the World Commission on the Social Dimension of Globalization, and the 2008 Declaration on Social Justice. While they only partially succeeded, as discussed below, the financial crisis of 2008 put new energy into their demand for greater coherence and more effective regulation of global economic integration.

The establishment of the World Commission on the Social Dimension of Globalization in 2001 was linked directly to the failure of the 1999 WTO Conference in Seattle. For fear of appearing to lend even indirect legitimacy to the link between trade liberalisation and its social dimension, the majority of WTO member countries had adamantly rejected proposals, put forward by the United States and the European Union, to open debate under WTO auspices on social or employment dimensions of trade liberalisation.[20] An initiative was subsequently taken by Juan Somavia to propose the creation of the Commission to the ILO Governing Body,[21] thereby allowed the debate to continue, while the Doha negotiations were ongoing, if not under the aegis of the ILO, at least under the Director-General's patronage.

When the Commission released its findings in 2004[22] they were indeed addressed beyond the ILO, to any and all organisations with a stake in the underlying questions. The Commission thus represented a very ambitious attempt by the ILO to influence the course of globalisation, applying its persuasive capacities beyond its usual comfort zone and especially beyond its traditional standards-based approach. The full lessons of this experience will be examined further on, especially in the discussion of the role of the ILO's analytical capacity. But what was its practical impact? No doubt, the report successfully attracted momentary attention from the organisations concerned. More difficult to say, however, is how far these

Declaration on Social Justice for a Fair Globalization' (2009) 20(3) *European Journal of International Law* 823, 837–39.

[20] Andrew J Samet, 'Doha and Global Labor Standards: The Agenda Item that Wasn't' (2003) 37(3) *International Lawyer* 757.

[21] This was 'an attempt to build consensus across a wide range of perspectives, North and South, national and international, business and labour, government and civil society, politicians and academics, on the key issues to be addressed and a feasible way forward' (Hamish Jenkins, Eddy Lee and Gerry Rodgers, *The Quest for a Fair Globalization Three Years On: Assessing the Impact of the World Commission on the Social Dimension of Globalization* (Geneva, ILO, 2007) 6.

[22] World Commission on the Social Dimension of Globalization, *A Fair Globalization: Creating Opportunities for All* (Geneva, ILO, 2004).

organisations went in implementing its numerous recommendations – save of course for the ILO, with the 2008 Declaration to be discussed in the next section.[23] The eruption of the financial crisis in 2008 and the litany of negative social consequences it entailed provided the ILO with an opportunity to say 'I told you so' given that the World Commission's analysis had failed to lead to any significant corresponding reforms. No doubt the point was fair game from a public relations standpoint.[24] However, the sudden swelling of the public debt dimension of the crisis only a short while later seemed to point to a crucial and obvious gap in the Commission's analysis.

D. 2008 Declaration on Social Justice for a Fair Globalization

If the World Commission's report was addressed *urbi et orbi*[25] to all the organisations concerned with the social dimension of globalisation, it would probably go too far to say that this meant its recommendations fared much better than any of those contained in the international system's regularly-produced high-level reports. Though the ILO may at most be described as the sponsor of the report, it was probably within the ILO itself where the report ultimately had the most concrete and durable impact. In fact, one slightly cryptic phrase buried in the mass of diverse proposals[26] served as the basis for reflections that, in turn, eventually lead to a second initiative aimed at giving the decent work strategy more concrete form: the 2008 Declaration, entitled, as a result of various vicissitudes, the 'Declaration on Social Justice for a Fair Globalization'. Without questioning the adequacy of the ILO's voluntary means, the adoption of this text was supposed to give the decent work concept a clearer legal status, with all the consequences this would entail as a matter of ILO constitutional practice. The result, however, ended up some distance from the intended goal, not least of all in the title that was finally adopted.[27]

[23] To some extent, the adoption of ILO Recommendation 202: Social Protection Floors Recommendation (Recommendation concerning National Floors of Social Protection) (101st Session, Geneva, 14 June 2012), can also be traced back to the World Commission.

[24] As fair as it was for others in the subsequent months to invoke the apparent but ultimately illusory end of the crisis to deny its systemic character.

[25] Indeed, as President Halonen of Finland came to emphasise in presenting the report to the ILC, 'the recommendations in the World Commission's report cover a much wider field than the ILO's direct scope' (cited in ILO, *Reply by the Director-General to the Discussion of His Report* (ILC, 92nd Session, Geneva, 1–17 June 2004) 25/2).

[26] In particular, it asks the ILO, 'taking advantage of its wide-ranging Constitution and its constituency of workers' and employers' organizations as well as governments, to develop new instruments and methods which can promote coherence between economic and social goals in the global economy, in coordination with other organizations of the multilateral system' (World Commission on the Social Dimension of Globalization, *A Fair Globalization* (n 22) 114, para 513).

[27] The instrument strives to present the entire range of practical implications that the concept might entail. Thus, just as the concept is intended to provide a synthetic, comprehensive structure to the ILO's objectives, the Declaration calls for an 'integrated' and interdependent approach to achieving the concept's incorporated objectives; it furthermore extends the logic of the follow-up to the 1998 Declaration on Fundamental Rights to the ILO's other policy objectives; to do so, it creates a new system

In fact, 'decent work' is curiously absent from the text's title, given that the document was intended to bring an end to the uncertain institutional status implied by the context of its original establishment.[28] In a surprising turn, its title instead revisited the concept of 'social justice'. the leitmotif of official rhetoric during the Cold War, which had (due perhaps to its 'collectivist' connotations) fallen into relative disfavour almost immediately after the fall of the Berlin Wall. There is no small irony in the fact that it was only the stubborn refusal of employers to grant 'decent work' the recognition of being included in the Declaration's title which ultimately led to 'social justice' making a spectacular comeback.[29]

It should be emphasised here that the financial crisis, already brewing at the time and boiling over in the weeks following the text's adoption, gave the outcome a retrospectively prophetic aspect.[30] Indeed, the tumult brought on by the crisis threw a stark light on growing inequality, as it (temporarily at least) removed access to the usual excuse that it ultimately contributed to the dynamism of the economy and the overall expansion of the common-weal.[31]

II. Have the Consequences of the Financial Crisis Rendered the Renewal Old News?

There is no denying that this diverse collection of initiatives helped renew the ILO's image and increase its visibility arousing no little controversy in the process.[32]

of recurring reports that evaluate the impact and shortcomings of the ILO's activities during a given period, including with respect to existing standards; that evaluation in turn is supposed to be conducted in a way that provides recipients a voice.

[28] ILO, *Report V: Strengthening the Capacity* (n 14) paras 143–44. To make this point clear, the concept was first developed by Juan Somavia in reports submitted annually by the Director-General to the ILC. These reports allow for an exchange of views, but cannot per se lead to a formal decision expressing the will of the organisation. Even though it does not always take the form of a standard, the ILO's will can be officially expressed only through a formal decision taken by the ILC pursuant to a question that appears on the agenda; although in a small number of cases where there is no prior agenda item, recourse can be had to a special resolution passed under s 17 of the Rules of the Conference.

[29] See Renée-Claude Drouin and Isabelle Duplessis, 'La régulation internationale du travail de 1998 à 2008: un Eldorado normatif ou un désert interprétatif' (2009) 14(2) *Lex Electronica* 18. The authors find particular fault in the decision to exclude the concept of decent work from the title of the 2008 Declaration, estimating that the Declaration would thereby encourage not only *soft* law but what they refer to as 'liquid law'. Their analysis does not seem to take into account the fact that decent work already lacked any clear legal status, never having been approved following an adversarial, tripartite debate at the ILC. In fact, the 2008 Declaration was the first time it was given any legal status, its absence from the document's title notwithstanding.

[30] It is no coincidence that the final report of the previous Director-General returns to this theme by announcing (with some recklessness, if one knows the history), 'a new era of social justice' (ILO, *A New Era of Social Justice: Report of the Director-General* (ILC, 100th Session, Geneva, 1–17 June 2011).

[31] Quite to the contrary, many prominent economists have pointed to the particular contribution made by inequality to the dynamics underlying the 2008 crisis. See, eg Raghuram Rajan, *Fault Lines: How Hidden Fractures Still Threaten the World Economy* (Princeton, Princeton University Press, 2010).

[32] See below, and the courteous exchange between Langille, Maupain and Alston in the *European*

Will that sufficiently enable it to pursue its raison d'être: of putting in place a regime capable of regulating globalisation? The financial crisis of 2008 clearly showed how far away from realisation this project remains. As unwelcome as it may have been, the *timing* of the crisis was a relative boon to ILO credibility. Indeed, starting at the summit in Pittsburgh, American and international trade unions were able to seize the moment and convince President Obama to get the ILO an invitation to the G20,[33] placing it 'in the big leagues' with the IFIs and the WTO. In validating the warnings made in the 2008 Declaration only a few weeks prior, the crisis highlighted the shortcomings of global financial 'regulation'. But by the same token, it framed the existing deficits in social regulation and threw a bright light on the inability of the ILO and its Members to ensure effective implementation of the universal 'rules' embodied in fundamental rights at work.

While highlighting the ILO's structural weaknesses, the crisis seems to have fallen at an opportune time to reinforce its underlying rationale, by increasing appetites both for regulation and for coherence in the financial, economic and social dimensions of the global market. The speech of French President, Nicolas Sarkozy, at the 2009 ILC, echoed by equally sharp statements he made at Davos in 2010,[34] epitomised this perspective. He said in effect 'the real pipe dreams of today – or let me go further, what is totally irresponsible today – is to believe that the crisis is merely a temporary hitch and that, once it is over, everything can go back to normal'.[35] From which he concluded: 'What do we need, in the end, if it is not rules, principles, a governance that reflects shared values, a common morality?'[36] As much as these comments were intended largely for domestic political consumption, one may wonder to what degree his inquiry is reflective of the increasingly minority position of the 'shrinking West', the group of developed and industrialised countries in decline, against which might be set the views of the 'booming rest' of emerging countries who are not exactly chomping at the bit for new forms of social regulation. Speaking some time later in *Le Monde* with a certain admixture of compassion and irony, Pascal Lamy, while claiming a sympathetic ear to the underlying anxiety, could not refrain from advising supporters of

Journal of International Law (Philip Alston, '"Core Labour Standards" and the Transformation of the International Labour Rights Regime' (2004) 15(3) *European Journal of International Law* 457; Brian A Langille, 'Core Labour Rights: The True Story (Reply to Alston)' (2005) 16(3) *European Journal of International Law* 409; Francis Maupain, 'Revitalization Not Retreat: The Real Potential of the 1998 ILO Declaration for the Universal Protection of Workers' Rights' (2005) 16(3) *European Journal of International Law* 439; Philip Alston, 'Facing Up to the Complexities of the ILO's Core Labour Standards Agenda' (2005) 16(3) *European Journal of International Law* 467. On the concept of decent work *cf* Guy Standing, 'The ILO: An Agency for Globalization?' (2008) 39 *Development and Change* 355; Louis, *Travail décent* (n 6).

[33] The ILO remains the only specialised agency of the United Nations entitled to this privilege.

[34] Nicolas Sarkozy, President of the French Republic, Speech delivered to the 40th World Economic Forum (40th World Economic Forum, Davos, 27 January 2010).

[35] Nicolas Sarkozy, President of the French Republic, Address to the International Labour Conference, 15 June 2009, reproduced in ILO, *Provisional Record* (ILC, 98th Session, 11th Sitting, Geneva, 15 June 2009) 11A/20.

[36] ibid.

'deglobalisation' that their views are 'minoritaire dans le monde. En Asie, en Afrique et en Amérique latine, on y voit surtout des perspectives positives'.[37] He added (unwittingly echoing comments made by Albert Thomas at the beginning of the Great Depression):[38]

> Des réponses aux perturbations douloureuses que vivent les populations occidentales sont nécessaires, mais en utilisant d'autres formes de protection que le protectionnisme, qui ne protège pas . . . Ce n'est pas la mondialisation qui fait problème, mais l'insuffisance de garde-fous, de régulations.[39]

Once the initial shock had passed, and dynamics (deceptively) seemed to regain their normal course, 'short-termism' quickly reasserted itself. Despite the hopes pinned on the G20, it turned out to be ill-equipped to provide the mediating role which would have made it a bona fide institutionalised decision-making system. Without the ability to reconcile a diversity of competing interests, it can hardly hope to introduce any new form of regulation, least of all in social matters.

Against the backdrop of this stalemate, the symbolically significant 100th Session of the ILC in June 2011 saw a new abortive attempt to move the ILO into the regulatory gap. A 'draft resolution concerning the coherence of the multilateral system' was introduced, shortly before the Conference began, by Switzerland, with support from France, South Africa, a few other countries and especially the Workers group.[40] This late initiative was, inter alia, prompted by the conviction that 'the overall increase of wealth made possible by globalization is resulting in too slow a reduction in poverty and inequalities and is not being translated into sufficient job creation to reduce unemployment'.[41] Beyond its specific terms, the move was tactically designed to insert the organisation into the debate a few months before the G20 at Cannes, thus hopefully pushing the theme of coherence away from the purely rhetorical and toward concrete engagement with its institutional roots.[42] Given how late it was launched, however, the initiative foundered in the shallows of the ILC's emergency procedure and, in the end, the expected debate

[37] That is, such views are 'part of a global minority. In Asia, in Africa and in Latin America, we see above all positive perspectives' (author's translation). Cited in Alain Faujas, 'Pascal Lamy: "La démondialisation est un concept réactionnaire"', *Le Monde* (Paris), 30 June 2011.

[38] 'What a strange idea it was of yours, Mr. Lambert-Ribot, to find a contradiction between the "labour protectionism" of the International Labour Office and the theory of free or freer trade for which the League stands.' Remarks by Albert Thomas in the ILC in 1930 (cited in Albert Thomas, *International Social Policy* (Geneva, ILO, 1948) 114).

[39] 'Positive responses to the unfortunate disruptions faced by the population of eastern countries are necessary, but using forms of protection other than protection, which does not protect at all . . . It is not globalisation that is the problem, but the insufficiency of safeguards, of regulations' (author's translation) quoted in Faujas, 'Pascal Lamy' (n 37).

[40] ILO, Provisional Record (ILC, 100th Session, Geneva, 1–17 June 2011) No 2.

[41] ibid 1.

[42] The text pointed to certain institutional dimensions of inconsistency, and applying the 2008 Declaration and reviving its follow-up showed the ways in which the ILO could play a concrete role in remedying them: '(A) strengthening partnerships with the organizations concerned; (B) enabling better policy coordination between and within member States; (C) strengthening universal implementation of the fundamental principles and rights at work as "rules of the game" for the social dimension of globalization; (D) implementing a Social Protection Floor' (ibid 2/2).

gave way to a suitably vague consensus statement from the tripartite Officers of the Conference, helped by the secretariat.[43]

Despite its immediate failure, the effort still left its mark on the work of the G20 at Cannes in November 2011. Traces appear, first in the recommendations adopted by the meeting of G20 Labour and Employment Ministers, held under the French Presidency on 26 and 27 September 2011;[44] the same perspective reappeared in their 2012 meeting in Mexico.[45] There is also an indication of its continued, even if somewhat attenuated, relevance in the first few paragraphs of the Final Declaration of the Cannes meeting, in a section devoted to 'fostering employment and social protection.'[46] Paragraph 6 of the same text specifically calls for greater coherence between the WTO, ILO, OECD and the IFIs.[47] If the formulation of the appeal appears stereotypical, it nonetheless conceals an issue which we will now see is of paramount importance to the ILO and its effectiveness in the context of a globalised economy.

[43] ILO, *Provisional Record* (ILC, 100th Session, Geneva, 1–17 June 2011) No 6, 5; ibid No 32, 16.

[44] In addition to section II, making a call to 'strengthen social protection' and section III, promoting 'effective implementation of social and labour rights' (including the fundamental principles and rights at work by reference to the 1998 Declaration), section IV was focused directly on strengthening the coherence of economic and social policies, and not only included references to the 2008 Declaration but, like the Swiss draft, advocated both for greater coherence in domestic policies *and* coordination between organisations. G20, 'Labour and Employment Ministers' Conclusions' (G20 Meeting, Paris, 26–27 September 2011).

[45] G20, *Labour and Employment Ministers' Conclusions* (G20 Meeting, Guadalajara, 17–18 May 2012) paras 16–17.

[46] G20, *Cannes Summit Final Declaration: Building Our Common Future: Renewed Collective Action for the Benefit of All* (G20 Summit, Cannes, 4 November 2011). Paragraph 5 in particular constitutes a suitably diplomatic compromise: while expressing a commitment to respect fundamental principles and rights at work, it encourages the ILO to continue promoting ratification and implementation of the Conventions (without giving a sense of who should be targeted by these efforts). There is, in particular, not even an intimation that the G20 should lead by example, no matter the French President's reported sentiments that he found it 'shameful' that the members of such a distinguished club had so consistently failed to ratify the fundamental Conventions. The result provides a strong control sample for the proposition that these questions can only be kept from falling through the cracks by continued attention at the ILC itself.

[47] There is, however, no evidence of the great ideas and reforms (apparently inspired by his adviser Henri Guaino) that the French President announced from the podium at the 2009 ILC whereby the ILO and other specialised agencies would be called upon to provide a preliminary ruling to the WTO when issues concerning the rights of workers arise in a commercial dispute. See ILO, Address, M. Nicolas Sarkozy (n 35) 11A/23. In the 2012 G20 Declaration, on the other hand, discussions of coherence were limited even further to cooperation on implementing 'nationally determined social protection floors' (G20, *G20 Leaders Declaration* (G20 Meeting, Los Cabos, 18–19 June 2012) para 22).

Part II
The Proliferation of Multilateral Actors and the Challenge of Coherence

Introduction

There is widespread recognition of the need to decompartmentalise the work of the global-level multilateral organisations. Setting aside any truly unavoidable conflicts between the ILO's social objectives and the economic and financial objectives of the international financial institutions (IFIs), the paucity of active coordination impacts the whole of the global institutional landscape. In this regard, the proliferation of international organisations and regimes has gradually developed an appetite for a 'Global Administrative Law' capable of moving overall practice from an 'austere law of coexistence' to a 'law of cooperation'.[1]

This tendency has manifested itself in numerous contexts, pushing against the self-referential myopia which is the natural inclination of most, if not all, international organisations. The epiphany that multilateral agencies do not exist in isolation has been most glaring in international trade jurisprudence, a legal context which had previously seemed to jealously guard its specificity; thus, even the WTO Appellate Body's fairly obvious recognition 'that the General Agreement is not to be read in clinical isolation from public international law'[2] inspired a surge of approving commentaries. If putting the matter this way seems far from extraordinary at first glance,[3] the formula's merit lies in opening the way for (albeit indirect) consideration of substantial public international law so that, as put by Sandrine Dubois-Maljean in her reading of a report of the International Law Commission, 'the jurisdiction of the WTO tribunals must be "controlled by the normative environment"'.[4] As we will see, such a change in orientation to international law was not without its implications for the ILO as well.

[1] Benedict Kingsbury and Lorenzo Casini, 'Global Administrative Law Dimensions of International Organization Law' (2009) 6(2) *International Organizations Law Review* 319, 327.

[2] *United States – Standards for Reformulated and Conventional Gasoline*, Report of the WTO Appellate Body (29 April 1996) WT/DS2/AB/R, 171.

[3] Indeed, Art 31(3)(c) of the Vienna Convention on the Law of Treaties (adopted 23 May 1969, entered into force 27 January 1980) 1155 UNTS 331, requires that, when a treaty's obligations are being interpreted, 'any relevant rules of international law applicable in the relations between the parties' are be taken into account in that interpretation.

[4] Sandrine Maljean-Dubois, 'Le spectre de l'isolation clinique: quelle articulation entre les règles de l'OMC et les autres instruments et principes internationaux' (National Conference, Taiwan University, Taipei, 12 November 2007) (author's translation) quoting Martti Koskenniemi and the International

This concern is also explicitly reflected in the increasing frequency of mutually supportive cross-referencing seen in international agreements, most noticeably in environmental regulation.[5] Such provisions reflect a clear desire for a more integrated legal regime at the international level.

What is to be done, however, in cases where such cross-references are absent or inexplicit or, what is worse, when provisions in the relevant charters seem to require functional rejection of anything other than what is contained in their respective mandates?[6] The rules of treaty interpretation are in this case of little help,[7] and as we shall see, little is to be gained from pretending that coherence can be guaranteed by establishing an *a priori* hierarchy of objectives.

Law Commission, *Fragmentation of International Law: Difficulties Arising from the Diversification and Expansion of International Law*, Report of the Study Group of the International Law Commission (13 April 2006) A/CN.4/L.682, 45. This was also an important motif in *EC – Biotech* (*EC – Measures Affecting the Approval and Marketing of Biotech Products*, WTO Panel Report (21 November 2006) WT/DS291/36), a case involving a European moratorium on approvals for the marketing of certain biotech products. In this regard, the European Union had, inter alia, invoked the Cartagena Protocol on Biosafety adopted in 2000, conceived as a kind of firewall against the liberalisation of trade in biotech products, but which is not binding on all WTO members (nor even on all parties to the dispute in question). A key question in that case was how this protocol should be taken into account when the panel was interpreting the parties' obligations under the WTO's covered agreements. In rejecting the European argument, the Panel acknowledged somewhat cryptically that external obligations could, though not invariably or exclusively, act as a 'tie breaker' in cases where two interpretations were possible (*EC – Biotech*, para 7.69). Regrettably, the Panel then severely narrowed this opening by placing strict conditions on the external agreements that could be taken into account, specifically requiring that such agreements had to bind not only all the parties to a dispute, but all members of the WTO! The unfortunate consequences of this approach are well captured by Martti Koskenniemi in his final report to the International Law Commission: 'The panel buys what it calls the "consistency" of its interpretation of the WTO Treaty at the cost of the consistency of the multilateral treaty system as a whole' (Koskenniemi, *Fragmentation of International Law*, (n 4) para 450).

[5] See Laurence Boisson de Chazournes and Makane Moïse Mbengue, 'À propos du soutien mutuel – les relations entre le protocole de Cartagena et les accords de l'OMC' (2007) 4 *Revue Générale de Droit International Public* 829. The article provides a helpful overview of various legal instruments in this area: (i) the Rotterdam Convention on Chemicals and Pesticides, whose Preamble states: 'trade and environmental policies should be mutually supportive with a view to achieving sustainable development'; (ii) the Cartagena Protocol: 'trade and environment agreements should be mutually supportive with a view to achieving sustainable development'; (iii) the Doha Declaration of the WTO, para 31 of which refers to the need for 'mutual supportiveness of trade and environment'; (iv) the UNESCO Convention on Cultural Diversity that incorporates a principle of mutual supportiveness of treaty obligations not only in its Preamble, but as *jus dispositivum* in Art 20.

Though these developments all affect the link between trade and environment (save the UNESCO Convention), we could well imagine transposing this reasoning to the link between trade and employment, in the name of promoting 'decent work', a concept which has been recognised at least as often as 'sustainable development'.

[6] One interesting issue here is what leads to such stark segregation. Might the silence of the 1994 WTO Agreement regarding its relationship with related and relevant treaties such as UNCLOS reflect, as some have suggested, 'arrogance, oversight, disagreement or a misplaced belief in the self contained character of WTO law'? As explained by Boyle and Chinkin, this silence may indeed be the result of a complex strategy deployed by players, including the United States, who wish their obligations to be exclusively governed by the laws of multilateral trade (Alan E Boyle and Christine M Chinkin, *The Making of International Law* (Oxford, Oxford University Press, 2007) 258).

[7] Although customary rules of interpretation are also explicitly adopted in the WTO's Dispute Settlement Understanding, it must be faced that many of these rules, especially those dealing with legal change across time, are often of little help in reconciling legal commitments that were designed from the very beginning to exist indefinitely and to 'overlap' one another more than 'opposing' one another.

This challenge – promoting functional coherence in the absence of legal congruence – is the subject of the following three chapters. The first discusses the ILO's unsuccessful attempt in 1945, after the frustrations it confronted during inter-war period,[8] to influence the course of economic policy by granting itself a kind of 'right of oversight' over the impact which economic, financial and trade policies of states and other organisations had on the achievement of its own objectives. That initiative essentially foundered on a perimeter of defences set up by the organisations concerned, aimed at preventing any outside interference in their mandate. Rather than becoming superior principles to be superimposed on other international efforts, social goals remained de facto country cousins of the economic objectives pursued outside the ILO. These experiences suggest that it is fultile to expect that the coherence problem could be solved by a hierarchy of objectives imposed from above (even if it can be claimed that such a shared hierarchy of values already exists in principle, as rightly suggested by Alain Supiot in his *Esprit de Philadelphie*).[9] Instead, success is more likely to flow from efficacy considerations drawing on the mutual interdependence of economic and social objectives, no matter the chagrin of those who find instrumental justifications for social goals distasteful.

One area where mandates intersect and where logic would seem to dictate a more direct and immediate path to cooperation is *employment*. We will, however, discover in the second chapter that this apparent common ground unfortunately lies on a kind of 'fault line' between fundamentally different approaches to socio-economic regulation.

The upshot of these explorations is that coherence can ultimately progress only by way of institutionalised dialogue. And, as discussed in the third chapter, the ILO has significant comparative advantages in this regard, which have yet to be systematically explored, or sufficiently exploited.

[8] A striking illustration of these perceived constraints is provided by comparing the tone and content of the Global Jobs Pact adopted by the ILC in 2009, with the resolution adopted by the Governing Body on the recommendation of its Committee on Employment and Social Policy: the latter begins with the unequivocal recognition that: 'the crisis can only be solved by the adoption of economic, financial and political measures which are outside the competence of the International Labour Organisation' (International Labour Organization, *Provisional Record* (Governing Body, 55th Session, 1931) 102).

[9] Alain Supiot, *L'esprit de Philadelphie: La justice sociale face au marché total* (Paris, Seuil, 2010).

4

Social Goals: Doomed to Remain 'Country Cousins' of Economic Objectives at the Universal Level?

The division of labour reflected in the respective mandates of the international organisations dealing with social, economic and commercial matters corresponds, at least theoretically, to effectiveness considerations. It is striking, however, that those same considerations, used at the ILO to justify 'desegregation' of social progress goals from economic development objectives, were in the case of a financial organisation like the World Bank used to maintain a protective barrier around its mandate aimed at preventing contamination from anything but purely economic considerations.

I. From the Pre-War Marginalisation of the ILO's Social Objectives to the Declaration of Philadelphia's Failed Attempt at a Hostile Takeover

Albert Thomas, the ILO's first Director-General, became aware at a very early stage of the limitations posed to the ILO's overall effectiveness by the narrow focus on worker protection expressed in its mandate and objectives.

The economic crisis of 1920–1923 offered him a first opportunity, drawing on International Labour Office expertise,[1] to affirm the dual social and *economic* dimensions of the organisation's mandate. A little later, during the discussions

[1] In June 1920 the Governing Body decided, on the proposal of the Director-General, to establish a set of expert commissions. One of them, the Commission on Unemployment, was to conduct surveys on the state of unemployment in all the Members. If the International Labour Office's expertise in employment, largely due to its collaboration with the International Association for Combating Unemployment and the International Institute of Statistics, preceded this early crisis, the tumult nonetheless accentuated the organisation's efforts on the issue. All of which put in place, according to Olivier Feiertag, the beginnings of a transnational economic regulatory regime. See Olivier Feiertag, 'Réguler la mondialisation: Albert Thomas, les débuts du BIT et la crise économique mondiale de 1920–1923' in Alya Aglan, Olivier Feiertag and Dzovinar Kévonian (eds), *Albert Thomas, société mondiale et internationalisme* (Paris, Les Cahiers Irice, 2008).

leading to the World Economic Conference of 1927 organised under League auspices, Thomas sketched a visionary overview, outlining an 'emerging "world economy" and "new economic organization" in which labor protections and free trade [would be] complementary'.[2] However, while the ILO was invited to meetings of the Conference's preparatory committee, it was not extended a full seat in its eventual work. Its role was instead confined to the production of certain documents (history here revealing its tendency to repeat itself), essentially providing symbolic support for the exercise from management and labour.

Thomas hoped to break this isolation by rooting the legitimacy of ILO intervention in the framework of productive relations. In a personal note written in 1927, he thus opposed the original design in which the protection of labour is presented solely in terms of the distribution of the wealth produced, in favour of considering such protection from the angle of 'production' itself:[3] 'It is evident that we face a new problem: it is the place of work in the process of production itself. If we take the economy as a whole, our isolation can no longer be accepted.'[4] These reflections lead him to a radical conclusion: 'In the end, I am forced to return to my earlier idea. The League of Nations should be divided into two main departments: one for political concerns and one for the economic – and it is the ILO which should be responsible for the second.'[5]

[2] Steve Charnovitz, 'The Neglected Employment Dimension of the World Trade Organization' in Virginia A Leary and Daniel Warner (eds), *Social Issues, Globalisation and International Institutions: Labour Rights and the EU, ILO, OECD and WTO* (Leiden, Martinus Nijhoff, 2006) 136, relying on Albert Thomas, *International Social Policy* (Geneva, ILO, 1948) 108, 114.

[3] A new approach in which one can perceive an echo of the opinion of the PCIJ in 1922 regarding the ILO's competence in agricultural work. See *Competence of the ILO to Examine Proposal for the Organization and Development of the Methods of Agricultural Production* [1922] PCIJ Rep Series B No 3, indicating that: 'The organisation and development of the means of production are not committed to the Organization . . . It does not follow that the International Labour Organisation must totally exclude from its consideration the effect upon production of measures which it may seek to promote for the benefit of the workers. If it should appear that a particular measure would involve a material diminution of production, this might be a matter proper to be considered by the Organization before deciding on its adoption, although it might be desirable in other respects' (reproduced in (1922) 6 *ILO Official Bulletin* 377, 381–82).

[4] Author's translation. Original: 'il est évident qu'un problème nouveau est posé: c'est la place du travail dans la production même. Si on prend l'économie dans son ensemble, notre isolement n'est plus admissible.' Albert Thomas, personal note of 9 May 1927, CAT 6, quoted by Denis Guérin, *Albert Thomas au BIT 1920-1932: De l'internationalisme à l'Europe* (Geneva, Europa, 1996).

[5] Author's translation. Original: 'Au fond, je reviens à mon idée. La Société des Nations doit être divisée en deux grandes sections: la section politique et l'économique, mais c'est l'Organisation internationale du travail qui devrait devenir la partie économique' ibid. It should be noted in this regard that the League had set up the Economic and Financial Organisation, consisting of a Permanent Secretariat of the League and two expert committees. This organization, whose economic and financial orientation stood some distance from that of the ILO, was greeted in 1920 with scepticism and caution by Albert Thomas, who saw it as an attempt to deprive the ILO of its economic mandate (Yann Decorzant, 'Répondre à la demande sociale et à la demande du marché : les prémisses de la régulation économique dans les années 1920' in Aglan, Feiertag and Kevonian, *Albert Thomas* (n 1)). According to the Director-General, it would not be unfair for some to describe the Brussels International Financial Conference which laid the theoretical foundations of the Economic and Financial Organisation (though of course he would never put it this way!) as 'a Conference of bankers, which was convened and worked in the capitalists' interests, and was hostile to those of the workers'. (See correspondence between Albert Thomas and Sir Eric Drummond of 9 November 1920, in ILO, 'The Brussels

Despite the fact that this analysis was taken over by Thomas' successor, Harold Butler, the impact of his vision seems to have remained marginal even during the context of the Great Depression.[6] Once again, it would not be until the cataclysm of the Second World War and the onset of the Cold War that it would see renewed attention.

At war's end, with the legitimacy undoubtedly bolstered in the eyes of the Allies by its move to Montreal, and the momentum the Atlantic Charter had given its reformist philosophy, the ILO launched an audacious takeover bid of the economic and financial system then under construction. The report of the interim Director-General Edward Phelan at the Philadelphia Conference in 1944 clearly expressed the new position, affirming from the first page that beyond continued differences regarding timing and method, there was broad agreement on 'the general proposition that economic policy is to be regarded as essentially a means for the achievement of certain social objectives'.[7] The famous Declaration of Philadelphia,[8] adopted at the end of this conference, elaborated the institutional consequences of this perspective, stating the ILO's veritable 'right of oversight' over economic, financial and commercial matters, and making it the organisation's responsibility 'to examine and consider all international economic and financial policies and measures in the light of this fundamental objective', i.e. in light of the understanding that 'lasting peace can be established only if it is based on social justice'.[9]

International Financial Conference and Unemployment Subsidies' (September–December 1920) 2(10) *ILO Official Bulletin* 14).

The Great Depression could obviously do little but sustain Thomas and his colleagues in their convictions. This is why he returned strongly to this point in his speech to the ILC in 1932: 'Then what is lacking? It is organisation; it is the possibility of bringing all these elements together' (Thomas, *International Social Policy* (n 2) 125). In the same vein, in a letter to Thomas, Assistant Director Harold Butler confirmed how it had become clear that standard setting alone was incapable of promoting the organisation's objectives in the context of the Great Depression: 'I do not feel that we can continue to rely on Convention as the principal test of our activity and progress. I think we ought to take this opportunity of shifting our centre of gravity, so to speak, from the purely social to the economic sphere by devoting the whole of our attention to the effects on the workers of the world depression' (Stephen Hughes and Nigel Haworth, 'A Shift in the Centre of Gravity: The ILO Under Harold Butler and John G. Winant' in Jasmien van Daele and others, *ILO Histories: Essays on the International Labour Organization and Its Impact on the World During the Twentieth Century* (Peter Lang, 2010) 301). After becoming Director-General himself, Butler drew much the same conclusion in his 1935 report to the ILC (ILO, *Report of the Director-General* (International Labour Conference, 19th Session, Geneva, 4–25 June 1935).

[6] Hughes and Haworth, 'A Shift in the Centre of Gravity' (n 5).

[7] ILO, *Report I: Future Policy, Program and Status of the ILO* (ILC, 26th Session, Philadelphia, 20 April–12 May 1944) 1.

[8] According to Jenks, 'the Declaration of Philadelphia is a fundamental part of the fundamental Charter of the ILO, binding upon the organisation, binding upon its member states, and binding upon the United Nations as a statement of the Organisation's mandate'. Wilfred Jenks, 'The Declaration of Philadelphia After 25 Years' (Temple Univeristy, Conference on Human Rights, Human Resources and Social Progress, Philadelphia, 8 May 1969) reproduced in ILO, *Social Policy in a Changing World: The ILO Response: Selected Speeches by Wilfred Jenks* (Geneva, ILO, 1976).

[9] Declaration concerning the Aims and Purposes of the International Labour Organisation (adopted 10 May 1944, annexed to the ILO Constitution in 1946) Principle II(d) ('Declaration of Philadelphia').

As noted with a touch of irony by Ernst B Haas, if those who had adopted the Declaration had been literally committed to its logic:

> the ILO would have developed into the master agency[10] among the emerging family of functional international bodies; it would have taken the place intended for the United Nations Economic and Social Council – though not in fact attained – by some of the drafters of the Charter.[11]

Some evidence suggests, however, that while governments may have assented to this language, they did not intend its consequences – or at least never intended that the ILO would be allowed to determine those consequences. The fate of the initiative intended to ensure institutional follow-up to the Declaration is rather revealing in this regard. Indeed, alongside the draft Declaration, the Conference was seized with a draft resolution to give effect to this 'right of oversight'. The proposed follow-up was supposed to take the form of a recurrent discussion at the ILC based on 'a report outlining developments in the economic and financial field having a bearing on the maintenance of full employment and the promotion of higher standards of living'.[12] This project passed quickly by the wayside on the ground that, in the architecture of the new United Nations, the coordination function was to be vested with ECOSOC. Haas' wry conclusions in 1964 regarding what the latter had been able to do unfortunately remain topical nearly half a century later.[13]

It is therefore tempting to wonder whether, as had already been the case in the Preamble to the Constitution and the Labour Charter of 1919, the Declaration of Philadelphia was intended first and foremost as a sort of pledge of loyalty to the popular forces in return for the sacrifices they had made during the war (and had yet to make, given the fighting was not yet over) from governments that remained privately convinced that economic, financial and commercial affairs were too serious a matter to be entrusted to an organisation whose mandate was confined to labour issues, and which, to make matters worse, was subject to a tripartite decision-making process.

One might also have a sense that history repeated itself with the financial crisis of 2008.[14] It was after all pressure from trade unions, and in particular the Secretary

[10] It is notable in this regard that, in his 1953 campaign to change the constitutional relationship of the United States to international treaty law, Senator Bricker targeted the ILO with peculiar virulence, claiming that it intended to become the 'economic overseer of all humanity' (quoted in Steve Charnovitz, 'Editorial Comments: The ILO Convention on Freedom of Association and its Future in the United States' (2008) 102(1) *American Journal of International Law* 90, 99).

[11] Ernst B Haas, *Beyond the Nation-State: Functionalism and International Organization* (Stanford, Stanford University Press 1964) 164.

[12] ILO, *Report I: Future Policy, Program and Status of the ILO* (n 7) 120.

[13] On the inability of ECOSOC to fulfil this coordination role, and UNCTAD's abortive attempts to occupy the normative space yielded by the failure of the Havana Charter, leading in the end 'from the commanding heights of international trade to the sprawling territory of a failed ECOSOC', see the very interesting article by Jacques Lemoine, a keen observer of the development system and its changes over nearly 50 years (Jacques Lemoine, 'International Trade Regimes in Retrospect' in Marcel A Boisard, Evgeny, Chossudovsky and Jacques Lemoine (eds), *Diplomatie multilatérale: système des Nations Unies à Genève: guide de travail* (The Hague, Kluwer Law International, 1998) 397.

[14] Another recent, and striking, example of how the activities of 'sister organisations' might work against a state's obligations to the ILO was highlighted in 2008 by the Committee of Experts: 'the

General of the International Trade Union Confederation (ITUC), which (as we have seen) led to the ILO being extended an invitation to the G20, the new self-proclaimed centre of international governance, for the first time since its inception in 1999. This decision was rightly hailed as a huge accolade for the ILO and its head, invited to sit alongside the Bretton Woods institutions and WTO – the 'organisations that matter' on the economic front. The actual course of events, however, could easily raise suspicions that this recognition will turn out to be just as illusory as the claims made in the Declaration of Philadelphia during the closing days of the war. In much the same way as it did then, the prominence given to the ILO lends the whole enterprise an atmosphere of moral support for the labouring masses, at precisely the moment when they might otherwise conclude they were being asked to bear the brunt of a crisis that was not of their making. Yet it is possible that the concrete results attributable to its presence may be negligible, bringing neither new regulations nor even effective protection of existing employment levels. Yet, if the concrete results attributable to its presence are not negligible as regards the emphasis placed on employment,[15] it is hard to detect any trace of the specific principles it stands for, and in particular, the need for a fair distribution of the sacrifices as well as of the benefits involved in recovery, as clearly restated in the 2008 Declaration.[16]

Rather than slipping with some observers into 'soft' conspiracy theory, and characterising the whole situation as part of a deliberate attempt by existing powers to keep the relevant multilateral organisations fragmented[17] through hyper-specialised mandates[18] and distinct bureaucracies, one is tempted to share instead the conclusion of the disillusioned Francis Blanchard. After the superhuman

Committee is concerned that international organizations working in the procurement area may use their technical guidelines and policy tools, which typically emphasize the aim of increasing the competition that takes place under procurement procedures in a transparent and corruption-free environment, as a justification for giving advice that may lead countries to disregard their ILO treaty obligations' (ILO, *Report III(1B): General Survey concerning the Labour Clauses (Public Contracts) Convention, 1949 (No 94) and Recommendation (No 84)* (ILC, 97th Session, Geneva, 28 May–13 June 2008) para 208).

[15] Or rather on 'jobs', in line with the Bank's rather than the ILO's terminology. See, eg G20, *The Los Cabos Growth and Jobs Action Plan* (19 June 2012). It is interesting to note that, according to the most recent World Development Report, 'jobs' are defined as any 'activities that generate income, monetary or in kind, and do not violate fundamental rights and principles at work' (World Bank, *World Development Report 2013: Jobs* (Washington DC, World Bank, 2013) 66). This definition certainly expresses a new opening in the Bank's position, but as we shall see does not necessarily imply that the Bank is committed to actively support all of these rights in its activities.

[16] For example, the G20 Leaders Declaration mentions only the need to protect 'the most vulnerable' (G20, *G20 Leaders Declaration* (G20 Meeting, Los Cabos, 18–19 June 2012) para 9).

[17] See Eyal Benvenisti and George W Downs, 'The Empire's New Clothes: Political Economy and the Fragmentation of International Law' (2007) 60(2) *Stanford Law Review* 595. This article most notably goes over the strategies of fragmentation put in place within international organisations by the most powerful states, aimed at protecting themselves against the numerical superiority of developing countries and thereby maintaining their dominant position in negotiations. The authors go so far as to speak of 'sabotage' of the international system by actors like the United States and the European Union.

[18] Maurice Bertrand, *L'ONU* (Paris, La Découverte, 2006). The author makes a sharp critique of the excesses of specialisation, the primary source, he suggest, of UN system ineffectiveness.

efforts he expended to establish a genuine partnership with the Bretton Woods institutions (addressed in Chapter 3), he came to feel, in fact, that it:

> ne servirait à rien de tenter de rendre les mandats de l'OIT et des institutions de Bretton Woods "compatibles". Leur refonte est hors de portée. Faute d'accord sur une stratégie prenant en compte la double dimension économique et sociale du développement, le malentendu hypocritement entretenu pendant des années persistera et l'OIT continuera à servir de bonne conscience.[19]

While this diagnosis rightly points towards the institutional roots of the problem, it may at the same time exaggerate the futility of reform efforts. Even taking the hard case represented by the World Bank (the IMF's Articles of Agreement do not include the same restrictions on taking into account non-economic considerations), it may be less a question of constraints inherent to the text, than it is an intentional and constructed barrier kept in place by a virtual 'quarantine' at the level of their respective objectives.

However, insofar as the situation results in large part from a 'constructed' segregation, the situation can be seen as at least potentially reversible. And all the more so, given there is a common dimension, even a shared aspiration, that can be discerned in the founding charters of each of these organisations – employment – an aspiration that has unfortunately been treated mainly as an economic byproduct in practices outside the ILO. But let us address each of these propositions in turn.

II. The 'Mandated' Segregation of Social Considerations in the (Former?) Practice of the World Bank

When it came to the policies of the competent economic and financial organisations, the post-war years not only saw the ILO fail to put the into practice the 'right to oversee', outlined by the Declaration of Philadelphia, but also saw these organisations arrogate to themselves, in the name of their economic mandate and objectives, a right to review Member state implementation of a wide collection of social objectives, even those considered to be fundamental by the ILO.

The case of the World Bank ('the Bank') is of particularly interest in this regard, because of well-known provisions in its charter. Under sections III 5(b)[20] and

[19] '[I]t would be of no use to attempt to make the ILO's mandate "compatible" with those of the Bretton Woods institutions. Their overhaul is out of the question. Failing some agreement on a strategy that takes into account the combined social and economic dimensions of development, the hypocritical entente maintained over the years will no doubt endure, with the ILO continuing to perpetuate it with a clear conscience.' Francis Blanchard, *L'organisation internationale du travail: De la guerre froide à un nouvel ordre mondial* (Paris, Seuil, 2004) 235 (author's translation).

[20] 'The Bank shall make arrangements to ensure that the proceeds of any loan are used only for the purposes for which the loan was granted, with due attention to considerations of economy and efficiency and without regard to political or other non-economic influences or considerations.'

IV(10)[21] of its Articles of Agreement, it is subject to a double constraint: on the one hand, it is prohibited from any political consideration or influence in lending decisions and loan administration; and on the other, it is required to make these decisions guided solely by economic considerations (narrowly interpreted in practice, it should be noted, in terms of 'efficiency' alone).

The Bank has applied these twin obligations in a seemingly rigorous manner, to the point of appearing, notably in the decolonisation context, to subject basic human rights to the imperatives of economic development[22] and 'the cold calculus of economic viability'.[23] This was achieved, however, without ever explicitly claiming any hierarchy between economic objectives and social considerations. It was enough, for all practical purposes, to invoke the 'exclusive' relevance which the Articles of Agreement allocate to economic considerations, which seemed sufficient to protect them with a kind of 'quarantine line' that placed them in a de facto position of pre-eminence. This approach is reminiscent of the PCIJ's candid explanation in its 1922 agricultural competence case of the necessary subordination of social progress, 'although it might be desirable in other respects', to considerations of overall production.[24]

Despite its undeniable legal basis, this approach was subject to a mounting wave of criticism, from the growing human rights movement and as well as the unions, that required it to adapt slightly as a result. These adaptation efforts demand a closer look from two directions: first, is the relaxation of this approach a matter of evolving interpretation or of shifts in political will? And second, could the relaxation of this doctrine actually lead the Bank to take into account certain social considerations, or even to apply certain conditionalities of a social nature?[25]

A. A Complex Question of Interpretation or a Straightforward Matter of Political Will?

The full extent of the difficulty can hardly be understood without recalling that, in the name of the legal strictures of its mandate, the Bank came to directly defy the

[21] 'The Bank and its officers shall not interfere in the political affairs of any member; nor shall they be influenced in their decisions by the political character of the member or members concerned. Only economic considerations shall be relevant to their decisions, and these considerations shall be weighed impartially in order to achieve the purposes stated in Article I.'

[22] See the comments below on the rather malicious indifference the Bank has shown towards certain fundamental rights recognised by the international community, whose results are hard to see as anything *but* an interference in the political choices embodied in the decisions of the entire international community.

[23] In the words of Ascher, cited in Philip Alston, 'Making Space for New Human Rights: The Case of the Right to Development' (1988) 1 *Harvard Human Rights Yearbook* 3, 18.

[24] *Competence of the ILO* (n 3) 386. The court did not say explicitly that the ILO had to subordinate social progress to economic considerations. But it essentially prohibited the organisation from considering the *positive* impact of labour protections on production, while suggesting that it was totally proper for the organisation to restrain labour protections where they might lead to *decreases* in production.

[25] Note that 'conditionalities' is intended here to have a meaning quite different from how it is normally understood in the financial institutions.

United Nations General Assembly by maintaining loans to colonial Portugal and apartheid-era South Africa despite resolutions and attendant political pressure expressly demanding that it stop doing so.[26] This precedent makes clear that, when the Bank derives from its Articles an absolute prohibition on conditionalities in its operations linked to respect either for human rights or for worker protection, that claim must be taken *very* seriously.

Since the 1960s, however, this position has evolved somewhat, in rhetoric if not in substance. In addition to mounting pressure from the human rights movement, the presidency of James Wolfensohn from 1995 to 2005 helped to significantly loosen up the Bank's approach, by sketching the need for greater coherence.[27]

It is against this background that one can scrutinise the efforts made by the long-serving General Counsel of the Bank, Ibrahim Shihata, to (at least partially) relax the doctrinal treatment of human rights considerations. According to him, the Bank had to consider itself authorised to intervene more directly in development projects, wherever the human rights under consideration were relevant to its overarching mandate or to the success of those projects. It was for just this reason that the Bank recognised the need to extend a minimal degree of participation to those who might be affected by the design and implementation of its projects.[28] Similarly, violations of political rights reaching proportions massive enough to risk an economic impact or a breach of legal obligations relevant to the Bank could, he proposed, justify the termination or denial of a project.[29]

[26] Starting in 1961, the year when the majority of colonial countries gained independence and became members of the United Nations, the General Assembly adopted a series of resolutions condemning both the apartheid regime in South Africa and Portugal's continued control over several African and Asian countries. In 1965, faced with continued financial and technical support of the regimes from the Bank and the IMF, a special committee of the General Assembly: 'Appeal[ed] to all the specialized agencies of the United Nations, and in particular the International Bank for Reconstruction and Development and the International Monetary Fund, and requests them to refrain from granting Portugal any financial, economic or technical assistance so long as the Portuguese Government fails to renounce its colonial policy, which constitutes a flagrant violation of the provisions of the Charter of the United Nations' (United Nations Special Committee, Resolution (10 June 1965) UN Doc A/AC.109/124 and Corr. 1). That appeal was repeated in slightly softer language by the General Assembly six months later (UN General Assembly, Question of Territories under Portuguese administration (adopted 21 December 1965) UN Doc A/RES/2107(XX)). When Bank management met to take a position on the lending, a majority of directors nonetheless decided to continue lending. Their justification? Article 4(10) of the Bank's statutes, prohibiting it from engaging in politics! All industrialised countries, supported by a number of Latin American countries, voted in favour of continuing the loans. In 1966, the Bank approved a loan of US$30 million for Portugal and US$20 million for South Africa (see, generally, Samuel Bleicher, 'UN v. IBRD: A Dilemma of Functionalism' (1970) 24 *International Organization* 31).

[27] Which led him to strongly emphasise in a noteworthy 1998 speech at the IMF, 'development is about putting all the components parts in place, together and in harmony'. James Wolfehnson, 'The Other Crisis', Speech to the Board of Governors of the IMF, 6 October 1998.

[28] *cf* Daniel Bradlow and Sabine Schlemmer-Schulte, 'The World Bank's New Inspection Panel: A Constructive Step in the Transformation of the International Legal Order' (1998) 54(2) *Heidelberg Journal of International Law* 353; Korinna Horta, 'Rhetoric and Reality: Human Rights and the World Bank' (2002) 15 *Harvard Human Rights Law Journal* 227.

[29] Ibrahim Shihata, *The World Bank in a Changing World* (Leiden, Martinus Nijhoff, 1998) vol 2. See in particular ch III, 'Limitations'.

These efforts were continued and expanded by his successors. Of particular interest, both in their content and in their fate, were relatively recent efforts made by Roberto Daniño.[30] He first attempted to take advantage of a university setting more conducive to open dialogue, to develop ideas that would broaden space at the Bank for human rights in the name of 'social equity' (which is supposed to go hand in hand with the Bank's goal of economic growth); he even went so far as to suggest that the notion of 'social justice' was inherent in the rule of law.[31] In January 2006 (literally the day he was to leave office) he ventured to send a document to Bank staff, a *Legal Opinion on Human Rights and the Work of the World Bank*,[32] which went far beyond the 'Shihata doctrine'. In that opinion, he recognised a real obligation on the Bank to take into account serious human rights violations, and went much further in the recognition of the indivisibility of human rights.[33] This led him to distinguish three levels of acceptable Bank engagement with human rights questions:

- at the first level, the Bank could be 'broadly supportive' of the human rights commitments of its members when they 'have an economic impact or relevance' (it being implied, no doubt, that the impact should be positive);
- at the second level, actual violations of these commitments or obligations *should* be taken into account, but again, only when they have an impact on the economy;
- on the third level (most strongly differentiating Daniño's opinion from his predecessor), in cases of the most serious violations, the Bank should withdraw support *regardless* of economic impact and subject only to the vague condition that the situation gets to the point where the Bank 'can no longer achieve its purposes'.

This opinion undoubtedly represented some significant progress in terms of desegregating 'economic considerations' from considerations of social equity. This development produces an image of a less insular legal order at the Bank, even if it comes more cautiously and indirectly than in the WTO *Gasoline* case mentioned above.[34] Yet it also suffers from a pair of caveats, one legal and one practical. As a matter of the opinion's legal status, it should be noted that for various reasons, it never gained the status of an official interpretation of the Articles of Agreement.[35] Not least among those reasons is that such endorsement was never

[30] World Bank, *Human Rights Indicators in Development: An Introduction* (Washington, World Bank, 2010) 6.

[31] Roberto Dañino, 'The Legal Aspects of the World Bank's Work on Human Rights', Lecture at NYU School of Law, 1 March 2004.

[32] See Galit Sarfaty, 'Why Culture Matters in International Institutions: The Marginality of Human Rights at the World Bank' (2009) 103 *American Journal of International Law* 647, 663–67.

[33] For Shihata, civil and political rights had for the most part remained confined behind the 'quarantine line'/

[34] See above, text to nn 3 and 4.

[35] It would have required, inter alia, the endorsement of the Bank's Board of Directors, followed by official diffusion to the Members (Sarfaty, 'Why Culture Matters' (n 32) 665–66).

canvassed from the Bank's board.[36] According to Sarfaty, leaving things this way is not uncharacteristic of the attitude of lawyers at the Bank, who tend to 'fly below the radar' so as to avoid direct confrontation with the economistic orthodoxy (that is, rule by economists) of the organisation.[37] It therefore seems clear that the relaxation of the doctrine – of what is in this regard difficult to even treat as a fixed 'doctrine' – relies more on the Bank's political leadership than it does on the ingenuity of its lawyers.

Moreover, save in cases of 'extensive and pervasive' violations, Daniño's opinion ultimately seems to leave in place the basic premise of the 'Shihata doctrine', that human rights considerations should remain derivative, as suggested by his conclusion that the Bank 'may take any type of human right into account *provided there is economic impact or relevance*'[38] (emphasis added). As explored in the next section, this kind of tiered treatment of rights leaves the Bank ample leeway, allowing it to apply heightened scrutiny to those rights that have long been a critical dimension of the ILO's overall approach: freedom of association and the right to collective bargaining.

B. Selective Treatment of Fundamental Rights

Responding to pressure from human rights advocacy organisations, pressure which has only increased since the end of the Cold War, the World Bank has exerted some effort in recent years to highlight the contribution of its development activities to realising rights in recipient countries. In line with the arguments developed by Shihata, it effectively defended its 'principled' approach to these rights through at least two decades of apparently ignoring them in practice. In particular, it insisted that even though it might do so indirectly, it made an important contribution to the realisation of human rights by providing loans for education, health, nutrition and anti-poverty projects.[39] It would be quite the leap, from

[36] The fact that the opinion was never brought forward to the Board was likely determined in no small part by the relationship its supporters may have had with the Bank's President, not to mention the general circumspection and lack of leadership shown by the legal department after Shihata's departure.

[37] Sarfaty, 'Why Culture Matters' (n 32) 674–76. It is no doubt in light of this experience that it is best to read the much more vague interpretation offered by Ana Palacio who, having just succeeded Dañino, quoted selectively from the 2006 opinion and characterised it as 'permissive' and therefore 'allowing, but not mandating, action on the part of the Bank in relation to human rights' (Ana Palacio, *The Way Forward: Human Rights and the World Bank* (Special Report, World Bank, 2006). It is also somewhat noteworthy that the dubious legal authority of the Dañino opinion does not prevent it from being referenced in the 'Human Rights' FAQ on the Bank's site, but again, the reference focuses only on the opinion's permissive dimensions and the opinion itself is not made available.

[38] Daniño, 'Legal Aspects' (n 31) 6. Setting aside the case of the ill-defined 'extensive violations of . . . pervasive proportions' it seems hard to see Dañino's opinion as truly at odds with the Shihata doctrine and even harder to understand how it might, as put by Sarfaty, 'clear the way for the Bank's adoption of human rights norms' (Sarfaty, 'Why Culture Matters' (n 32) 665).

[39] As argued by the World Bank, 'The Bank contributes directly to the fulfilment of many rights articulated in the Universal Declaration. Through its support of primary education, health care and nutrition, sanitation, housing, and the environment, the Bank has helped hundreds of millions of

this kind of diachronic and passive link between development and human rights (which seems rather anachronistic and restrictive in light of the supposed 'integrated' vision of development put forward by J Wolfensohn) to active support of 'collective rights' for workers which the Bank believes may be 'economically harmful'. As we shall see, this gap is still clearly far from being spanned.

For reasons amply explored in Part III, the ILO attaches special importance to the implementation of fundamental labour rights, and to freedom of association and collective bargaining in particular, to the extent that they are considered as a necessary precondition for effectively claiming other rights at work. Yet to ensure the adoption of the 1998 Declaration, even the question of *whether* it should be officially communicated to the Bretton Woods institutions and the WTO had to be bypassed by a legal sleight of hand.[40] Nonetheless, it was clear that the effective implementation of these rights had much to gain from a positive development of thinking at the Bretton Woods institutions, and especially at the Bank under the stewardship of James Wolfensohn.

In much the same way as the OECD,[41] the Bank's 'doctrine' remained true to a position of principle according to which it can support fundamental rights at work, subject to the caveat that they must contribute to efficiency and economic growth. This criterion leads to unequivocal respect for the 'individual' fundamental rights: the eradication of child labour that cuts into the potential productivity of future generations, and the elimination of discrimination and forced labour that stand in the way of efficient labour market functions.[42] Things are not quite so clear cut, however, for the collective rights of freedom of association and the right to collective bargaining, whose impact on economic efficiency has given rise to heated debate. The Bank 'doctrine' in this regard was expressed for the first time with clarity in the *World Development Report* of 1995. While acknowledging the

people attain crucial economic and social rights. In other areas, the Bank's contributions are necessarily less direct, but perhaps equally significant. By helping to fight corruption, improve transparency and accountability in governance, strengthen judicial systems, and modernize financial sectors, the Bank contributes to building environments in which people are better able to pursue a broader range of human rights' (World Bank, *Development and Human Rights: The Role of the World Bank* (1998) 3). See also Laurence Boisson de Chazournes, 'Banque mondiale et développement social: les termes d'un partenariat' in Pierre de Senarclens (ed), *Maîtriser la mondialisation: la régulation sociale internationale* (Paris, Presses de Sciences-Po, 2000).

[40] This concern explains the part of para 3 in the 1998 Declaration that limits distribution solely to those organisations with which the ILO has 'established relations'. This formulation made it possible to exclude, without saying so, both the Bretton Woods institutions and the WTO.

[41] Which, despite its 1996 study (OECD, *Trade, Employment and Labour Standards: A Study of Core Workers' Rights and International Trade* (1996)) 'remains equivocal about the value of unions and collective bargaining: while core labor standards can support economic development if properly implemented, the economic effects of freedom of association and the right to collective bargaining are variable, as such rights can also introduce market distortions' (Kerry Rittich, 'Core Labour Rights and Labor Market Flexibility: Two Paths Entwined?' in International Bureau of the Permanent Court of Arbitration (ed), *Labor Law Beyond Borders: ADR and the Internationalization of Labor Dispute Settlement* (The Hague, Kluwer Law International, 2003) 176–77).

[42] As a matter with some relation to forced labour, the Bank did cease operations in Myanmar in the late 1990s, but this decision had no direct link to the establishment of the ILO's Commission of Inquiry or the findings and recommendations in the Commission's 1997 final report.

positive role of trade unions on non-discrimination and even productivity, the Bank lists a number of negative effects linked to so-called 'monopolistic' behaviour by unions, that allegedly cause distortions of the labour market and translate into an unjustified 'wage premium' for 'insiders' at the expense of the unorganised and those in informal sector.[43]

Despite ongoing ILO efforts following the adoption of the 1998 Declaration,[44] it does not appear that this position has fundamentally changed; the Bank did introduce some formal nuances, and the practice of all international financial institutions has shifted in a positive way,[45] but there is no clear evidence that it has repudiated its doctrine. To this end, the World Bank did concede shortly thereafter (in a form that can still be found on its website) that: '[i]nspired by the 1998 ILO Declaration on the Fundamental Principles and Rights at Work, the World Bank promotes an atmosphere conducive to the achievement of core labor standards'.[46] This does not prevent it from then proceeding to sift through these rights, justifying itself with reference to the fact that 'the Bank is obliged by its legal framework to base lending considerations on the basis of their demonstrable economic impact. Under such criteria, Bank research supports the standards related to harmful child labor, forced labor, and gender equality in the labor market'.[47] Freedom of association and collective bargaining continue to be regarded as civil rights which Bank activities might facilitate, but it still believes that it is not in its mandate to actively promote them, and even less so where they might interfere with economic performance.[48]

This is not necessarily incompatible with the recent and positive move already noted in the last *World Development Report* according to which activities involving the violation of fundamental workers rights and principles at work cannot be defined as a job.[49] If the tone of the Bank's collective rights objections has been turned down at the political level, the priority accorded to the economic considerations which underlie them still seem to very much inspire the Bank's operational

[43] World Bank, *World Development Report 1995: Workers in an Integrating World* (New York, Oxford University Press, 1995).

[44] Of particular note here is a Washington meeting held with chief executives of the IMF and the Bank in the autumn of 1998.

[45] *cf* Franz Christian Ebert and Anne Posthuma, *Labour Standards and Development Finance Institutions: A Review of Current Policies and Activities*, International Institute of Labour Studies, Discussion Paper 204, (Geneva, 2010).

[46] World Bank, *Core Labor Standards and the World Bank* (2000).

[47] The World Bank research relied on here, it should be noted, was for the most part *inconclusive* (see Toke Aidt and Zafiris Tzannatos, *Unions and Collective Bargaining: Economic Effects in a Global Environment* (Washington DC, World Bank, 2002).

[48] 'Freedom of Association/Collective Bargaining. The Bank's treatment of union rights is complicated by (a) the potential political nature of the standards and (b) research showing ambiguous economic outcomes. Consistent with other findings such as that of the OECD, recent analytical work done by the Bank has found no simple relationship between unions and collective bargaining, on the one hand, and economic performance, on the other. The Bank survey of research found that there is no strong correlation, either positive or negative, between union density and economic performance indicators, although there does appear to be a negative correlation with earnings inequality.' (World Bank, *Core Labor Standards* (n 46)).

[49] World Bank, *World Development Report 2013* (n 15).

activities and analytical work. Its *Doing Business* report, a flagship project designed to help investors choose between potential investment locations, has given rise to additional complexities which are far from being fully resolved. These annually-produced reports are supposed to assess the economic efficiency of national regulations and, based on indices collected with that purpose in mind, provide rankings intended to inform investment choices. Among the most controversial of these measurements is the 'rigidity of employment' indicator which is based, inter alia, on whether employees can be hired on the basis of fixed-term contracts, regardless of their length of service.[50] On this basis, social rights that make it harder to fire or dismiss employees have generally been assigned a negative coefficient in the overall ranking. If this methodology is particularly questionable,[51] it may be excessive to go as far as Alain Supiot's characterisation of the rankings as an expression a genuine 'normative Darwinism' in line with Friedrich Hayek.[52] Indeed, the World Bank has tried to respond (at least partially) to the recurrent criticisms their methods have received from the ILO and the ITUC, given the deterrent effect which the *Doing Business* criteria placed on ratification of ILO Conventions by Members.[53] Thus, in *Doing Business 2011*, the 'employing workers' criterion, though it continues to appear in the body of analysis, was completely removed from the 'ease of doing business' ranking.[54]

[50] Yaraslau Kryvoi, 'The World Bank and the ILO: Two Visions of Employment Regulation' in Roger Blanpain and Claire Grant (eds), *Fixed-Term Employment Contracts: A Comparative Study* (Bruges, Vanden Broele, 2009) 47.

[51] See the methodological criticisms made by Kerry Rittich (Kerry Rittich, 'Global Labour Policy as Social Policy' (2008) 14(2) *Canadian Labour and Employment Law Journal* 272) and Kryvoi, 'Two Visions' (n 50).

[52] Alain Supiot, *L'esprit de Philadelphie: La justice sociale face au marché total* (Paris, Seuil, 2010) 64 ff.

[53] See Alvaro Santos, 'Labor Flexibility, Legal Reform and Economic Development' (2009) 50 *Virginia Journal of International Law* 43. The ILO is particularly critical where a country satisfying the terms of an ILO Convention would be ranked lower than one which had not put in place such protections. As a result, the Bank undertook in 2004 to address these criticisms by making small modifications to its indices (concerning hiring, working conditions and employee discharge) so as to better integrate, or at least stop vilifying, the so-called 'rigidity' factors (and particularly their social contributions).

By 2008, the World Bank Independent Evaluation Group had come to recognise that, as much as the *Doing Business* methodology may have been in compliance with the letter of ILO Conventions, it violated their spirit, by assigning classifications which systematically penalised countries with high levels of social protection. Thus, the World Bank launched a search to complete a set of indicators on the integration of core labour standards into national legislation. This research focused initially on Conventions Nos 138 and 182 dealing, respectively, with the minimum age and the worst forms of child labour. This research aimed to expand to other areas covered by the basic standards and involve the participation of an 'advisory group with a broad representation of stakeholders'. Kryvoi, however, has noted the repeated inconsistency between the views of the ILO and the World Bank in the regulation of employment, illustrated in the *Doing Business* report precisely by the unilateral nature of the programme. While the ILO, with its tripartite composition, represents the interests of three parties, the Bank takes only the employer perspective: 'the World Bank's rigidity of employment index is intentionally skewed in favour of one party, namely the employer, which could be the main reason for the ILO's and international unions' criticism'. After all, the main objective of the *Doing Business* report is to successfully create 'a more employment-friendly climate for business', not to promote the principle of freedom of association (Kryvoi, 'Two Visions' (n 50) 49 and 57).

[54] Despite an agreement with the ITUC that 'labour market flexibility indicator' would not be used as part of Bank policy or lending decisions (an agreement referenced, but apparently no longer

C. An Unlikely Move Towards 'Workers Rights Conditionality'

The above analysis shows that, at the cost of significant efforts, it is possible to get the Bank to slightly relax the selective treatment it applies to fundamental rights at work on the basis of their expected economic impact. It would be a bit of stretch, however, to expect the Bank to move from this (not exactly benevolent) neutrality to the type of positive conditionality[55] some have fancied, most notably perhaps in President Sarkozy's appeals to the ILC in 2009 and at Davos in 2010.[56] As much as development in this direction may benefit from a number of reasonable arguments, achieving any sort of conditionality in practice seems highly unlikely, notwithstanding arguments that can be drawn from the practices of sister organisations.

Counter to the *Doing Business* report, certain forms of positive conditionality have indeed been developed in the activities of the regional banks, especially the Asian and African Development Banks[57] and this trend is even more evident in the activities of the 'secular arm' of the World Bank group, responsible for financing private projects. Indeed, the International Finance Corporation (IFC) and the Multilateral Investment Guarantee Agency (MIGA), respectively responsible for supporting private initiatives and guaranteeing foreign direct investment (FDI), now apply a real social conditionality to their loans and insurance, explicitly based on the ILO's 1998 Declaration. For its part, the IFC has adopted a series

available, online), the 2010 *Doing Business* report not only placed Rwanda at the head of the pack of overall reformers, but also put it first among reformers in the 'employing workers' category – because the country had made it easier to use an indefinite number of fixed term contracts, and had removed the right to consult on redundancy decisions (see, eg International Trade Union Confederation, *Doing Business 2010: World Bank Discourages Extension of Social Protection* (Press Release, 9 September 2009), available at www.ituc-csi.org/doing-business-2010-world-bank.html?lang=en.

As for *Doing Business 2011*, 'Regulations affecting 11 areas of the life of a business are covered . . . The getting electricity and employing workers data are not included in the ranking on the ease of doing business index in *Doing Business 2011*' (World Bank and International Finance Corporation, *Doing Business 2011: Making a Difference for Entrepreneurs* (Washington DC, World Bank, 2011). Following these changes, Sharon Burrow, the new General Secretary of the ITUC, requested that the World Bank continue the process of revising *Doing Business* criteria, suggesting that 'the Bank should carry through on the positive step it has made in *Doing Business 2011* by removing the EWI from all future editions and, instead, adopting policies on labour issues that recognise and reward the importance of adequate labour regulations and comprehensive social protection' (ITUC, *ITUC Calls on World Bank to Complete Overhaul of 'Doing Business'* (Press Release, 5 November 2010). The most recent issue also excludes the 'rigidity of employment' index from the overall ease of doing business rankings, and does not provide a ranking of countries by this index (World Bank and IFC, *Doing Business 2013: Smarter Regulations for Small and Medium-Size Enterprises* (Washington DC, World Bank, 2013) 2 and 129).

[55] The term conditionality should not be understood here in the usual sense used by the Bank or the IMF, referring to the subordination of the granting of soft loans on specific packages of economic and other policy, but in the sense that the social conditionality we commonly refer to as 'social clauses'.

[56] See Chapter 3, text to nn 34 and 35. The contrast between the cold silence that met this suggestion, and the broad applause which greeted his vaguer proposals to change the order of priorities speaks volumes about the persistence of the taboo regarding social conditionalities.

[57] ILO, *Report V: Strengthening the Capacity of the ILO to Assist its Members' Efforts to Promote its Objectives in the Context of Globalization* (International Labour Conference, 96th Session, Geneva, 30 May –15 June 2007) 30 Box 4.3.

of initiatives to promote respect for the fundamental Conventions with its client companies.[58] Under the 'Performance Standards 2' it has applied since 2006,[59] these efforts include promoting respect for freedom of association and the right to collective bargaining. Since 2007, similar provisions have been compulsory terms of MIGA funding.[60] All of which, according to Ebert and Posthuma, has apparently been very well received by client companies.[61] Might a similar pattern be possible at the Bank proper, whose clients are governments and public authorities?

Though the prospect may seem promising, it stumbles in the face of realities which seem much less accommodating. In the first place, we must realise that 'social conditionalities' like those practised by the international financial institutions (IFIs) have an inherent limit that became all the more salient in the case of freedom of association, considered by ILO constituents as the most important of fundamental workers rights. Indeed, the IFIs are already required to apply a 'special approach' to the implementation of freedom of association, to avoid putting their clients in the awkward position of being at odds with national legislation prohibiting workers from forming unions.[62] Essentially, the standard on freedom of association is satisfied in such a case so long as the borrowers develop so-called 'parallel procedures' giving the effected workers some degree of voice.

Moreover, even if the Bank was tempted in its own relations with public authorities to take guidance from the IFC's practices vis-à-vis private companies, it would run into political and economic realities which would, to put it lightly, be less than favourable. Indeed, in the current context, the Bank's attractiveness as a lending institution finds itself (perhaps temporarily) already weakened by a global savings glut and the rise of rather less-discerning lenders, China foremost among them. All of which would make it all the more difficult to justify social conditionalities already likely to be considered as overly intrusive.

Three concluding thoughts emerge from these complex and seemingly contradictory dimensions of the Bank's approach.

First, the figurative game of 'hide and seek' played by Bank management and its lawyers and the evolving practice just mentioned, make it fairly clear that Bank activities do not follow the line of any coherent, stable doctrine applicable from the top to the bottom of the hierarchy, be it at the Bank's headquarters or in the field. Instead, given the difficulty of openly amending (or reversing) its official doctrine to deal with the numerous divergent interests at play, what is most easily discerned is a public relations policy with an unenviable task: pasting over an incoherent practice with a facade that gives everyone the impression that their

[58] Franz Christian Ebert and Anne Posthuma, *Aligning Private Sector Investment and Labour Standards? The Case of Policies of the Development Finance Institutions*, ILO and IILS Conference Paper (Geneva, 2011) 3 and 4.

[59] ibid.

[60] Multilateral Investment Guarantee Agency, *Performance Standard 2: Labor and Working Conditions' Performance Standards on Social & Environmental Sustainability* (1 October 2007), available at www.miga.org/projects/index_sv.cfm?stid=1589.

[61] Ebert and Posthuma, *Aligning Private Sector Investment* (n 58) 13.

[62] ibid 5.

concerns are being addressed.[63] The conciliatory comments delivered by the Bank's President to the ILO Governing Body not so long ago probably have to be read in this light.[64]

Secondly, some have expressed concerns that that the ILO may be carried away from its own principles by engaging too closely in the logic of its interlocutors as it strives to demonstrate, no matter the cost, the compatibility and even convergence between economic efficiency and respect for human rights.[65] That temptation might be all the stronger given that socio-economic realities, at least at the macro level, often appear to provide a fairly easy case for these rights.[66] Indeed, the risk of chasing economic vindication is that the ILO might thereby end up consistently on the defensive. Thus, without in any way shrinking away from the debate, it seems essential not to undermine more fundamental considerations concerning the legitimacy of the Bank's approach in principle, rather than trying to focus the fight on efficiency questions alone.

One issue raised in this regard is that, from a legal point of view, there is a legitimate argument that the criterion of economic efficiency is only one of the possible interpretation of the 'economic considerations' dictated in the Bank's Articles of Agreement.[67] Not to mention that adopting a broader reinterpretation could strengthen the Bank's ability to carry out its mission, add to its value and bolster its legitimacy.

[63] So would it not be surprising, given the (more or less isolated) pressures for new social conditionalities which reveal themselves from time to time (see below) to see the re-emergence of proposals aimed at distributing 'toolkits' to constituents?

[64] In March 2008, during a meeting of the Governing Body, World Bank President, Robert Zoellick, made a point of mentioning the points of convergence between the agendas pursued by the World Bank and the ILO: 'It obviously connects quite well with the Decent Work Agenda, and we have been very pleased, as Juan mentioned, to try to build a closer working relationship with the ILO and the World Bank across an agenda that also involves other partner' (Robert B Zoellick, World Bank Group President, Speech at the International Labour Organization, Geneva, 17 March 2008). These comments also provide an excellent illustration of how the conceptual flexibility of 'decent work' can smooth over otherwise important doctrinal differences. It is interesting to note that the 2013 World Development Report contains a box (World Bank, *World Development Report 2013* (n 15) 158 Box 5.3) devoted to the concept of 'decent work' based on the ILO literature, but where one is surprised to learn that it is 'now part of the ILO Constitution!'. The report, however, chooses not to use the concept in practice, even though it clearly insists on the principle that 'not all forms of work are acceptable' (ibid 14).

[65] *cf* Guy Davidov, 'Comment on Alan Hyde: The Perils of Economic Justifications for International Labor Standards' (2009) 3(2) *Law and Ethics of Human Rights* Art 3.

[66] That is, in contributing to a more equal distribution of global wealth, respect for fundamental rights, and especially for freedom of association and collective bargaining, could make a significant contribution to stimulus to address the crisis, setting aside concerns sometimes raised about micro-level distortions brought about by certain union practices.

[67] As noted by Jordi Agusti-Panareda, a broader view of these terms is possible, which would amount to a simple evolution of the Bank's theoretical foundations that would in no way come into conflict with its duty of impartiality (Jordi Agusti-Panareda, 'La Banque Mondiale' in Jean Marc Thouvenin and Anne Trebilcock (eds), *Droit international social* (Brussels, Bruylant, 2013) ch 4). In this regard, the (at least usually) well-founded charges of 'mission creep' levelled against the Bank's ongoing extension of its activities into new areas (Jessica Einhorn, 'The World Bank Mission Creep' (2001) 80(5) *Foreign Affairs* 22) suggest that the content and limits of its mandate may be surprisingly versatile. Indeed, it seems hard to understand how its mission as currently expressed – 'working for a world free of poverty' – can be derived from a mandate which the Bank has always rigorously sought to define in purely economic terms.

It is arguable, more fundamentally, that the somewhat monomaniacal interpretation of the strict 'economic considerations' requirement has led the Bank to drift away from the other limiting condition of its mandate, one it has tried to cleave to with at least as much force as the first. This is, of course, the terms imposed under Article IV(10) of the Articles of Agreement, according to which '[t]he Bank and its officers shall not interfere in the political affairs of any member'. It may be argued that by persisting in an attitude of what might be described as latent distrust toward workers' collective rights[68] under the pretext of disregarding 'non-economic influences or considerations' the Bank actually ends up violating the injunction imposed by this latter provision.[69]

Thirdly, these potential avenues for broader social engagement beyond the ILO do not mean that the ILO can itself evade the debate on the efficiency impacts of fundamental rights; quite to the contrary. They imply that it must engage in that debate within a much clearer and rigorous framework, including two specific considerations. First off, assessments should focus on particular practices,[70] leaving aside the abstract question of the economic efficiency of the underlying principles as such.[71] Furthermore, the debate should occur in an appropriate institutional framework: it is clear in this regard that the simple exchange of analyses, conducted according to idiosyncratic methodologies, or through journals acting as proxies, cannot substitute for face-to-face debate conducted in an adversarial manner and according to accepted methodologies between all those concerned. To end current forms of institutional myopia, it is essential that everyone accept that a small amount of mutual influence is liable to occur in any discussion[72] that can genuinely be called a 'dialogue'. If such a framework does not exist at present, we shall see in Chapter 6 just how readily it might be grafted onto existing ILO procedures and practices.

[68] Even though the organisation responsible for labour regulation has recognised these rights as fundamental, and despite the pledge of the community of states to respect and promote them.

[69] The basic structure of this rather compelling argument is that, in accordance with its duty of impartiality and its commitment to non-interference in the political affairs of its members, the Bank's activities should not conflict with commitments its members have made elsewhere in the international system (see Daniel Bradlow, 'The World Bank, the IMF and Human Rights' (1996) 6 *Transnational Law and Contemporary Problems* 47; John D Ciorciari, 'The Lawful Scope of Human Rights Criteria in the World Bank Credit Decisions' (2000) 33 *Cornell International Law Journal* 331).

[70] Thus, it may be reasonable to examine union practices which are not only 'inefficient' but also in some sense 'anti-social' insofar as they favour what might be called 'rent seekers' (not to question the role of shareholders here of course!) at the expense of those who are not so protected.

[71] In other words, assessment should focus on (i) the objective evaluation of the economic impacts of certain practices; and (ii) whether or not those practices are inseparable from respect for fundamental principles and rights.

[72] Louis Veuillot is well-known for introducing a paradox of pluralistic governance, which might be phrased: 'When I am the weaker I ask you for my freedom because that is your principle; but when I am the stronger I take away your freedom because that is my principle'. The debate regarding the possible introduction of positive social conditionalities on Bank loans seems to allude to the same logic, but played in reverse: 'I demand conditionalities on your activities in the name of my principles, but I refuse them for myself in the name of yours.' In this regard, might the claim for conditionalities in favour of the ILO's fundamental objectives not actually benefit from conceding the point regarding their economic impact? The arguments to this effect are not lacking, especially if one takes the long-term view which takes into account the degree to which social and economic rights have been shown quite capable of promoting social cohesion and political legitimacy, insofar as they make wealth distribution more equitable.

5

Employment: Functional 'Common Ground' or Policy Fault-Line?

If achieving comprehensive coherence among the objectives and activities of the universal multilateral organisations may seem a utopian enterprise, there remains one area in which such coherence seems natural, or even legally imposed: employment. Among policy objectives, it not only acts as a singular hinge between the economic and social spheres, but is also alone in its common appearance in the respective charters of the social, economic, financial and trade organisations, as seen in Box 5.1.

Box 5.1 Social objectives appearing in the introductory provisions of the constitutional charters

Articles of Agreement of the International Bank for Reconstruction and Development, Article 1 – Objectives

(iii) To promote the long-range balanced growth of international trade and the maintenance of equilibrium in balances of payments by encouraging international investment for the development of the productive resources of members, thereby assisting in *raising productivity, the standard of living and conditions of labor in their territories.* (emphasis added)

Articles of Agreement of the International Monetary Fund, Article 1 – Purpose

(ii) To facilitate the expansion and balanced growth of international trade, and to contribute thereby to *the promotion and maintenance of high levels of employment and real income* and to the development of the productive resources of all members as primary objectives of economic policy. (emphasis added)

Agreement Establishing the World Trade Organization, Preamble

Recognizing that their relations in the field of trade and economic endeavour should be conducted with a view to raising standards of living, *ensuring full employment and a large and steadily growing volume of real income and*

> *effective demand*, and expanding the production of and trade in goods and services, while allowing for the optimal use of the world's resources in accordance with the objective of sustainable development, seeking both to protect and preserve the environment and to enhance the means for doing so in a manner consistent with their respective needs and concerns at different levels of economic development. (emphasis added)

The best that might be said in practice is that realities do not quite match the rhetoric.[1] It is hard to describe the situation except in terms of collective failure. One explanation for this contradiction is that the explicit reference to employment and rising living standards in the IMF and WTO charters bear the mark of the Keynesian ideas in vogue at the time of their origins – ideas almost totally disavowed with the rise of the Washington Consensus. During the 1980s, the neoliberal vision served by the Washington Consensus policies coming out of the international financial institutions (IFIs) came to supplant the Keynesian vision which had provided the cement of the international system following the Second World War. The shift in international orthodoxy toward the neoliberal perspective resulted in the creation of a similar tension, if not an actual split, in understanding regarding the appropriate role for the state. For its part, the ILO continued to see a key role for the state in maintaining employment demand (as notably expressed in Convention No 122, already discussed),[2] a perspective in clear opposition to the primarily supply-side prescriptions envisioned by the financial, trade and economic organisations. And these conflicting allegiances led to a dual tension.

The first concerns the relative priority to be allotted to employment among economic and social objectives. The tension arises between the ILO's initial approach, which understood employment as a free-standing goal requiring targeted macro-economic policy choices, and the conception of the other organisations, among which employment (except perhaps in times of crisis) was regarded simply as a sort of byproduct of an otherwise balanced macro-economic policy.

The second related to *the type of job* in question. Here, the ILO has most consistently committed to achieving a balance between creating a supply of work sufficient to meet the need, and a refusal to sacrifice job quality in order to increase supply. Nonetheless, it has faced, and continues to face, pressures aimed at shifting the balance toward purely quantitative concerns.

[1] As noted in the previous chapter, unemployment and informal work are not only stagnant, but are actually increasing in many countries, and the financial crisis has only exacerbated the situation.

[2] Convention No 122 on Employment Policy (adopted 9 July 1964, entered into force 9 July 1965) 569 UNTS 65, Pt I, c 2, s B.iii.

I. Employment: Free-standing Policy Objective or Economic Windfall?

A. ILO View: Employment as an Objective in Its Own Right

In the original text of the ILO Constitution, employment made only a passing appearance, in the form of an expressed need for 'the prevention of unemployment'. The Great Depression, though, and its devastating impact on employment, quickly revealed the myopic inadequacy of this vision.[3] More generally, it showed the inadvisability of expecting an improvement in the plight of workers without an active employment policy.[4] In response, the Declaration of Philadelphia proclaims the ILO's urgent task:

> to further among the nations of the world programmes which will achieve: (a) full employment and the raising of standards of living; (b) the employment of workers in the occupations in which they can have the satisfaction of giving the fullest measure of their skill and attainments and make their greatest contribution to the common well-being.

As supplemented by the various declarations adopted during the ILO.s history, the constitutional texts thereby established employment as more than just a way for workers to ensure their living. It came to represent a goal in its own right,[5] insofar as, through employment, individuals could reach their 'personal fulfilment' and contribute to 'the common wellbeing'.[6] Without work, in the words of Wilfred Jenks, 'the whole fabric of society' unravels.[7] Recognition of the social and personal function taken on by work of course leaves open the question of what form it is supposed to take.[8] This way of thinking leads naturally to the belief that job creation should be at the forefront of macro-economic policies, even to the point (we will return to this) of dictating the choice of 'appropriate' technologies.

[3] This perception of the immediate post-war period is reflected in the predictions of Cordell Hull that '[t]here will be the inevitable seeds of future wars in the form of vast unemployment and hunger throughout the world' (Cordell Hull and Andrew Henry Thomas Berding, *The Memoirs of Cordell Hull* (New York, Macmillan, 1948) 1477).

[4] Well captured in the formula used in a 2001 speech by Director-General Juan Samovia: 'No decent work without work!'.

[5] Note that the question of whether the work could or should be considered a Rawlsian 'primary good' (that is, of the sort that can claim a theoretical basis sufficient to outweigh all other considerations, including efficiency measurements) has been addressed directly by Hugh Collins (Hugh Collins, 'Theories of Rights and Justifications for Labour Law' in Guy Davidov and Brain A Langille (eds), *The Idea of Labour Law* (Oxford, Oxford University Press, 2011) 137 ff).

[6] ILO, Declaration on Social Justice for a Fair Globalization (adopted 10 June 2008) IA(i) (2008 Declaration). It is interesting to compare this statement to the analysis contained in the Bank's recent World Development Report (World Bank, *World Development Report 2013: Jobs* (Washington DC, World Bank, 2013) 8, Figure 4) illustrating the 'transformational' character of jobs.

[7] ILO, *Social Policy in a Changing World: The ILO Response: Selected Speeches by Wilfred Jenks* (Geneva, ILO, 1976) 252.

[8] The notion of employment, too, can be used to refer to either salaried or unsalaried work, in a formal or informal setting. That being said, in the ILO setting, at least, it has traditionally been applied so as to capture the possibility of working in a dependent relationship.

To truly understand the priority the ILO accords to employment, it is important to remember that, in contrast to other subjects which 'naturally' lead to conflict, such as the level of wages or how stable and permanent the employment relationship is expected to be, it inherently offers an unparalleled common ground between workers' and employers' interests.[9] This shared interest, helped along by the high unemployment rates in the multiple newly independent countries that acceded to ILO membership in the early 1960s, no doubt goes a long way toward explaining the priority this goal was assigned during the post-war years.[10] It was this context that led the ILO to take a further step in the formal recognition of employment, in the words of the 1959 speech by David Morse, as 'the central issue of social policy'.[11] Specifically, the organisation turned toward standard-setting, and adopted Convention No 122 (already discussed) with the hope that its Members would recognise the central role employment played not only in social policy, but in economic policy more generally.[12]

This activism brought the ILO into an undisputed leadership role in the United Nations system,[13] receiving the Nobel Peace Prize in 1969 on the occasion of its fiftieth birthday, and launching the World Employment Programme[14] the following year as a way to 'reclaim the high ground' in international development work.[15]

[9] See Alain Supiot (ed), *Beyond Employment: Changes in Work and the Future of Labour Law in Europe* (Paris, Flammarion, 1999). This obviously does not mean that their respective visions of employment policy naturally and automatically coincide. This was evident especially during the years of the World Employment Programme and the basic needs strategy for development, whose radicalism provoked strong resistance from employers. Today, however, any employer hostility to the ILO's approach has since fallen to the wayside: indeed, since at least 1999 employment has considered as somewhat of an employer fiefdom. The direction of the International Labour Office's Employment Department (now the Employment Sector, which includes numerous subdepartments) has been entrusted to people whose sensitivity if not origins are closer to those of the employers. On these subjects, see the (very pointed) comments by Guy Standing, 'The ILO: An Agency for Globalization?' (2008) 39 *Development and Change* 355, 363.

[10] See above, Part I, Introduction, text to n 13.

[11] ILO, *Reply of the Director-General following the Discussion of his Report* (ILC, 43rd Session, Geneva, 3–25 June 1959) 560. The phrase is more powerful in the French, claiming that employment is 'au cœur de la politique sociale'.

[12] Indeed, there is probably significant insight to be gleaned from closer examination into the processes and motivations that led International Labour Office economists, despite their relative cultural segregation from standards work, to nonetheless pursue their belief in employment's deserved policy priority by way of the standards power. Some hint is provided in the sense that standard-setting was almost the only way to earn the ILC's attention – and thereby to gain access to associated resources.

[13] The will to maintain that leadership and consolidate the place of employment in an unfavourable environment led the ILO to mobilise its 'tripartite strike force' through two audacious attempts at high-level conferences in 1976 and 1987, addressed in Chapter 6.

[14] The notion that employment was at one and the same time a method and purpose was at the centre of the programme, as stated by its 'high priest', Louis Emmerij, 'Employment was both a means and an end' quoted in Ashwani Saith, 'Reflections: Louis Emmerij' (2005) 36(6) *Development and Change* 1163.

[15] See Eddy Lee, 'Employment and Poverty Reduction' in Gerry Rodgers and others, *The ILO and the Quest for Social Justice* (Geneva, ILO, 2009) 186.

The fact is, in any case, that since that time, fundamental rights aside, there is no goal to which the ILO has accorded a higher priority. It is listed second among the four strategic objectives introduced in the 2000s.[16] The organisation has expended considerable resources in service of this objective. In addition to related standards activities, a very significant portion of its budgetary resources and staff time are devoted specifically to employment: no fewer than 23.5 per cent of the 2012–2013 strategic budget was allotted for the sole purpose of employment[17] (a slightly lower proportion compared to the early 2000s[18] but still considerable), and it has successfully attracted substantial extra-budgetary resources since the launch of the World Employment Programme in the 1970s.[19] Employment has been the subject of a vast research programme: the ILO has played a key role in improving knowledge of the problem in all its dimensions. It was a pioneer in drawing attention to and conceptually framing the phenomenon of informal work.[20] Employment has now been the subject of countless meetings at all levels, including, until a recent reform, at the Committee on Employment and Social Policy, a standing committee of the ILO's Governing Body. And finally, it has often been the subject of solemn proclamations of principle, which in the last decade alone have included both the Global Employment Agenda adopted by the Governing Body in 2003, and the 2009 Global Jobs Pact.

B. View Outside the ILO: Employment as a Reward for Sound Economic Policy?

As noted above (Box 5.1), the charters of the IMF and the WTO make explicit reference to employment and rising living standards. In the first case at least, one can see the very clear imprint of Keynesian-era origins. In the post-war period and during much of the post-war boom, the influence of this perspective was almost universal (outside the Soviet Bloc, of course). More particularly, the 'embedded liberalism' of the period constituted the very basis of an international system

[16] The strategic objectives are: (i) promote and realise standards and fundamental principles and rights at work; (ii) create greater opportunities for women and men to decent employment and income; (iii) enhance the coverage and effectiveness of social protection for all; (iv) strengthen tripartism and social dialogue.

[17] ILO, *Programme and Budget for the Biennium 2012–13* (ILC, 100th Session, Geneva, 1–17 June 2011) 3.

[18] For 2002–2003, the share of employment in the regular budget was 26.2 per cent and 35.3 per cent of extra-budgetary resources (ILO, *Draft Programme and Budget 2002–03 and Other Financial Questions* (ILC, 89th Session, Geneva, 5–21 June 2001) viii). This share fell slightly in 2004–2005 and stabilised at 22 per cent in 2006–2007 (ILO, *Programme and Budget for the Biennium 2006–07* (ILC, 96th Session, Geneva, 31 May–16 June 2005) 23).

[19] This made it possible to ensure the programme was not stopped dead in its tracks by the non-payment and then withdrawal of the US contribution.

[20] Guy Standing attributes authorship of the concept to Keith Hart (Standing, 'Agency for Globalization?' (n 9) 363).

modelled on an 'internationally constructed national autonomy'[21] that many have described as 'Adam Smith abroad – John Maynard Keynes at home'.[22] In this context, international regulation provided an active counterweight to cross-border economic integration, allowing states to protect themselves from the destabilising effects of the expanded trade (including through the power to control the movement of capital and limit some imports) thereby enabling the development of effective industrial relations mechanisms and generous welfare programmes,[23] all while helping to promote and support employment. All in line, in other words, with ILO objectives.

This Keynesian economic culture, however, was sharply challenged by a succession of economic shocks beginning in the 1970s. For reasons both political and pragmatic, the transformation of the global economic environment led IFI orthodoxy away from the conceptions popular at the ILO[24] and from the Keynesian model of an interventionist state. Under this new conception, employment presupposed the existence of firms and entrepreneurs, and employment policy took on the limited form of establishing conditions for sustainable economic activity, rather than trying to manipulate macro-economic balances or intervene directly by expending public resources on somewhat contrived job creation. The primary aim in this framework was to develop an institutional environment which encouraged initiative, creativity and economic efficiency, cast together as the sole source of productive and sustainable job creation. According to the reformed view, and quite contrary to the Keynesian policies of yesteryear, the fight against inflation would be placed at the heart of good macro-economic policy, even if the cost of this prudence was a certain degree of unemployment. In short, this vision confined public institutions to the mainly complementary task of 'creat[ing] a more employment-friendly climate for business',[25] by fostering the adaptability of the

[21] David M Trubek, Jim Mosher and Jeffrey S Rothstein, 'Transnationalism in the Regulation of Labor Relations: International Regimes and Transnational Advocacy Networks' (2000) 25 *Law and Social Inquiry* 1187, 1190.

[22] Adelle Blackett and Christian Lévesque, 'Introduction: Social Regionalism in the Global Economy' in Adelle Blackett and Christian Lévesque (eds), *Social Regionalism in the Global Economy* (Routledge, 2011) 6. The classic source on embedded liberalism is, of course, John G Ruggie, 'International Regimes, Transactions, and Change: Embedded Liberalism in the Postwar Economic Order' (1982) 36(2) *International Organization* 379.

[23] ibid.

[24] According to some authors, not only did IFIs change their perspective, they actually embarked on a crusade against the ILO. François-Xavier Merrien claims that 'les politiques publiques défendues par l'Organisation internationale du travail sont l'objet d'une intense campagne de délégitimation' led by the World Bank, which itself 'souligne leur inefficacité, leur incapacité à faire face aux défis démographiques, leur effets anti-économiques' and 'propage mondialement un nouveau programme de politique sociale' ['public policies promoted by the International Labour Organization are subject to an intense campaign of delegitimization' [led by the World Bank, which itself] 'emphasizes their inefficiency, their failure to cope with demographic challenges, their anti-economic effects' [and] 'that spreads worldwide, a new social policy agenda', trans] (François-Xavier Merrien, 'Nouveau régime économique international et devenir des États Providence' in Pierre de Senarclens (ed), *Maîtriser la mondialisation: la régulation sociale internationale* (Paris, Presses de Sciences-Po, 2000) 94).

[25] World Bank, *MILES: A Multi-Sector Approach to Foster Job Creation, Poverty Reduction and Growth* (4 October 2007), quoted in Yaraslau Kryvoi, 'The World Bank and the ILO: Two Visions of Employment

workforce to technological innovations, rapid changes in production methods and consumer preferences.[26]

Thus, in 1979 the G7 set the stage for the World Bank and the IMF to begin implementing structural adjustment programmes.[27] Fed by successive crises in Asia and Latin America, a monetarist, export-oriented, liberalisation-focused paradigm gradually coalesced in these institutions in the form of an ascendant 'Washington Consensus'. The same logic also lead to the dismantling of institutions deemed inefficient, including a wide array of international and national regulations restricting the free functioning of markets.[28] In the countries subjected to this regime, the conditionality attached to loans from the Bank and the IMF imposed tough constraints, with respect to social policy and interventions in favour of employment in particular, all ostensibly aimed at restoring the balance of payments, ending trade imbalances, balancing state budgets and putting an end to the debt crisis.

This kind of reversal of perspective finds expression in three emblematic aspects of the orthodoxy that has established itself in the 'international community' for nearly two decades: first, the priority given to trade liberalisation as an engine of sustainable employment creation; secondly, the fight against poverty; and thirdly, the policy of workforce adjustment typified by the framework of the OECD 'jobs strategy'.

(i) Promoting Further Trade Liberalisation

The priority given to full employment in the immediate post-war period found its way shortly after the creation of the IFIs into the Havana Charter, originally intended as the foundation of a new global trade regime that would eliminate the risk of returning to pre-war protectionism. Drawing from the Keynesian perspective, the

Regulation' in Roger Blanpain and Claire Grant (eds), *Fixed-Term Employment Contracts: A Comparative Study* (Bruges, Vanden Broele, 2009) 49.

[26] Indeed, so unwavering is the focus on the qualities of the labour supply that, as one scholar put it regarding the 2004 report of the World Commission, 'we are invited to conclude that a skilled labour force creates its own market' (Kerry Rittich, 'Rights, Risk, and Reward: Governance Norms in the International Order and the Problem of Precarious Work' in Judy Fudge and Rosemary J Owens (eds), *Precarious Work, Women, and the New Economy: The Challenge to Legal Norms* (Oxford, Hart Publishing, 2006) 43). Despite the new emphasis that the most recent WDR places on 'jobs', appearing in some sense to put jobs at the very foundation of development, underlying the three pillars of living standards, productivity and social cohesion (World Bank, *World Development Report 2013* (n 6) 8), the Bank very much sticks to the orthodoxy when it comes to choosing economic policy priorities, a point well illustrated by the pyramid (ibid 23, Figure 16) with three distinct layers of policy: macro-economic stability, an 'enabling business environment' and the rule of law as the basis of the pyramid, labour policies that 'avoid misguided interventions' in the middle, and specific employment challenges considered last.

[27] Gustave Massiah, *Grandeur et décadence de l'ajustement structurel: Les programmes d'ajustement structurel et le développement* (Association internationale de techniciens, experts et chercheurs (AITEC), 2000).

[28] Of course, the flagship report of the *Doing Business* programme discussed above draws directly from this perspective. The result is that countries known for how little they think of fundamental rights of workers, including Belarus and China, find themselves in a better position in these evaluations than most Western European nations!

Charter made 'fair employment' a real objective of that system, even to the point of justifying certain temporary restrictions on full trade liberalisation.[29]

As for the GATT, the sole survivor of the Havana Charter's stillborn 'International Trade Organization', the Preamble only 'makes a bow to ensuring full employment'.[30] Nor did the creation of the WTO 50 years later fundamentally change the situation: while much hay can be made of the opening to sustainable development and the environment manifested in its Charter's Preamble, Charnovitz's conclusion on the WTO's employment dimension is likely just as applicable to those issues: 'none of the actual rules drafted during the Uruguay round do anything concrete to achieve this goal'.[31] Beyond a massive communications effort holding out the promise to the public of millions of jobs that were to result from the Marrakesh agreement, 'not a single procedure was foreseen that would permit the impact of creating a free flow of goods and capital on a global scale with regard to standards of living, employment levels, or incomes'.[32] The underlying reason is, again according to Charnovitz, that the 'WTO epistemic community tends to look at employment as an output generated by trade negotiations'.[33] Or to put it another way, job creation and rising living standards are not viewed as autonomous goals to be pursued but as (albeit beneficial) byproducts of economic liberalisation and growth, the latter being the only goals worth actively pursuing.

[29] In the Charter: 'The Members recognize that measures relating to employment must take fully into account the rights of workers under inter-governmental declarations, Conventions and agreements. They recognize that all countries have a common interest in the achievement and maintenance of fair labour standards related to productivity, and thus in the improvement of wages and working conditions as productivity may permit. The Members recognize that unfair labour conditions, particularly in production for export, create difficulties in international trade, and, accordingly, each Member shall take whatever action may be appropriate and feasible to eliminate such conditions within its territory'. In this regard, see also Jacques Lemoine, 'International Trade Regimes in Retrospect' in Marcel A Boisard, Evgeny, Chossudovsky and Jacques Lemoine (eds), *Diplomatie multilatérale: système des Nations Unies à Genève: guide de travail* (The Hague, Kluwer Law International, 1998).

[30] Steve Charnovitz, 'The Neglected Employment Dimension of the World Trade Organization' in Virginia A Leary and Daniel Warner (eds), *Social Issues, Globalisation and International Institutions: Labour Rights and the EU, ILO, OECD and WTO* (Leiden, Martinus Nijhoff, 2006) 153 (discussing similar language appearing in the WTO Preamble).

[31] ibid 127–32. To this analysis one can probably add, as recently observed in the *International Herald Tribune*, that the marginalised probably do not possess sufficient political strength to tip the balance.

[32] Author's translation. Original: 'aucune procédure n'[était] prévue, qui permettrait de mesurer l'efficacité de la généralisation de la libre circulation des capitaux et des marchandises à l'échelle du monde au regard des objectifs de niveau de vie de taux d'emploi ou de revenus'. Alain Supiot, *L'esprit de Philadelphie: La justice sociale face au marché total* (Paris, Seuil, 2010) 63–64. Measuring such impacts was exactly what the Office had in mind when it put forward the resolution in 1946 that would have allowed the Conference to conduct a recurring tripartite discussion on the social impacts of international economic policies – a task, it will be recalled, that was rejected on the grounds that it fell to ECOSOC's coordinating functions.

[33] Charnovitz, 'The Neglected Employment Dimension' (n 30) 19. This explains Art XII:3(a) of the GATT, which requires members to take into account 'the desirability of avoiding an uneconomic employment of productive resources' and XII:3(d), which attempts to provide some room for policies aimed at 'full and productive employment'. We find much the same philosophy in the subsidies agreement, which exempts subsidies dealing with acute social problems in industries affected by trade liberalisation, though these subsidies are supposed to be limited and temporary.

The experience of the past two decades can only lend credence to the impression that this vision proceeds from a kind of article of faith, both impervious to empirical verification[34] and tending to gloss over the serious normative questions raised by the (re)distribution of gains and losses it seems to generate.[35]

The eagerness and vigour with which this orthodoxy reaffirmed itself following the shock of the 2008 crisis, and the attendant doubts it raised, seem particularly revealing in this regard. The financial crisis had led to a temporary 'return of the state' in a kind of employment policy scramble, sometimes at the cost of certain protectionist deviations which everyone had an interest in ignoring. The severity of its consequences for the most vulnerable gave birth to a fleeting conviction that 'nothing would be as it had been before' and faith that new regulations would inevitably be given their turn, as called for in President Sarkozy's 2009 speech to the ILC.[36] Thus, at the height of the crisis, the G20 Declaration in Pittsburgh ended up proclaiming that: '[w]e cannot rest until the global economy is restored to full health, and hard-working families the world over can find decent jobs'.[37] The warm welcome which greeted the Global Jobs Pact adopted by the ILC in June 2009 (which we will return to at the end of this chapter) can easily be understood as part of the same general clamour.

Yet commitment to the perspective in these resolutions started to unravel from the first sign (however illusory) of global recovery. In its June 2010 statement in Toronto, the G20 bluntly returned to the previous order of things. In this regard, it clearly insisted that: 'open markets play a pivotal role in supporting growth and job creation, and in achieving our goals under the G20 framework for Strong, Sustainable and Balanced Growth. We ask the OECD, the ILO and the WTO to report on the *benefits* of trade liberalization for employment and growth at the Seoul Summit' (emphasis added, but capitals in the original text!)[38]

[34] Consider, for example, a joint report (WTO and ILO, *Trade and Employment: Challenges for Policy Research* (Geneva, WTO, 2007)) conducted late and not without some reluctance by the two secretariats in 2007, following the intervention of the ILO's Working Party on the Social Dimension of Globalization, and from which it emerged that the record is not as bright as it was made out to be at the Marrakesh Conference.

[35] Indeed, as Rittich eloquently puts an insight she takes from Kapstein and Pogge, 'if the generation of winners and losers is as routine, and even as systemic, as it appears to be, liberalized trade and globally integrated economies may be hard to defend normatively in the absence of some institutionalized commitment to redistribution' (Rittich, 'Global Labour Policy' (n 26) 253).

[36] ILO, Address, Mr Nicolas Sarkozy, President of the French Republic (ILC 98th Session, 11th Sitting, Geneva, 15 June 2009).

[37] G20, *G20 Leaders Statement* (G20 Summit, Pittsburg, 24–25 September 2009). This position had already been affirmed by the G8 in July 2009, where heads of state and government had recognised that '[t]aking forward the ILO Decent Work Agenda, building on the ILO resolution on "Recovering from the Crisis: A Global Jobs Pact", is relevant to respond to the crisis at worldwide level and advance the social dimension of globalisation' (G8, *G8 Leaders Declaration: Responsible Leadership for a Sustainable Future* (G8 Summit, L'Aquila, 8 July 2009) para 37).

[38] The Declaration made at Cannes the following year (G20, *Cannes Summit Final Declaration: Building Our Common Future: Renewed Collective Action for the Benefit of All* (G20 Summit, Cannes, 4 November 2011)) while referring in the section on the multilateral trading system (paras 65–66) to the Toronto commitments 'to roll back any new protectionist measure that may have risen' does not show the same lyricism regarding trade's 'pivotal role'.

The term 'benefits' seems particularly significant here. This phrasing abjures objective, empirical analysis of the *impacts* of trade liberalisation in favour of the assumption that it necessarily has a positive impact on employment. This 'spin' is all the more striking given that the joint work carried out at the secretariat level of the ILO and WTO had already led to the conclusions (albeit timidly stated) that the effects of trade liberalisation on employment were not wholly positive, particularly in terms of its potential augmentation of informality.[39]

The joint report (mentioned above) submitted to Seoul by the IFIs and the ILO[40] concluded for its part with an unequivocal plea in favour of completing the Doha Round.[41]As one commentator observed, the impression given was that the social dimension, that is to say, the consequences of the reference to employment contained in the founding charters, is completely relegated to the national level, leaving international organisations to play a consulting role at most.[42]

This episode cannot help but give credence to Francis Blanchard's hypothesis (mentioned above) that, despite what may be laid out in the Declaration of Philadelphia, the ILO's expected role in the system is not so much contributing to collective progress by assessing the impact of globalisation through the lens of its own objectives (particularly employment), as it is to act as a kind of social 'alibi' for the whole process. Yet the mere fact that its sanction is deemed necessary can constitute an invaluable asset, as long as the ILO knows how to use it. To this we will return.

(ii) Prioritising 'the Eradication of Poverty'

A second symptomatic aspect of this shift of perspectives is the way in which the fight against poverty rose, with the active support of the World Bank, to the premier rank among priorities expressed by the Millennium Development Goals.

Direct interest in poverty, of course, is nothing new to the ILO. One of the Declaration of Philadelphia's most famous mottos is that 'poverty anywhere constitutes a danger to prosperity everywhere'. The fight against poverty was also

[39] ILO and WTO, *Globalization and Informal Jobs in Developing Countries* (Geneva, WTO, 2009). When the report came before the ILO, and the Governing Body's Working Party on the Social Dimension of Globalization in particular, in November 2010, Pascal Lamy, among the panelists, emphasised the importance of this step, given that it could signal closer cooperation between the ILO and the WTO. Without making direct reference to the conclusions of the G20 in Toronto or Lamy's intervention, the workers nevertheless focused on the shortfalls, recalling the uneven impacts of trade liberalisation, particularly in developing countries that had to focus on industrialisation strategies rather than liberalisation. That position was echoed by the workers' spokesperson on 17 November 2010. See ILO, *Report of the Working Party on the Social Dimension of Globalization* (Governing Body, 300th Session, Geneva, November 2007).

[40] ILO, World Bank and WTO, *Seizing the Benefits of Trade for Employment and Growth: Final Report* (G20 Summit, Seoul, 11–12 November 2010).

[41] The plan that the G20 annexed to its most recent communiqué (G20, *The Los Cabos Growth and Jobs Action Plan* (19 June 2012)) seems to reflect some loss of faith in the outcome of the Doha Round, merely proclaiming the Group's commitment 'to resist protectionism in all forms and promote open trade'.

[42] Centre d'études sur l'intégration et la mondialisation (CEIM), 'Lien commerce-emploi: les organisations internationales se prononcent' (December 2010) 1(2) *Chronique Humaniser le commerce* 3.

at the heart of the basic needs strategy developed under the World Employment Programme framework in the 1970s. The thrust of this strategy incited strong resistance at the time, on the whole levelled against its radicalism and very proactive vision regarding the state's responsibilities in general,[43] and its active role in choosing 'appropriate' technologies in particular (matters addressed more directly below).

Such 'radicalism' is unsurprisingly absent from the World Bank-inspired strategy to eradicate poverty, endorsed by the United Nations system at Millennium Summit held in 2000.[44] It is significant in this context that the ILO was essentially left out of the loop during the run-up to the summit. Instead, preparations relied heavily on *A Better World for All*, a report developed jointly by the United Nations, the OECD and the Bretton Woods institutions that virtually ignores both ILO texts, and its efforts. Indeed, as put by Marieke Louis, the omission is so glaring that employment, having been relatively neglected in Copenhagen,[45] appears as 'le grand absent du Sommet du Millénaire',[46] no matter that employment has subsequently been described as (according to a rather memorable formula) 'the best anti-poverty programme'.[47]

The emergence of the fight against poverty as a kind of relatively autonomous policy goal is a subject of some perplexity. Without a doubt, the fight against poverty has important links to policies that promote employment; promoting education and training, for example, can enable the parties involved to escape from poverty by improving their ability to find (or create) a job, thus targeting the source of the problem. Yet the link between employment and poverty reduction is not as unambiguous as this assessment suggests, given that 50 per cent of workers find themselves in precarious situations, just as a significant fraction of those not falling into the recognised categories of working relationships nevertheless manage to support themselves.[48] Of course, these questions raise the more general problem of knowing what is respectively included in 'employment' and 'work', issues already admitted to be beyond the scope of this book.[49]

[43] For an overview of the strongly negative responses to portions of the World Employment Programme, especially from the side of the United States, see Robert Cox, 'Labor and Hegemony' (1977) 31(03) *International Organization* 385, 417–20.

[44] UN Millennium Declaration (adopted 8 September 2000) UNGA Res 55/2.

[45] Louis Emmerij, Richard Jolly and Thomas George Weiss, *Ahead of the Curve? UN Ideas and Global Challenges* (Blomington, IN, Indiana University Press, 2001).

[46] Marieke Louis, *L'organisation internationale du travail et le travail décent: Un agenda social pour le multilatéralisme* (Paris, L'Harmattan, 2011) 92 ff.

[47] ILO, *UN General Assembly adopts Resolution on World Commission Report on Fair Globalization* (Press Release, 7 December 2004).

[48] This is much the point made by Nomaan Majid, 'The Working Poor in Developing Countries' (2001) 140(3) *International Labour Review* 271. This situation is clearly contemplated by the Preamble to the ILO Constitution which targets 'conditions of work *involving* such injustice hardship and privation' and thereby implying that work can be a contributory *cause* of poverty, not only a response to it.

[49] No doubt, confusion is only likely to increase as a result of the choice made by the World Bank in its *World Development Report 2013* to use 'jobs' as the baseline category that seems to include almost any kind of (rights-respecting) productive or reproductive work (World Bank, *World Development Report 2013* (n 6) 66).

It is nonetheless worth asking whether the emphasis on this objective, rather than on employment (or 'jobs'), does not above all reflect underlying differences regarding the nature (and limits) of the responsibilities to be placed on public authorities. Through the lens of 'the fight against poverty', the target of government intervention moves away from potentially 'misguided'[50] *economic* measures that view poverty primarily through a lens of a lack of adequate jobs, and toward *social* measures that (without necessarily ignoring the diversity of its causes) seek instead to address its various social manifestations and to prioritise assistance for the poorest households.[51]

It is striking to note that, to the extent that the call to promote 'decent work' could leave room for an interpretation legitimising a greater involvement on the part of public authorities in the creation of such jobs, references to the concept are immediately matched by a kind of antidote in the form of the adjectives 'productive' and 'useful',[52] the significance of which will be discussed below.

(iii) And a Special Emphasis on 'Workforce Adjustment'

A third example emblematic of the new consensus is the approach taken to by the OECD's 'jobs strategy'.[53] Though the prospects of an aging population led to the 2006 refinement of the OECD's Jobs Strategy to encourage workforce

[50] Once again, this is the phrasing of the warning against any form of policy that would interfere with fundamentals, including 'a business friendly economic environment' and macro-economic stability. World Bank, *World Development Report 2013* (n 6) 23.

[51] In her own way, Francine Mestrum has hit the nail on the head in pointing to the shift of state responsibilities toward 'non-monetary forms of poverty'. Eradication of poverty is thereby regarded as a residual of growth: in other words, 'aujourd'hui, développement, lutte contre la pauvreté et croissance sont utilisés comme s'il s'agissait de synonymes' ['nowadays, development, fight against poverty and growth are used as if there were synonyms', trans].The issue of income inequality between social groups, the redistribution of wealth, and the role of the state in the definition of social policy: all of these are thereby set aside. (Francine Mestrum, 'La pauvreté multidimensionnelle: La dynamique sémantique dans le discours de la Banque mondiale' (2008) 88 *Mots* 2, 4). See also Louis, *Travail décent* (n 46) chs 3 and 5.

[52] Thus, the Millenium Declaration's reference to 'decent and productive work', the text of the 2005 follow-up (UN 2005 World Summit Outcome (2005) UNGA Res 60/1) to 'full and productive employment and decent work' and in a 2010 statement from UN Secretary-General Ban Ki Moon, to 'decent and productive work' (United Nations, *Economic Uncertainty, Fiscal Austerity Not Excuses for Doing Less, But Reasons to Do More, Secretary-General Says, in Message for Poverty Eradication Day* (Press Release, 12 October 2010) SG/SM/13176, DEV/2839, OBV/922). On the other hand, as indicated in a review of the decent work concept by Jean-Claude Javillier, part of the tension comes from original formulation of the concept by Director-General Somavia in 1999, suggesting that the 'primary goal of the ILO today is to promote opportunities for women and men to obtain decent *and productive* work, in conditions of freedom, equity, security and human dignity' (Jean-Claude Javillier, 'The Employer and the Worker, the Need for a Comparative and International Perspective' in Brian A Langille and Guy Davidov (eds), *Boundaries and Frontiers of Labour Law* (Oxford, Hart, 2006) 355, 371). On the more or less successful 'export' of the Decent Work Agenda to the United Nations, the WTO and the Bretton Woods institutions, see Louis, *Travail décent* (n 46).

[53] See Organization for Economic Cooperation and Development, *OECD Jobs Study: Evidence and Explanations* (Paris, OECD, 1994). The 10 recommendations in the 1994 Jobs Study were confirmed as the 'OECD Jobs Strategy' the same year. See OECD, *OECD Jobs Strategy: Pushing Ahead with the Strategy* (1996).

participation by, inter alia, taking a hard line against early retirement,[54] the focus remained on providing incentives and skills to keep people at work, even as job security crumbled. While the approach had been intended to respond to the situation in industrialised countries, it does not fundamentally differ from that taken by the IFIs, and by the IMF in particular.[55] Until recently, the OECD has continued to maintain that what workers need most in the context of globalisation is not more protection against risks in general or unemployment risks in particular, but simply a greater ability (and incentives) to learn the new skills dictated by the market's needs.

If this strategy seems largely a matter of common sense, it leaves open a concern articulated quite sharply by Kerry Rittich, that it might result in companies outsourcing, rather than absorbing, the costs of restructuring and redeployments.[56] Even if companies are coerced into contributing their fair share of these costs, it seems clear that it will take considerable public expenditure, not to mention time, to create institutions capable of managing labour market adjustment, before the necessary training can be provided to workers.[57] Yet in practice, where there are insufficient means to build the skills at the foundation of quality jobs, the risk is that states will be driven to sacrifice quality for quantity by pursuing a one-sided 'return to work' strategy.

Now, as we shall see, another dilemma facing policy-makers is precisely that of striking a balance between these two ends.

II. The Evolving Employment Dilemma: Quantity vs Quality

The question here is, of course, related to an earlier one of whether the recognition of work as a social objective implies that any job is better than no job at all. The answer is 'obviously not', but the reasons that make the answer certain at the ILO

[54] OECD, *Boosting Jobs and Incomes: Policy Lessons from Reassessing the OECD Jobs Strategy* (2006).

[55] See International Monetary Fund, *World Economic Outlook: Advancing Structural Reforms* (Washington DC, IMF, 2004) and in particular ch III 'Fostering Structural Reforms in Industrial Countries'. Under the direction of Dominique Strauss-Kahn, however, the IMF's approach during the financial crisis moderated, recognising the need not to jeopardise a fragile recovery at the risk of catastrophic increases in unemployment. Most notably at the high profile joint summit with the ILO in Oslo in September 2010, the IMF explicitly recognised the risks of giving up employment support measures too quickly.

[56] Rittich, 'Global Labour Policy' (n 26) 254.

[57] As stated by Kerry Rittich, 'Policies to get workers into jobs that are suitable and provide decent wages typically require sustained efforts over the long run as well as significant amounts of financing and deep connections between firms and industrial sectors on the one hand, and the institutions that provide training and education to their workforces on the other' (Rittich, 'Global Labour Policy' (n 26) 258). Following the same line of argument, she notes elsewhere that although the OECD approach requires states to promote quality primary and secondary education, it demands nothing in terms of funding or public programmes to develop human capital (ibid 251).

have a slim margin of overlap with those making it obvious for the IFIs or the WTO.[58]

As illustrated by the prior discussion of Convention No 122, the ILO has always striven to strike a balance between the quantitative and qualitative aspects of employment. It is startling to observe, however, how the meaning and nature of 'quality' has evolved with developments and shifts in the international system and the global economy. At the time Convention No 122 was adopted, the 'quality' of jobs had to take into account a Western point of view that focused on their efficiency and productivity, in order to discredit the claim of the Soviet model that it had achieved 'full employment'; with the rise of emerging economies, however, 'quality' has today become associated more closely with questions of 'decency'. Conversely, the concept of decency may now be seen as an obstacle in the way of policies designed to fight unemployment and underemployment, especially insofar as they stand in the way of incentives for a 'return to work' recommended as part of the strategy of the OECD and the IFIs.[59] These two aspects of the controversy deserve individual attention.

A. Quantity vs Productivity?

Compatibility between full employment and productivity growth was a major political issue in the background of ILO standard-setting efforts, culminating in the adoption of Convention No 122. In this respect, the organisation was placed in a dilemma. Before decolonisation brought about an influx of newly independent countries and the cohort of particular problems they faced, it had committed to the idea that (full) employment should be 'at the heart of any social policy'. Yet it was pulled in the opposite direction by Western constituents who feared that such commitments would pave the way to much greater state intervention, if not Soviet-style planning. For them, employment policies had to be part and parcel of overall strategies for economic growth and development.[60]

Convention No 122 was intended to steer a middle way between these currents. The text begins by stating that employment policy must aim to provide work 'for all who are available for and seeking' it.[61] Secondly, it establishes that work must be 'as productive as possible' and that freedom of choice be respected.[62] The Convention also recognises 'the mutual relationship between employment objectives and other economic and social objectives' and allows national policy to 'be pursued by methods that are appropriate to national conditions and practices'.[63]

[58] As for the World Bank, it has already been mentioned that the 2013 WDR recognised that 'not all forms of work are acceptable' (World Bank, *World Development Report 2013* (n 6) 14) but it prefers to talk in terms of 'good jobs for development' rather than in terms of 'decent work'.

[59] See, generally, ILO, *General Survey Concerning Employment Instruments in Light of the 2008 Declaration on Social Justice for a Fair Globalization* (2010) 551–76.

[60] Victor-Yves Ghebali, *The International Labor Organization* (Geneva, Georg, 1987) 127 ff.

[61] Convention No 122 (n 2) Art 1(2)(a).

[62] ibid.

[63] Convention No 122 (n 2) Art 1(3). Note that the English version mentions a 'mutual relationship' which goes beyond the 'existing relationship' articulated in the French version.

The tension between employment and productivity later re-emerged from the very different perspective of the choice of appropriate technology, which essentially highlighted the value of using labour-intensive technologies to reduce unemployment in developing countries.[64] Despite efforts to make the idea widely amenable, trying on adjectives ranging from 'intermediate technology' to 'labour-intensive technology', before landing on the decidedly neutral 'appropriate technology', the conceptions was not introduced without meeting some serious difficulties. There were, first, technical difficulties insofar as, for example, appropriate technologies may not be the same for export as for local consumption,[65] but there were also legal, psychological and political complications. Put simply, many developing countries saw in these discussions a further ruse on the part of developed countries directed at perpetuating their dependence by limiting access to the most advanced technologies.[66]

B. Quantity vs Decency?

We will not return here to the analysis and significance of the concept in terms of the constitutional mandate and objectives of the organisation.[67] Suffice it to recall that: (i) the use of the word 'work' rather than 'labour'[68] is supposed to expand the quantitative dimension to all forms of useful activity performed for others (though there may be some disagreement about whether it includes only remunerated, productive activity);[69] and (ii) the term 'decent', though it has not been without some dissent,[70] refers to a rather obvious qualitative dimension, of meeting those conditions already identified in the Preamble to the Constitution by the term 'humane'.

The primary value-added of the concept as consolidated in the 2008 Declaration was to provide a kind of global, synthetic vision to ILO objectives by affirming the

[64] One might ask why the question is not asked more generally, given that studies from France's Insee (Institut national de la statistique et des études économiques) have estimated that change in technologies account for three-quarters of job destruction, with trade liberalisation counting for only one-quarter. For some comparative data on the role of technology, financial liberalisation and other factors in the growth in inequality over the last 30 years, see IMF, *World Economic Outlook October 2007: Globalization and Inequality* (Washington DC, IMF, 2007) ch 4.

[65] Emmerij, Jolly and Weiss, *Ahead of the Curve?* (n 45) 64.

[66] It is suitable in this regard that 'the Global Employment Agenda' adopted by the ILO's Governing Body in March 2003 and identifying key principles of making employment more productive, comes down clearly in favour of technological change, which is supposed to contribute to 'higher productivity *and* job creation *and* improved standards of living'. ILO, *Global Employment Agenda* (Governing Body, 286th Session, Geneva, March 2003) para 17 (emphasis added).

[67] Louis, *Travail décent* (n 46).

[68] Guy Standing claims responsibility for the choice of 'work' – with the aim of better covering all forms of useful activity, rather than other terms which would traditionally have covered only activities performed under a contract of employment (Standing, 'Agency for Globalization?' (n 9) 370).

[69] By recalling that this implication is far from clear outside the ILO, one can discern a tendency to refer to decent 'work' and decent 'employment' somewhat interchangeably.

[70] Louis, *Travail décent* (n 9) 46–47. Most notable of these objections might be a 2003 speech to the ILC which certainly ruffled some feathers, in which Malaysia's Prime Minister, Mahathir bin Mohamed, went so far as to give it a neo-colonialist connotation. See ILO, *Provisional Record* (ILC, 91st Session, 11th Sitting, 3–19 June 2003).

inseparability and interdependence of their quantitative and qualitative dimensions.[71] If the concept in principle leaves little room for criticism – the exact reason for its quick rise to such wide popularity – it is also quite clear that the right proportion between these two dimensions to achieve optimum results leaves room for diverse interpretations. And so it is not surprising that beyond a façade of consensus, the concept still leaves in place two fundamental dilemmas: first, whether the 'quality' of employment is now to be assessed solely according to humanistic criteria[72] or still leaves room for questions of efficiency;[73] and secondly, how optimally to reconcile the improvement of the quality of work through progressive social legislation and increasing the number of (paid) jobs available.

As previously noted, this ambivalence may explain why the leitmotif of decent work has been almost systematically outflanked by the terms 'useful' and 'productive' in official documents from the United Nations, and from ECOSOC especially.[74] The discourse seems motivated by resistance to government interventions that, under the guise of decency, might be at cross purposes with IFI recommendations to encourage hiring by relaxing legislative protections on working practices or, in the same vein, OECD recommendations to encourage 'return to work' by restricting access to unemployment benefits.[75]

The paradox here is that, as aging drives up the relative cost of supporting dependants for the remaining population of active workers, industrialised countries are, as noted above, pushed by the OECD in particular to give priority to the

[71] For a 'scientific' assessment of the concept's added value, we should probably question both what it has done and what would not have been possible without it. It is difficult to say that the practical activities carried out under its flag would never have happened absent the decent work frame, although bringing them together under the concept may have attracted more resources than might have otherwise been possible. It is almost axiomatic, moreover, that any contributions to ILO visibility facilitated through the numerous references to the concept in UN texts and literature would have otherwise been very hard to attract.

[72] To some extent, the term *decency* places the concept clearly on the field of moral values (hence the preference of some for the use of the word 'dignified'). One notes with some interest in this regard the use of this adjective in a legal publication of France's CGT (Michèle Bonnechère, 'L'optique du travail décent' (February 2007) *The Right Worker* 57) and . . . in the latest papal encyclical! (Benedict XVI, *Caritas in veritate [Charity in Truth]* (2009) para 66).

[73] Especially given that the 'productivity' was already present in the description of the concept in the Director-General's report where it first appeared. See Javillier, 'The Employer and the Worker' (n 52)).

[74] In addition to the cases noted above (n 52), see the resolutions of the Economic and Social Council: ECOSOC, Resolution Promoting Full Employment and Decent Work for All, Res 2008/18 (24 July 2008); Resolution on Recovering from the Crisis: A Global Jobs Pact, Res 2009/5 (21 July 2009).

[75] As previously mentioned, the OECD's jobs strategy established in 1994 stems from the belief that poor performance in the labour market stems from excessive rigidity of institutions which, far from serving social justice, have resulted in creating an impassable barrier between 'insiders' and 'outsiders'. The 'Euro-sclerosis' of the 1980s is intended to provide an example of this dynamic (and an appropriate foil). Although the evidence of the negative consequences on job attainment of certain institutions such as minimum wages or collective bargaining have turned out to be rather ambivalent, and even if the OECD's policy report *Boosting Jobs and Income* recognises the viability of the European model, its strategy continues to show a clear preference for labour market flexibility that cleaves more or less to the American model. In line with the priority given to the eradication of poverty, this led it to support the implementation of social safety nets targeted to the poor rather than the traditional systems of social protection which, according to this view, tend to weaken the monetary incentive to seek employment (Rittich, 'Global Labour Policy' (n 26) 249–50).

quantitative consideration of reducing unemployment rates by changing incentives for workers. The question thus raised is to what degree such 'incentives' may amount to a deterioration in the quality of jobs (including salary reductions liable to swell the ranks of the working poor).[76] By a kind of historical irony, such attempts to improve the quantitative performance of employment policy in developed countries could be open to a complaint that parallels those previously levelled against the Soviet model; not because the relative quantitative surplus is, as in the Soviet case, being paid for with deficits on the productivity side, but because some reduction in 'decency' is now expected to be the price paid for pursuing 'full employment'.

III. The Financial Crisis: An (as Yet) Unexploited Opportunity to Give Social Objectives their Due

Though it represents a persistent social challenge, there is little in the above evidence to corroborate the convergence implied by employment's common appearance in the founding charters of the relevant international organisations. Notwithstanding the apparent consensus that has coalesced around the concept of decent work,[77] employment has yet to offer an exemplary platform of cooperation and coherence at the international level. Even beyond the diversity of variables and interests the subject inherently puts into play, the evidence gives an inkling that such cooperation turns significantly on an ideological dimension, and that differences revolve primarily around the appropriate role of the state. The good news, however, is that the situation is far from static. It might even offer the ILO a new perspective on its work, provided it can break away from its role as (perhaps somewhat unwilling) social underwriter, and set out a coherent, compelling path that might be followed by others. Three points seem particularly salient in this regard.

First, it cannot be forgotten that the rather constrained role assigned to the state by IFI and OECD orthodoxy in the years before the crisis was a contingent outcome, the result of strategic choices made in the context of the normative upheavals of the late 1970s. This limited view is by no means written in stone. Quite to the contrary: one can neither ignore the legal salience of the references to employment (and even full employment) laid out in the Preambles to their charters, nor relegate those references to merely decorative significance.[78] Even if it would go too far

[76] See, in this regard, the comments of the Committee of Experts in the above General Survey (ILO, *General Survey* (n 59) para 557 ff) and the emphasis it rightly places on the need for 'strong measures to ensure access to quality training opportunities' for the unemployed.

[77] Though the World Bank has not taken up the banner of decent work in its own analysis, it does admit that the 'decent work agenda has gained considerable traction and international policy buy-in over the past decade' (World Bank, *World Development Report 2013* (n 6) 158, Box 5.3).

[78] As suggested in particular by the important role that the WTO's dispute settlement bodies have given to the terms of the Preamble in their interpretations of operative provisions in the covered

to read in employment as a directly-binding objective that dictates organisational policies and programmes, interpreting these references in good faith would seem to leave the organisations concerned a rather wide margin of discretion to engage in genuine institutional dialogue with the ILO.

The most promising prospects in this regard seemed to be taking shape until recently at the IMF, under the influence of Dominique Strauss-Kahn. These developments found their start in the dialogue he was invited to attend at the ILO Governing Body in March 2009.[79] This rapprochement was subsequently borne out by a high profile 'Summit' held in Oslo in September 2010, which allowed for the display of a certain amount of convergence on the need not to give up too quickly on measures supporting employment in post-crisis policies, and even raising the possibility of establishing a 'social protection floor',[80] whose content and outline remained to be specified.[81] The latest twists in the debt crisis in Europe, however, have led some observers to announce that the Washington Consensus has returned with a vengeance, under the concerted direction of the IMF and a European Commission which seems at times to have taken the leading role.[82] Even the World Bank's *World Development Report 2013*, as much as it may cleave to the ILO's perspective when it emphasises the 'transformational' role of jobs, nonetheless strikes a cautiously orthodox note in its underlying policy framework.[83]

This turn of events (assuming things have actually turned) confirm the fragility of any progress that is disconnected from an institutional framework capable of ensuring long-term, consistent policies on employment through all the inevitable vicissitudes of the economy.

Secondly, if the debt crisis seems to have subjected European states to some amount of top-down trusteeship, it also seems to have entailed some relegitimisation of the state's role in safeguarding and promoting jobs. Besides the immediate

agreements (ILO, *Report V: Strengthening the Capacity of the ILO to Assist its Members' Efforts to Promote its Objectives in the Context of Globalization* (International Labour Conference, 96th Session, Geneva, 30 May–15 June 2007) 117).

[79] Over the course of the session there was little hesitation to openly tackle some of the complaints levelled against the fund almost as a matter of routine at ILO meetings (ILO, *Report on the High-level Tripartite Meeting on the Current Global Financial and Economic Crisis* (Governing Body, 304th Session, Geneva, 23 March 2009).

[80] Discussed in Part I.

[81] Alain Faujas, 'Le très libéral FMI vire-t-il social démocrate?', *Le Monde* (Paris), 15 September 2010. Media coverage of the event did not fail to fuel speculation about his residual interest in French electoral politics, prospects that must have at least had some impact on the rather circumspect comments from ITUC Secretary General Sharon Barrow (ITUC, *ILO-IMF Conference on Employment: Concrete Action Must Follow Announcement of Good Intentions* (Press Release, 14 September 2010)).

[82] See Rémi Barroux, 'Le G20 fait de l'emploi des jeunes et de la mise en place d'un socle de protection sociale une priorité', *Le Monde* (Paris), 5 November 2011, citing among others Philippe Egger, Director of Programming and Management for the ILO. For samples which provide an interesting comparison of the Commission's recent approach to that of the IMF's, see a recent piece from the Vice President for economic monetary affairs, Olli Rehn, 'Austerity is working: Europe must stay the course', *Financial Times* (London), 11 December 2012, and the reconsideration of macro-economic contributions to employment levels in the IMF's most recent World Economic Outlook (IMF, *World Economic Outlook 2012: Coping with High Debt and Sluggish Growth* (Washington DC, IMF, 2012) 159–60).

[83] See above (Chapter 4 n 15).

need to act against the consequences of the situation in terms of employment, the success of China's 'market Leninism' has provided some additional food for thought, although the ILO demonstrated undeniable public relations savvy when it seized the opportunity offered by the crisis and provided a temporary impression of consensus restored by adopting the Global Jobs Pact in 2009.[84] It is clear, however, that this kind of success can only be fleeting[85] unless the ILO can demonstrate a long-term ability to provide the concrete support states need to fulfil the role accorded to them, and especially to help them make more informed trade-offs which they will inevitably face.

Thirdly, if the real challenge for Members is choosing (and coordinating on) enlightened policies, the ILO's key task will be to determine *how* to offer its Members assistance more concrete than objectives broad enough to avoid any controversy (such as the intentions listed in the Global Jobs Pact to 'accelerat[e] employment creation, jobs recovery and sustaining enterprises . . . build social protection systems and protect people . . . strengthen respect for international labour standards'). Precisely because they are broad, aspirational and uncontroversial, such 'objectives' can offer little useful guidance on how to achieve them in the specific circumstances, or how to find an optimal equilibrium between maintaining satisfactory quantities of employment and pursuing other goals vital to the vitality of the social fabric.

Though it would likely be unrealistic for the ILO to attempt to provide a ready-made recipe applicable to each specific situation, but it can certainly do better than just providing the ingredients, as it did (with some success) in the Global Employment Agenda.

The answer to this question is probably again that the ILO should make a more inventive use of its institutional comparative advantages. Its institutional potential

[84] It is really more of a resolution than a Pact in any proper sense: the text takes up elements of earlier texts and places them into a general framework of possible economic and social policies, calls for 'decent work responses' (or slightly less vaguely in the French, for 'ripostes fondées sur le travail décent') – and contains no real reciprocal commitments.

[85] Beyond the more or less captive references made to the text by ECOSOC and the G20 boasted about by the Office (*cf* ILO, *A New Era of Social Justice: Report of the Director-General* (International Labour Conference, 100th Session, Geneva, 1–17 June 2011) para 162), its real impact is less than obvious. As for the 15 or so pages of the text itself, its long list of good intentions and oft-recited, perfectly laudable goals make it resemble more of a long letter to Santa Claus than the plan or agreement advertised in its title. Its set of 'decent work responses [to the crisis]', though presented as a general framework of economic and social policies, inevitably leaves open the essential question of how priorities are to be determined and resources allocated.

That being said, the text does contain one paragraph which brings things back to earth and could therefore still have concrete value. Section 25 (which would justify the name Pact) provides that 'Giving effect to the recommendations and policy options of the Global Jobs Pact requires consideration of financing. Developing countries that lack the fiscal space to adopt response and recovery policies require particular support. Donor countries and multilateral agencies are invited to consider providing funding, including existing crisis resources, for the implementation of these recommendations and policy options.' Unfortunately, such a perspective seems not to have materialised so far, and the ongoing developments of the crisis are not likely to improve its prospects. The recent review of the 'impact' of the Global Jobs Pact at the Governing Body, while stressing its 'continued importance' gave no consideration to this aspect of the document. (See ILO, *Staving Off Renewed Crisis: The Role of the ILO* (Governing Body, 313th Session, Geneva, March 2012).

is not limited to a form of coordination comparable to what Deakin calls 'competitive federalism'; it extends to what the same author calls 'reflexive harmonisation'[86] which very closely corresponds to what had been more awkwardly referred to in earlier ILO documents as the pooling and confrontation of concrete experiences on a voluntary basis. Beyond the Danish model of 'flexicurity' which has had its heyday, the comparison of national experiences may help combine doctrinal analysis of possible solutions into a small number of models, as done by Leah Vosko drawing on work by Gerhard Bosch and Alain Supiot.[87] In the absence of a power to propose predetermined formulas combining the various ingredients, the ILO can still make a vital contribution to each Member's search for a mixture adapted to their situation, by synthesing other countries' experiences and drawing out potential lessons. As we will have the opportunity to see, it has already embarked on this path but, especially as empowered by the 2008 Declaration, could expand these efforts much further in association with other organisations.[88]

As we will see more in detail in the next chapter, this approach could perfectly (especially in the light of the innovations introduced by the 2006 ILO Maritime Labour Convention) be accommodated within the framework of an ILO Convention or Recommendation.

This leads to one final point on inter-agency coherence. Without a cataclysm of the kind that gave rise to the ILO in 1919 or to the United Nations system in 1945, it seems pointless to expect major moves toward comprehensive institutional coherence in the near future.[89] Anyone who needs convincing on this point can simply consider the difficulties that confronted United Nations reform efforts over the last 10 years. It seems clear, moreover, that the path to greater coherence cannot be a one-way street: it cannot be dictated by any one organisation. It is a matter of patiently establishing institutional dialogue and mutual persuasion. However, there is nothing to prevent such institutional dialogue from developing within the existing constitutional framework. In this regard, the ILO's tripartite structure, and the universal and tripartite parliament that the International Labour Conference can legitimately claim to be, already provides it with a formidable 'strike force' too seldom deployed in pursuit of greater coherence with the economic, trade and financial organisations.

[86] Simon Deakin, 'Social Rights in a Globalized Economy' in Philip Alston (ed), *Labour Rights as Human Rights* (Oxford, Oxford University Press, 2005) 41.

[87] Leah Vosko, *Managing the Margins: Gender, Citizenship, and the International Regulation of Precarious Employment* (Oxford, Oxford University Press, 2010). This does not prevent her from attempting to identify the weaknesses of these models compared to the one she herself proposes. For a critical reading of this book, see Marieke Louis, 'Intégrer les marges', *La Vie des Idées* (Paris, 9 December 2010), available at www.laviedesidees.fr/Integrer-les-marges.html.

[88] World Bank, *World Development Report 2013* (n 6) at 18–19 proposes a 'typology of jobs challenges' for countries in different historical, geographical and demographic situations and at different levels of development, which seems to at least begin to set out on the appropriate path.

[89] Jacques Attali, *Demain, qui gouvernera le monde ?* (Paris, Fayard, 2011) 20.

6

Boosting the ILO's Capacity to Promote Coherence

In his 2011 report to the ILC, ILO Director-General, Juan Samovia, explored how regulatory inadequacies and policy inconsistencies in the international system had led to a situation of 'inefficient growth', where economic expansion was not matched by social progress, economic stability or environmental sustainability. According to Samovia, this '[i]nefficient growth reflected a deeper flaw in the conventional policy strategy. Economic goals have taken precedence over social and environmental ones. Growth was inefficient because it was conceived in isolation from everything else'.[1] The remainder of his report prescribed what should be done to remedy the situation. Yet, apart from some references to enhanced cooperation with the IMF in the wake of the Joint Conference held at Oslo in September 2010, the question of which institutional paths lead to likely remedies for this 'inefficiency' was not really addressed.

This is precisely the crux of any effort to create lasting change. Without losing sight of the fact that greater coherence cannot be a one-way street, three types of initiative[2] might allow the ILO to contribute, albeit slowly and partially at best, to greater coherence between economic, commercial and social objectives.

First of all, the ILO can act at the level of its own Members to promote greater coherence in their own policies, directly contributing to greater coherence in the system-wide implementation of social, economic and trade objectives. Doing so could only make the ILO more effective at implementing its own objectives.

Secondly, the ILO could act to promote a genuine institutional dialogue with, and among, the competent international organisations, providing a context for such dialogue, the sole forum that brings together all the representatives of the 'real economy'.

[1] ILO, *A New Era of Social Justice: Report of the Director-General* (International Labour Conference, 100th Session, Geneva, 1–17 June 2011) paras 133–34. It may have been better to use 'ineffective' given the association of 'efficiency' with the economic imperative of growth.

[2] Which were already outlined in the draft resolution submitted by Switzerland to the 100th Session of the ILC (*Draft Resolution Concerning the Coherence of the Multilateral System* (ILC, 100th Session, Geneva, 1 June 2011)) partly incorporated into section IV of the G20 *Labour and Employment Ministers' Conclusions* (G20 Meeting, Paris, 26–27 September 2011), as annexed to the Cannes Declaration (G20, *Cannes Summit Final Declaration: Building Our Common Future: Renewed Collective Action for the Benefit of All* (G20 Summit, Cannes, 4 November 2011)), and reiterated in their 2012 Los Cabos Declaration (G20, *The Los Cabos Growth and Jobs Action Plan* (19 June 2012) para 22.

The third tack the ILO might take would be to develop its own capacity for analysis and research, with the goal of contributing to an 'epistemic community' capable of competing with (and hopefully supplanting!) the Washington Consensus orthodoxy whose legitimacy has been weakened by the crisis.

I. Promoting State-level Coherence

A. Encouraging Consistency in their International Activities

We have already pointed to the hypothesis advanced by some analysts that maintaining a siloed, incoherent UN system serves the interests of the major powers by leaving them greater overall control.[3] There are, however, less convoluted explanations: states, or rather their governments, might participate in international organisations in an inconsistent, if not contradictory, manner simply because they lack *internal* coherence. Without totally rejecting the idea that it could be deliberate, this lack of consistency could just as easily be an accidental artefact of functional differentiation at the state level. It is hardly a secret that ministries of labour, in principle the interlocutors with the ILO under the Constitution, generally find themselves in a position of relative inferiority in their respective governments.[4] Given this possibility, it makes sense that officials would attempt to use the ILO as a platform to bolster their relative prominence in national administrations vis-à-vis ministries of finance or foreign affairs. Conversely, governments are more willing to adopt socially progressive positions within the ILO when they know they can count on the financial organisations to put the breaks on their implementation.[5]

Though these phenomena are rooted largely in the nature of national and international bureaucracy, this does not doom efforts to overcome those problems to failure. In many if not most cases, the inconsistent positions taken in different organisations is simply a reflection of insufficient (or the complete absence of!) internal coordination, rather than a result of deliberate strategy or bad faith. It is with this view in mind that the 2008 Declaration explicitly calls on members to ensure that the commitments they have undertaken (in unanimously adopting the Declaration) are not affected by inconsistent positions they may take in other organisations.[6]

[3] See Chapter 4 n 17.

[4] A remarkable exception (they are few and far between) is Switzerland, where social affairs are linked directly to economic planning. It is not hard to surmise that this strategy has some connection with the quite enviable results the country maintains in employment rates.

[5] The way in which individual members of the European Union tend to take the easy way out on unpopular measures adopted jointly within the Union's central organs illustrates exactly the same phenomenon.

[6] To this end, section B(iv) of Part II requests 'adequate coordination between positions taken on behalf of the member State concerned in relevant international forums and any steps they may take under the present Declaration'.

The question is how to prevent this exhortation from becoming a dead letter. Despite the various provisions in the Declaration concerning the follow-up and impact assessment it is supposed to receive,[7] the ILO's Governing Body has yet to be provided with any proposal enabling it to give practical effect to the various possibilities envisaged.[8] In addition to the framework agreements for the promotion of decent work discussed above,[9] one of the possibilities outlined during preparations for the 2008 Declaration, and alluded to in section II A(iii) and section II D(ii) of the Annex,[10] seems particularly relevant: the premise is that a mechanism for peer review of policies implemented by the Members could be grafted onto a voluntary standards instrument. But it is likely useful to discuss in more detail what form such a mechanism might take.

B. Voluntary Framework to Pool the Lessons of National Experience

Breaking down the siloed pursuit of shared objectives using a voluntary institutional framework that can create mutual learning out of the lessons of individual experience is an idea that has seen many manifestations, but one that still lacks concrete implementation at the global level. Proposals in this vein have, however, received more than passing interest; two proposals that have gained traction both seem to point in the direction of doing so through an explicitly-negotiated mechanism.

(i) From a Social Dimension of Trade Policy Review to a Trade Dimension in Social Policy Review?

Workers acting through the International Trade Union Confederation (ITUC, formerly ICFTU) have sought for years to promote greater consistency between social and trade considerations in the positions held internationally by individual states, exploring mechanisms that would allow states to take obligations to one organisation into account when they are acting in another context. The main target of these efforts has been the WTO's Trade Policy Review mechanism, established in Annex 3 of the Marrakesh Agreement. The advantage of this mechanism is (or was) that

[7] Part III(B) and (C) make the Governing Body and the Director-General responsible for establishing the modalities for implementing the various provisions, subject to ILC review and oversight. Part III of the Annex dictating the required follow-up also provides that the impact of the Declaration be regularly evaluated by the Conference on the basis of a report covering the implementation of measures taken by the organisation and its Members.

[8] It being too early to know whether the abortive resolution on coherence submitted by Switzerland to the 100th Session of the ILC will receive more substantial follow-up.

[9] ILO, *Report V: Strengthening the Capacity of the ILO to Assist its Members' Efforts to Promote its Objectives in the Context of Globalization* (International Labour Conference, 96th Session, Geneva, 30 May–15 June 2007) Box 3.2.

[10] Which discusses a kind of 'peer review' mechanism that Members may wish to establish on a voluntary basis to share experiences and best practices.

it provides a framework for the 'regular collective appreciation and evaluation of the full range of individual Members' trade policies and practices'.[11] Such reviews are conducted periodically, with the periods determined by reference to the country's portion of total international trade. The term 'collective' corresponds in this context to a procedure for evaluating states' trade policy to their peers, that is to say, other Members. Given the advantages of its structure, the ITUC has sought to add a social dimension to this review by submitting and systematically distributing information on how a country under review addresses workers' rights and especially human rights, in the hope that the discussion would take account of this information. That hope has thus far met largely with disappointment: making such a link is anathema to many WTO members, and invitations to engage in these issues have so far repeatedly been confronted by flat refusal.

These attempts have, however, given rise to the idea of applying a countervailing logic, but on a purely voluntary basis, within the ILO's tripartite framework. If the prospect of such an approach to promoting greater coherence between states' policies seems permanently stalled on the WTO side, nothing appears to stand in the way of establishing a symmetrical mechanism through a social policy instrument at the ILO. In a way, the components of such a mechanism already exist in the organisation's past practice, including the 'country studies' into the impact of trade liberalisation on efforts to promote ILO objectives, first conducted between 1997 and 1999 and recently reprised in a slightly amended form by the International Institute of Labour Studies (IILS).[12] It was according to this logic that the 2007 report submitted to the ILC to inform the first discussion of what would become the 2008 Declaration raised the possibility of institutionalising a system of peer review to maximise 'synergies' between the different components of decent work by the 'cross fertilisation of experiences'.[13] It was envisaged that peer review could be the final stage of a process combining independent external evaluation with tripartite discussion within the country. The 2008 Declaration adopted this idea in general terms in section II D(ii) of the Annex, listing arrangements 'such as peer reviews which interested Members may wish to establish or join on a voluntary basis' among the measures that the organisation would be required to take. If no proposals have been made to the Governing Body to implement these ideas, the recent favour showered on the theme of institutional coherence, including at the G20 Labour Ministers meetings in France and Mexico, could give such avenues another chance.

[11] As the objectives are described in s A(i).

[12] These studies, conducted with the cooperation of the individual countries concerned, aimed at realising a kind of in-depth audit of how they try to reconcile their social policy objectives with economic development in the context of globalisation (taking into account constraints) so that all Members could draw lessons and learn from best practices after their consideration by the Governing Body. See Raymond Torres, *Towards a Socially Sustainable Global Economy: An Analysis of the Social Pillars of Globalization*, Studies on the Social Dimensions of Globalization (ILO, 2001). On the more recent overview of the 'Studies on Growth with Equity' see International Institute for Labour Studies, *Making Recovery Sustainable: Lessons from Country Innovations* (ILO, 2011).

[13] ILO, *Strengthening the Capacity* (n 9) paras 74–90 and 152–53.

(ii) Within the Framework of a Possible Coherence Instrument?

The idea of engaging in reflection regarding a possible 'coherence instrument' surfaced in response to the 2010 General Survey on employment. While the Survey is fairly routine, conducted annually by the Committee of Experts under the auspices of Article 19 of the Constitution, the 2010 report was nonetheless a first. This is because it was supposed to simultaneously provide the necessary normative background for the 'recurrent discussion' introduced by the follow-up to the 2008 Declaration; with the discussions rotating among the four strategic objectives, 2010 was both the first of these discussion, and the first on employment. According to the Declaration's logic, the Survey was intended to facilitate evaluation of existing ILO employment instruments and, in particular, to determine whether they needed to be supplemented or revised. The logic of such a review was even stronger given that the financial crisis had broken out in the interim, setting off a host of negative social consequences, perhaps most notably the serious rise in unemployment figures. In this context, the discrepancy between the economic reality, in which the employment situation for most members was strongly conditioned by growing economic interdependence, and the 'state-centrism' maintained by the corpus of existing instruments, could not have appeared more flagrant.

However, while the Committee of Experts' conclusions in the General Survey did address the issue of bringing the employment instruments up to date, the two suggestions they made appeared somewhat out of tune with the overall context.[14] The first was, in essence, to carry out a 'consolidation' of the existing collection (an option simultaneously implying continuity with the existing approach and commitment to a major, long-term undertaking); and the second (doubtlessly inspired by the precedent of post-war reconstruction) was to develop a new instrument on the crisis itself.[15]

It is against this background that the Workers' group, supported by France and a number of other governments, launched an idea to get to the root causes of the situation and address the coherence issue through a possible normative instrument.[16] Given coherence is not a unidirectional objective, however, such a project could make sense only to the extent that all the organisations concerned were involved with its development, and even its implementation.[17]

However, the idea met with strong resistance, for two interrelated reasons. On the one hand, for many (including some within the International Labour Office) the sermon had already been delivered with the prior year's adoption of the Global Jobs Pact, and it was important not to interfere with the cheerful sense of consensus communicated by the earlier text. Perhaps more fundamentally, the subject of

[14] ILO, *General Survey Concerning Employment Instruments in Light of the 2008 Declaration on Social Justice for a Fair Globalization* (2010) paras 806–7.

[15] See in this regard ILO Recommendation R071: Employment (Transition from War to Peace) (International Labour Conference, 26th Session, Philadelphia, 20 April–12 May 1944) of doubtful relevance in the context of the financial crisis aftermath.

[16] See ILO, *Provisional Record* (ILC, 99th Session, Geneva, 2–8 June 2010) No 16 Part 1.

[17] There is a precedent in this regard, elaborated in Box 6.1.

coherence, as self-evident and necessary as it may appear, also touches on interests as numerous as they are divergent, and any deep reflection was bound to bring them to the fore. The idea was therefore purged from the conclusions of the debate.

The second failed attempt (mentioned above and discussed in further detail in the next section) was that made by Switzerland at the 100th Session of the ILC, in the form of a draft resolution submitted with the accord of the French Presidency of the G20.[18] This proposal addressed various institutional aspects of reinforcing coherence between social, economic and commercial objectives in the overall rules of the game, both at the state level and among international organisations. Though the resolution was not adopted, commitments made by the tripartite officers of the ILC led to an Office-prepared document on the issue being placed before the Governing Body that November. This text, was however, silent on the institutional dimension of the problem.[19] Though the important role played by *institutional* coherence at both levels received slightly more explicit mention in the 2011 conclusions of the G20 Labour and Employment Ministers,[20] it was subsequently diluted in the catch-all reference to 'coordination' between organisations in the final Cannes declaration, with the references to state-level policy coherence disappearing completely.[21]

If none of these developments put into question the legitimacy or technical feasibility of some sort of a coherence instrument, they do suggest such an endeavour could easily come up against serious obstacles unless the ILO Director-General, aided by circumstances, gave it sustained personal attention. Box 6.1 is intended merely to illustrate that ILO standards may in any event be a tool which fits this enterprise rather nicely. Indeed, the proposal helps provide evidence that the ILO's normative tool is sufficiently flexible to promote coherence between social, economic and trade objectives on the basis of mutually and voluntarily shared experience among interested members.

[18] The issue of coherence was a priority in the objectives of the Presidency. See the end of Part I for a short overview of the proposal.

[19] See ILO, *Policy Coherence in the Multilateral System* (Governing Body, GB.312/HL/1, 312th Session, Geneva, 3–18 November 2011). The paper raises the possibility of initiatives working through one of five 'channels': better cooperation between secretariats; the introduction of devices such as 'reciprocal invitations' which could 'where appropriate' be expanded to include 'institutional mechanisms' (not detailed) for policy convergence; better country-level coordination between the ILO and other UN agencies (but not including the IMF, the World Bank or the OECD); better coordination of Member positions in various international forums; and finally, assistance to those desiring to promote the ILO strategic objectives by acting in concert (particularly bilateral or multilateral agreements). That is, it suggested ways that the ILO could act differently, but provided no specific ideas about how international organisations might approach the social-economic balance differently, or how the ILO could help its Members do so.

[20] See G20, *Labour and Employment Ministers' Conclusions* (n 2) paras 27–28, evoking in particular the possibility that the organisations concerned enter into cooperation agreements with a view to strengthening the consistency.

[21] See para 6 of the Summit's final declaration which calls for 'international organisations to intensify their coordination and make it more effective. In view of a greater coherence of multilateral action, we encourage the WTO, the ILO, the OECD, the World Bank and the IMF to enhance their dialogue and cooperation' (G20 , *Cannes Summit Final Declaration* (n 2)).

Box 6.1 Possibility of promoting policy coherence of social, economic and trade policies by way of an ILO Recommendation[a]

The general objective of such an instrument would be to encourage each member country to design a coherent social policy, to optimise the social benefits that it derives from economic interdependence, and in particular to improve the capacity of its workers (and employers) to anticipate and confront the changes inherent to an open economy. Apart from fundamental rights – the precondition for workers to obtain their fair share of those benefits – pursuing this objective would require a mix of education and training facilities, social protection and employment policies. Though the mix appropriate to each country's situation may best be decided at the national level, those decisions can usefully be informed by experiences, successes, failures and choices of other countries.[b]

The ILO contribution to this goal could thus take the form of a Recommendation which would both encourage all Members to develop such a comprehensive policy (on a tripartite basis, and taking into account appropriate ILO instruments), but more specifically, would guide those efforts by providing a framework to pool or 'mutualise' their experiences by way of a voluntary but reciprocal peer review mechanism.[c]

To be consistent with the concept of coherence, other interested organisations would also have to be given the opportunity to have some association with the framing of the instrument and even with its implementation, a possibility with a precedent in the Social Policy (Aims and Standards) Convention (No 117, 1962).

[a] For a more elaborated sketch of the proposal, see Francis Maupain, *L'OIT à l'épreuve de la mondialisation financière, peut-on réguler sans contraindre?* (Geneva, ILO, 2012) 126–27, Box 6.1.

[b] For many years the ILO sought to address this need through the 'country studies' conducted since 1997 and recently included under the name of 'pilot country studies' by the IILS. See n 12. A 'coherence' instrument would provide a step towards the institutionalisation of the country study approach.

[c] One precusor, *ILO Recommendation R70: Social Policy in Dependent Territories Recommendation* (ILC 26th Session, Philadelphia, 20 April–12 May 1944), now shelved, includes in its Art 3 a sui generis monitoring system that places the text halfway between a Convention and a classic Recommendation. For its part, ILO Convention No 117 on Social Policy (Basic Aims and Standards) (adopted 22 June 1962, entered into force 23 April 1964) incorporates and extends the provisions of Recommendation 70. The recent ILO Maritime Labour Convention (adopted 23 February 2006, entry into force 20 August 2013), has quite masterfully illustrated the ability of the traditional normative activities to cover a very broad subject matter in an integrated, transnational approach. To this end, it has taken up quite innovative formulas (see Lisa Tortell, Rudy Delarue and Jeffrey Kenner, 'The EU and the ILO Maritime Labour Convention: "In Our Common Interest and in the Interest of the World"' in Jan Orbie and Lisa Tortell (eds), *The European Union and the Social Dimension of Globalization: How the EU Influences the World* (Routledge, 2009) 113–30).

II. Pursuing Coherence Through Inter-organisational Dialogue

It is impossible to commit to the ideal of coherence without accepting exposure to the influence of others while optimising one's capacity to influence them.

As alluded to in the discussion above of the ILOs new relationship with the IMF under the direction of Dominique Strauss-Kahn,[22] such dialogue is unlikely to have lasting top-to-bottom effects on how the participating organisations perform their responsibilities unless the interaction is rooted in a somewhat formalised framework. Beyond the more or less ritualised call to 'strengthen coordination', such institutionalised dialogue could find a foundation in formally negotiated agreements, yet there might also be a surprising amount to be gained from simply seeking increased involvement from other international organisations in the ongoing definition of appropriate social policy at the tripartite 'parliament' of the International Labour Conference.

A. On the Basis of Formal Inter-Agency Agreements

Nothing more effectively captures the current state of relations between the ILO, the Bretton Woods institutions and the WTO than the following irony: in the immediate post-war period, the ILO was a pioneer, becoming the first international organisation to create a formal arrangement with the United Nations. The agreement it signed was a treaty of cooperation and reciprocal representation, approved by the representative bodies of both organisations, becoming a model for subsequent agreements between the United Nations and its specialised agencies.[23] The ILO has since developed a network of similar agreements with sister organisations at the universal level and extended this cooperation to numerous regional organisations, in most cases fast on the heels of their establishment. Yet the only organisations with which it still lacks any formal agreement are those which, as a matter of achieving its objectives, are probably the most relevant at the universal level.[24]

This anomaly prompted a (small) number of Western governments to urge the ILO to remedy the situation by requesting observer status at the WTO.[25] At first glance, such a request is simply common sense. It would provide the ILO (until

[22] See Chapter 5 nn 76–79 and text to notes.

[23] Louis B Sohn, 'The Contribution of the International Labour Organization to the Concept of Economic, Social and Cultural Rights' in René-Jean Dupuy and Linos-Alexandre Sicilianos (eds), *Mélanges en l'honneur de Nicolas Valticos: droit et justice* (Pedone, 1999) 604–5.

[24] This is particularly striking given the recent proliferation of heterogeneous 'memoranda of understanding' with a plethora of organisations whose link with ILO objectives is not always obvious.

[25] See, eg the intervention of the President of Switzerland, Micheline Calmy-Rey, ILO, *Provisional Records No 28* (ILC, 100th Session, Geneva, 1–17 June 2011) 3.

now invited only to the Ministerial Conference on the basis of precedents dating back to the Havana Conference) automatic representation at the General Council and its committees. More generally, formal agreements with the WTO and the Bretton Woods institutions could provide an opportunity not only to discuss matters of common interest, but to define terms of cooperation on the goals that find shared expression in their respective charters, including, as we have seen, employment – even 'full employment'. It is even possible to imagine reciprocal agreements that would include a formal undertaking from the parties not to obstruct 'exogenous' obligations their members hold with the other parties.[26]

In the face of this litany of solid justifications, it should be no surprise that the absence of any formal arrangement is no simple accident. Among the obstacles to actually concluding such agreements are a host of complicated legal issues, including structural asymmetries standing in the way of the reciprocal representation in the various organs that would generally give such agreements substance. Such technical difficulties cannot explain everything, however.[27]

Indeed, the negotiation of such an agreement is hampered by political complexities as much at the ILO (where the former Director-General has studiously refrained from taking any initiative), as at the WTO. In the latter case, assent to engage in such a process would take a decision of the General Council, therefore requiring an absolute consensus.[28] However, for many countries, the conclusion of a *separate* agreement allowing the ILO to be represented at the General Council and other organs would likely be interpreted as a step, albeit symbolic, towards the eventual legitimisation of a 'social dimension' in the WTO. As a result, such a decision will in all likelihood continue to face reluctance if not straight-out refusal from many WTO members (even if they are also members of the ILO). Pascal Lamy himself has noted how the issue is a bit of a minefield, recalling that it is hardly realistic to imagine the realisation of such a direct link with social norms at the WTO, particularly due to the continuing reticence of developing countries. However, he diplomatically put the ball back into the ILO's court, noting that this should not preclude the matter from being considered on the ILO side. For what it's worth, he specified that:

[26] This idea was actually tendered by the ILO at the September 1998 high level discussions held with the financial institutions in Washington, where it tried to develop the idea that all United Nations-associated organisations should at the very least have a negative duty not to oppose or weaken international commitments made by members in other fora. It is notable that while World Bank practice does not appear completely resistant to such an approach, that flexibility seems limited to environmental concerns. It might even be proposed that, at least for organisations attached to the United Nations system, such an obligation already exists, with or without a formal agreement: given their common goals, they could be understood to have an embryonic obligation of '(con)federal loyalty' (analogous to the German *Bundestreue*) which should lead them to refrain from deliberately inducing members to violate commitments made to sister organisations.

[27] After all, such structural asymmetry did not prevent a highly significant agreement with what was then the EEC. See Francis Maupain, 'Particularismes institutionnels et vocation universelle: les défis croisés des relations CEE-OIT' (1990) 1190(1) *Revue générale de droit international public* 50.

[28] See Arts V.1 and IX.1 of the Marrakesh Agreement Establishing the World Trade Organization (signed 14 April 1994).

> The ILO can thus seek to draw closer to the WTO and its members can commit not to compete by putting social standards in question. This approach, embodied in the 2008 Declaration,[29] is interesting because it creates a state of affairs whereby the ILO enters into the domain of trade.[30]

The difficulty of such an agreement in practice is why the 2008 Declaration was careful not to directly address this possibility. It placed much more emphasis on generalised reinforcement of existing partnerships with United Nations organisations,[31] emphasising the contribution that such cooperation could make to promoting decent work.[32] On this basis, according to the resolution accompanying the Declaration addressed to the Governing Body and the Director-General, the International Labour Office was supposed to make a (yet to be conducted) inventory of its various partnerships and eventually advance proposals to buttress those relationships, even seeking observer status where appropriate. This approach was designed to make it possible to address the issue of agreements in a broad perspective, rather than immediately shining the spotlight on the WTO and the Bretton Woods institutions, and having to immediately confront the potential roadblocks such efforts would throw up. This is also the reason why it would be particularly worthwhile to explore other avenues, and in particular, to consider bringing these organisations to the ILO table notwithstanding the absence of any agreement on reciprocal representation.

[29] This reference to the 2008 Declaration is particularly significant. Indeed, in Part IIC, it refers to the issue specifically, emphasising the contribution these organisations can make to the implementation of the so-called 'integrated approach', and tasking the ILO with inviting them to promote decent work to the extent consistent with their mandates. And Part IIIC of the Annex takes matters one step further – a significant step – by providing that interested multilateral organisations will be given the opportunity to participate both in the evaluation of the Declaration's impact and in the institutional discussion of that impact at the ILC.

[30] Author's translation. Original: 'L'OIT peut ainsi chercher à se rapprocher de l'OMC et ses membres peuvent s'engager à ne pas se faire concurrence sur la base d'une remise en cause des standards sociaux. Cette démarche, réalisée avec la Déclaration de l'OIT de 2008, est intéressante car elle crée un état de fait à travers lequel l'OIT entre dans le domaine commercial.' Pascal Lamy, 'Statement: "Quels leviers de régulation mondiale pour le social"' (Roundtable of L'Observatoire Social International, Paris, 12 April 2010). Lamy did not hesitate in characterising the seat granted to the ILO at the G20 as progress, and enthusiastically suggested that 'if the emerging markets that are G20 members, can accept that the ILO represents a source of authority on coherence, there is an opportunity for trade, the environment, financial regulation, social standards, etc. to be debated and brought into congruence' ibid (author's translation). Original: 'si les pays émergents, membres du G20, acceptent qu'il [l'OIT] constitue une instance de cohérence, il existe une opportunité pour que commerce, environnement, régulation financière, standards sociaux, etc. soient débattus et mis en cohérence'. Unfortunately, by 2012 even the reference to coherence between international organisations that had appeared in the 2011 G20 Declaration had been limited to the much narrower, albeit still worthwhile, project of establishing national social protection floors. See G20, *G20 Leaders Declaration* (G20 Meeting, Los Cabos, 18–19 June 2012) para 22.

[31] Section IIA(v) and s IIA(v) of the Annex.

[32] Section IIC(i) of the Annex.

B. By Proactively Including Them in ILC Discussions and Optimising the 'Strike Force' of Tripartism

The failure of the Declaration of Philadelphia to establish the ILO as the 'master agency' lording over the social review of international policies shows the futility of pretending that the ILO can dictate coherence of its own accord. Such coherence can instead be built up only through dialogue among the relevant international organisations, states and social partners. This dialogue must be established around shared knowledge, and joint, rather than unilateral, assessments of how diverse fiscal, economic and trade policies impact on the achievement of social objectives. Beyond the different lenses through which it can be understood, employment in particular provides a purpose common to their respective mandates, and therefore constitutes an unavoidable test of their collective success or failure.

As already observed above, the ILO has a comparative advantage in providing the framework for such dialogue. First, of course, because the interests and dialogue between opposing views is innate to its constitutional make-up. Yet it is also especially suited to such a task as the sole forum bringing together those who create jobs, those who hold them and those who regulate them[33] – or, to use concepts that have recently seen increasing use in official ILO communications, it is the only forum that brings together all the players in the so-called real economy, as opposed to players in the 'virtual' or 'financial' economy.

As such, there would be some sense in enlisting this unique tripartite structure to the cause of seeking coherence, turning it into a framework to discuss issues of common interest to the multilateral organisations with competence in economic, commercial and financial matters and especially, of course, in matters of employment.

This possibility, which might be thought of as a kind of 'organ loan',[34] would not be without precedent in the ILO's long history of procedural innovations.[35] Such an opening would be facilitated by the ILO's well-established, ecumenical constitutional practice, developed at times by very generous readings of the text, clearly differentiating it from many other organisations (and from the WTO in particular). Of most help here would be the now-routine practice of inviting outside organisations to participate in the deliberations at the Governing Body and the ILC, notwithstanding the absence of any formal agreement providing for reciprocal representation. By bringing representatives of these organisations to the

[33] Subject to the question of how effective such representation is, a matter which receives some of the further attention it deserves in the book's conclusion.

[34] As suggested by the description of previous examples in René-Jean Dupuy (ed), *Manuel sur les organisations internationales* (Dordrecht, Martinus Nijhoff, 1998) 531.

[35] See the completely original experience of the ILO Tripartite Conference for the development of the European Social Charter organised by the ILO on behalf of the Council of Europe (Nicolas Valticos, 'La Charte sociale européenne: sa structure, son contenu, le contrôle de son application' (September–October 1963) 26 *Droit social* 466.

table, the ILO and its tripartite constituents could directly influence the representatives of the organisations involved.[36]

It seems safe to assume that the organisations concerned would have a hard time staying away from a dialogue which required them neither to renege on their own principles nor (especially unlikely in current circumstances) to sign an agreement for reciprocal representation. In fact, they would probably be well advised to participate, given the extent that they face (the WTO in particular) general scepticism, and a growing crisis of popular legitimacy.

The idea of making better use of the 'strike force' of tripartism vis-à-vis other international organisations could take more unusual forms, two of which were already tested during the World Employment Programme years. The first was the World Employment Conference, held simultaneously but separately from the International Labour Conference in 1976,[37] thereby maximising impact while minimising costs.

The second took place a decade later, in 1987, at Francis Blanchard's initiative. He hoped to find a targeted way to rally formal support from the economic organisations for the ILO's employment efforts.[38] This idea was taken one step further, by gathering all the stakeholders at a high-level tripartite meeting whose ambition

[36] And not only their respective secretariats, just as was done with respect to the ILO representation in the G20 or the coordination between the UN executive heads. The attendance of these international organisations is usually organised at the secretariat level, or in the best case, at the level of executive heads, which have occasionally been invited to participate in tripartite discussions at special sessions held for this purpose at the Governing Body or the Conference. It is true that this approach does not establish a direct dialogue with the decision-making bodies of the relevant organisations. Yet provided it is organised more systematically (eg in the context of standard-setting) this option could nevertheless provide both a relay and a sounding board of effective tripartite discussion with other organisations. In particular, it could help to address inconsistencies and/or contradictions, if not outright duplicity, of Members and their administrations (who sometimes seem to be using international organizations as proxy battle grounds for their own internal turf wars).

[37] The purpose of this Conference was to revise and extend the objectives of the Global Employment Programme, in a difficult political and economic context marked by the deteriorating global economic situation, the tension between Western countries and the Group of 77 reflected in the project for a 'New International Economic Order' and, of specific concern at the ILO, the threat of withdrawal by the United States. Some saw the Conference 'as a great triumph. Heads of State, religious leaders such as the Pope and many prominent social thinkers lined up to attend the three-week event'. In this sense at least, '[i]t did undoubtedly mark a certain kind of triumph' (Guy Standing, 'The ILO: An Agency for Globalization?' (2008) 39 *Development and Change* 355, 362). It should not be too surprising that the result of this ambitious initiative reflected in the eventually adopted 'programme of action' was rather mixed. For those most closely associated with the project, the thinness of its impact was attributable mainly to the ILO's failure to follow up at the country level in accordance with the mandate it had been given. When a new development paradigm came to the fore at the dawn of the 1980s, employment and basic needs faded into the background in favour of other priorities. See ILO, *Declaration of Principles and Programme of Action Adopted by the Tripartite World Conference on Employment, Income Distribution and Social Progress, and the International Division of Labour* (ILO, 1976).

[38] 'Plus que certains de [ses] plus brillants collaborateurs.' Francis Blanchard was convinced that all ILO efforts to put employment at the heart of the debate through the World Employment Program would not prevent the programme from being left at the margins by the structural adjustment policies being imposed across the developing world by the Bretton Woods institutions, and to a lesser extent, the OECD. (Francis Blanchard, *L'organisation internationale du travail: De la guerre froide à un nouvel ordre mondial* (Paris, Seuil, 2004) 22526).

was reflected in the title's inclusion of a subject which become almost taboo at the ILO: structural adjustment.[39]

Like its predecessor, this ambitious initiative saw little substantial success in establishing a common vision. Two reasons may explain this failure. First of all, the meeting was quickly followed by the radical change in political and economic context represented by the collapse of the Berlin Wall and the rising tide of trade liberalisation as the new keystone of development. Secondly, the conference owed its existence to the energy Francis Blanchard expended on it, rather than on any pre-existing institutional framework that could have made it sustainable.

The key difference today is that such an institutional framework does exist: it is provided for in the 2008 Declaration which, as we have seen, pushes toward stronger collaboration at the universal level, and explicitly recognises an important role for organisations with related mandates in the implementation of an integrated approach.[40] This is why the Conference explicitly provided for the communication of the 2008 Declaration to the organisations in question,[41] and indicated that they would be asked in due course to participate in the assessment of its impact.[42] This general framework, combined with constitutional practice permitting international organisations to attend the ILO's key meetings without an expectation of reciprocity, should facilitate a much more active and systematic participation by international organisations in the work of the International Labour Conference. This might be particularly fruitful in carrying out one of its assigned functions, of discussing recurrent reports to assess the needs of its members, and evaluate programmes related to each strategic objective, including employment.

One could equally imagine, as envisaged by the draft resolution Switzerland submitted to 2011 ILC[43], and as already contemplated in the Declaration of Philadelphia, that the International Labour Conference might be called upon from time to time to assess the impact of economic, financial and trade policies on the strategic objectives, based on reports jointly prepared by the secretariats of the relevant organisations, and with their active participation in discussions.[44]

Finally, if the ILO were one day to pursue the idea of adopting an instrument on the coherence of economic, trade and social policies aimed at Members,

[39] See ILO, *Record of the Meeting on Employment and Structural Adjustment* (World Employment Programme Meeting, Geneva, 23–25 November 1986) WEP 2-46-04-03. In the end, the meeting came close to being derailed by the workers' attempt to insert a paragraph linking trade liberalisation and compliance with international labour standards, which they agreed to withdraw subject only to a promise that the ILO would address this issue at a later date (see Eddy Lee, 'Employment and Poverty Reduction' in Gerry Rodgers and others, *The ILO and the Quest for Social Justice* (Geneva, ILO, 2009) 200 ff).

[40] ILO, Declaration on Social Justice for a Fair Globalization (adopted 10 June 2008) IA(i) (2008 Declaration) s IIC.

[41] ibid s IIIA (Final Provisions).

[42] ibid Annex, s IIIC.

[43] ILO, *Draft Resolution on the Coherence of the Multilateral System* (n 2) 3.

[44] To date, the G20 Labour and Employment Ministers meeting in Paris on 26 and 27 September 2011 have only called for 'multilateral organisations with an employment and social mandate [to] be consulted when appropriate to assess the social impact of economic and financial policies advocated by other international organisations' (G20, *Labour and Employment Ministers' Conclusions* (n 2) para 28).

the other organisations should be fully involved in the development of such a text.

The field for partnership-building is wide open. All that is required to start the ball rolling is the will of the constituents and an official invitation from the ILO Director-General to each of his fellow chief executives.

III. Actively Supporting the Emergence of a Relevant 'Epistemic Community'

As Charnovitz justly noted in his analysis of the subordinate place given to employment,[45] it appears that a genuine 'epistemic community'[46] has developed among the Bretton Woods institutions, the WTO and the OECD.[47] That community has generally not included the ILO. Proof of the proposition can be gleaned from the fact that, to be heard in discussions at the G20, the ILO had to cast its analysis according to the models used by the international financial institutions (IFIs).[48] One might also wonder, for example, why nobody seems to have thought to ask the ILO at the end of the 1990s about the possible impact France's implementation of a 35-hour working week might have on employment.

Might it be otherwise? Faced with the crisis, its ongoing twists and turns, and the concerns expressed about the current revival of protectionism, might not the ILO play a role in defining a new paradigm, which neither replicates Keynesian models nor hitches its wagon to IMF orthodoxy?[49] Expressing such an ambition may appear rather unseemly for the secretariat of an international organisation.[50] The goal may be all the more unattainable given that the universal search for

[45] Steve Charnovitz, 'The Neglected Employment Dimension of the World Trade Organization' in Virginia A Leary and Daniel Warner (eds), *Social Issues, Globalisation and International Institutions: Labour Rights and the EU, ILO, OECD and WTO* (Leiden, Martinus Nijhoff, 2006).

[46] In the words of Peter Haas, 'Epistemic Communities and International Policy Organization' (1992) 46(1) *International Organization* 1.

[47] Beyond the frame of the 'epistemic community', other analysts have relied on the Weberian concept of 'social closure' to explain the subordination of social policy to economic concerns, with reference to the combination of the neo-functionalist structure and institutional technocracy of international governance (see, eg Robert O'Brien, 'Organizational Politics, Multilateral Economic Organizations and Social Policy' (2002) 2(2) *Global Social Policy* 141, especially 146–47).

[48] It was an observation of this kind that led former Director-General Hansenne to envisage the assignment of oversight over employment instruments to an ad hoc group of experts composed, in contrast with the existing Committee, not of legal experts, but of internationally-respected economists and social scientists, that could in the end bolster the ILO's credibility and influence. It was perhaps forgotten that supervision cannot escape from the texts as they already exist, nor ignore the prestige of the Committee of Experts and the weight of tradition.

[49] It is neither by maintaining a claim to be the 'master agency' that deploys its heightened credibility to promote coherence between economic and social objectives, nor by quietly taking a seat at the far end of the G20 table, that this will be achieved.

[50] After all, according to Alston, 'International Organizations are, for several reasons, notoriously unsatisfactory incubators for intellectual ideas' (Philip Alston, 'Making Space for New Human Rights: The Case of the Right to Development' (1988) 1 *Harvard Human Rights Yearbook* 3, 10).

compromise apparently imposed by the organisation's tripartite structure might also inevitably imply compromising the integrity of research, as well.[51]

This inherent infirmity is accentuated at the current juncture by the concurrent complexity and speed of the transformations that have developed since the triumph of financial capitalism. These practices form a nested problem so complex that it has paralysed not only governments but also (as some commentators have pointed out) the European Commission. There is no inherent reason to believe that the ILO is in a better position, especially given the limited resources at its disposal. And this can only strengthen the temptation to find refuge in further, more or less catch-all public relations or exhortatory exercises.[52]

Yet even without giving too much weight to analyses reflecting the International Labour Office's sometimes self-indulgent vision of itself,[53] the ILO's secretariat is – or at least has been – a special case among intergovernmental organisations,[54] particularly in comparison with an organisation such as the WTO.[55] Under the guidance of its Director-General, the Constitution accords the Office a substantial degree of autonomy. And across the years constitutional practice has lead to the broadening and consolidation of this autonomy, to the point of establishing it as the organisation's hallmark.

This distinction was evident early on in matters of research broadly conceived. Faced with disappointing results on the normative front (and the failure of his door-to-door campaign to extract ratifications from Members), Director-General Albert Thomas pinned hopes on the role that the consolidation of data and quality research could play in the ILO's work.

If Thomas imagined that the Office could play a role in bolstering the relatively limited analytical capacity possessed by workers and their organisations (especially in contrast to the substantial resources available to major industry), the Office and its successive Directors-General have nonetheless demonstrated consistent resolve in claiming a responsibility to define a common interest or vision that rises above the lowest common denominator to be found in the expressed interests of the three groups. They have in some cases been notably successful, with the 'basic needs' era and the responses it met in both the academic world and among the

[51] According to a reference book on the subject, it is almost in their nature for the reports of international organisations 'to be replete with half truths' (José Alvarez, *International Organizations as Law Makers* (Oxford, Oxford University Press, 2005) 643).

[52] In this vein, it is striking to see the proliferation, in the face of massive political and economic turbulence, including the financial crisis and the Arab Spring, of ILO titles like *The Financial and Economic Crisis: A Decent Work Response*; *ILO Decent Work Response to the Situation in North Africa and the Horn of Africa* and *Challenges in the Arab World: An ILO Decent Work Response – Creating Opportunities in the Middle East and North Africa.*

[53] According to Georges Scelle, the Office was invested with a power of persuasion backed up by 'le souci du bien public, la possession de la vérité technique (sic!), la discipline de l'objectivité' ['the concern for public good, the technical truth possesion (sic!), the discipline of objectivity', trans] (Georges Scelle, *L'Organisation internationale du travail et le BIT* (Paris, Editions M Rivière, 1930) 37).

[54] Francis Maupain, 'L'OIT, la justice sociale et la mondialisation' (1999) 278 *Recueil des Cours de l'Académie de Droit International* 331, 363–67.

[55] Indeed, the WTO's Director-General never misses an opportunity to remind his critics that he heads 'a constituent-led organisation'.

financial institutions providing a clear case of the ILO's capacity for conceptual leadership.[56] In a different way, the decent work strategy showcased the organisation's capacity to creatively develop an appealing consensus on the social dimensions of globalisation.

Even with its particular advantages, the challenge is immense. The vast transformations wrought by transnational financial capitalism, the erosion of the wage labour model tied to industrial capitalism, the reconsideration of the 'affordability' of the European social model – all seem to demand the elaboration of a vision that neither falls in line with the Washington consensus, nor returns to a Keynesian substitute tied to an international system which no longer exists.

Is it realistic to imagine that the ILO might meet this need? The answer depends on two conditions – a critical mass of resources and a high degree of autonomy – which both seem indispensable to credibly confront such a challenge, yet whose prospects leave little room for optimism.

Critical mass required. The ILO can hardly hope to act as a counterweight to dominant models without teams of researchers who can measure up in these areas. This obviously depends on available resources. Yet, at least in terms of the regular budget, research resources seem doomed to relative stagnation. To the degree the ILO faces a zero-sum game on the income side, increasing resources for research can come only at the cost of starving other specific demands, often more concrete and popular among constituents;[57] or by shrinking the so-called 'support services' which absorb a significant share of resources. Since the 1990s, the 'active partnership' policy[58] launched by Michel Hansenne and continued by his successor Juan Somavia (including through decent work country programmes) has created a spiral of direct and indirect costs; as a result of path dependencies, it is likely that the expectations and demands generated by these policies now represent the main obstacle to reinforcing an analytic capacity capable of constituting the required critical mass.[59] These conflicting demands on the institution's resources mean that putting ILO research on a more equal footing with the financial institutions might require a turn toward philosophy, i.e. to those who have pondered unstoppable forces meeting immovable objects. Less pessimistically, three pathways might provide a way out of the dilemma, or at least ameliorate its effects.

[56] On the basic needs approach, see Ashwani Saith, 'Reflections: Louis Emmerij' (2005) 36(6) *Development and Change* 1163.

[57] It should not be forgotten that the ILO faced a crisis during the 1970s brought about by the United States' suspension of its contributions and subsequent withdrawal. For example, in the early 1970s, the Office's attempts to address what was already a gap in its research capacities came into competition with the desire of employers to receive relative parity of resources with workers, to fund programmes supporting the development of employers' organisations in developing countries. In this regard, see the discussions between the Director-General and the employer's representative, Mr Neilan (ILO, *Report II: Draft Program and Budget 1970–1971 and Other Financial Questions* (ILC, 53rd Session, Geneva, 4–25 June 1969); ILO, *Draft Program and Budget 1972–1973* (ILC, 56th Session, 2–23 June 1971).

[58] See ILO, *Provisional Record* (Governing Body, 252nd Session, March 1992); Michel Hansenne, *Un garde-fou pour la mondialisation: Le BIT dans l'après-guerre froide* (Paris, Zoe, 1999) 93.

[59] Lee, 'Employment and Poverty Reduction' (n 39) 200 ff.

The first possibility is to use a process that enjoys considerable favour among international organisations. Specifically, the organisation could rely on consultants or outside authorities whenever it needs to address issues where it feels less than totally assured of its own expertise. The experience of the World Commission on the Social Dimension of Globalization provides a useful case study. The creation of the Commission, as we have already noted, represented an uncharacteristically ambitious enterprise for the ILO, and a commendable attempt to fill in the conceptual shortfalls and policy vacuum left behind by the fiasco at the 1999 WTO Ministerial in Seattle. In this regard, when it comes to nothing less than presenting as coherent a vision as possible of the 'social dimension of globalisation', the reliance placed on the authority of internationally renowned experts and public figures had its advantages, but also inherent limitations.

The establishment of the Commission was itself an impressive accomplishment, not only because it gathered together a notably diverse and distinguished group of experts and personalities,[60] but also because the project had to attract considerable funding before it could be launched.[61] It is also indisputable that, at least for a while, the Commission contributed significantly to the ILO's visibility within the overall international system, and that this amplified visibility probably made more than a negligible contribution to securing it a place at the G20 starting in 2010.

Yet, as will be elaborated under the rubric of 'autonomy' below, solutions of this sort are unable to fill gaps in analytical capacity on anything approaching a permanent basis. In a certain way, they actually put the cart before the horse: such a distinguished body can optimally contribute to the construction of a new paradigm only to the extent that the way has been carefully paved by preliminary research prepared by an Office that itself already enjoys the required scientific authority to exercise the necessary leadership.

The second avenue would be to turn to extra-budgetary resources. It was extra-budgetary resources, particularly the active support of UNDP, in the first period of the World Employment Program and basic needs strategy, which helped launch a programme with some other major and coherent research projects on employment.[62] More recently, following the global financial crisis of 2008, the ILO opened an experimental Regular Budget Supplementary Account (RBSA) supplied by voluntary contributions, to meet the needs of the Members and 'overcome the lack of resources due to the lack of real growth – a necessary growth – in the regular budget'.[63] This additional budget item allows the organisation to 'expand and deepen decent work priorities and outcomes',[64] particularly in the context of

[60] The Commission's members included a Nobel Prize-winning economist (Joseph Stiglitz) and two heads of state (Benjamin Mkapa and Tarja Halonen, Presidents of Tanzania and Finland, respectively).

[61] All the more impressive given it is so difficult, lest we forget, to obtain an increase in budgetary resources needed for longer-term strengthening of analytical capacity of the Office!

[62] Louis Emmerij, Richard Jolly and Thomas George Weiss, *Ahead of the Curve? UN Ideas and Global Challenges* (Blomington, IN, Indiana University Press, 2001).

[63] ILO, *Background Information: The Regular Budget Supplementary Account*, available at www.ilo.int/public/english/bureau/pardev/download/rbsa/rbsa_background.pdf.

[64] ibid.

country programmes to promote these (Decent Work Country Programmes, DWCPs): US$53 million was pledged and made available by six donor countries (all European) in 2010, up from the initial amounts allocated in 2008–2009. So the Office has been successful in attracting extra-budgetary resources, but apparently less successful in making use of the funds on time,[65] which in turns begs the question of the possible link between this state of affairs and the Office's analytical and operational capacity. In an interesting development, it seems that the 2014–2015 budget proposals may give priority to research in the allocation of RBSA resources.

The third and final track, which is probably the most realistic and is, moreover, a matter of simple common sense, would be to reorganise or at least rationalise the use of research resources and capabilities currently widely dispersed across the Office. It appears, on the one hand, that total resources devoted to research at the ILO are far from negligible (possibly exceeding that of the OECD), but are distributed across a multitude of programmes. On the other hand, the International Institute of Labour Studies, despite a relatively limited resources and a small staff, has demonstrated that a strategy focused on addressing a few key questions can contribute to real break-throughs, manifested, inter alia, in the ranking of the *International Labour Review* among the premier journals in its field.

Sufficient autonomy. A second essential precondition for the development of an ILO 'epistemic community' capable of influencing common thinking on social and economic policy is that its research enjoy sufficient protection from both political and technical interference.

First of all, it goes without saying that it must be free from the pressures and influences of external policies. During the Cold War years, when it was extremely difficult to deviate from a form of 'official thought', the need for autonomy led to irreconcilable differences between the new Director-General, Wilfred Jenks, and the Director of the IILS, Robert Cox.[66] In a context of intensified ideological confrontation, where the mere appointment of a Soviet to the position of Assistant Director-General was enough to cause the United States to withdraw its contribution (eventually snowballing into the total withdrawal of the United States from the organisation), Jenks felt that allocating unlimited freedom of inquiry and expression to one unit was simply not worth the existential risk it created for the institution as a whole.[67]

[65] See ILO, *ILO Regular Budget Supplementary Account, November 2012 RBSA Update* (2012) 5.

[66] Robert Cox later became a well-respected professor of international relations theory. The International Institute of Labour Studies had been founded by the previous Director-General, David Morse, with the stated goal of meeting education and training goals. It owed its (very relative) autonomy to this mandate, making it one of few spaces where independent thinking was possible in the context of the Cold War. It was in the name of protecting the embryonic academic freedom enjoyed by the institute that Cox came into confrontation with Jenks, himself a broad-minded intellectual and an international lawyer of high calibre, which lead to Cox's eventual resignation.

[67] To fully understand the height that tensions reached during the period, consider that in a 1962 discussion between Director-General David Morse and George Meany, then President of the AFL-CIO, not only did Meany accuse Morse of showing a shameful leniency vis-à-vis the Soviet Bloc, but the Director-General responded by accusing Meany of anti-Semitism! (Edward C Lorenz, *Defining Global*

If the Cold War's tensions have dissolved, the risk of interference still exists in another, albeit milder, form. The hazard lies in the nature of the relationship between the conduct of research, and the institutional commitment to tripartite compromise.

Without a doubt, it is perfectly acceptable, and even beneficial, for the choice of research topics and the results to be subject to tripartite debate: *ex ante*, it prevents resources from being spent on topics of purely academic interest; *ex post*, it helps to ensure that the results are valid by demonstrating that they hold up under conditions of relative adversity (or not, as the case may be). The risk is however that, in anticipation of a negative reaction from one group or another, certain topics might be given up completely, or that controversial conclusions might be emasculated. Instead of providing ideas in accordance with the responsibilities it has been accorded not only by tradition but according to constitutional practice, the Office is thus gradually brought by its anticipation of possible negative reactions to engage in endless 'informal tripartite consultations' ostensibly aimed at filling the vacuum of ideas and addressing the need for reform, but with the least possible risk. Though this risk manifests itself perhaps most seriously with respect to reform proposals and initiatives with a potential effect on existing institutional practices, the same dynamic could just as easily impact on research.[68]

It is easy to imagine that such 'upstream' excess of tripartite zeal allays the possibility of any truly contentious tripartite debate happening 'downstream', as the smoothing out of any truly rough patches in the planned debate reduces the incentive for high level leadership to take part in the debates once it becomes public. Thus, as much as it may avoid conflict, such preliminary review ultimately undermines one of tripartism's essential comparative advantages.[69]

A second sense of autonomy has already been touched on in the discussion of the resource question above. The ILO must have an analysis and research capacity sufficient to avoid reliance on outside consultants and authorities whenever a new topic comes up. There is a balance to be reached in this regard. On the one hand, the acquisition of the necessary analytical capacity on a given subject is a cumulative process largely incompatible with outsourcing; on the other, there is a real risk that as time goes by, the analytical capacity thus painstakingly built up will become less relevant to meet new problems and shifting priorities.

Justice: The History of US International Labor Standards Policy (Notre Dame, University of Notre Dame Press 2001) 192).

[68] Thus, the prospect of a hostile reaction from one group or the other may, more often than not, cut short any effort or inclination to innovate at the institutional or conceptual level.

[69] It is probably no coincidence in this respect that almost no original ideas regarding economic regulation have come out of the ILO since the era of 'basic needs' (Kerry Rittich, 'Rights, Risk, and Reward: Governance Norms in the International Order and the Problem of Precarious Work' in Judy Fudge and Rosemary J Owens (eds), *Precarious Work, Women, and the New Economy: The Challenge to Legal Norms* (Oxford, Hart Publishing, 2006)). Is it any accident that nobody came to ask the ILO what it thought a 35-hour working week might contribute to job creation? More recently, it preferred to decline the invitation it was extended to participate alongside the IMF in discussions with the government and the Greek unions on measures to restore the balance of accounts.

As much as the broad audience of the World Commission (not only the ILO but the whole UN system) makes it a sui generis case, the experience nonetheless provides interesting insights into these concerns.

Beyond the immediate attention it attracted, the outcome confirmed that without some kind of harmonising themes, the competing voices in such a diverse chorus make it hard to do more than juxtapose each participant's favourite refrain.[70] The desire nonetheless to have everyone singing the same tune condemns the exercise (and this was Kerry Rittich's criticism) to 'fiddl[ing] at the margin' instead of attacking the heart of the problem in a way that affects the dominant paradigm.[71] Without real trade-offs, the result simply adds to a corpus of sanctimonious literature that, as put by Martin Wolf, is 'long on pious aspirations and short on rigorous analysis'.[72] Unless a minimally shared sense of the nature of the problem informs their thinking from the start, it seems unrealistic to expect a coherent vision to emerge spontaneously from the collaboration of eminent but diverse minds; of course, this returns us to the question of the Office's ability and willingness to propose just such an outline.[73]

To conclude, it is worth recalling that the 2008 Declaration, in this field as in others, endeavoured to address the problem by identifying a method and procedure to advance its objectives. The solution proposed was a systematic evaluation of the impact of previous research, and of ongoing needs in this area. It was intended that the 'recurrent reports' on each strategic objective would provide just such an evaluation.

In light of the foregoing, one conclusion seems called for: through its procedures, its tradition, and the potential 'strike force' residing in the unique tripartite parliament on the real economy provided by the ILC, the ILO has a considerable and largely untapped capacity for promoting greater coherence through persuasion.

The active exploitation of this potential is obviously a matter of resources, but it is also a question of political will, and there is no doubt that the former is unlikely to be forthcoming unless the latter is present. One key political dimension of this dynamic, it must be said, remains in the hands of the employers. Albert Thomas used to compare the ILO to a car in which workers are the motor, the government

[70] On the other hand, reducing the diversity represented in this kind of an assembly risks a substantial reduction in the credibility and legitimacy of the results.

[71] For Rittich, the message to be taken away from the report is that globalisation is good for workers, but that it should be made even better through 'better governance' (Rittich, 'Rights, Risk and Reward' (n 69)).

[72] Martin Wolf, 'Growth requires painful choices, not platitudes', *Financial Times* (London), 2 March 2004).

[73] Certain segments of the report contain what might be thought of as the main themes of such an outline. This is particularly true of the analyses and recommendations dealing directly or indirectly with the institutional capacities of states (World Commission on the Social Dimension of Globalization, *A Fair Globalization: Creating Opportunities for All* (Geneva, ILO, 2004) paras 249–51, 255–59, 269–77). Choosing such an orienting theme could (logically) have led to an earlier identification of the public debt issue, a matter that is conspicuously absent from the report, but which has less than 10 years on arisen as a crucial issue for European states and the sustainability of their social model.

the steering wheel, and the employers the brakes. This image is as eloquent as it is questionable: the ILO cannot be a full participant in the UN system if employer participation is focused on slowing the pace of innovation or if their positive motivations are limited to the individual benefit they might draw, or the support such participation may provide to national employers' organisations.[74]

Here also the 2008 Declaration sought to engage employers within the ILO on the collection of information, the validation of facts and analyses, and the sharing of experiences through tripartite debate. The active support employers lent to the text seemed promising. This support, however, seems to have substantially waned following the financial crisis and the lack of any systematic monitoring of the Declaration.

And yet the financial crisis and its aftermath should quite to the contrary provide fertile ground for a renewed convergence of workers' and employers' interests on an optimised role for the ILO. The threat posed to the relatively impoverished 'real economy' by the excesses of a financialised economy, and the need to correct the 'inefficiency' of current growth patterns (in the terminology of the previous Director-General), should provide sufficient common ground for a shared request to the Office to develop a credible and consistent model that can reconcile an increase in aggregate demand with respect for the environmental and equity between the various stakeholders.

This supposes, of course, that current realities of tripartite representation at the ILO justify its claim to represent the real economy. Even *raising* this issue is sure to ruffle some feathers, but it must be addressed nonetheless. That discussion, however, will have to wait for the book's conclusion.

[74] Such as securing resources for the creation and development of employers' organisations in developing countries, or of obtaining 'more staff from the employer community' as put by a recently designed pamphlet which was supposed to introduce the group's perspective regarding the desired profile and priorities of Juan Somavia's successor.

Part III
ILO Influence and the Enduring Demand for Universal 'Rules of the Game'

Introduction

At this point in the analysis, two tentative conclusions seem to emerge. Part I made clear just how much energy the ILO has expended searching for new modes of regulation to address the global economy's social deficits and imbalances. These efforts, moreover, have relied on a very broad application of its persuasive abilities, rather than on an explicit redirection of its traditional normative activities. The observations of the second Part, on the other hand, brought to light the significant opportunities still open to the ILO if it puts those persuasive capacities at the service of enhancing coherence in the work of the multilateral organisations with social, trade and economic objectives. All that is required is the establishment of an appropriate institutional framework.

Nonetheless, it would be a bit hasty to infer that this capacity to persuade will be sufficient to address globalisation's myriad challenges. It is especially unclear whether the options outlined in the previous two Parts can overcome continuing regulatory deficits in matters of employment and social protection, each admittedly exacerbated by the global financial crisis, but neither unique to it. Even *were* new institutional instruments to be successful, seeking the optimal application of the organisation's persuasive endowments requires persistent, long-term efforts on several fronts. All the while, the dynamics of ongoing political and social evolution leave open the ever-present possibility that these efforts will all be for nought. The timescale and scope of the challenge will inevitably increase the temptation to take some sort of short-cut or apply a quick fix. With hopes of turning the ILO into Haas' so-called 'master agency' for international socio-economic regulation more or less dashed, the sole conceivable short-cut left is one that drives to the heart of the problem, ie the 'prisoner's dilemma' which traps states as soon as they begin relying on the benefits of relatively open markets.

The need for a fix-all seems particularly acute when it comes to an issue the ILO has placed at the core of its credibility: the 'rules of the game' on workers' rights it has proposed as a normative baseline in the global economy.

As we have already seen, the 1998 Declaration represented a bold attempt by the ILO (whose impact stretched much beyond it) to address the challenges of globalisation and respond to demands from workers for universal regulation.

Although this was not the stated objective at the time, the Declaration noticeably nudged ratification rates upwards for the relevant Conventions, as illustrated by Figure III.1. Yet the graph's curves also reveal a gradual levelling off before rates reaching universal ratification. Moreover, if the focus of analysis moves from the number of ratifying states toward the actual population benefitting from an internationally enforceable guarantee of the rights provided by ratification, the picture darkens considerably. Indeed, the picture is downright gloomy for freedom of association and collective bargaining. Taking into account the numerous large countries (Brazil, the United States, China and India) which have still not ratified Convention No 87, the ratification rate by population in relation to freedom of association fails to reach even 50 per cent.[1]

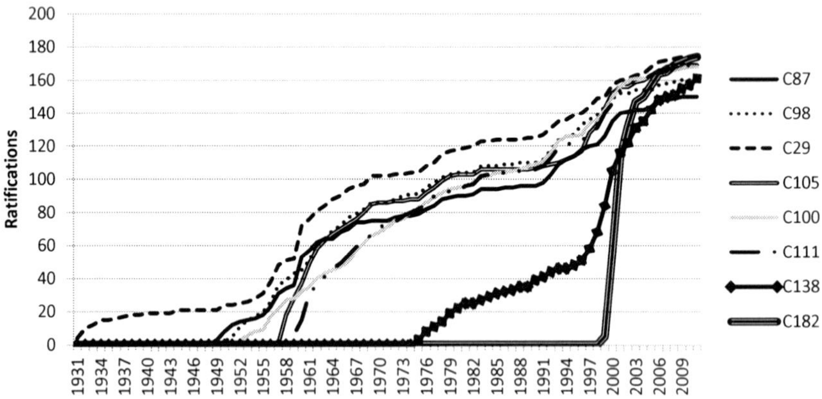

Figure III.1 Ratifications of ILO fundamental conventions

This data seems to lead to the inescapable conclusion that the time has come for persuasion to give way to a more binding alternative, possibly in the form of a limited set of universally applicable rules. But assuming that universal protection does indeed call for universal rules, the harder and more important question is *how*? On this point, the ILO finds itself, so to speak, trapped by its own logic. If the ILO's persuasiveness has successfully procured general and widespread recognition that these rights perform the function of inescapable rules of the game, the organisation now has to face a sobering reality: after nearly 15 years these ostensibly universal rules of the game remain far from universally enforceable.

[1] See ILO, *Report VI: Fundamental Principles and Rights at Work: From Commitment to Action* (International Labour Conference, 101st Session, Geneva, 30 May–14 June 2012) 18, Table 2.3. This report contains tables and statistics which will pique the interest of those seeking trends not only in ratification rates by country, but the impact of these ratifications in terms of the proportion of the world's population who live in countries which have ratified. As it turns out, despite recent ratifications, this proportion remains below 50 per cent for Conventions Nos 87 and 98, though it peaks at 95 per cent for Convention No 100.

The limits of persuasion and the merits of coercion are further illustrated by developments related to another matter that has impacted the lives of many workers: the deadly risks inherent in the use of asbestos. On the face of it, it would seem hard to find a clearer example of the contrast between the two approaches than by placing the ruthless efficacy of the European ban endorsed by the WTO Appellate Body[2] against the slow and uncertain impact of Convention No 162 (1986), purporting to promote the 'safe use' of asbestos – though a closer analysis shows how deceptive the comparison is.

Especially in light of this counterpoint, there seems no way to avoid the proposition that universal respect for fundamental rights should not be given a status equivalent to the binding rules governing market liberalisation, especially since it is these very trade rules which place states in the prisoner's dilemma. In other words, it seems unavoidable to address the prospect of making, in the multilateral trade regime set up under the WTO Agreements,[3] what for a long time been called (a) 'social clause(s)'.

The history of this extremely delicate subject has rightly been described by Charnovitz as 'one long string of false starts, hollow promises, and forgotten laws'.[4]

The first 'false start' was the stillborn Havana Charter, negotiated more than 60 years ago.[5] Considering the two issues to be legally and economically inseparable, the UN Economic and Social Council convened a Conference on Trade and Employment in 1947. The Havana Charter, produced by the conference the following year, contained a call to arms on employment, compelling each Member to 'take action designed to achieve and maintain full and productive employment and large and steadily growing demand within its own territory through measures appropriate to its political, economic and social institutions'.[6] More importantly, Article 7 contained a 'social clause' concerning fair labour standards, even providing a system of dispute settlement where one Member complained that another's standards were too low and therefore unfair.[7]

[2] See *European Communities – Measures Affecting Asbestos and Asbestos-Containing Products*, WTO Appellate Body Report (5 April 2001) WT/DS135/AB/R ('*EC – Asbestos*').

[3] Under the WTO's 'single undertaking', the more than a dozen agreements annexed to the Marrakesh Agreement establishing the WTO form an integral part of a whole agreement systematically binding all ratifying states of the Marrakesh Agreement. Save for a small number of so-called 'plurilateral' agreements in Annex 4 the single undertaking allows neither exclusion from any individual agreement, nor reservations to any individual provision.

[4] Steve Charnovitz, 'The Influence of International Labour Standards on the World Trading System: A Historical Overview' (1987) 126(5) *International Labour Review* 565, 580.

[5] See Jacques Lemoine, 'International Trade Regimes in Retrospect' in Marcel A Boisard, Evgeny Chossudovsky and Jacques Lemoine (eds), *Diplomatie multilatérale: système des Nations Unies à Genève: guide de travail* (The Hague, Kluwer Law International, 1998) 399.

[6] See United Nations, Final Act and Related Documents (Conference on Trade and Employment, Havana, 21 November 1947–24 March 1948) UN Doc E/CONF/2/78, Art 3.1.

[7] Article 7 provides: '1. The Members recognize that measures relating to employment must take fully into account the rights of workers under inter-governmental declarations, Conventions and agreements. They recognize that all countries have a common interest in the achievement and maintenance of fair labour standards related to productivity, and thus in the improvement of wages and working conditions as productivity may permit. The Members recognize that unfair labour conditions, particularly in production for export, create difficulties in international trade, and,

Since 1947, the economic context has changed profoundly, and though trade barriers have lowered, the situation bears little resemblance to the so-called 'first globalisation'.[8] As pointed out by Brian Langille among others, it is less appropriate than ever to model countries as if they were firms forced to compete on the basis of social costs.[9] Due to the development of transnational production involving multiple networks, we no longer find ourselves in a world (if we were ever in one) where countries exchange final goods produced mainly within their own borders.[10]

This situation explains why even the possibility of disciplining market access based on social realities or workers' rights protections gives rise to such radically divergent interests. These differences arise not only between developing countries and emerging markets but also, within developed countries, among employers and workers (and even within each group) depending on their degree of reliance on international trade.[11]

It should be emphasised that what is problematic is not the principle that 'competitiveness of new imports from developing countries should not be achieved to the detriment of fair labour standards'.[12] Indeed, that principle was recognised as far back as 1976 in the Declaration of Principles and Programme of Action adopted by the ILO-organised World Employment Conference.[13] What has been more problematic is the idea of conditioning access to developed country markets on respect for this principle. As for developing countries, they level the accusation that the push for this type of condition (referred to as 'conditionalities' in the French or Spanish literature) is a way for industrialised countries to camouflage protectionist impulses behind a veneer of concern for justice and social progress. One can hardly ignore the apparent willingness of certain countries to impose social and labour standards on the developing world almost immediately after the

accordingly, each Member shall take whatever action may be appropriate and feasible to eliminate such conditions within its territory. 2. Members which are also members of the International Labour Organisation shall cooperate with that organization in giving effect to this undertaking. 3. In all matters relating to labour standards that may be referred to the Organization in accordance with the provisions of Articles 94 or 95, it shall consult and cooperate with the International Labour Organisation.'

[8] Dani Rodrik, *The Globalization Paradox: Democracy and the Future of the World Economy* (New York, WW Norton & Company, 2011).

[9] Brian A Langille, 'The ILO is Not a State, Its Members are Not Firms' in George P Politakis (ed), *Protecting Labour Rights as Human Rights: Present and Future of International Supervision* (Geneva, ILO, 2007).

[10] See Chavagneux's analysis of the complex opportunities for conflict and convergence between firm and state interests (Christian Chavagneux, 'L'instabilité du monde: inégalités, finance, environnement' in *Esprit* (Paris, December 2011) Pt I, n 38).

[11] For a recent summary of the arguments involved on all sides, see the excellent compilation put together by George Tsogas (George Tsogas, 'Labour Standards in International Trade Agreements: An Assessment of the Arguments' (1999) 10(2) *International Journal of Human Resources Management* 351. See also Rabiî Haji, *Normes du travail, commerce et développement*, Centre d'études sur l'intégration et la mondialisation Research Paper 10-01 (2010), available at www.ieim.uqam.ca/spip.php?article6114.

[12] ILO, Declaration of Principles and Programme of Action adopted by the Tripartite World Conference on Employment, Income Distribution and Social Progress, and the International Division of Labour (1976) 189, para 72.

[13] ibid.

success of their prior efforts to sell the benefits of open markets! It is not surprising that developing countries are left suspicious that one hand ultimately threatens to take away what was supposedly being promised with the other. Countries like India have gone even further in their criticism of the apparent hypocrisy of this position. They have suggested that if developed countries were as concerned as they claimed to be about improving the lot of workers in developing countries, they would have a very simple way of demonstrating it: they could open their labour markets to workers from developing countries, who could then enjoy the proposed standards directly![14]

All kinds of nuances and variations have, of course, been grafted onto these two fundamental themes. It is striking that, in this view, the same arguments have found their way to both sides of the supposedly watertight barrier separating the mandates of the WTO and ILO. One finds similar themes in debates in both contexts reaching back to the early 1990s, unsurprising given the numerous discussions (albeit informal, but nonetheless substantial) between the ILO's Director-General, Francis Blanchard, and the Director-General of the GATT at the time, Arthur Dunkel, inspired by the ascent of globalisation as a serious concern in the late 1980s.[15] It is interesting to note that the way these debates played out at the ILO generally had employers adopting a perspective closer to that of developing countries, while governments in industrialised countries (with the notable exception of the United Kingdom) mostly found their position put them in the workers' camp.[16]

One episode[17] can help to understand the sensitivities these themes now provoke. Few will remember that the ILO was actually somewhat of an early-adopter in these matters, addressing the question of attaching fundamental rights 'conditionality' to its own activities, and to its technical cooperation work in particular, as early as 1992. Beyond research and standards, of course, technical cooperation provides another of the various ways in which the ILO can pursue its objectives by

[14] Christopher Arup, *The New World Trade Organization Agreements: Globalizing Law Through Services and Intellectual Property* (Cambridge, Cambridge University Press, 2000) 126. See also Government of India, 'India is the Founder Member of ILO', available at labour.nic.in/upload/uploadfiles/files/footergallery_pdf/India%20is%20founder%20member%20of%20ILO.pdf, noting that 'India and other developing countries had taken the position that labour standards at the international levels can be appropriately addressed only in the ILO, not in the WTO. The social clause is not within the mandate of the WTO. In response, India had countered that the relationship between trade and immigration policies may also be examined in the WTO. The issue was not pursued seriously by the US for sometime thereafter.'

[15] Francis Blanchard, *L'organisation internationale du travail: De la guerre froide à un nouvel ordre mondial* (Paris, Seuil, 2004).

[16] This is not, on reflection, as obvious as it may seem. After all, don't companies (or at least some of them), have an incentive to agree on a number of basic rules of the game, as came to be the case in the maritime industry? The answer to this question can be found in part in the composition of the Employers group at the Conference and the Governing Body, and specifically might be attributed to the dearth of representation from important multinationals. The lack of empirical studies on this issue, not to mention the composition and representativeness of the other two groups, is as surprising as it is regrettable.

[17] A history no doubt unknown to the President of France when he launched his call for social conditionalities from the podium of the ILC in 2009!

applying its persuasive capacities. Under ILO practice, however, this particular application of its persuasive capacities had only been loosely related (if at all) to the implementation of specific organisational objectives. (see Box III.1). Michel Hansenne, Director-General at the time, was convinced that being consistent with the organisation's principles required a more direct link between technical cooperation and standards.[18] Among the proposed implications of such a link was the possibility of limiting expenditures out of the ILO budget, and expenditures on technical cooperation in particular, only to countries demonstrating sufficient respect for fundamental rights. The idea gained support from the workers,[19] but only at the cost of almost universal opposition from governments, and particularly ferocious resistance from employers who saw the plan as contrary to the discretionary nature of Convention ratification.[20]

Box III.1 Technical cooperation, between persuasion and conditionality

Article 10 of the Constitution provides little guidance regarding the particular forms technical cooperation (TC) is to take.[a] Such activities were only actually developed after the Second World War, at the impetus of David Morse, who hoped to promote a less Euro-centric, more development-oriented image of the ILO to its developing world constituents. Since its inauguration, TC was seen as an additional tool of persuasion for the ILO, offering Third World countries expertise and resources on legal and administrative institutions they may otherwise have lacked, and were often keen to obtain.

The extent to which this additional tool of persuasion actually served the ILO's specific objectives, contributed to the implementation of standards or bolstered social development more generally, is a more complex and fraught question. Initially, Morse seems to have viewed technical cooperation primarily as a 'containment' device against the progress of communism, which would help persuade the countries concerned to 'go the ILO way' towards

[18] ILO, *Report of the Director-General* (ILC, 79th Session, Geneva, 3–23 June 1992) 27.

[19] ILO, Minutes (Governing Body, 252nd Session, Geneva, February–March 1992), II/1-II/11, III/1-III/13.

[20] The debate came to a decisive end in 1994 when Hansenne, in his presentation to the 81st Session of the International Labour Conference, recalled that '[a]ction to bring them closer together does not imply, and has never implied, imposing a condition of ratification or application for extending technical cooperation, or for brandishing technical cooperation as a reward or punishment, or banning a member State from technical cooperation'. Though it seemed the idea did not die completely: he also emphasised that '[t]he idea of partnership, which is implicit in technical cooperation, requires a mutual acceptance of certain commitments. In cases where those commitments are not fulfilled, *where for example there are serious and persistent violations of freedom of association or the other main human rights standards, there may well be a need to review technical cooperation activities* to determine whether certain specific projects should be reoriented, accelerated, slowed down or discontinued in order to facilitate a return to a situation more compatible with reciprocally accepted commitments' (ILO, *Defending Values, Promoting Change: Report of the Director-General* (ILC, 81st Session, Geneva, 7–24 June 1994) 87–88, emphasis added).

modernisation and social progress, supported of course by heavy involvement and financing from the United States.[b] This may go some way to explaining a recurrent theme in ILO literature regarding the uneasy coexistence of normative activities and technical cooperation as two separate cultures within the Office.[c]

While the Cold War turned out to be a golden age for technical cooperation activities as much as for standards,[d] the fact is that links between TC and specific aspects of the ILO's mandate loosened in the process, a disconnect exacerbated by the budget crisis of the 1970s and 1980s. Especially during this period, technical cooperation activities had a tendency to become their own justification, providing a source of income (through so-called 'agency costs') that allowed the maintenance of existing staff levels.[e]

The Cold War marked a break for technical cooperation as much as it did for standards activities. This was the context of Michel Hansenne's proposed 'conditionality' approach: he quickly questioned the relevance of TC activities that seemed to have drifted away from the ILO's core mandate (including, for example, TC projects for the development of hostelry and tourism), and went so far as envisaging that any TC financed from the ILO's regular budget might be subject to a condition of respect for core standards.

While the attempt to create a hard connection between the two areas of work ultimately fizzled, only shortly thereafter TC nonetheless became a key element in the promotion of fundamental rights at work under the 1998 Declaration (which proclaimed in its paragraph 3 the ILO's obligation to assist Members' efforts) and its follow-up.[f] The ILC has since repeatedly affirmed the principle that the ILO's technical cooperation work is 'a fundamental means of action to achieve its mission and realize its objective'.[g] The Decent Work Country Programmes should ideally have provided the missing institutional framework to coherently 'operationalise' that principle.[h] As noted, they seem however to have been caught in the (financial) logic of 'self-service normativity' (à la Supiot) dictated by the fickle and fluctuating priorities of both donors and beneficiaries,[i] instead of addressing regulatory deficits in recipient countries in any systematic way.[j]

[a] Paragraph 2 of the Constitution provides that, as directed by the Governing Body, the Office shall '(b) accord to governments at their request all appropriate assistance within its power in connection with the framing of laws and regulations on the basis of the decisions of the Conference' and extend similar assistance on 'the improvement of administrative practices and systems of inspection'. Of course, under para 3, the Office also has whatever powers are assigned to it by the Conference and the Governing Body.

[b] Daniel Maul, *Human Rights, Development and Decolonization: The International Labour Organization, 1940–70* (Geneva, ILO, 2012) 121–51.

[c] Indeed, given the surprising insight into the contributions that a similar 'cultural divide' may have made to the World Bank's particular policy trajectory, there is space for some fascinating research on the realities and impact of this divide at the ILO. See Galit Sarfaty,

'Why Culture Matters in International Institutions: The Marginality of Human Rights at the World Bank' (2009) 103 *American Journal of International Law* 647.

[d] In his Cornell lectures (1969), Morse points out that the share of technical cooperation in the ILO global budget had grown from 2 per cent in 1949 to 45 per cent in 1968. David A Morse, *The Origin and Evolution of the I.LO and its Role in the World Community* (Ithica, NY, Cornell University,1969) 47–48.

[e] See in this connection the sceptical question posed by Philippe Séguin (a pre-eminent French political figure and atypical Chairman of the ILO Governing Body) in his preface to Blanchard's memoir (Francis Blanchard, *L'organisation internationale du travail: De la guerre froide à un nouvel ordre mondial* (Paris, Seuil, 2004)), regarding the long-term impact of this enormous investment and effort.

[f] An overview of the range of technical cooperation (TC) resources and activities relating to Fundament Principles and Rights at Work (FPRW) is provided in the recurrent Report VI submitted to the ILC.

[g] See ILO, *Supplement to Report VI: The Role of the ILO in Technical Cooperation* (ILC, 87th Session, Geneva, 1–17 June 1999); ILO, *Report VI: The Role of the ILO in Technical Cooperation: Promoting Decent Work Through Field and Country Programs* (ILC, 95th Session, Geneva, 31 May–16 June 2006), where the same ideas are repeated.

[h] Leaving aside the specific case of the use of TC and expertise to facilitate the implementation of ratified conventions. See ILO (International Labour Standards Department), *Improving the Impact of International Labour Standards Through Technical Cooperation: A Practice Guide* (Geneva, ILO, 2008).

[i] See also ILO, *Report VI: The Role of the ILO in Technical Cooperation: Promoting Decent Work Through Field and Country Programs* (ILC, 95th Session, Geneva, 31 May–16 June 2006) paras 165–68.

[j] Though note that of 'Conclusions' appended to the Resolution at the end of the 2012 ILC, discussion of the recurrent report on fundamental principles and right at work did specifically point to the desirability of a more 'systematic' approach to the inclusion of FPRW in Decent Work Country Programmes. ILO, *Provisional Record* (ILC, 15th Session, Geneva, May–June 2012) 15/90-15/97, para 20(a).

Given this background, spending more time on a potential link between trade and social conditions may seem futile, like beating a horse which by all evidence is already dead. Yet the necessary precondition in the search for potential alternatives, including the strategy of 'decentralising' the link, which has actually enjoyed relative favour over the past decade, is to understand how and why including minimum social benchmarks in the universal trade regime seems definitively doomed to failure. This is precisely the purpose of the next three chapters.
Indeed, this part of the book focuses on three interrelated issues worth distinguishing if the 'link' question (and its continuing relevance) is to be fully appreciated:

- precisely what rights could anchor the link at the universal level: we will see in this context that, by recognising the 'special significance' of fundamental principles and rights at work, the ILO made a significant contribution to clarifying a debate that had previously become a dialogue of the deaf;
- whether and how such a link could be established at the universal level: what

quickly becomes clear is that, while nothing bars such rights from being grafted onto the universal trading regime in principle, doing so might have less than unequivocally beneficial consequences in practice, even if some miracle were to suddenly jump-start its political feasibility. Ultimately, the sole way that progress can realistically be imagined in this direction takes the form of one of various somewhat 'clandestine' connections which might manage to develop in the interstices of existing provisions;

- the implications of the 'decentralisation' of the link in bi- or multilateral agreements for the ILO and its objectives.

7

From the Impasse of the Social Clause Debate to the Delimitation of Fundamental Rights at Work as Shared 'Rules of the Game'

The idea of the social clause starts off from a simple (and on closer examination, simplistic) idea: that the failure of developing countries to maintain decent standards gives them an unfair, or even unjust, competitive advantage in international trade. This premise runs up against the challenge of delineating what rights are relevant in the determination of 'fairness'. Without trying to provide a complete inventory of the myriad justifications advanced in that regard,[1] it seems useful to dwell on two that have probably had the widest uptake. The first is a (dubious) rationale which draws an analogy between low social standards and the economic concept of *dumping*. The second argument makes a legal-ethical claim (unfortunately almost as dubious), based on the existence of 'internationally recognised' labour rights. In refocusing the debate on fundamental principles and rights at work, the ILO primary's success on this front was to break the gridlock which had previously stalled the debate. To bring the ideas elaborated below to a sharp point, fundamental rights are the precondition for the achievement and the recognition of other rights, regardless of a country's level of development. In the words of the report introducing them in a first draft, these principles and fundamental rights are 'not fundamental because the Declaration says so; the Declaration says that they are fundamental because they are'.[2]

[1] For an exhaustive presentation of justifications see George Tsogas, 'Labour Standards in International Trade Agreements: An Assessment of the Arguments' (1999) 10(2) *International Journal of Human Resources Management* 351; Christian Barry and Sanjay G Reddy, 'International Trade and Labour Standards: A Proposal for Linkage' (2006) 39 *Cornell International Law Journal* 545.

[2] ILO, *Consideration of a Possible Declaration of Principles of the International Labour Organization Concerning Fundamental Rights and its Appropriate Follow-up Mechanism*' (ILC, 86th Session, Geneva, 2–18 June 1998) 10).

I. From the Misleading Analogy of 'Social Dumping'

The texts of the multilateral trade regime of course contain no provisions of immediate relevance to labour standards. Once traditional jurisprudence had ruled out the possibility of introducing relevant distinctions,[3] proponents of the social clause were reduced to casting inadequate labour standards as an inherent violation of trade rules, by drawing on the concepts of 'subsidies' or 'dumping' dealt with respectively under Articles VI and XVI of the GATT.

The most common structure taken on by these arguments uses the 'social dumping' label to invoke an analogy between low labour standards and violations of the dumping provisions under Article VI. Unfortunately, the concept has to date suffered from a somewhat 'journalistic' usage;[4] as put by WTO Director-General Pascal Lamy, it constitutes a conceptual 'melange'[5] which has certainly not helped to clarify the debate.[6] This loose analogy nevertheless has the advantage of drawing attention to the crux of the problem.

To understand why, note that the concept of dumping as defined in Article VI of the GATT establishes the right of a country to take compensatory measures when 'products of one country are introduced into the commerce of another country at less than the *normal* value'.[7]

The transposition of this concept to the field of worker protection therefore supposes that products from a country not respecting what are supposedly 'normal' labour standards have an unfair price advantage compared to those produced under working conditions meeting the relevant standard.[8] Even if the concept of

[3] The well-known case is *Belgian Family Allowances* (1952) GATT BISD 39S/155.

[4] Marie-Ange Moreau, *Normes sociales, droit du travail et mondialisation: confrontation and mutations* (Paris, Dalloz, 2006) 64 ff.

[5] Alain Faujas, 'Pascal Lamy: "La démondialisation est un concept réactionnaire"', *Le Monde* (Paris), 30 June 2011.

[6] See also Bob Hepple, *Labour Laws and Global Trade* (Oxford, Hart Publishing, 2005) 13–15.

[7] Emphasis added. The full text of Art VI(1) provides that: 'The contracting parties recognize that dumping, by which products of one country are introduced into the commerce of another country at less than the normal value of the products, is to be condemned if it causes or threatens material injury to an established industry in the territory of a contracting party or materially retards the establishment of a domestic industry. For the purposes of this Article, a product is to be considered as being introduced into the commerce of an importing country at less than its normal value, if the price of the product exported from one country to another (a) is less than the comparable price, in the ordinary course of trade, for the like product when destined for consumption in the exporting country; or, (b) in the absence of such domestic price, is less than either (i) the highest comparable price for the like product for export to any third country in the ordinary course of trade, or (ii) the cost of production of the product in the country of origin plus a reasonable addition for selling cost and profit. Due allowance shall be made in each case for differences in conditions and terms of sale, for differences in taxation, and for other differences affecting price comparability.'

[8] As stated in the study led by Jean-Marc Siroën, '"Social Dumping", a term subject to some controversy, may be defined as an impingement of workers' rights applied for the purposes of boosting competitiveness, in both the import and export markets alike. *It is thus a means of putting pressure on social costs and production costs*' (Jean-Marc Siroën and others, *The Use, Scope and Effectiveness of Labour and Social Aspects and Sustainable Development Provisions in Bilateral and Regional Free Trade Agreements*, Final Report of the European Commission (2008) 36 (emphasis added).

normality had to be and eventually was clarified in the trade regime itself,[9] it seems rather futile to try to find an uncontroversial definition of 'abnormal'[10] (or sub-standard) when it comes to workers' rights (one exception is export zones, where 'normality' can be clearly defined with reference to the law applying everywhere else within the national territory).[11] Some authors have nevertheless made attempts at such a definition, eg:

> Unlike conventional dumping which means selling abroad below cost or at lower prices than charged in the home market, 'social dumping' refers to costs that are for their part depressed below a natural level by means of 'social oppression' facilitating unfair pricing strategies against foreign competitors.[12]

It seems doubtful, however, that there is ultimately much to be gained from substituting the word 'normal' with 'natural'.

Looking at the question from an ILO perspective, it might seem an obvious step to simply use international labour Conventions as the benchmark of 'normality'. This would be a mistake. Indeed, these instruments are designed to define what is *desirable*. Their content was determined in light of the fact that they cannot be made mandatory. It cannot be forgotten that their voluntariness had a significant impact on the level of obligations they set out, even if that level is sometimes presented as establishing a minimum. (We will return to this point later.) What is considered normal by one country may not be by another. To take an example with an obvious impact on overall costs of labour, Western European practice in social security matters may have for a long time been considered 'normal' by this group of countries. Yet they were obviously never thought of that way in the United States,[13] and are increasingly in question on both sides of the Atlantic.[14] On

[9] Indeed, within the confines of the GATT, the term 'normal' is deceptively simple, substitutable by a dual condition that the price not be set (i) below production costs, nor (ii) below the prevailing price in the exporting country.

[10] Section 7 of the Havana Charter (signed 24 March 1948) had little to say about what was normal, aimed instead at 'the achievement and maintenance of *fair* labour standards related to productivity' (emphasis added). Members also recognised that the 'unfair labour conditions, particularly in production for export, create difficulties in international trade, and, accordingly, each Member shall take whatever action may be appropriate and feasible to eliminate such conditions within its territory'.

[11] Thus, '[a] strict definition would imply that such an impingement refers to "normal" practice in the producing country: violation of national laws, exemptions granted to certain export industries; it may also refer to a "normal" salary evaluated according to the level of labour productivity in the producing country or according to the wages paid in comparable sectors' (Siroën and others, *Use, Scope and Effectiveness* (n 8) 36). By contrast, it is interesting to note that Michael J Trebilcock and Robert Howse consider the prohibition on dumping to be *inherently* irrational, save in cases of anti-competitive practices pursued by selling below cost, which, they point out, can be prohibited by national laws without reference to country of origin (Michael J Trebilcock and Robert Howse, *The Regulation of International Trade*, 3rd edn (London, Routledge, 2005) 250–60).

[12] Harald Grossmann and Georg Koopman, 'Social Standards in International Trade: A New Protectionist Wave?' in Harald Sander and András Inotai (eds), *World Trade After the Uruguay Round: Prospects and Policy Options for the Twenty-first Century* (Routledge, 1996) 116.

[13] See Antony Alcock, *The History of the International Labour Organization* (New York, Macmillan, 1971), shedding light on the United States' stance against Convention No 102.

[14] Despite the passage of ILO Recommendation R202: Social Protection Floors Recommendation (International Labour Conference, 101st Session, Geneva, 14 June 2012), there is little evidence of a reversal in this trend.

the other hand, judging 'normality' by reference to rules preventing 'social oppression' seems more promising: in many ways this reasoning corresponds well with the identification of fundamental rights as 'enabling rights', a prospect discussed further below.

II. Or Ambiguous References to 'Internationally Recognised Worker Rights'

To circumvent the difficulties inherent to the 'social dumping' analogy, the United States focused their strategy on the concept of 'internationally recognised workers' rights'. At first, this concept seems to usefully replace the subjectivity of 'normal' with an apparently objective concept rooted in an international consensus.[15] In reality, this conception remains highly ambiguous. As explained lucidly by Laurence Dubin,[16] one can see this terminology as the result of a legal high-wire act intended to subject US trade partners to standards which: (i) would not be based on the relevant international labour Conventions, which the United States for the most part had not yet ratified, and was still disinclined to ratify;[17] and (ii) would not prejudice the US position that, unlike fundamental human rights, fundamental workers' rights cannot be considered part of customary international law, but should rather, according to their position, be treated as general principles of law justifying a legal response only to constant and gross violations.[18]

While flying under cover of reference to an international consensus, the concept as implemented under section 301 of the Omnibus Trade and Competitiveness Act (OTCA) can easily change its stripes to suit the circumstances.[19] As a matter of the level of protection required or the specific rights protected, its selective character poses two clear problems. Perhaps most important for the ILO, the list's coverage of the catalogue of fundamental rights notably leaves out non-discrimination. As a matter of multilateral trade disciplines, however, section 301 also raises problems because of its inclusion of 'acceptable conditions of work

[15] This consensus can be said to exist, insofar as the entire list of rights is covered by the International Covenant on Social, Economic and Cultural Rights (signed 16 December 1966, entered into force 3 January 1976) 993 UNTS 3, which the United States has also not ratified.

[16] Dubin's version is usefully compared to Lance Compa and Jeffrey Vogt, 'Labor Rights in the Generalized System of Preferences: A 20 Years Review' (2001) 22(2–3) *Comparative Labor Law and Policy Journal* 119, 202–8.

[17] For the reasons (or perhaps excuses) which were offered in this regard, including American federalism, see Francis Maupain, 'Fédéralisme et Conventions internationales du travail' (1987) 126(6) *International Labour Review* 701.

[18] Laurence Dubin, *La protection des normes sociales dans les échanges internationaux* (Presses Universitaires d'Aix-Marseille, 2003) 63–69. See also Steve Charnovitz, 'Editorial Comments: The ILO Convention on Freedom of Association and its Future in the United States' (2008) 102(1) *American Journal of International Law* 90, 98–103.

[19] Philip Alston, 'Labor Rights Provisions in US Trade Law: Aggressive Unilateralism?' (1993) 15(1) *Human Rights Quarterly* 1.

with respect to minimum wages, hours of work, and occupational safety and health'.

Here we come up against a difficulty analogous with that which faced the 'social dumping' argument: questions related to working hours, and especially those related to wages, have historically been considered as largely dependent on a country's level of development. The example of the rapid progress made by some Asian countries, especially South Korea, confirms the trend. The inclusion of these subjects of regulation, therefore, leaves the entire category open to constant suspicion, and absolutely subject to allegations,[20] that the category is intended to respond first and foremost to protectionist motivations incompatible with the philosophy of the Marrakesh Agreement, accounting neither for international realities, nor for issues of true fairness.

III. To the ILO's Functionalist Approach, Turning on 'Fundamental Rights as Enabling Rights' (and as Potential Rules of the Game)

The impasse met by both of the approaches highlighted above makes clear just how valuable it was for the ILO to successfully focus the debate on fundamental rights and principles at work. The merit of the approach was not only that it offered a category with an intrinsic conceptual coherence, but that the underlying framework was directly relevant to the achievement of the WTO's primary objective of transnational economic integration. The fact that the success came somewhat indirectly does not detract from that achievement. To elucidate the unique contribution the new category brought to the debate, it is worth considering three aspects: (i) the circumstances which explain the emergence of the category; (ii) its internal coherence; and (iii) its relevance to the social dimension of trade liberalisation.

A. Emergence of the Category

The genesis of fundamental principles and rights at work as a specific category has a long history. The often virulent controversies of the debate were largely focused, within the ILO and outside it, on the *advisability* of a social clause. Indeed, it was only when the workers' vice-chair of the ILO Governing Body, Lord Brett, agreed to a truce on the subject (a decision that itself attracted substantial criticism) that the search for a solution was finally able to take root.[21]

[20] DiCaprio may find that the motivations of labour provisions in US trade policy is not motivated by protectionism, but unfortunately, much seems to turn on a rather loose definition of the term: Alisa DiCaprio, 'Are Labor Provisions Protectionist? Evidence from Nine Labor-Augmented US Trade Arrangements' (2004) 26(1) *Comparative Labor Law and Policy Journal* 1.

[21] See in this regard the exchange between Hans-Goran Myrdal, Swedish employers' representative, arguing that with this decision 'the social clause issue is practically dead', and Lord Brett's statement that

Contrary to a common reading of events, the origin of the concept goes even further back than 1995 and the World Summit for Social Development in Copenhagen.[22] While the idea of 'core labour rights' had been in the air for a long time at the ILO, it took hard work and a confluence of circumstance to help the concept crystallise. Negotiations floundered for many reasons, perhaps chief among them the fundamental principle that international labour Conventions had equivalent status as treaties, along with the correlative difficulty of establishing any formal hierarchy among them.[23]

The first important step was a Director-General's report prepared in the run-up to the ILO's 75th anniversary, and released during the ongoing Uruguay Round of trade negotiations. Through this document, Michel Hansenne daringly inserted himself into the debate on the social clause already raging within the GATT. Though the report was to be discussed at the ILC that June, it was finalised and distributed before the Marrakesh Conference which was to establish the World Trade Organization in April 1994.[24]

His report proposed a new approach to the social clause issue, one that foreshadowed the distinction between rights that depend on economic progress and those which make social progress possible.[25] When the ILC had the chance to comment on the report that June, the Director-General's position (described in a PhD thesis as

the suspension was 'only for the time being' and only within the forum of the ILO itself. Hans-Goran Myrdal, 'Social clause issue "practically dead"', *Financial Times* (London), 4 May 1995; Lord Bill Brett, 'Letters to the Editor: social clause delayed, but not dead', *Financial Times* (London), 10 May 1995.

[22] The Copenhagen Declaration has been described as 'the first formal international recognition of the special status of these rights, which became accepted as the core labour standards' (Gerry Rodgers and others, *The ILO and the Quest for Social Justice* (Geneva, ILO, 2009) 219). As shown in the text below, the ILC had already recognised the special significance of these rights in 1994, and the rationalisation of their status as 'enabling rights' did not result from the Copenhagen text, which referred to them only as among 'basic rights'. Rather, that justification was first found in a document submitted to the Governing Body in November 1994, offering the formula which was eventually codified in the Preamble to the 1998 Declaration. See ILO, *The Social Dimensions of the Liberalization of Trade* (Governing Body, 261st Session, Geneva, November 1994); Francis Maupain, 'L'OIT, la justice sociale et la mondialisation' (1999) 278 *Recueil des Cours de l'Académie de Droit International* 331, n 115.

[23] Klaus Samson, 'The Protection of Economic and Social Rights Within the Framework of the International Labour Organization' in Franz Matscher, *Implementation of Economic and Social Rights: National, International and Comparative Aspects* (Engel Verlag, 1991) 123, 125–26. See also Francis Maupain, 'La "valeur ajoutée" de la Déclaration relative aux principes et droits fondamentaux au travail pour la cohérence et l'efficacité de l'action normative de l'OIT' in Isabelle Daugareilh (ed), *Mondialisation, travail et droits fondamentaux* (Brussels, Bruylant, 2005) 20–21.

[24] ILO, *Defending Values, Promoting Change: Report of the Director-General* (ILC, 81st Session, Geneva, 7–24 June 1994) especially 56–63.

[25] In his report, which painted a broad picture of the problems that the ILO had faced in the last quarter of the century, Hansenne expressed his conviction that the ILO could not ignore this debate, particularly given the likely impact of the issue on organisations of employers and workers. Yet, he expressed doubts about the advisability of trying to use the ILO to counter alleged 'social dumping' by putting in place a compulsory *outcome* which would equalise social protection (ibid 57–58). Instead, he advanced a solution based on a common obligation of *means* and behaviours which would effectively link trade liberalisation and labour standards, consistent with respect for freedom to choose national priorities (ibid 59–60). Indeed, he specifically invoked the idea of promoting the universal application of fundamental rights beyond freedom of association, which was of course already protected by a special procedure (ibid 51–54).

'interventionist')[26] collided with a 'neoliberal' perspective grounded in an uncharacteristically heterogeneous group of countries and interests. Despite the absence of consensus on the substance of the debate, agreement was captured on two points: first, a compromise with the workers allowed the adoption of a resolution clearly linking the four fundamental rights to a list of specifically enumerated Conventions;[27] and secondly, and more importantly, a decision was taken to continue the discussion in a Working Party on the Social Dimensions of the Liberalization of International Trade created under the auspices of the Governing Body. As an extension of the reflections initiated in the Director-General's Report, the International Labour Office document submitted to the working group that November again stressed that the issue should not be framed in terms of defining and imposing a top-down, uniform level of protection that would ignore each Member's level of development and its legitimate priorities. Instead, the issue was defined as a matter of identifying the rights without which there is no possibility for individual and collective preferences to be effectively expressed. Given the context of economic liberalisation, these rights would thus provide the indispensable tools for the social partners to obtain fair compensation for their contribution to common prosperity. [28]

Delineating the rights in question follows directly from this characterisation of the problem. We find (unsurprisingly) freedom of association and collective bargaining rights (enshrined in Conventions Nos 87 and 98), but also the prohibition of forced labour (enshrined in Conventions Nos 29 and 105, with the exploitation of children also annexed here, given their reduced autonomy), and finally, the prohibition of discrimination (established by Conventions Nos 100 and 111) as an infringement of freedom of workers to receive fair compensation for their work. The eventually-adopted model of fundamental rights, organised around the strategic function of ensuring an automatic linkage between economic and social development, earned gradual vindication. First, at the World Summit for Social Development in Copenhagen in 1995, the 'programme of action' adopted by the participants lent significant political clout to this version, emphasising the importance of this group of rights to achieving 'truly sustained economic growth and sustainable development'.[29] The OECD then added analytical heft to the model,

[26] Gerda Van Roozendaal, Social Challenges to Trade: Trade Unions and the Debate on International Labour Standards (DPhil thesis, University of Amsterdam 2001) 194 ff.

[27] ILO, Resolution concerning the 75th Anniversary of the ILO and its Future Orientation (ILC, 81st Session, Geneva, 22 June 1994). See also van Roozendaal, 'Social Challenges to Trade' (n 26) 194.

[28] ILO, *The Social Dimensions of the Liberalization of Trade* (n 22) 26–29.

[29] See para 54(b) of the Programme of Action adopted by the World Summit: 'Governments should enhance the quality of work and employment by . . . [s]afeguarding and promoting respect for basic workers' rights, including the prohibition of forced labour and child labour, freedom of association and the right to organize and bargain collectively, equal remuneration for men and women for work of equal value, and non discrimination in employment, fully implementing the Conventions of the ILO in the case of states Parties to those Conventions, and taking into account the principles embodied in those Conventions in the case of those countries that are not States parties to thus achieve truly sustained economic growth and sustainable development' (UN, Programme of Action of the World Summit for Social Development (World Summit for Social Development, Copenhagen, 6–12 March 1995) Annex II; United Nations, *Report of the World Summit on Social Development* (19 April 1995) A/CONF.166/9, cited in ILO, *Consideration of a Possible Declaration* (n 2) 13).

with the economic findings it made in its 1996 report addressing the relationship between these 'core rights' and trade.[30] Finally, by renewing their 'commitment to the observance of the internationally recognised core labour standards' in their Singapore Ministerial Declaration,[31] washing their hands of any active role in the matter, and recognising the ILO's competence to 'set and deal' with them, WTO negotiators unwittingly paved the way for the ILO to officially confirm the special status of fundamental principles and rights at work two years later.[32] All in all, the vision set out in 1994 is expressed rather faithfully in the Preamble to the 1998 Declaration, which states that 'it enables the persons concerned, to claim freely and on the basis of equality of opportunity, their fair share of the wealth which they have helped to generate, and to achieve fully their human potential'.

B. Its Internal Coherence

Ever since it was crystallised in the 1998 Declaration, the category of 'fundamental rights' has been the subject of wide criticism, especially on the basis that it is too restrictive and ultimately arbitrary. [33] Addressing these criticisms head on cannot only dispel some misunderstandings, but also clarify the internal logic that gives the category its coherence.

First of all, the inclusion of child labour has been described by many authors in developing countries as a reflection of the ongoing Western cultural bias which consistently afflicts the ILO.[34] As a matter of fact, such views find support even from developed-country authors as reputable as Alain Supiot.[35] On the other hand, the constructed category excludes certain subjects that many would claim are just as 'fundamental'; which might, indeed, in some sense be considered as 'vital'. Why not include health and safety (the asbestos example mentioned in Part III Introduction being particularly evocative) or, as Supiot himself put forward in an ILO-commissioned report, social security?[36]

[30] Organisation for Economic Co-operation and Development, *Trade, Employment and Labour Standards: A Study of Core Workers' Rights and International Trade* (1996); OECD, *International Trade and Core Labour Standards* (2000).

[31] WTO, *Singapore WTO Ministerial 1996: Ministerial Declaration* (13 December 1996) para 4.

[32] See Brian A Langille, 'The ILO and the New Economy: Recent Developments' (1999) 15(3) *International Journal of Comparative Labour Law and Industrial Relations* 229, 240–41.

[33] For an overview of critiques, see Claire La Hovary, *Les droits fondamentaux au travail* (Paris, Presses Universitaires de France, 2009) 44–45.

[34] Moreover, as recalled by Andrew Brown and Robert Stern, 'the concept in Western countries of childhood as a time for education and play is, after all, a comparatively recent notion' (Andrew Brown and Robert Stern, 'What Are the Issues in Using Trade Agreements to Improve International Labour Standards?' (2008) 7(2) *World Trade Review* 331, 339). On economic critiques regarding child labour, see Aminata Cissé-Niang, 'L'interdiction internationale du travail des enfants vue d'Afrique' (2002) 1095 *Semaine Sociale Lamy* 9.

[35] Alain Supiot, 'La place de la sécurité sociale dans le système des normes internationales du travail' in Alain Supiot (ed), *Protection sociale et travail décent: Nouvelles perspectives pour les normes internationales du travail* (Supplement No 1272, *Semaine Sociale Lamy*, 2006) 7, 8.

[36] ibid.

It should be noted, first, that the inclusion of child labour was never a foregone conclusion. According to the jurisprudence of the Committee of Experts, child labour was initially understood to be covered (at least in its most reprehensible forms) by the prohibition against forced labour.[37] It soon became clear, however, that public relations practicality and political expediency made it essential to grant child labour separate recognition, as it was in 1995 in Copenhagen.[38] Fortunately, and most importantly, its inclusion had no impact on the overall coherence of the category. Indeed, the common thread connecting these rights and ensuring the category's conceptual integrity is that they all relate to safeguarding the autonomy of the will, granted that will is exercised collectively in the case of freedom of association and collective bargaining.[39]

This is obviously not to say that the category's exclusion of other important rights was exclusively dictated by a desire to preserve its coherence. It is clear that practical and political reasons played a substantial role. Indeed, there was a real risk that, rather than consolidating the rather rapidly emerging consensus, any attempt to expand the category could have easily toppled the entire exercise.

Regardless of whether it is a simple result of circumstance or actually represents a principled derivation from underlying principle, the category establishes an important link with multilateral trade disciplines. This goes some way to explaining the significant impact of the 1998 Declaration as a baseline for determining the social dimension in regional or bilateral trade agreements – successes discussed more fully below. It was, indeed, for this reason that the Declaration 'emerged as the centrepiece of international efforts to remedy the plight of vulnerable workers in the global economy'.[40] Without the crystallisation of a consensus on the 'core labour rights', it is unlikely that it could have come to represent the sole 'global regulatory project in respect of work and labour market' that is considered a credible alternative to the dominant model of the IFIs and the OECD.[41]

[37] ILO, *The Social Dimensions of the Liberalization of Trade* (n 22) para 29.

[38] Philip Alston in particular has argued that the list of fundamental rights that ultimately made their way into the 1998 Declaration was, in reality, a simple copy-and-paste of the US priorities already reflected in the Trade Act of 1974 (Philip Alston, '"Core Labour Standards" and the Transformation of the International Labour Rights Regime' (2004) 15(3) *European Journal of International Law* 457, 466–69, 485 and 498). It is true that the United States made the inclusion of child labour a sticking point early in the debate, but they were hardly alone in this regard. Moreover, they were much less enthusiastic about the inclusion of non-discrimination which, as discussed below, has been a sticking point for them in both multilateral and bilateral trade agreements. Of course, this conclusion also misses the long list of other labour rights enumerated in the Trade Act which did not make it into the consensus category.

[39] As well-reflected in the terms of the 1998 Declaration's Preamble, emphasising that they 'enable the persons concerned to claim freely and on the basis of equality of opportunity their fair share'.

[40] Kerry Rittich, 'Core Labour Rights and Labor Market Flexibility: Two Paths Entwined?' in International Bureau of the Permanent Court of Arbitration (ed), *Labor Law Beyond Borders: ADR and the Internationalization of Labor Dispute Settlement* (The Hague, Kluwer Law International, 2003) 159–60.

[41] Kerry Rittich, 'Global Labour Policy as Social Policy' (2008) 14(2) *Canadian Labour and Employment Law Journal* 272.

C. And its Relevance from the Perspective of Implementing WTO Objectives

When international trade ministers, meeting under the auspices of the newly formed WTO, designated the ILO as 'the competent body to set and deal with' core labour standards, they almost certainly did not expect the statement to be understood as a call for the ILO to break new ground in its own work. The designation was not meant to 'hand things over' so much as it was intended simply to 'pass the buck' – to get rid of a problem that had shown so much discord in WTO negotiations. They can hardly have anticipated the ILO Director-General's effort to take the Ministerial Declaration and 'run with it' toward what became the 1998 Declaration.[42] It almost goes without saying that the speed of his response and the ironic ingenuity of simply *taking the text at face value*[43] caught some of its authors off guard; it also attracted a surplus of attention to the negotiations leading to the 1998 Declaration.

Indeed, even if the underlying motivations were a mix of suspicion and enthusiasm, the heightened attention meant negotiations were conducted at an uncharacteristically high level for the ILO, with active participation by a number of key ambassadors active in the WTO context. The authority and prominence of the negotiators made it possible for a number of key emerging economies, including both India and Brazil, to accept a preliminary sketch of the final text during preliminary consultations.[44]

This short history makes it clear that major WTO players were all acutely aware that, as much as the universal responsibility to 'respect, promote and realise' the fundamental principles and rights at work was invoked as a legal obligation inherent in ILO membership, they are also directly relevant to the WTO framework, in at least two ways.[45]

First of all, no participant in the debate claimed that respect for this category of rights was or should be linked to a country's level of development.[46] As a result, the Declaration made it difficult to apply the much-rehearsed reproach which had previously coloured calls for universal and effective respect of labour rights as thin camouflage for protectionist motivations.

[42] As the Director-General stated explicitly: 'The ball is now in our court and . . .we have no intention simply to hang on to the ball. We are going to play it', quoted in Tsogas, 'Labour Standards' (n 1) 370.

[43] A tactic which earned quite direct praise from some quarters (see, eg Langille, 'The ILO and the New Economy' (n 32) 240–411; Brian A Langille, 'Core Labour Rights: The True Story (Reply to Alston)' (2005) 16(3) *European Journal of International Law* 409, 420–21).

[44] Those consultations, held under the skilled and impartial guidance of the Canadian Ambassador to the United Nations, Mark Moher, earned Moher the chair of the ad hoc committee of the Conference which drafted the Declaration. It was only because negotiations were unable to overcome stubborn resistance from a final trio of diehards (Pakistan, Mexico and Egypt) that the ILC had to adopt the text by majority vote rather than consensus.

[45] Almost the entire ILO membership carries 'the obligations of membership' concurrently with those flowing from their participation in the WTO.

[46] An objection that, as it turns out, may not be so ridiculous when it comes to child labour.

Secondly, and more positively, the logic of 'enabling rights' affirmed during the discussion and appearing in the text actually has conceptual resonance with the implementation of WTO purposes expressed in the Preamble to the Marrakesh Agreement.[47] As explored further below, these rights can also be framed by the *functional* role they must play if the 'raised standards of living' and 'steadily growing . . . real income' promised in the WTO Preamble are to be translated into concrete realities for those who will inevitably be affected, for better or for worse, by expanded trade.

Indeed, this approach is the key to correctly reading the language in paragraph 5 of the Declaration, according to which 'nothing in this Declaration and its follow-up shall be invoked or otherwise used for [protectionist trade purposes]; in addition, the comparative advantage of any country should in no way be called into question by this Declaration and its follow-up'.[48]

The parallels between this paragraph and the most disconcerting aspects of the Singapore text drew sharp criticism, especially because it seemed to force the ILO to dance to the WTO drum.[49] In this regard, it is easy to see how heavy borrowing from the text of the Singapore Declaration in the first paragraph of the 1998 Declaration would give the impression that the protection of comparative advantage had trumped respect for fundamental rights.

One crucial aspect of both texts needs to be underlined in this respect: like the Singapore text before it, the opening of the paragraph refers, unlike the rest of the document, not to fundamental rights but to labour standards in general. It seems a fair deduction that this paragraph is meant to address the position expressed by many delegates throughout the Conference, especially those from developing countries, that labour standards are generally dependent on each Member's level of development and particular capacities. In this sense, the text is meant to assuage any residual concerns by solemnly recognising that criticism of a country's labour standards *in general* would not, by dint of the Declaration, suddenly become a legitimate basis for protectionist policies.

At the same time, however, the overall push of the Declaration makes clear that this logic does not and cannot apply to the category of fundamental rights, because of the specific function they fulfil under the Preamble: as enabling rights they are

[47] That resonance had already been outlined in the memorandum submitted by the ILO to the G7 Conference on Employment (ILO, 'The Social Dimension of the Liberalization of International Trade' (G7 Conference on Employment, Lille, April 1996) G7/E.C./1996/1, 3). Specifically, among the justifications deployed for the unconditional nature of these rights, Hansenne invokes 'economic congruence, since recognition of these fundamental rights appears to be based on the same principles as those underlying the international trade system itself. The prohibition of forced labour and recognition of freedom of association are thus the prerequisites for freedom and transparency in the labour market and may also be seen as the natural extension of free trade in the world market'.

[48] ILO Declaration on Fundamental Principles and Rights at Work (adopted June 1998) para 5.

[49] See Steve Charnovitz's criticism of the Singapore text in 'Trade, Employment and Labour Standards: The OECD Study and Recent Developments in the Trade and Labour Standards Debate' (1997) 11(1) *Temple International and Comparative Law Journal* 131, 156–57. Charnovitz's argument is extended to para 5 of the Declaration in Langille, 'The ILO and the New Economy' (n 32) 250–51. See also La Hovary, *Les droits fondamentaux* (n 33) 23–25.

recognised as a *necessary condition* for achieving progress toward other rights. Their violation deprives those concerned of the right to freely demand gradual improvements in their working conditions and income, in accordance with opportunities arising out of increased prosperity those expected from trade liberalisation in particular. Despite the general claim of paragraph 5, the failure to guarantee these rights cannot be claimed as a legitimate source of comparative advantage without destroying the premise of the argument.

As strong as this argument may be, the somewhat equivocal wording of the paragraph is hard to deny. Fortunately, any lingering uncertainty (undoubtedly essential to securing adoption at the ILC in 1998) was clearly and definitively eliminated with the adoption of the Declaration on Social Justice for a Fair Globalization in 2008, and the last paragraph of section IA(iv) in particular, which succinctly declares 'that the violation of fundamental principles and rights at work cannot be invoked or otherwise used as a legitimate comparative advantage', even while reiterating 'that labour standards should not be used for protectionist trade purposes'.[50]

It seems fairly obvious that such an unequivocal statement could not be made without having some consequences for the relative status of these rights in relation to trade rules. These consequences will be further explored in the following chapters.

[50] If one remembers the militant opposition of some Asian countries to para IA(iv) of the 2008 Declaration (noting that 'the violation of fundamental principles and rights at work cannot be invoked or otherwise used as a legitimate comparative advantage'), it is remarkable that this formula was accepted with relatively good grace by China, so long as the relevant phrase from the 1998 Declaration ('labour standards should not be used for protectionist trade purposes') was reiterated.

8

Can the Social 'Rules of the Game' be Made More Effective by Linking Them to Basic Trade Rules?

If there is, as we have seen, a real affinity between the implementation of fundamental rights at work and the WTO's objectives of raising living standards and pursuing sustainable development, the question that inevitably arises is: what should the consequences of that link be? Does this connection justify, or even demand, that formal recognition of these rights should be grafted onto existing agreements, or even that new agreements be added to the single undertaking? If the answer does not lie in this kind of radical surgery, is it possible to draw *any* consequences within the universal trading system as it already exists?

In what follows, we attempt to show that, under the multilateral trade disciplines as they exist: (a) transplanting formal clauses that aim to ensure universal respect for fundamental rights directly into the WTO agreements would be legally compatible with the existing multilateral trade regime; (b) any expansion in the *effectiveness* of protection that would result from such a formal transplant would come at a high price in terms of the *level* of protection offered: trade-offs that cut into the attractiveness of such proposals; (c) especially given how politically contentious a transplant remains, a more promising option is to foster connections under the existing framework and within the interstices of existing mechanisms, preferring informal (if not clandestine) connections over explicitly-approved links expressly enshrined in the texts.

I. Legitimacy, Perceptions and Barriers to a Possible Legal Transplant

To get a solid handle on this issue, it is necessary to return to the starting point, that is to say, to the assumption that such a transplant would assure a more effective implementation of fundamental rights. Such a gain would theoretically be accomplished, first of all, by incorporating those rights into the WTO framework so as to make them mandatory for all WTO members, irrespective of a country's ratification of the relevant Conventions; and by thereby allowing the possibility for trade measures that would deter violators or compensate for possible violations.[1] It is easy to understand why such a prospect would be so attractive to some workers, especially given the apparent contrasts with the ILO's more exhortatory approach exemplified in the asbestos case already alluded to above.[2] As we shall see, however, the cost–benefit analysis of such a transplant turns out on closer examination to be more complicated than the asbestos case might imply.

The first question which arises in this respect is whether the relevant principles can be added in without coming into conflict with existing trade disciplines and thereby undermining the coherence and efficacy of the trade regime as a whole. We shall see that the transplant would not only be compatible with the logic of individual trade disciplines but, in light of the regime applied to intellectual property, would be a perfectly legitimate addition to the overall regime as well. Paradoxically, it appears that what such integration would put most seriously into question is not the coherence of the trade system, but the nature of the ostensible improvement in the implementation of fundamental workers' rights – leaving aside, of course, the challenge of finding the requisite political assent.

A. Legitimate Transplant as a Matter of Principle

The main objection to the establishment of a link or conditionality between international trade and labour rights regimes is that such a link would introduce a species of deadly virus into the heart of the system, threatening to destroy the logic on which global trade integration is based.

It is true that non-discrimination and national treatment, the two key disciplines of international trade law derived in turn from the system's two underlying principles of comparability and comparative advantage, seem at first to doom this type of transplant to rejection. The first concept, applicable at the *product* level, requires similar ('like') products to be treated the same way; the second, which lies at the *country* level, requires that any States accepting the same rules be granted the same market access. In this regard, the transplantation of labour rights as conditions on trading rights ('conditionalities') has two possible, and possibly cumulative, implications. At the *product* level, the appearance and physical properties of a product remain from an orthodox point of view the only acceptable criteria for establishing comparability; a labour link would lift the veil, as it were, turning attention to the conditions of production. At the *country* level, the link would put

[1] Indeed, many have considered recourse to the dispute settlement system of the WTO, seeing it as a jack-of-all-trades which could be just as effective on environmental and social issues as it is in trade disputes. As stressed by Donald McRae, however, such a possibility is both 'remote and largely unpractical' (Donald McRae, 'The Place of the WTO in the International System' in Daniel Bethlehem and others (eds), *The Oxford Handbook of International Trade Law* (Oxford, Oxford University Press, 2009) 75). These proposals nonetheless emphasise the relative clout of the WTO in the international system.

[2] For more detail on the nuances of the case and its implications, see below.

into question the legitimate comparative advantage that some countries draw from their less advanced level of development, and relatively less advantageous working conditions.

(i) 'Impermeable Barrier' of the Product/Process Distinction

It was long believed that the integrity of the multilateral trade regime could only be protected from fatal contamination by surrounding it with an impermeable barrier formed by a distinction that has been a bit like the *summa divisio* of the system: the conceptual divide between *products* and their associated production *processes.* And indeed, this distinction seems rather evident in its simplicity.

At least in principle, the working conditions of those who create a product have no direct, measurable effect on the end product (although a senior World Bank official once boasted that he could easily identify a carpet made by children, by its incomparably fine weave). As a result, working conditions have been categorised as 'unincorporated' processes and production methods (PPMs), the label given in the literature to processes that have no impact on the physical characteristics of the final product. Unlike 'incorporated' PPMs, which leave some residue which can be detected by the consumer, the consideration of unincorporated PPMs in internal trade policies has long been treated with suspicion in the WTO system (and the GATT before that). According to jurisprudence which seemed well established until recently, the similarity of the goods simply does not depend on similarities (or differences) in their PPMs.[3] Or, put another way, a PPM is not a relevant criterion in determining whether two products are 'similar'[4] and cannot form the basis for a regulatory distinction.[5]

As we shall see, however, the barrier thus created is not as impermeable and inviolable as it appeared even a few years ago. Indeed, not only has WTO jurisprudence introduced a certain element of subjectivity into the 'likeness' determination, but most importantly, that jurisprudence has given way to allegedly more important considerations under the TRIPS Agreement, a central part of the single undertaking created during the Uruguay Round.

(ii) Easily Permeated by Subjective Considerations

As just noted, the distinction is not drawn from the text of the agreements themselves, but is the result of a progressive judicial construction which has relaxed the principle of non-discrimination. While the GATT case law that prevailed before the founding of the WTO declared the illegality of *any* differentiation between products

[3] *United States – Restrictions on Imports of Tuna,* GATT Panel Report (1991) GATT BISD 39S/155, unadopted ('GATT *United States – Tuna I*'); GATT, *United States – Restrictions on Imports of Tuna,* GATT Panel Report (1994) GATT DS29/R, unadopted ('GATT *United States – Tuna II*').

[4] GATT *United States – Tuna I* (n 3) paras 5.12–5.15. See also GATT *United States – Tuna II* (n 3) paras 5.8 and 5.9.

[5] *United States – Measures Affecting Alcoholic and Malt Beverages,* GATT Panel Report (1992) GATT BISD 39S/206, paras 5.72 and 5.73.

proved to be similar, according to the Appellate Body a difference in treatment between similar products no longer automatically implies the existence of less favourable treatment.[6] So could it be that a measure establishing different treatment of similar products no longer automatically constitutes a violation of Article III:4 of the GATT, to the extent that this difference in treatment can be explained by something other than the product's origin?[7] It may be that if a country applying measures with a detrimental impact on certain imports can clearly show the connection of those impacts to the objective intended by the internal measure, that the claim of less favourable treatment would not prima facie be established.[8] The burden of proof would then shift to the complainant to show that the detrimental impact was in fact explained by the origin of the products in question.

If it still seems highly unlikely that this case law could be successfully invoked to justify the introduction of a total restriction based on the presumed aversion of its consumers to certain modes of production,[9] it nonetheless opens up a perspective which we will be explored in greater detail below. Just as importantly, this legal development lends additional credence to the compatibility between the multilateral trade regimes and the possible non-discriminatory system of social labelling to be discussed in the final chapter.

(iii) And Cut Right Through by the TRIPS Precedent

The second problem with the impermeable barrier set up by the product/process distinction is much more significant: a total breach of its underlying logic in the

[6] See, eg *European Communities – Measures Affecting Asbestos and Asbestos-Containing Products*, WTO Appellate Body Report (5 April 2001) WT/DS135/AB/R ('*EC – Asbestos*') para 100. The Appellate Body continues in the same paragraph that 'A complaining Member must still establish that the measure accords to the group of "like" imported products "less favourable treatment" than it accords to the group of "like" domestic products. The term "less favourable treatment" expresses the general principle, in Article III:1, that internal regulations "should not be applied . . . so as to afford protection to domestic production". If there is "less favourable treatment" of the group of "like" imported products, there is, conversely, "protection" of the group of "like" domestic products.'

[7] See *Dominican Republic – Measures Affecting the Importation and Internal Sale of Cigarettes*, WTO Appellate Body Report (19 May 2005) WT/DS302/AB/R, para 96. In this case, the Appellate Body, confirming the findings of the Panel, held that 'the existence of a detrimental effect on a given imported product resulting from a measure does not necessarily imply that this measure accords less favourable treatment to imports, if the detrimental effect is explained by factors or circumstances unrelated to the foreign origin of the product', and concluded in accordance with the Panel that, in this case, the unit cost of the bond was higher for the importer of Honduran cigarettes than for two domestic producers and therefore the difference in result was not sufficient to establish that the requirement to deposit gave a less favourable treatment to imported cigarettes.

See also the application of the same logic in the Panel Report in *European Communities – Measures Affecting the Approval and Marketing of Biotech Products*, WTO Panel Report (21 November 2006) WT/DS291/36 ('*EC – Biotech*') paras 7.2509–7.2516. More particularly, the Panel concluded very clearly in para 7.2514 that 'it is not self-evident that the alleged less favourable treatment of imported biotech products is explained by the foreign origin of these products rather than, for instance, a perceived difference between biotech products and non-biotech products in terms of their safety'.

[8] As discussed in below, recent case law under the Technical Barriers to Trade (TBT) Agreement has further complicated the question of when a detrimental impact on foreign products may constitute 'less favourable treatment' and the degree to which regulatory purposes play a role in that determination.

[9] At least not without recourse to Art XX of the GATT, a possibility explored further below.

name of protecting intellectual property. Indeed, the TRIPS Agreement ultimately seems to imply that the distinction has only a contingent value, capable of yielding in favour of sufficiently powerful interests. As Maskus bitingly summarises the process leading to the TRIPS Agreement:

> [t]hree powerful and easily organized industries (pharmaceuticals, recorded entertainment and software) presciently recognized the opportunity afforded by the Uruguay Round to protect their intellectual property in the future and made IPR a core issue for the United States Trade Representative.[10]

What they got for their efforts was a set of universally applicable minimum standards of intellectual property protection, therefore requiring all Members to ignore the product/process sanitary cordon, at least where intellectual property was at stake. As we have seen elsewhere, hunting down counterfeit goods is not always easy, since it is almost impossible for a non-specialist to distinguish some (good) reproductions from the genuine on the basis of appearance and physical qualities alone.[11] What distinguishes the two instead is something intangible, a matter of production processes that do not follow intellectual property dictates. As well summarised, again by Maskus: '[u]ltimately . . . TRIPS will result in trade sanctions imposed against failures to prevent the use of illegal production processes'.[12]

One can naturally maintain that the protection of intellectual property rights (like competition law) has a greater impact on trade flows and market access than protection of the environment – and much stronger than labour standards (though the strength of this position turns on the degree to which trade is seen as an end in itself).[13] No doubt, this observation weakens the political argument for the inclusion of labour standards among international trade rules,[14] but it cannot change the legal salience of this precedent in terms of the legitimacy of the potential transplant to protect workers' rights. And even if we cleave to the economic logic of this reply, it does not become obvious why distorting free market access for products from all sources to the benefit of one societal interest, namely, the need to

[10] Keith E Maskus, 'Regulatory Standards in the WTO: Comparing Intellectual Property Rights with Competition Policy, Environmental Protection, and Core Labor Standards' (2002) 1(2) *World Trade Review* 135, 137.

[11] See Francis Maupain, 'Is the ILO Effective in Upholding Workers Right? Reflections on the Myanmar Experience' in Philip Alston (ed), *Labour Rights as Human Rights* (Oxford, Oxford University Press, 2005) 85, 133–34; Gabrielle Marceau, 'Trade and Labour' in David Bethlehem and others (eds), *The Oxford Handbook of International Trade Law* (Oxford, Oxford University Press, 2009) 547 n 26; Alain Supiot, *L'esprit de Philadelphie: La justice sociale face au marché total* (Paris, Seuil, 2010) 156–57.

[12] Keith E Maskus, *Regulatory Standards in the WTO*, Peterson Institute for International Economics Working Paper 00-1 (2000), under 'Other Standards Under Consideration'.

[13] ibid 142–44.

[14] Yet it seems only fair to qualify this observation. Certainly, protection of intellectual property has a clear trade dimension. Yet if it took a specific agreement to protect it, that meant that intellectual property could not be caught by the existing categories and rules of the multilateral trade system. In other words, it is difficult to draw out this argument in any legitimate way without admitting at the same time that workers' rights, or at least some of them, also have an important commercial dimension. Yet this is precisely the crux of the problem, and the source of the disagreement.

perpetuate future innovation by rewarding it in the present, could not just as easily justify the protection of the capacities of future generations of workers[15] (including their capacity for innovation!). No doubt, once the focus is expanded beyond the narrow interests of the companies involved, society does have a legitimate interest in protecting inventions in the name of encouraging innovation. From an axiological point of view, however, there is no reason why the social rights of workers, especially those rights enshrined as fundamental, should be any less deserving of protection.[16]

These controversies aside, it seems clear that any obstacles placed in the way of linking trade liberalisation to fundamental rights cannot be a matter of underlying trade principles. Instead, the refusal to put in place such a link is without question a political choice. The arguments in favour of transplantation of fundamental rights of workers are no less strong in terms of principles than those which led to the TRIPS Agreement or otherwise. Yet this point is not enough to tip the balance in favour of performing such a transplant in practice.

B. But Likely to Come with Many Undesirable Consequences in Practice

(i) A Significant Price to Pay in Terms of the Protection Afforded

In terms of level of protection. If the TRIPS precedent seems a powerful foil, sufficient in principle to vindicate the logic of grafting fundamental rights onto the multilateral trade system, it is not clear that the argument can proceed much further than that principle. As we shall see, the possibility of grafting on a clause that extends an obligation to respect fundamental rights to all trading partners, regardless of their ratification of the relevant ILO Conventions, would almost certainly entail some expensive trade-offs. Indeed, it could easily impact the content and level of protection available to workers, even without guaranteeing the gains in the effective level of protection foreshadowed by the asbestos example.

Putting in place a linkage between fundamental rights and multilateral trade rules at the universal level would inevitably involve changing the Marrakesh Agreement establishing the WTO (unless actors were to opt for the 'Hansenne' solution addressed below). This prospect has raised some understandable anxieties. Some observers have stressed, and not without good reason, that the WTO lacks expertise in labour matters, with some even describing it as *particularly* ill-equipped to deal with labour issues.[17] Indeed, that shortcoming seems to have

[15] That is, by prohibiting child labour.

[16] Especially to the extent where they bear on the rights which are the condition for progress towards other rights, they must have at least some relationship with the 'capabilities' concept developed by Amartya Sen. It is thus hard to see why they would represent an inherently less important social concern than encouraging innovation by providing limited rents to inventors. On using Sen's approach to labour law, see Introduction, n 27.

[17] Andrew T Guzman, 'Trade, Labor, Legitimacy' (2003) 91 *California Labor Review* 885, 899.

been precisely acknowledged by the Singapore Declaration's legal hand-off of these issues to the ILO.

On the other hand, jurisdictional expertise is not the most onerous problem. That issue hides a much more fundamental tension between an obligation's level of protection and its voluntary acceptance.

When the ILO's founders took a gamble on achieving social progress by way of voluntary standard-setting, it was less a choice than a dictate of political realities. As detailed in Part I, the dream of proper 'international labour legislation' which would have established a collection of universal, mandatory rules (subject only to a temporary 'opt out' clause) was abandoned because they realised that such a solution might lead to results contrary to the intended objectives, ie to the adoption of a lowest common denominator rather than a universal progressive uplifting of labour rights. Modern proponents of the 'social clause' do not seem to have grappled with how difficult it is to escape from this dilemma. The content of protection which comes out of the long and arduous negotiations in the context of the ILC is not only a function of a tripartite framework where the Workers group provides a driving force, but also depends on the same voluntary character of acceptance that led efforts during the Cold War away from 'ratifiability' and toward 'magisterial' authority. What this means, as we have seen, is that willingness to take a progressive stance in negotiations, from governments and employers both, is directly conditioned on their awareness that governments retain final control over whether they will be subject to the resulting obligations. This goes some way toward explaining why the Cold War years and its attendant ideological competition saw employers and governments of Western countries often vote in favour of progressive solutions which they had no intention tying themselves to at the international level by way of ratification.

At the universal level, therefore, the real risk is that transplanting the rights concerned would offer a dreamed opportunity to redefine the content of those rights and lower the level of protection they offer. Even in the best case scenario where the contents of the hypothetical social clause grafted into the WTO agreements was set by reference to ILO Conventions, the situation would still be welcomed by some as an opportunity to cast off the weight of a 'jurisprudence' established by the ILO supervisory bodies that has not, to put it lightly, been universally accepted as an authoritative interpretation of the relevant Conventions.[18] There is every reason to

[18] Even within the bounds of freedom of association and collective bargaining, it must be remembered in this regard that Conventions Nos 87 and 98 are extremely terse. Contrary to Art 8(1)(d) of the Covenant on Economic, Social and Cultural Rights adopted in 1966, the right to strike is not *expressly* listed but was inferred in the 'jurisprudence' of the Committee on Freedom of Association and Committee of Experts. The terms and limits of the rights exercise resulting from this jurisprudence, including in respect of essential services, is extremely rich and detailed but is increasingly and quite radically being put into question both by the employers and by a number of governments. In fact, the legal status and use of this 'jurisprudence' inside the ILO (and, though the point was made less explicitly, outside it) was the basis of the 'crisis' of the ILO supervisory system seen in the summer of 2012 that saw the Conference's Committee on the Application of Standards unable to complete its supervisory work (see ILO, *Report of the Committee on the Application of Standards* (ILC, 101st Session, 30 May–14 June 2012) paras 134–236). On these issues, see Francis Maupain, 'Une Rolls Royce en mal de révision?

fear that the definitive rejection of this 'jurisprudence' could be an unfortunate side-effect of transplanting the underlying rights into the trade regime.

The various developed-country initiatives to make fundamental rights more binding by tying them to preferential market access under regional, bilateral or multilateral agreements provide ample demonstration that these risks are far from imaginary. The experience of the 'decentralised links', given fuller treatment in Chapter 9, shows that the pressures inherent to reciprocity or, more specifically, in the concessions 'paid' in return for access to the partner's markets has inevitably led the parties with more advanced legislation to knock down the level of their requirements regarding the content or substance of the 'social dimension' in those agreements. And, given that they were introduced within a unilateral framework, the admittedly very progressive standards in the 'conditionalities' provided under the European Generalised Scheme of Preferences (GSP) provide a telling negative case.

In terms of scope ratione personae (with the potential of increasing the dualisation of the economy). The second risk raised by an explicit 'link' is that boosting the effective implementation of workers' fundamental rights might be detrimental to the *scope* of that protection, though admittedly this risk seems less inevitable than the previous one. The realisation of that risk would depend on whether a link was established according to a logic of undistorted ('free') trade applied in existing agreements, or within a framework of 'fair' trade.

In the first case, the link could consist in extending or extrapolating the concept of *dumping*, so that it explicitly covered specified situations or practices where workers' rights were violated or insufficiently protected: for example, trade benefits might be denied to products or services where unequal or oppressive working conditions distort competition and provide an unfair competitive advantage, as a result of either failure to guarantee fundamental rights or exemptions from labour laws (as in export processing zones).[19] If this was the frame used to extend the dumping logic, the scope of protection might end up being limited to workers who contributed to the production of goods and services integrated into international markets.[20] Certainly, this would have much more than a negligible impact, but it should at the same time be borne in mind that the vast majority of workers, especially those working in the informal economy, do not work directly for export. Under a link based on the dumping analogy, this working majority would generally end up

L'efficacité du système de supervision de l'OIT à l'approche de son centenaire' (2010) 3 *Revue générale de droit public* 465, 489 ff.

[19] Strictly speaking, the GATT's dumping provisions do not allow for the application of quantitative restrictions in general, or a ban on imports in particular. Indeed, unlike the retaliatory tariffs that are the general form of the 'enforcement' measures under the GATT, the dumping provisions provide for the application of countervailing duties against the goods being sold 'below cost'. These distinctions have no significant impact on the analysis here, insofar as the measures create similar incentives to change practices only in firms working for export and not in the economy as a whole.

[20] One can certainly argue that subjecting workers to oppressive conditions always contributes to unfair trade advantages: though it may be indirect, oppressive conditions in workplaces not producing for export arguably lower overall costs of living in the country concerned. Yet, if this argument failed to convince the US Trade Representative it is unlikely to perform better vis-à-vis trading partners even less eager to make the relevant concessions.

significantly less well-off than those involved in firms and industries working for export. Even in the absence of any overarching changes in the national legislation applicable to them, those working for export would be able to avail themselves of the 'socially responsible' practices (or at least, commitments) of firms seeking to ensure an adequate share of global export markets.[21] In the well-known example of child labourers, the category of workers both most vulnerable and most often in the mind of supporters of the link, only a very small minority (roughly estimated to be 5 per cent by the ILO)[22] are involved in the manufacture of products for export. From this point of view, a solution of this nature thus largely misses its target.

It is quite conceivable, however, that the link could be designed so that all workers in a country, whether or not they were involved in the production of exported goods and services, could benefit from the guarantee of fundamental rights or the relevant conditions of work. This can be done by drafting a specific agreement stating that, beyond the prevailing conditions in a single firm, Members must have laws guaranteeing those conditions across the workforce. In fact, this is the model followed under the TRIPS Agreement: the measure of compliance is the existence of legislation protecting intellectual property derived from a number of WIPO-based agreements, not the production standards of particular products.[23]

Looked at in another way, this solution is analogous in structure to a proposal advanced by Michel Hansenne, who suggested that ratification of ILO core Conventions (or at least some of them) should be made a condition of WTO membership.[24] As we shall see later on, as much as this solution had a certain undeniable logic, it no longer holds much water, especially since China's accession to the WTO. It would simply raise further complications, not least of which as regards the fate of the ILO's 'jurisprudence', currently inseparable from the ratification of Conventions.

(ii) *And for What Effective Gain in Implementation?*

At least when enacted in the form of a ban on imports, the deterrent power of trade measures is prima facie superior to that of moral suasion or 'mobilisation by shame'. The asbestos prohibition example seems particularly telling in this regard, at least at first glance. While the ILO's Convention No 162 strove only to protect workers against the risks attached to using this product,[25] the WTO, by recognising

[21] For some further consideration of the possibilities and limitations of corporate social responsibility, see Part IV.

[22] ILO, *A Future Without Child Labour: Global Report Under the Follow-up to the ILO Declaration on Fundamental Principles and Rights at Work* (ILC, 90th Session, Geneva, 4–20 June 2002) para 66.

[23] The relevant agreements are listed in Art 1(3) of the Agreement on Trade-Related Aspects of Intellectual Property Rights, Annex 1C to the Agreement establishing the World Trade Organization (signed 15 April 1994, entered into force 1 January 1995).

[24] The suggestion was put forward at the 1995 Copenhagen Summit (Robert Taylor, 'WTO urged to stress labour standards', *Financial Times* (Londo)n, 9 March 1995, 8, stating, however, that 'time is not yet right for including a social clause').

[25] One can hardly deny the credit due to ILO Convention No 162 on Safety in the Use of Asbestos (adopted 24 June 1986, entered into force 16 June 1989) for rallying international attention to a health problem of significant importance which had been largely overlooked up to that point. Under pressure

the legality of measures taken by France under the framework of European regulations to prohibit importation,[26] eliminated its use in one fell swoop.

Yet, as an example, the case is deceptive.[27] First, the case addressed a product which was inherently harmful not only to workers involved in its production, but for the general public as well. Where the potential harms are not inherent in the product but located further 'upstream', the effectiveness and advisability of solving the problem by refusing or limiting market access raises more complex issues. The arguments, pro and con, have been well-rehearsed.[28]

Secondly, and perhaps more importantly, where 'non-dangerous' goods are produced in dangerous conditions, or in *any* conditions contrary to accepted labour standards, the question is whether applying the WTO's existing enforcement mechanism of decentralised and uncoordinated trade measures can effectively address the underlying problem.

At the risk of oversimplifying, two logics can be distinguished which work somewhat at odds in this scenario. First of all, there is the logic of retaliation or compensation for the breach of an obligation. The decentralised logic of the WTO agreements allows each aggrieved trading partner to decide unilaterally whether to turn to the settlement procedures for restitution.[29] Whether an individual country actually does so will depend on an evaluation of their interests, [30] including the potential impact on the relationship with an important trading partner.[31]

from, inter alia, its largest exporter (Canada), the Convention nevertheless settled on a philosophy of risk mitigation and prevention, well indicated by the chosen title, 'Convention Concerning Safety in the Use of Asbestos'. As everyone knows, the approach it proposes has unfortunately not been sufficient to eliminate the underlying risk.

[26] For a quick summary, see *EC – Asbestos* (n 6) para 4.

[27] In this case, the ban was intended to protect the population in the importing country, not to prevent any ongoing risk in the country of production (even though the extent of that risk may have been limited by the decline in effective global demand). Furthermore, the effectiveness of the original decision depended strongly on the compulsory, collective rule adopted by EU Member States invoking the public health exception under Art XX. There was, in other words, no question of Canadian non-compliance with an obligation under the GATT or any other WTO agreement. It should be noted that the Appellate Body simply found that the asbestos products in question were not 'like' other products, rendering the Panel's decision on other issues somewhat moot.

[28] See, eg ILO (Working Party on the Social Dimensions of the Liberalization of International Trade), *Overview of Global Developments and Office Activities Concerning Codes of Conduct, Social Labelling and Other Private Sector Initiatives Addressing Labour Issues* (Governing Body, 273rd Session, Geneva, 27 October–6 November 1998) 129.

[29] If a social clause were in fact to follow the enforcement logic of the subsidies provisions under Art VI of the GATT, countervailing duties could be applied unilaterally by an aggrieved country. This does not affect the analysis, insofar as it would still lie in the hands of individual countries to decide whether to attempt to enforce the labour provisions in the hypothetically-reformed agreement.

[30] This point should not be confused with a related concern about standing. The DSU has been interpreted in a way that gives a very wide scope for countries to bring claims, even where they are not directly targeted by a measure. The concern here is not about whether a country could bring a claim, but about whether any individual country would be *willing* to do so given the potential impacts on their *de facto* trade relationships.

[31] Thus, as much as the concept of MAED (Mutual Assured Economic Destruction) is used to cool fear about the possibility of conflict between the two countries, the factors underlying the relationship (the involvement of US multinationals in China and China's large and growing collection of American debt) would seem to foreclose the possibility of US trade sanctions against China. See, eg Alain Frachon and Daniel Vernet, 'Le grand malentendu' (2012) 35(140) *Commentaire* 1189, 1193.

On the other hand, the logic of implementing fundamental workers' rights is supposed to make their enforcement a question of public order. The credibility of the category would seem to depend on the severity and likelihood of enforcement having some sort of correlation with *the seriousness of the breach*, rather than turning primarily on commercial or strategic interests of particular countries. The capacity of the link to actually establish a 'level playing field' in practice would be severely undermined if enforcement measures were left to the goodwill or discretion of a particular country vis-à-vis specific trading partners, in turn dependent on a complex of ulterior motives, commercial, strategic or otherwise. A link that could undergird a level playing field would require collectively exercised, relatively rational actions.

The case of Myanmar offers an excellent illustration of the underlying tension. The ongoing severity of forced labour practices applied by the army following its (renewed) takeover in the early 1990s could have severely undermined international confidence in the ILO's ability to bring a country to heel on the obligations it had under the relevant Conventions. It was that risk which led the organisation for the first time in its history to put in place enforcement measures under Article 33 of its Constitution.[32] The resulting resolution endorsed by the ILC in June 2000[33] asked all Members (and through them employers and workers) to review their relations with Myanmar, and take 'appropriate measures' to ensure that such relations would not perpetuate or extend the system of forced or compulsory labour whose existence had been established by the Commission of Inquiry. It was, inter alia, by reference to this resolution that the United States Congress justified the 'Burmese Freedom and Democracy Act' passed in July 2003. Unlike actions taken elsewhere, including measures adopted by the European Union, the Act introduced a total embargo on trade with Myanmar. Though the Act had no apparent impact on the prevalence of forced labour in Myanmar at the time, it is perfectly plausible that the marginal impact followed not from some inherent deficiency in trade measures, but rather from the relative isolation of the United States in taking such a drastic step.[34] After all, one can hardly discount the fact that India and China, Myanmar's largest trading partners, both treated the situation as an

[32] The measures were adopted in order to force Myanmar to comply with the conclusions and recommendations of the Commission of Inquiry. The Commission report, released two years earlier, had clearly established serious breaches under Convention No 29. See ILO, *Report of the Commission of Inquiry Appointed under Article 26 of the Constitution of the International Labour Organization to Examine the Observance by Myanmar of the Forced Labour Convention, 1930 (No 29)* (2 July 1998) reproduced in (1998) 81 *ILO Official Bulletin* Series B (Special Supplement).

[33] ILO, Resolution concerning the Measures Recommended by the Governing Body under Article 33 of the ILO Constitution on the Subject of Myanmar (ILC, 88th Session, Geneva, 30 May–15 June 2000).

[34] It can be argued here that their lack of efficacy results from the fact that the trade embargo was implemented in isolation by the United States. However, the attitude of both Japan and the Europeans shows at the same time how completely unrealistic it would have been for the ILO to try to force all its Members to implement sanctions, rather than leaving the details of the measures taken more or less at their discretion. The responses to the episode also had the substantial merit of confirming that, through the combined effects of Art 33 of the ILO Constitution and exceptions in Art XX of GATT, implementing trade measures to punish violations of a ratified Convention is not only legally possible, but difficult to attack on political, as much as on legal, terms.

opportunity to expand bilateral trade and solidify their relationship with the regime then in power.[35]

The next question which arises is whether stronger measures could possibly have been justified. Though it may have been legally possible, a solution which went beyond *permitting* trade sanctions for fundamental rights violations to making those measures *mandatory* seems close to politically unthinkable. At first glance, the broad wording of Article 33 of the ILO Constitution seems to offer the Conference total discretion regarding the nature of the measures it might take itself, or request from Members, to bring a Member into compliance. Sticking to the text of the Article, the Conference could thus theoretically have requested that all Members apply equivalent measures to make the Commission of Inquiry's recommendations effective, rather than the approach they actually take, which was to leave the decision regarding what measures were best suited to achieving the stated purpose to the discretion of each individual country (using an excuse based on the diverse realities of Myanmar's trade relations with each Member). Even though implementing Article 33 only requires a simple majority at the ILC, it would be unrealistic, even in the case of such a politically isolated 'pariah' state,[36] to imagine that a majority might have been cobbled together in favour of a resolution purporting to impose an enforcement action on all Members, without any room for exceptions.

All this seems to confirm conclusions already made about these questions by Bob Hepple.[37] Having shown that the unilateral application of sanctions for the violation of workers' rights is neither desirable in principle nor highly effective in practice, he rightly pointed out that this does not mean that such sanctions 'should be absent from the system of transnational labour regulation. On the contrary persuasion and conciliation will not work unless there is ultimately a sanction that can be invoked'.[38] From this point of view, the solution which follows from Article 33 of the ILO Constitution and the experience of its implementation in the case of Myanmar seems realistic, balanced and judicious.[39] This is particularly so since its implementation requires only a simple majority (almost automatically reached if

[35] According to the cynicism (or candour) of statements made by Myanmar's Minister of Labour to the ILO team which visited to negotiate the role of a proposed 'ILO Liaison Officer' who would review and monitor individual allegations of forced labour, authorities attached no importance to trade measures from Western countries, not only because their markets represented such a small part of the country's trade, but because of a sense that the economic future of the whole world seemed to be taking shape right at Myanmar's borders! See Richard Horsey, *Ending Forced Labour in Myanmar: Engaging a Pariah Regime* (London, Routledge, 2011).

[36] To borrow the title of Richard Horsey's book, ibid.

[37] This is also perfectly consistent with the views expressed by the Commission on International Labour Legislation in 1919, which was keen to devise the procedure in such a way so as 'to avoid the imposition of penalties, except in the last resort, when a State has flagrantly and persistently refused to carry out its obligation under a Convention'. See ILO, 'The Brussels International Financial Conference and Unemployment Subsidies' (September–December 1920) 2(10) *ILO Official Bulletin* 14, 266.

[38] Bob Hepple, *Labour Laws and Global Trade* (Oxford, Hart Publishing, 2005) 274.

[39] Indeed, what can be clearly discerned from the Myanmar experience is that the *threat* of sanctions or, perhaps more accurately, the 'suspended application' of sanctions by the ILO pursuant to the June 2000 resolution proved to be most effective in winning concessions and seeing significant progress. See Maupain, 'Is the ILO Effective' (n 11) 100–16; Horsey, *Ending Forced Labour* (n 35).

workers and employers can come to agreement at the ILC) and it also has the advantage in terms of credibility of not being (directly) influenced by commercial considerations.

C Though Only if it Somehow Ceased to be a Political Dead-End

The question which has plagued the ILO, ever since the end of the Cold War heralded the advent of a globalised market, is in a sense whether history can be rewritten. When one considers that the Havana Conference was attended by only 56 states,[40] there is reason to believe that the opportunity to establish a constitutional 'linkage' was forever lost by those who have since fought most strenuously to restore it.[41] Strident resistance continues to greet any attempt to put the issue back on the agenda. Indeed, transplanting such an obligation into the WTO system would be all the more inconceivable, in that it would not only be politically unacceptable but could also spoil the WTO's dispute resolution mechanism, vindicating those worried that using the Dispute Settlement Understanding (DSU) as a 'jack of all trades' to resolve inevitably controversial social and environmental issues would mean losing the effectiveness that makes it so attractive.[42] For the time being, everyone seems equally alive to the fact that insisting on a social clause would achieve little more than driving a final nail into the coffin of the Doha Round (or doom any future negotiations should some miracle allow Doha to succeed).

The procedural difficulty which immediately comes to mind is that any change in the WTO agreements would require consensus among a membership which now includes almost every member of the United Nations. But this procedural question can also be phrased as a substantial one: what kind of *quid pro quo* would have to

[40] In fact, the Final Act of the Conference which brought the Havana Charter into existence was signed by only 53 countries.

[41] Keeping in mind that it was the US failure to ratify the Havana Charter which ultimately doomed the ITO. On the reasons for this failure, see Christophe Bezou, *La clause sociale: la négociation internationale menée par l'OIT* (Paris, ESKA, 2008).

[42] See, inter alia, Guzman, 'Trade, Labor, Legitimacy' (n 17). Between these paths laid out in this chapter – extrapolating from existing obligations and transplanting external duties – there is a middle path offered which might attempt to exploit other options which already exist in the agreements, including Art XXIII on the nullification and impairment of benefits. These provisions could be invoked either in the case of fundamental rights violations, following the reasoning in the 2008 Declaration characterising such violations as creating an illegitimate comparative advantage, or in any case where a country tries to improve its competitive position by bringing in legislative amendments that reduce existing protections for its workers. As we will discuss further in Chapter 9, both of these possibilities are provided for in certain bilateral and multilateral trade agreements. Nothing furthermore prevents them from being given universal scope. One can also imagine creating a link which, rather than cleaving to the logic of public policy exceptions, would instead provide an organising principle of international public order, setting minimum social standards of behaviour to be admitted as part of the 'club'. This was essentially the logic offered by Hansenne when he suggested that the ratification of the fundamental conditions should be a precondition of WTO membership (see Taylor, 'WTO urged' (n 24)). Introducing such a membership condition moving forward would, however, be rather difficult, given that the club in question has already been constituted.

be on offer before a transplant became acceptable to the large cohort of countries who have consistently expressed hostility to its fundamental principle? To put the measure of the challenge in perspective, would France, or any EU Member State for that matter, be willing to liberalise its agricultural markets in return for seeing some fundamental rights protections annexed to the overall WTO deal?

The difficulty of making such a bargain explains why most ILO Members balk at turning in the cards they have already been dealt. One might even say they prefer the flexibility of the market-access commitments they have already made, because it allows them to pursue the social dimension of trade liberalisation through the side door – by way of bilateral, multilateral or regional agreements that relate to their specific interests. However, as we shall see in Chapter 9, this way of approaching the problem quickly comes up against its own limitations.

II. Reading Between the Lines: From a Formal Marriage of Trade Rules and Labour Rights to a Possible (Clandestine) Liaison?

The multiple possibilities of developing a legally-founded social dimension on the basis of the Preambles, exceptions and other legal crevices of the multilateral trading system have been the subject of an abundant literature. These possibilities are highlighted by the WTO Secretariat and its Director-General, who have understandably seen the development of the social dimension by way of a grafted social clause as a political 'hot potato'. Thus, a balanced overview of the subject from Gabrielle Marceau, a senior advisor at the WTO, underlined that '[t]he WTO system appears to be receptive to good faith and non-protectionist labour considerations within several trade measures'.[43] Pointing out how the Preamble 'gives colour, texture and shading to the rights and obligations of Members under the WTO agreement', she has highlighted its potential to ground a progressive interpretation of WTO provisions.[44] These optimistic jurisprudential perspectives, as real as they may be, cannot help but leave some lingering doubts.[45]

For the WTO, such musings help put to rest a perennial issue, one that has sown disorder and contributed indirectly to disaffection not only with ongoing negotiations but with the entire system. Indeed, relying on a hypothetical and somewhat remote jurisprudential evolution can hardly remedy the widespread legitimacy

[43] Marceau, 'Trade and Labour' (n 11) 542.

[44] ibid 543, quoting from and relying on *United States – Import Prohibition of Certain Shrimp and Shrimp Products*, WTO Appellate Body Report (6 November 1998) WT/DSF8/AB/R, paras 153–55 ('*United States – Shrimp/Turtle*').

[45] Indeed, such readings appear sometimes much like the homage vice pays to virtue: do they not amount to admitting, at least implicitly, that it is legitimate to apply the tool which allows restriction on market access for purposes other than trade expansion, thereby recognising in the final account that trade liberalisation is not the end in itself?

deficit the multilateral trading system seems to have earned by almost totally ignoring the social dimension[46] since the failure of the Havana Charter.[47] For that matter, even if it were to come to pass, a favourable evolution in the DSU's orientation to social concerns could only go so far toward protecting labour rights, unless it was able to take advantage of an external 'prosthesis' of expertise which might be provided by the ILO.

This logic holds for each of three possible directions for legal evolution. The first direction is offered by the exceptions under Article XX of the GATT, which may allow for specific limitations on market access for products from a country violating obligations to protect fundamental rights; the second possibility lies along the pathway opened up by Article XXIII of the GATT, which extends to every WTO Member the right to bring a 'representation' challenging a 'situation' where a country's failure to realise relevant labour rights impairs benefits under the agreement, even (hypothetically) where those impairments do not otherwise violate GATT obligations. Finally, the third direction would be to explore the narrow path of consumer perception open by the widening breach into the product/process distinction. The implications of these three scenarios will be considered in turn.

A. GATT Article XX Exceptions: A Possible Auxiliary Force to the Rescue of Compliance with Ratified ILO Conventions?

Article XX of the GATT, and sections (a)[48] and (b)[49] in particular (see Box 8.1), have afforded domestic authorities a broad margin of freedom. Indeed, as put by

[46] Exacerbated to some extent by the sluggish opening of the environmental dimension.

[47] Guzman, 'Trade, Labor, Legitimacy' (n 17) 888.

[48] Article XX(a) establishes that efforts to protect 'public morality' can justify a limitation on the application of WTO rules. Some authors have suggested that only 'inherently immoral' products, such as child pornography, should be taken into account by this provision, to the exclusion of any consideration of conditions of production. The immorality of products which have been manufactured using (exploitative) child labour is in this regard not axiomatic, yet the risk aimed at by the measure which is claimed to interfere with the objective of, for example, the prohibition on child labour, is located less in the product as such than in the process of its production. It should, however, be noted that nothing in WTO law appears to limit the sovereign discretion of Members to define the content of public morality or the appropriate level of protection to implement. See, eg David Luff, *Le droit de l'Organisation Mondiale du Commerce: Analyse critique* (Brussels, Bruylant, 2004) 176–77; *United States – Gambling*, WTO Panel Report (20 April 2005) WT/DS285/R (affirmed in *United States – Gambling*, WTO Appellate Body Report (20 April 2005) WT/DS285/AB/R, para 6.461), addressing a similar exception provided for in Art XIV of the GATS; *China – Measures Affecting Trading Rights and Distribution Services for Certain Publications and Audiovisual Entertainment Products*, WTO Panel Report (19 January 2010) WT/DS363/R, para 7.759; *Korea – Measures Affecting Imports of Fresh Beef, Chilled and Frozen*, WTO Appellate Body Report (10 January 2011) WT/DS161/AB/R, WT/DS169/AB/R, para 176 ('*Korea – Various Measures on Beef*'); *EC – Asbestos* (n 6) para 168. It is then for the Member invoking the public morality exception to prove the legitimacy of the objective. This might be demonstrated, regarding workers' rights, either by invoking the ILO Conventions which it has ratified or, if applicable, by invoking its responsibilities as a Member of the ILO pursuant to the 1998 Declaration on Fundamental Principles and Rights at Work.

[49] In the same way, Art XX(b) could be invoked to the extent that it is possible to establish a causal link between a violation of fundamental rights at work and specific harms or risks to workers' lives or

the Appellate Body in *US – Shrimp/Turtle,* the sections allow measures which abrogate from substantial provisions of the GATT wherever 'the domestic policies embodied in such measures have been recognized as important and legitimate in character'.[50] The exhaustive literature analysing the meaning and extent of these exceptions means that the explorations here can cleave to the most salient dimensions.

Box 8.1 GATT Article XX: General Exceptions

Subject to the requirement that such measures are not applied in a manner which would constitute a means of arbitrary or unjustifiable discrimination between countries where the same conditions prevail, or a disguised restriction on international trade, nothing in this Agreement shall be construed to prevent the adoption or enforcement by any Contracting Party of measures:

(a) necessary to protect public morals;
(b) necessary to protect human, animal or plant life or health;
(c) relating to the importations or exportations of gold or silver;
(d) necessary to secure compliance with laws or regulations which are not inconsistent with the provisions of this Agreement, including those relating to customs enforcement, the enforcement of monopolies operated under paragraph 4 of Article II and Article XVII, the protection of patents, trade marks and copyrights, and the prevention of deceptive practices;
(e) relating to the products of prison labour;
(f) imposed for the protection of national treasures of artistic, historic or archaeological value;
(g) relating to the conservation of exhaustible natural resources if such measures are made effective in conjunction with restrictions on domestic production or consumption;
(h) undertaken in pursuance of obligations under any intergovernmental commodity agreement which conforms to criteria submitted to the Contracting Parties and not disapproved by them or which is itself so submitted and not so disapproved[51];
(i) involving restrictions on exports of domestic materials necessary to ensure essential quantities of such materials to a domestic processing industry during periods when the domestic price of such materials is held below the world price as part of a governmental stabilization plan;

health. While it is easy to imagine establishing such a connection, it remains inconceivable that the violation of fundamental rights in the territory of the exporting country can affect the health and lives of persons in the territory of the importing country.

[50] *United States – Shrimp/Turtle* (n 44) para 121.

[51] The original text presents an asterisk referring to/explaining this exception

Provided that such restrictions shall not operate to increase the exports of or the protection afforded to such domestic industry, and shall not depart from the provisions of this Agreement relating to non-discrimination;

(j) essential to the acquisition or distribution of products in general or local short supply; Provided that any such measures shall be consistent with the principle that all Contracting Parties are entitled to an equitable share of the international supply of such products, and that any such measures, which are inconsistent with the other provisions of the Agreement shall be discontinued as soon as the conditions giving rise to them have ceased to exist. The Contracting Parties shall review the need for this sub-paragraph not later than 30 June 1960.

Despite the breadth of policy allowed for under the exceptions, their application is strictly circumscribed by criteria whose purpose is to balance each Member's right to protect essential non-commercial interests against the rights of other Members to reap the rewards they have negotiated under the agreement as a whole. The overall aim is to ensure that whenever the exceptions are relied upon, they are justified on the basis of precise criteria, rather than being used as a back door to usher in illegitimate trade advantages under the cover of moral considerations, public health concerns, environmental objectives or any other reason.

Proving the legitimacy of an exception therefore requires a State to run a gauntlet of legal tests. Is the moral (or public health) objective real? Are the measures taken truly necessary and proportionate to the intended goal,[52] taking into account the barriers that they per hypothesis will set up against the free movement of goods and products?[53] Do they pass an overall smell-test of being both created and implemented in 'good faith'?[54] Most importantly for our purposes, does the measure in essence export internal public morality concerns, ie does it constitute

[52] *Korea – Various Measures on Beef* (n 48) paras 152–85.

[53] The case of *Brazil – Retreaded Tyre* once again demonstrated that the necessity of even a highly restrictive trade measure may be allowed if it pursues an important interest or value, and makes a material contribution to the achievement of this important goal. The necessity test is determined on a case-by-case basis. *Brazil – Measures Affecting Imports of Retreaded Tyres*, WTO Appellate Body Report (17 December 2007) WT/DS332/AB/R

[54] This is the noted aim of Art XX's introductory paragraph: guarding against abusive application of measures which seem to justify a violation of GATT objectives by reference to one of the legitimate aims listed in the paragraphs of Art XX. The analysis of whether the application of a measure results in arbitrary or unjustifiable discrimination is supposed to centre on the cause of discrimination, ie the rationale advanced to justify its existence. Indeed, in the *US – Shrimp/Turtle* affair, the Appellate Body laid down a condition of flexibility in implementation. A Member invoking an Art XX exception has to demonstrate that the application of its measure does not discriminate or that the resulting discrimination is neither arbitrary nor unjustifiable. *United States – Shrimp/Turtle* (n 44) paras 158–60.

extraterritorial application[55] of considerations that are legitimate only in the domestic sphere?[56]

Without going into a detailed analysis of each of these conditions, a quick summary might be that a Member hoping to rely on an exception to justify restrictions or a full ban on market access for manufactured products will find it virtually impossible to meet these conditions without relying on some third party authority. In most cases, in this regard, the threat posed to the moral values or to the 'standards of right and wrong conduct maintained by or on behalf of a community or nation'[57] is not immediately manifest in the character or external appearance of a product (though this may be the case for pornographic materials,[58] drugs, foods forbidden by religious or moral standards, or even substances hazardous to health, such as asbestos). It is not too much of a stretch to make the same point about services, even those offering online access to gambling.

The European ban on products derived from the seal hunt,[59] motivated by the objective aim of protecting animal welfare as much by the subjective reactions of the European public to the unavoidable brutalities of the slaughter, effectively illustrates the difficulty.[60] Certainly, such a measure can claim a legitimate connection to public morality.[61] With changing attitudes, it seems legitimate in this regard to extend the ambit of such considerations to all forms of cruelty (starting with the most gratuitous) when exercised against living beings other than humans.

[55] The legitimacy of a country using its domestic market in an attempt to achieve goals abroad that have no instrumental effect within its own borders had been controversial under the GATT; while such 'extraterritorial' activities were explicitly endorsed under the TBT Agreement in *United States – Measures Concerning the Importation, Marketing and Sale of Tuna and Tuna Products,* WTO Appellate Body Report (12 June 2012) WT/DS381/AB/R ('*United States – Tuna II*') as discussed further below, it is not clear to what degree this TBT jurisprudence will 'cross-pollinate' back into adjudication of the GATT's exceptions. Much harder to overcome will be the clear position taken by the WTO Appellate Body in *US – Shrimp/Turtle*, that the attempt to unilaterally impose a single regulatory model, standard of practice or policy approach on importing countries constitutes 'unjustifiable discrimination' under the chapeau of Art XX (*United States – Shrimp/Turtle* (n 44) paras 161–63).

[56] A short exposition of these arguments is made in Douglas A Kysar, 'Preferences for Processes: The Process / Product Distinction and the Regulation of Consumer Choice' (2004) 118 *Harvard Law Review* 525, 596–97.

[57] Quoted approvingly from the *Shorter Oxford English Dictionary* by the WTO Appellate Body in *US – Gambling* (n 48) para 296.

[58] See Kysar, 'Preferences for Processes' (n 55) 567, relying on Robert Howse, 'The World Trade Organization and the Protection of Workers' Rights' (1999) 3 *Journal of Small and Emerging Business Law* 131, 143–44.

[59] European Parliament and Council Regulation (EC) 1007/2009 of 16 September 2009 on trade in seal products [2009] OJ L286 bans the marketing of seal products within the European Union, with the exception of products derived from 'hunts traditionally conducted by Inuit and other indigenous communities and [which] contribute to their subsistence' or resulting from non-profit hunting regulated by national law conducted for the sole purpose of sustainably managing marine resources. A WTO Panel was composed in October 2012 to address the justifiability of the ban.

[60] For an overview of the European legislative response to the seal hunt, see Nicolas Fairise, L'exception de moralité publique dans les accords de l'OMC et son application dans le différend canado-européen sur la chasse au phoque (Master's thesis, Université de Montreal, 2010) 56–73.

[61] ibid 81–85. For a robust argument in favour of the justification of the European policy under the WTO agreement, see Robert Howse and Joanna Langille, 'Permitting Pluralism: The Seal Products Dispute and Why the WTO Should Accept Trade Restrictions Justified by Noninstrumental Moral Values' (2012) 27(2) *Yale Journal of International Law* 367.

From this starting point, it would seem that the path is wide open for the application of this public morals exception to the protection of workers. Indeed, why would workers, especially children, not be entitled to at least as much empathy as seals receive from consumers and the general public? Do workers exposed to asbestos during its removal not deserve just as much compassion as sea mammals, no matter how cute they may appear in photos?

There is, however, a twofold difference between the two cases, touching first of all on the materiality of the link between the product and the claimed moral harm, and secondly on the 'necessity' of the measure put in place to address that harm.

When it comes to the seal hunt, one argument that may help justify the ban (though one disputed by Canada) is that the product is inherently inseparable from the cruelty involved, inasmuch as the seals have to give their lives for the products to be made.[62] The norms and standards of a given community might therefore consider the purchase of the resulting products as intrinsically immoral, no less than, for example, pornography. In such a case, it is absurd to argue that the embargo or boycott fails to pass the test of necessity: no question, it prevents consumers from becoming moral accomplices to the impugned behaviour, but it also contributes to a total reduction in the number of victims, if not eradicating the practice itself.

The same simply cannot be said of products resulting from child labour or forced labour (or even worker exposure to asbestos at some stages of production) except to the degree that the immoral or dangerous practice is somehow a *sine qua non* of making the product in question. Supposing it was even possible to identify the subset of products made by children, there is a real risk that a ban might assuage consumer conscience without significantly impacting on the scale of the reprehensible practice, because it might simply allow production that involves the impugned practice to consolidate and expand toward internal markets.[63] Canadian markets simply cannot make up for reduced global demand in seal products; yet a country's production *can* be reorganised so that an impugned 'process' occurs more in sectors and firms bound for internal production.[64] One would, in such a situation, be led to conclude that for products or services that cannot be regarded as inherently immoral, a truly effective ban should not target goods or services per se, but legislation violating the standards in question.[65] However, such logic in

[62] Opponents of the hunt claim it is simply impossible to put in place less cruel (ie quick and painless) slaughter practices, because of the extreme conditions under which the hunt takes place. This statement is, however, disputed by producer countries who claim to authorise only technically 'humane' techniques backed up by scientific studies.

[63] This is above and beyond the oft-deployed argument that eliminating child labour can harm children and their families by removing an important source of income. *cf* Nicholas Kristof, 'Dreaming of sweatshops', *International Herald Tribune* (Paris), 5 January 2009 (arguing that labour standards can take work away from people who would prefer jobs with poor standards to no job at all).

[64] Indeed, the fact that, as previously noted, only 5 per cent of global production involving child labour makes its way into international markets indicates that many economies have already adapted in this way.

[65] Without prejudice to the potential case of practices which violate legislation that is otherwise compliant with the ethical considerations in question.

turn runs into a major obstacle, if not an outright contradiction: it would amount to the recognition that one country can validly impose a legislative norm on another.[66] Such a step would not only be contrary to existing trade disciplines, but would also undercut the voluntary character of ILO Conventions (including in the case of child labour and the fight against exposure to asbestos).[67]

Overall, this suggests that when a violation is not obvious or intrinsic to the nature or characteristic of a product, an objective demonstration would be needed to show that the public morality standard has in fact been violated (or not). This means two things: first, the standard of assessment must be a shared determination, not left to the subjective judgement each country may have of what is needed to pursue the moral ends in question; next, the constitutive facts of the moral violation must be open to objective determination (the violation can hardly be established by the country relying on the exception; by assumption, those facts are beyond their jurisdiction). This latter point probably provides part of the explanation for the failure of an amendment proposed during the preparations leading to Convention No. 105 on forced labour. While the amendment would have added a prohibition on international trade in products of forced labour to the Convention text, there was little clarity about how the existence of impugned practices might be objectively determined[68] (see Box 8.2).

Box 8.2 A reversible link? Putting a 'commercial clause' into an international labour Convention

Given the difficulty of introducing social clauses into the trade regime, might it be conceivable, vice versa, to introduce commercial clauses into ILO Conventions? Such a provision would authorise any State which had ratified the relevant Convention to apply a trade embargo to products representing a danger to health (for those who produce or those who use them) or which have otherwise been manufactured contrary to substantial obligations under the Convention.

Legally speaking, such a prospect seems well-grounded. During the preparatory work on Convention No 105 on the Abolition of Forced Labour (1957), an amendment to the draft was proposed which would have pursued exactly

[66] Though, as already mentioned, the applicability of recent TBT case law to GATT adjudication is up in the air; one of the clearest lessons to be drawn from *United States – Tuna II* (n 54) would seem to be the difficulty of applying an extraterritorial *policy goal*, which the WTO Appellate Body accepted, without also forcing other countries to adopt a unilateral *policy practice*, which the Appellate Body has had a hard time seeing as 'even-handed' (for the purposes of the TBT Agreement) or as 'justifiable' (under the chapeau of Art XX of the GATT).

[67] This is, besides, why the 2006 ILC resolution on asbestos provided that 'Asbestos Convention, 1986 (No 162), should not be used to provide a justification for, or endorsement of, the continued use of asbestos' (ILO, Resolution Concerning Asbestos (ILC, 95th Session, 31 May–16 June 2006) 47–56).

[68] See in this regard the proposals from the United States Government delegate at the ILC (ILO, Provisional Record: Appendix IX (ILC, 39th Session, 6–28 June 1956) 746.

this line of reasoning. Nor was that proposal explicitly rejected or voted down: the method of its introduction led it to languish in procedural limbo.

One challenge confronting such an approach would be deciding how to apply the clause vis-à-vis non-ratifying countries, where ILO constitutional procedures would provide no clear method to establish the existence of a violation. This difficulty disappears, however, if we allow for the heart of the matter, ie the determination of a violation, to be referred to a court in the ratifying country. Such is the case of merchant ships which do not meet certain safety standards under Convention No 147 of 1986, or the relevant standards established by the Maritime Labour Convention of 2006. Thus, a state where a ship is docked has the competence, after inspection, to take appropriate measures to prevent that ship from sailing again until the problem is rectified, whether or not the flag state has ratified the Convention.[69]

In light of the twin needs to 'avoid dualisation' and 'make an objective determination' of the existence of a violation, it is hard to see how national governments could take advantage of an Article XX exception without relying, directly or indirectly, on an external authority like the ILO.[70] The Myanmar/forced labour episode provides an enlightening negative case. First of all, as a matter of facts on the ground, Myanmar's violations of Convention No 29 had already been clearly established by the Commission of Inquiry, and had not been contested by way of the procedures set out in Article 29.2 of the ILO Constitution.[71] Just as importantly, however, as was highlighted in the document upon which the Governing Body would decide to set proceedings in motion under Article 33, the violation of these rights by its nature and magnitude, 'shocked the conscience'.[72] In June 2000, the International Labour Conference adopted a resolution under Article 33[73] inviting ILO Members to take appropriate action to force Myanmar to fulfil its obligations under Convention No 29. And it was, inter alia, on that basis that the United States Congress decided three years later to place a full embargo on Burmese imports.[74]

[69] Specifically, under Arts V(4) and V(6).

[70] This dimension is glossed over somewhat in the analysis of Howse and Genser (Robert Howse and Jared Genser, 'Are EU Trade Sanctions on Burma Compatible with WTO Law?' (2008) 29(2) *Michigan Journal of International Law* 165).

[71] Article 29(2) allows a country to contest the findings of a Commission of Inquiry before the International Court of Justice.

[72] Strictly speaking, the resolution initiating enforcement procedures under Art 33 of the Constitution with respect to Myanmar stated that the continuing failure to address the situation described by the Commission of Inquiry 'inspired . . . disapproval . . . in everyone's conscience' (ILO, Measures, Including Action under Article 33 of the Constitution of the International Labour Organization, to Secure Compliance by the Government of Myanmar with the Recommendations of the Commission of Inquiry Established to Examine the Observance of the Forced Labour Convention, 1930 (No 29) (Governing Body, 277th Session, Geneva, March 2000).

[73] Maupain, 'Is the ILO Effective' (n 11).

[74] See above.

Despite the turmoil it caused among some of Myanmar's neighbours and the doubts expressed by some experts regarding compatibility of the US law with Article III of the GATT,[75] the reluctance of the most interested party – Myanmar itself – to challenge the US legislation before the Dispute Settlement Body (DSB) speaks volumes about the legitimacy the embargo derived from the ILO's authorisation. [76]

There is also a more general take-away from this episode: insofar as it refers to an ability to impose trade sanctions for violations of an international labour Convention, *a social clause already exists*, without the need for a specific provision endorsing it.

However, it must be admitted that such an approach has a limited ambit. Putting it into action requires satisfying numerous preconditions, each more onerous than the last. It presupposes, of course, the ratification of the relevant instrument by the State in question; that a violation has been found by a Commission of Inquiry at the end of the drawn-out complaints procedure under Article 26; that any challenge brought before the International Court of Justice (ICJ) in accordance with Article 29.2 has been resolved; and finally, that a decision under Article 33 to assure the Member's compliance with its obligations has been referred by the Governing Body to, and then passed by, the ILC.

And yet, among several examples of undisputed breaches found through the complaints process (the only procedure which can properly make a legal determination of such a violation), Myanmar provides the sole example where the ILO pursued the full extent of the constitutional consequences from such a finding.

The application of Article 33 also has somewhat ironic consequences: it leads, in effect, to the application of a sort of 'double jeopardy' for ratifying countries compared to those which spare themselves such attention simply by choosing not to ratify in the first place. The latter group notably includes the United States, certainly at the head of the pack on these issues when it comes to rhetorical fervour, but hardly beyond reproach as a matter of its own law and practice, especially on freedom of association.[77]

Thus, even if jurisprudence evolved to make reliance on the Article XX exceptions less difficult, two snags would remain: (i) the approach would still offer no obvious pathway to act against countries that have not ratified the relevant Conventions; and (ii) it would only marginally increases coercive capacities vis-à-vis those countries which had ratified.

[75] See Christine Kaufmann, *Globalisation and Labour Rights: The Conflict Between Core Labour Rights and International Economic Law* (Oxford, Oxford University Press, 2007) 139.

[76] As noted in Howse and Genser, 'EU Trade Sanctions' (n 69) 178.

[77] Lance Compa has provided a useful summary of problems with the situation of freedom of association in the United States. One conclusion of his analysis seems to be that the situation for workers is more likely to improve if association and bargaining rights are seen in terms of 'human rights' rather than from the angle of 'enabling rights' (Lance Compa, 'Workers' Freedom of Association in the United States: The Gap between Ideals and Practice' in James A Gross (ed), *Workers' Rights as Human Rights* (Ithaca, Cornell University Press, 2006) 23).

This conclusion, however, does not close the book on possible liaisons and synergies between the ILO and WTO systems. Indeed, they simply represent the way a State can respond to a situation occurring *beyond its borders* by taking actions which would otherwise be in conflict with WTO obligations. Yet there is another possibility for action: to respond to the material consequences such a situation might represent for its *internal* affairs, by way of GATT Article XXIII.

B. GATT Article XXIII: A Path Worth Re-exploring?

Given the current state of the law, it appears that the violation of workers' rights by a WTO Member, and especially the violation of fundamental rights, does not constitute a failure to comply with any enumerated obligation under WTO agreements. Moreover, we have just seen that it is difficult for a Member to rely on the exceptions to the multilateral trade rules to justify labour-based trade restrictions, unless the situation or breach it is responding to has been objectively established or verified through an internationally recognised procedure. The GATT and the GATS, however, theoretically offer another option to address inadequate labour rights protection in other countries, even where such a 'situation' does not otherwise constitute a violation of an explicit obligation under the covered agreement. Under GATT Article XXIII (see Box 8.3), this procedural avenue opens whenever a Member country frustrates another Member's legitimate expectations regarding the potential benefits of WTO membership or impairs one of the agreement's underlying objectives.

Box 8.3 GATT Article XXIII: Nullification or Impairment

1. If any Contracting Party should consider that any benefit accruing to it directly or indirectly under this Agreement is being nullified or impaired or that the attainment of any objective of the Agreement is being impeded as the result of:

(a) the failure of another Contracting Party to carry out its obligations under this Agreement, or
(b) the application by another Contracting Party of any measure, whether or not it conflicts with the provisions of this Agreement, or
(c) the existence of any other situation,

the Contracting Party may, with a view to the satisfactory adjustment of the matter, make written representations or proposals to the other Contracting Party or Parties which it considers to be concerned. Any Contracting Party thus approached shall give sympathetic consideration to the representations or proposals made to it.

> 2. If no satisfactory adjustment is effected between the Contracting Parties concerned within a reasonable time, or if the difficulty is of the type described in paragraph 1(c) of this Article, the matter may be referred to the Contracting Parties. The Contracting Parties shall promptly investigate any matter so referred to them and shall make appropriate recommendations to the Contracting Parties which they consider to be concerned, or give a ruling on the matter, as appropriate. The Contracting Parties may consult with Contracting Parties, with the Economic and Social Council of the United Nations and with any appropriate inter-governmental organization in cases where they consider such consultation necessary. If the Contracting Parties consider that the circumstances are serious enough to justify such action, they may authorize a Contracting Party or Parties to suspend the application to any other Contracting Party or Parties of such concessions or other obligations under this Agreement as they determine to be appropriate in the circumstances. If the application to any Contracting Party of any concession or other obligation is in fact suspended, that Contracting Party shall then be free, not later than sixty days after such action is taken, to give written notice to the Executive Secretary to the Contracting Parties of its intention to withdraw from this Agreement and such withdrawal shall take effect upon the sixtieth day following the day on which such notice is received by him.

The idea that the failure to respect workers' rights would constitute the type of 'situation' contemplated by this provision is hardly a novel one. The point was raised repeatedly as far back as the early 1950s by those, including the United States, who felt that 'the existence of unfair labour conditions, particularly in production for export, would be a situation justifying recourse to Article XXIII'[78] and moreover that '[t]rade based on denial of worker rights and artificially low labour standards . . . runs counter to the GATT objective of raising standards of living'.[79] These claims, however, were never given effect.[80]

Some of the developments in the intervening years, in particular the adoption of the Social Justice Declaration in 2008, may slightly shift the perspective, and bolster the case for using this procedure to deal with a country that is seeking to acquire a comparative advantage either by (i) infringing fundamental rights at work; or (ii) revising its labour and welfare laws downward.

(i) In a 'Situation' of Non-Compliance with Fundamental Labour Rights by a State Not Bound by a Relevant Convention

As supplemented and clarified by the 2008 Declaration, the 1998 Declaration highlights three important aspects of fundamental rights: (i) they have a

[78] GATT Special Committee on Agenda and Intersessional Business, *Report on the Accession of Japan* (13 February 1953) GATT doc L/76, para 12.

[79] GATT, *Preparatory Committee: Worker Rights* (25 June 1986) GATT doc. PrepCom(86)W/43, 2.

[80] Laurence Dubin, *La protection des normes sociales dans les échanges internationaux* (Presses Universitaires d'Aix-Marseille, 2003) 221–22.

'particular significance' as 'enabling rights' that are necessary (if not sufficient) to assert and vindicate other rights at work; (ii) they must be respected by all ILO Members, whether or not they have ratified the relevant Conventions; and (iii) their violation can in no case be invoked as the basis of a legitimate comparative advantage.

Measures which effectively prevent workers from claiming fair compensation for their contribution to increasing prosperity seems to fit exactly within the framework provided by Article XXIII. After all, such measures would seem to impair a WTO objective, by denying these workers the Preamble's promise of 'raising [their] standard of living'. More than this, however, the fact that such a situation represents an injury first and foremost to workers in the country failing to protect their rights does not prevent the expectations of workers in other countries from being frustrated as well, insofar as the practice provides the guilty country an illegitimate competitive advantage.

From there, the use of the 'non-violation complaints' mechanism could offer two potential advantages from the ILO point of view. The first is that it would allow proceedings to be brought against any State, even those which had not ratified the relevant international Convention.[81] The second would be to establish a link between the dispute settlement mechanism and the ILO, by way of a back door referral[82] relying on Article XXIII:2 of the GATT and Article 13 of the Dispute Settlement Understanding.[83] Admittedly, however, the path leading in this direction is fraught with pitfalls, for the WTO and the ILO both.

[81] A state might also decide to take *unilateral* action against what they perceive to be a violation of fundamental rights, or of 'internationally recognised workers' rights', but which were not necessarily claimed to violate an ILO fundamental Convention, because they see non-compliance as an unfair distortion of competition. In the last 10 years, the United States has considered two such proposals put forward by the AFL-CIO, aimed at China's alleged failure to comply with fundamental labour rights under s 301 of the Trade Act of 1974. In the first of these cases, measures were seriously considered but the request was ultimately refused, not on the basis that the underlying claims were unjustified but, according to the United States Trade Representative, because they were undesirable: 'initiation of an investigation would not be effective in addressing the acts, policies, and practices raised in the petition' but, given China's steady progress in this area, 'initiation would instead hamper those efforts' (United States Trade Representative, Petition under Section 302 on Workers' Rights in China; Decision Not to Initiate Investigation (11 May 2004).

It is true that the legality of such measures within the WTO regime could be questioned in light of earlier case law on s 301 (Gabrielle Marceau, 'WTO Dispute Settlement and Human Rights' (2002) 13 *European Journal of International Law* 756, 760). But challenging such measures on the basis of this jurisprudence could only call into question their validity under the Dispute Settlement Understanding (Understanding on Rules and Procedures Governing the Settlement of Disputes, Annex II to the WTO Agreement (signed 15 April 1994, entered into force 1 January 1995) (DSU)) ironically leaving their permissibility under substantial WTO doctrine an open question. The best-case scenario of a challenge to such unilateral measures would amount, more or less, to endorsement of non-transparent unilateralism. Basing a complaint on Art XXIII(c), on the other hand, would have the advantage of allowing direct multilateral resolution of the underlying issues.

[82] Unlike the 'preliminary ruling' proposed by President Sarkozy in his 2009 speech to the ILC (ILO, Address, Mr Nicolas Sarkozy, President of the French Republic (ILC 98th Session, 11th Sitting, Geneva, 15 June 2009)), which would be impossible in the absence of procedural amendments (highly unlikely given the current progress of negotiations) to the existing WTO framework.

[83] Hepple, *Labour Laws* (n 38) 149.

On the WTO side, the key challenge would lie in finding a procedural solution permitting a Panel, where a claimed issue of non-compliance with core labour standards seemed to make it necessary, to refer the underlying determination to the ILO.[84] The Appellate Body has emphasised that the final decision on procedural questions are to be resolved by the Panel itself, subject only to an obligation to provide legal certainty, a duty to consult the parties, and a general responsibility to find a balance between efficiency and thoroughness.[85] Despite such leeway, were a complainant to suggest during a preliminary consultation that the existence of an alleged violation of core labour standards should be referred to the ILO, their claim could easily fall victim to the demonstrated tendency for Panels to retain control of such interpretative decisions.[86] That being said, the specific context of a question on core labour standards would certainly aid a country in pressing their proposal for a reference to the ILO.[87] And, to some extent, the 2008 Declaration further clears the path toward this procedural option.[88]

A symmetrical difficulty arises on the ILO side. Except in the case of complaints concerning freedom of association, the ILO can only avail itself of internal fact-finding procedures in relation to a country when it has ratified the relevant Conventions. This difficulty is not necessarily insurmountable. A quick historical survey reveals notable precedents, including the procedure of the Fact-Finding and Conciliation Commission on Freedom of Association (FFCC), which makes

[84] A departure of this sort from 'ordinary' procedure would be entirely consistent with the provisions of the DSU as a whole. While a default procedure is provided in the DSU's appendix, the agreement itself is clear that procedural questions are to be determined by the Panel itself.

[85] *European Communities – Measures Concerning Meat and Meat Products (Hormones)*, WTO Appellate Body Report (13 February 1998) WT/DS26/AB/R WT/DS48/AB/R, para 152, n 138. '[T]he DSU, and in particular its Appendix 3, leave panels a margin of discretion to deal, always in accordance with due process, with specific situations that may arise in a particular case and that are not explicitly regulated. Within this context, an appellant requesting the Appellate Body to reverse a panel's ruling on matters of procedure must demonstrate the prejudice generated by such legal ruling.' Section 12.1 of the DSU establishes a framework for panel proceedings, but leaves a large measure of discretion: 'Panels shall follow the Working Procedures in Appendix 3 unless the panel decides otherwise after consulting the parties to the dispute.' Section 12.2 dictates that Panel discretion regarding procedural questions is limited only insofar as '[p]anel procedures should provide sufficient flexibility so as to ensure high-quality panel reports, while not unduly delaying the panel process'. Finally, under Art 11, Panels are expected to 'consult regularly with the parties to the dispute and give them adequate opportunity to develop a mutually satisfactory solution'.

[86] Indeed, as much as it may rely on expert opinion, the Panel has generally retained the final say even on technical, non-legal issues.

[87] In this regard, it should be kept in mind that the link is a 'hot potato' not only because of opposition from developing countries to any doctrine which might legitimise limitations on access to developed country markets, but also because of the threat posed to the WTO system as a whole by the recurring criticisms levelled against Panels, putting into question their ability to effectively balance member States' specific goals with the common aim of promoting trade. It would thus be politically prudent to hand over the task of establishing a violation of core labour standards to the ILO. Beyond political expedience, the Panel would also have particularly strong legal grounds for a referral, in particular the Singapore Ministerial Declaration's clear indication that '[t]he International Labour Organisation (ILO) is the competent body to set and deal with these standards'.

[88] Particularly Pt IA(iv), mentioned above, which, in clearly delineating the line between legitimate and illegitimate bases for comparative advantage, almost calls out for the ILO to be consulted on the trade impact of certain national practices related to fundamental rights at work.

it possible to investigate allegations of violations of trade union rights even in countries that have not ratified the relevant Conventions.[89] No legal or conceptual barrier would prevent the Governing Body from establishing a similar body on an ad hoc basis to investigate allegations of infringement related to other fundamental rights in response to a request of a Panel.

The difficulty of the FFCC procedure, however, is that it requires the consent of the State against which the allegations are made. This condition represented a crippling defect for the Commission, to the point of making it almost irrelevant. Ironically, it could nonetheless become an asset in the present context. Were an impugned country (which has not ratified the relevant Convention) to refuse an ILO request to investigate an alleged fundamental rights violation, it would be quite reasonable for the Panel to draw its own conclusions, especially where the request originated with the Panel itself. And it would in particular be completely consistent with positions taken in prior cases for them to draw an adverse inference from such a refusal.[90]

To fully appreciate the possible consequences of these measures, it is important to realise that they are likely to remain largely symbolic. Even were a Panel to come to a favourable conclusion under Article XXIII:1(c), its report would have little chance of being adopted by the DSB.[91] This likelihood does not, however, substantially diminish the possible value that the procedure could contribute to the underlying objective: it would probably be insufficient to justify trade restrictions against a country found in violation of fundamental rights, but it would still meet the (main) objective, of shining a bright light on a situation which, in the absence of ratification, could not be captured by the ILO's conventional procedures.

The greatest weakness of this solution, however, is that putting it in place depends completely on the determination and commitment of the injured State to set in motion a procedure whose details are somewhat hazy, whose outcome is unpredictable and with a result that would be symbolic at best. Even when significant interests are at play, there appears little risk such bold steps will be taken. Consider that a government as powerful as the United States seemed to think twice before even *putting in question* a trade relationship as important as the one it has with China.[92] Twice petitioned by the AFL-CIO to put in place unilateral sanctions allowed for under section 301 of the country's Trade Act, in response to alleged 'unreasonable practices' by China,[93] the competent authorities chose to not even

[89] Nicolas Valticos, *Droit international du travail*, 2nd edn (Paris, Dalloz, 1983) para 788 ff.

[90] See, eg *Canada – Measures Affecting the Export of Civilian Aircraft*, WTO Appellate Body Report (20 August 1999) WT/DS70/AB/R, para 204.

[91] Article 26:2 of the DSU provides that 'non-violation' complaints brought under Art XXIII:1(c) of the GATT are subject to rules which, unlike other complaints, can only be adopted by the unanimous support of the DSB, including the country against which the complaints were originally levelled.

[92] Unsurprising, perhaps, given the *strategic* importance of trade between the two countries. See the comments on MAED above (n 31).

[93] The second of the two petitions discussed above (n 80) (American Federation of Labor and Congress of Industrial Organizations (AFL-CIO), Section 301 Petition (6 June 2006)) sheds interesting light on the numerous and persistent violations of international standards in China, including 'Denial of Free Association and Rights of Collective Bargaining', 'The Subclass of Migrant Factory Workers:

investigate further, notably citing positive developments for the situation of workers in the country.[94] This was despite the claim made by the authors of the petition that 'the Chinese government's labour repression accounts for the loss of approximately 973,000 manufacturing jobs and approximately 1,235,000 total jobs in the United States and perhaps many more – based on conservative assumptions about wage, price, and output effects'[95] and despite the existence of a US trade deficit at US$70 billion and rising.[96] This episode gives just a hint of the scale of resistance which would have to be overcome before a country might implement Article XXIII:1(c) procedures.

(ii) In the Form of a Universal 'Ratchet Clause' to Prevent any Manipulations to Weaken National Labour Protection?

A number of bilateral and multilateral trade agreements (many negotiated by the United States) include 'ratchet clauses' prohibiting any manipulations that would weaken national labour legislation so as to gain a competitive advantage; we will have an opportunity to review the overall impact and effectiveness of such clauses in the next section. In light of the foregoing, however, it seems worth investigating whether Article XXIII already creates an opening for a universally-applicable 'ratchet clause'. In this regard, it is easy to imagine that manipulations operating so as to abridge workers' rights, particularly changes which would weaken fundamental rights protections supporting realisation of other worker claims, might also create a 'situation' relevant under Article XXIII1:(c). Such a possibility seems all the more compelling insofar as it would apply to such a 'manipulating' country even where it had not ratified the relevant ILO Conventions. It would even be relevant where a country, having ratified a Convention, would otherwise consider denouncing it in order to proceed in peace with its rights-weakening reforms.[97] One issue that arises with particular acuity here is that such a device might be used by developing countries to tie developed countries to their existing legislative protections. But we shall return to this potentially ironic result a bit further below.

Bonded Labor', 'Failure to Provide Standards for Minimum Wages and Maximum Hours', 'Failure to Provide Standards for Occupational Safety and Health', 'Failure to Provide Child Labor Standards', 'Failure to Enforce Rights Against Forced Labor in the Penal System'.

[94] The response to the 2006 petition, which does not appear to have been published in the Federal Register, provided more justification than the first. It suggested that US efforts had yielded 'real progress' and argued that 'wage rates in China are rising, and China has enhanced labor inspections as a result of US engagement' (see United States Trade Representative, *Statement from USTR Spokesman Regarding China Labor Petition* (Press Release, 21 July 2006), available at www.ustr.gov/archive/Document_Library/Press_Releases/2006/July/Statement_from_USTR_Spokesman_Regarding_China_Labor_Petition.html.

[95] AFL-CIO, Section 301 Petition (n 92) 119.

[96] ibid 106.

[97] A possibility well-illustrated by the reactions in France and elsewhere following the conclusions of the tripartite committee established under Art 24 of the ILO Constitution to address a representation made by the union Force Ouvrière regarding the incompatibility of the proposed 'New Hiring Contract' (CNE) with the provisions of Convention No 158 ratified by France (see Maupain, 'Une Rolls Royce' (n 18) 483).

C. Narrow Path Opened by Consumer Perceptions

This would ultimately be the most radical way of loosening the stranglehold of the multilateral trade doctrines: to take working conditions directly into account at the product or country level. The question here is the extent to which consumer perception of production processes can be leveraged to differentiate between products with otherwise identical physical characteristics, without thereby coming into conflict with national treatment and non-discrimination principles.

One way of framing the issue is as matter of specifying when the conditions under which such products were made could affect perceptions so significantly as to impact on the evaluation of similarity (or 'likeness') under GATT Article III:4. In its *Asbestos* decision, the WTO Appeals Body provided a framework for analysing the 'likeness' concept that seemed to open the door to differential treatment of superficially similar products on the basis of consumer perceptions.[98] Indeed, based partially on the reasoning in that decision, Charnovitz and his co-authors have put forward the premise that 'if there is sufficient evidence that consumers distinguish between products produced in conditions consistent with social criteria or would distinguish these products if they had perfect information, one might argue that the former products are "unlike" the latter'.[99]

As it turns out, however, the expansion of the 'likeness' concept may only provide a narrow opening, or might even lead to a dead-end. The Appellate Body's reasoning in no way indicated that consumer perceptions could operate on their own to determine 'likeness', and was explicit that the relevant factors were non-exhaustive, interrelated and to be evaluated on a case-by-case basis.[100] As applied in the *Asbestos* case itself, the comprehensive consideration of the differences between the two products in question reached beyond consumer perceptions, and included explicit reference to the objective, differential health risks connected to the products in question.[101] Thus, '[w]hile consumers may at times distinguish based on production processes, and some competitive effect is quite possible', Gabriel Marceau has rightly cautioned that 'it is difficult to envision a circumstance where the effect would be great enough to render physically similar products un-like'.[102]

Yet the development of the 'likeness' jurisprudence may turn out to be somewhat moot. As discussed above, significant 'policy space' for States may have been

[98] See also Jessica Karbowski, 'Grocery Store Activism: A WTO Compliant Means to Incentivize Social Responsibility' (2008) 43(2) *Virginia Journal of International Law* 760.

[99] *cf* Steve Charnovitz, Jane Earley, and Robert Howse, 'An Examination of Social Standards in Biofuels Sustainability Criteria' (International Food and Agricultural Trade Policy Council, Poznan, 9 December 2008) 10.

[100] *EC – Asbestos* (n 6) para 102. The criteria to be included in the determination include '(i) the properties, nature and quality of the products; (ii) the end-uses of the products; (iii) consumers' tastes and habits – more comprehensively termed consumers' perceptions and behaviour – in respect of the products; and (iv) the tariff classification of the products' (ibid paras 101–2).

[101] *EC – Asbestos* (n 6) paras 113–16 and 128–31.

[102] Marceau, 'Trade and Labour' (n 11) 547.

opened up by an expanding consideration of regulatory purpose in the assessment of 'less favourable treatment'. A triplet of decisions under the Technical Barriers to Trade (TBT) Agreement[103] have generated a flurry of debate on how much fairly-applied and fairly-designed (or 'even-handed') regulatory schemes might be justified under the GATT without reference to Article XX,[104] even where it is clear that imported products would do better in the absence of that scheme.[105] Unsurprisingly, however, some difficult questions remain, in particular regarding: (i) the degree to which the conditions required under TBT and GATT national treatment provisions are cumulative;[106] (ii) the extent to which these decisions actually set a lower bar as regards the use of regulatory purpose in the determination of 'less favourable treatment'.[107]

Some tentative conclusions can nonetheless be drawn: first, it is unlikely that the Appellate Body will retreat from its holding that measures explicitly differentiating on the basis of origin are inconsistent with Article III:4;[108] secondly, since 'less favourable treatment' is almost certain to be found if the specific detrimental impact on imports is not justified by the specific regulatory distinction applied,[109]

[103] *United States – Tuna II* (n 44); *United States – Measures Affecting the Production and Sale of Clove Cigarettes*, WTO Appellate Body Report (24 April 2012) WT/DS406/AB/R ('*US – Clove Cigarettes*'); *United States – Certain Country of Origin Labelling (COOL) Requirements*, WTO Appellate Body Report (23 July 2012) WT/DS384/AB/R, WT/DS386/AB/R.

[104] Though the width of the gap between the two approaches could also conceivably narrow as a result of the recent decisions, Marceau and Wyatt have pointed out that the wider range of admissible policy objectives permitted by Art 2.2 of the TBT Agreement (along with the absence of a minimum threshold for the contribution a rule needs to make to a policy objective to be considered 'legitimate') 'make TBT article 2.2 more accommodative of members public policy objectives than GATT art. XX' (Gabrielle Marceau and Julian Wyatt, 'The WTO's Efforts to Balance Economic Development and Environmental Protection: A Short Review of Appellate Body Jurisprudence' (2013) 1(1) *Latin American Journal of International Trade Law* 291).

[105] Weihuan Zhou has argued, based on similarities in the language of TBT Art 2.1 and GATT Art III:4 that the most recent decisions 'have important implications for the interpretation of "less favourable treatment" under Article III:4', even though those decisions were taken under the TBT Agreement, not the GATT. Weihuan Zhou, 'US – Clove Cigarettes and US – Tuna II (Mexico): Implications for the Role of Regulatory Purpose under Article III:4 of the GATT' (2012) 15(4) *Journal of International Economic Law* 1075.

[106] The Appellate Body has held that a finding of compliance under the TBT Agreement does not suffice to show that a regulatory measure is also in compliance with the GATT itself, meaning that a provision found to be TBT compliant could still be challenged, and would need independent evaluation, under the GATT itself (see *United States – Tuna II* (n 44) para 405). There has yet to be a case, however, where a provision found to be compliant with the TBT provisions was found to be in violation of the GATT, and it is hard to imagine a context where such a finding could be both legally sound and politically feasible.

[107] Even if the Appellate Body holds to its view that TBT compliance is not dispositive of GATT compliance, that leaves open the question of how a finding of TBT compliance will affect the adjudication of the latter issue within an individual case, and more importantly, whether the interpretation of 'less favourable treatment' under the TBT Agreement in recent cases will impact future interpretation of the same language under the GATT itself. As Wyatt and Marceau have stressed, it is clear that the interpretation of the TBT Agreement has drawn on earlier interpretation of the GATT, but 'it remains to be seen whether and, if so, how much this new TBT jurisprudence may cross-fertilize back into the GATT case law' (Wyatt and Marceau, 'The WTO's Efforts' (n 103) 13).

[108] *Thailand – Customs and Fiscal Measures on Cigarettes from the Philippines*, WTO Appellate Body Report (17 June 2011) DS371, para 133.

[109] Wyatt and Marceau, 'The WTO's Efforts' (n 103) 10–11.

then it seems that States will be able to act with more confidence to the degree that measures are aimed at informing consumers about product differences (so as to allow them to exercise their preferences) rather than trying to substitute for those preferences; thirdly, given the difficulties of putting in place an 'even-handed' comparison of foreign and local production processes,[110] it will be easier to implement legitimate social and environmental objectives to the degree that states choose to apply standards based in the framework of an international agreement or on the basis of an international standard adopted by a competent body.[111]

Thus, beside the very narrow and uncertain path that seemed to emerge from the *Asbestos* approach to likeness, it seems the way may be open for a legitimate and non-discriminatory promotion of the 'rules of the game'[112] by allowing regulatory differences that empower consumer preferences. In short, it would seem entirely consistent with the logic developed by the Appellate Body to allow consumer preferences to be legitimately exercised on the basis of information regarding underlying production methods, so long as that information turns on origin-neutral, objective, non-discriminatory standards established on a multilateral basis.[113] Just such a proposal will be the subject of the final part of this text. Otherwise, these reflections seem to converge toward the same conclusion: without an external intermediary or the addition of an institutional prosthesis, any options which depend on an optimistic outlook regarding jurisprudential evolution at the WTO remain a distant mirage. That being said, as much as such prosthesis may seem less elegant than a made-to-order genetic alteration of the WTO regime, it offers a set of prospects which will be addressed in the conclusion.

[110] This was the reason that the WTO Appellate Body found against the United States labelling initiative in *United States – Tuna II* (n 44).

[111] This is all the more true given that Art 4.2 of the TBT Agreement requires States to apply relevant international standards wherever they exist. Though the WTO Appellate Body created a relatively high bar to standards that qualify for (almost) mandatory usage, the reality remains that the application of an international standard is likely to contribute strongly to claims that a measure is pursuing a legitimate, non-protectionist regulatory goal (see Wyatt and Marceau, 'The WTO's Efforts' (n 103) 13–14).

[112] It is important in this regard to realise that the compatibility issue arises not only in relation to multilateral trade doctrines but also in relation to international labour standards. To be legitimate, any account made for consumer perceptions cannot give free rein to their subjective judgment. They must correspond with the preferences recognised by the authorities, in turn internationally recognised as legitimate. To quote an extreme (but authentic) example, it is possible that consumers could believe rugs woven by children to be *superior* to carpets fabricated by adults or machines; it would nonetheless seem difficult to invoke the jurisprudence just canvassed to warrant a label certifying that the carpet bearing the mark was indeed made by children.

[113] As noted by Christine Kaufmann, 'One way of looking at this issue is to view labels as parts of the product, similar to its packaging and/or content. In this view, all social labels become "product related", even if they pursue a goal that is process-related such as the abolition of child labour' (Kaufmann, *Globalisation and Labour Rights* (n 74) 219).

9

Decentralised Linkages: A Mixed Blessing for the ILO?*

Buffeted by international competition that has only been exacerbated by globalisation and weakened by reduced institutional capacity, it is only natural that states might turn to collective solutions that provide an attractive half-way house to full global liberalisation,[1] offering the advantages of a larger market while allowing a certain social model to be safeguarded or otherwise putting up a shield or buffer against the abrupt social disruptions threatened by global trade expansion.[2]

The recurring failure to insert a social clause into trade agreements at the universal level followed by the impasse of the Doha Round have inevitably contributed to the development of more decentralised initiatives to achieve the same purpose.[3] This is indeed one aspect of a more general phenomenon[4] described in cosmological terms by Peter-Jan Kuijper: 'the seeming impossibility to make

* The author wishes to express his sincere thanks to Franz Ebert of the International Institute of Labour Studies for his valuable comments and suggestions on this chapter.

[1] Arrangements of this sort created within the framework of a regional agreement are specifically accommodated by WTO rules (under Art V of the GATS, and more directly relevant for our purposes, Art XXIV of the GATT). Specifically, inasmuch as they are believed to promote international trade liberalisation, both free trade areas and customs unions are allowed (Pieter Jan Kuijper, *Conflicting Rules and Clashing Courts: The Case of Environmental Agreements, Free Trade Agreements and the WTO*, International Centre for Trade and Sustainable Development Issue Paper 10 (2010) 19). The preferential treatment facilitated by the Treaty of Rome establishing the European Economic Community, now European Union (EU), provides an archetypal example of the type of arrangement allowed by Art XXIV.

[2] This dimension was underlined in the early 2000s by the Prime Minister of Barbados, speaking on economic integration in the Caribbean (Prime Minister of Barbados, Owen Arthur, Address at the Opening of the CSME Unit Office (Central Bank of Barbados, Bridgetown, 14 October 2002), available at www.caricom.org/jsp/speeches/csmeunit_arthur.jsp).

[3] Indeed, the United States long ago intimated that the ongoing failure to put the issue on the agenda of the universal trading regime would contribute to a unilateral approach to the issue on their part (see GATT, Communication of the United States Concerning the Relationship between International Human Rights Workers and International Trade (GATT doc C/M/2/12, 6 August 1987) para 11), a fact already illustrated in s 301 of the US Trade Act of 1974 as amended by the Omnibus Trade and Competitiveness Act (OTCA) adopted by the US Congress in 1988, and whose ratification of the WTO agreement has not led to withdrawal.

[4] As pointed out in the introduction to an excellent compilation on the social dimensions of regional integration, the growth of regional and bilateral free trade agreements mirrors a general shift toward a liberalised approach to trade, a tendency solidified but not initiated by the establishment of the WTO. Adelle Blackett and Christian Lévesque (eds), *Social Regionalism in the Global Economy* (London, Routledge, 2011) 3.

progress through negotiations at the galactic level pushed internal tensions up to the point where a supernova developed that projected great numbers of Regional Trade Agreements outward'.[5]

While this phenomenon may result from the failure to reach results at the universal level, it may at times also contribute to that failure in turn: in particular, it can reduce the incentive for states to pursue universal solutions, and displace negotiating energies in favour of extracting the best possible deal from the individual countries with particularly attractive markets. It not only leads to a partitioning of international trade[6] but also gives rise to an intractable tangle of universal, regional, bilateral and unilateral legal relations some have described as a 'spaghetti bowl'.[7] Whatever the underlying motivations, it is understandable that the pursuit of such agreements has also inspired tangled feelings among WTO officials; its Director-General, Pascal Lamy, has gone so far as to describe the trend as a 'mixed blessing'.[8]

Could the same not be said for the ILO, and the decentralisation of social clauses?

Two aspects need to be distinguished to answer this question. The first aspect comprises the ILO's institutional and functional interests. From this point of view, regional economic and political integration may to some extent be viewed as a way to partially escape the prisoner's dilemma.[9] This view is part of the explanation for the ILO's early interest in European political and economic integration;[10] there was a conviction that the project was inspired by the same underlying *values* as the ILO itself, that it would pull common prosperity up out of the ruins of the Second

[5] Kuijper, *Conflicting Rules* (n 1) vii.

[6] To the extent that such agreements systematically exclude third parties, they inevitably lead to some amount of trade distortion, or what Trebilcock and Howse describe as 'trade diversion' (Michael J Trebilcock and Robert Howse, *The Regulation of International Trade*, 3rd edn (London, Routledge, 2005) 193–98).

[7] Jagdish N Bhagwati, *Free Trade Today* (Princeton, Princeton University Press, 2002).

[8] Pascal Lamy, 'The WTO Needs Your Scrutiny' (Steering Committee of the Parliamentary Conference on WTO, IPU Headquarters, 22–23 September 2005), available at www.wto.org/english/news_e/sppl_e/sppl02_e.htm. In a much more recent speech (given July 2011) the criticisms of the illusory advantages and clear disadvantages of these preferential agreements gets to the point that it appears at times as if the Director-General has moved from seeing such agreements as a 'mixed blessing' to considering them an unmitigated curse for the universal trade regime. See Pascal Lamy, 'Lamy Says Trade Pacts Pose New Challenge to the Multilateral Trading System' (Launch of the World Trade Report 2011, 20 July 2011), available at www.wto.org/english/news_e/sppl_e/sppl202_e.htm.

[9] Some have claimed that '[t]he proliferation of labour provisions in trade arrangements . . . could constitute an important leverage towards the realisation of the ILO objectives' (Eric Gravel, Tomi Kohiyama and Katerina Tsotroudi, 'The Role of International Labour Standards in Rebalancing Globalization: A Legal Perspective' in ILO (ed), *The Global Crisis, Causes, Responses and Challenges* (Geneva, ILO, 2011) 217). Lorand Bartels has been more explicit that 'it is therefore to be welcomed that this inevitable discussion is being taken up in negotiations at the regional level, where parties with an interest in the matter are more able to experiment with different forms of regulation' (Lorand Bartels, 'Social Issues: Labour, Environment and Human Rights' in Simon Lester and Brian Mercurio, *Bilateral and Regional Agreements: Commentary, Analysis and Case Studies* (Cambridge, Cambridge University Press, 2009) 364).

[10] Demonstrated by the very significant agreements it concluded in 1953 with the European Coal and Steel Community and, a relatively short time later, with the EEC.

World War, and direct it towards the ILO's objective. At the same time, however, it seems obvious that the proliferation of trade agreements, each with its own slightly different 'social clause' and its own idiosyncratic relationship with ILO standards, would involve some problematic institutional consequences for the ILO, and for the integrity of its standards and supervisory procedures in particular – a challenge with some parallel with the WTO's perspective. The first section below will try to assess the meaning and impact of the phenomenon from the viewpoint of ILO institutional interests and functions.

That being said, the ILO's institutional interests are one thing, and social progress is (to some degree) another. It would be somewhat self-defeating to ignore or play down the improvements brought about by the social clauses contained in bi- or multilateral trade arrangements, just because they have been won outside of ILO standards and procedures. After all, the presence of a 'mixed blessing' for the ILO implies that these agreements make at least some contribution to promoting the organisation's objectives vis-à-vis workers. As we shall see in the second section, the extent of this blessing seems in many cases to boil down to an additional but not necessarily very effective guarantee as regards the implementation of the rights already enjoyed under national law by the workers concerned (and in certain respects, by their employers). Yet, in concluding comments, there is some exploration of the implications this way of doing things might have for the protection of guarantees offered by ILO procedures.

I. A Mixed Blessing from the Viewpoint of Implementing ILO Standards and Procedures

Despite the ILO's early interest in the phenomenon, it has dedicated little time or energy to specifically addressing the question of its possible impact and significance for its own standards and procedures.[11] It was only in the report submitted to the ILC in 2007 pursuant to the discussion that led to the Social Justice Declaration the following year, that questions were first raised about the trend's salience for the ILO and its standards.[12] That report noted, inter alia, that while the social aspects of these agreements often took the form of specific references to ILO principles, and even sometimes to ILO standards, the organization had never had the opportunity to assess their overall impact on the organisation's discharge of its

[11] And this is true even though the Governing Body's Working Group on the Social Dimension of Trade Liberalization (first established in 1994) had a section on its agenda to address regional integration and other multilateral agreements involving social legislation, for almost five years worth of meetings. In the end, however, this information gave rise to no real discussion regarding the potential impact of these developments on ILO objectives, or on the effectiveness of its standards. In 1999, the agenda item was simply abandoned when the working group was renamed the 'Working Group on the Social Dimension of Globalization' to avoid implying any connection to the 'social clause'.

[12] ILO, *Report V: Strengthening the Capacity of the ILO to Assist its Members' Efforts to Promote its Objectives in the Context of Globalization* (International Labour Conference, 96th Session, Geneva, 30 May–15 June 2007) paras 96–108.

mandate.[13] The report did not, however, capture a sense that a decentralisation of the social dimension should give the ILO the same conflicted feelings that they had inspired at the WTO.

The 2008 Declaration put a sharper focus on the issue. Addressing possible amelioration of institutional practices, Part IIA(iv) suggests that the International Labour Office could '[provide] assistance to Members who wish to promote strategic objectives jointly within the framework of bilateral or multilateral agreements'. The provision, however, clarifies that assistance with such agreements is 'subject to their compatibility with ILO obligations'.

More recently, the 2009 *World of Work Report* provided an overview of the growing practice, highlighting the diversity of normative references used in these agreements.[14]

What seems to emerge from the 2009 analysis, and the vast literature that has gradually appeared to address the phenomenon, is the limited extent to which ILO instruments (especially Conventions) and procedures are used to frame the social clauses in these agreements. Despite (or perhaps because of) the wealth of literature, it remains difficult to get a clear picture of why this is so, and of what impact it may have on the effectiveness of ILO efforts.

We will consider first the extent to which the situation may be explained by the sponsors' will and strategies, and more specifically, the extent to which these strategies reflect some 'loyalty' to the ILO, its objectives and its standards. For that purpose, we will compare the respective experiences of the two main sponsors of these clauses, the United States and the European Union,[15] to try and understand the institutional and other motivations which may have inspired the inclusion of these clauses. While recent years have seen the phenomenon expand in all regions,[16]

[13] ibid para 97. See also the short discussion of the ILO's role in Gravel, Kohiyama and Tsotroudi, 'The Role of International Labour Standards' (n 9) 219–20.

[14] ILO and International Institute for Labour Studies, *World of Work Report 2009: The Global Jobs Crisis* (Geneva, ILO, 2010) ch 3.

[15] As regards the European Union: 'Europe is the region with the largest number of RTAs, accounting for almost half of the agreements notified to the WTO and in force' (Roberto V Fiorentino, Luis Verdeja and Christelle Toqueboeuf, *The Changing Landscape of Regional Trade Agreements: 2006 Update*, WTO Trade Policies Review Division, Regional Trade Agreements Section, Discussion Paper 12 (2006) 13).

[16] Regional *integration* has been proceeding in other parts of the world for some time (see ILO and IILS, *World of Work Report 2009* (n 14) 70–74). It may be that the early movement in the European Union and the United States toward 'regional social integration' (if one considers the United States as itself to be a social integration project) qualifies them as models, but the role of fundamental social rights in other regional groupings (MERCOSUR, CARICOM, ASEAN and the AU) is an important subject of study, even if they will not be the focus in the text that follows. Overall, however, studies on the issue are still limited. The following can be identified: John DR Craig and Michael Lynk (eds), *Globalization and the Future of Labour Law* (Cambridge, Cambridge University Press, 2006); Anne Trebilcock (ed), *Labour and Employment Implications of the ASEAN Free Trade Agreements* (Geneva, ILO, 2005); Blackett and Lévesque, *Social Regionalism* (n 4). One point deserving particular attention concerns the principle of free movement of workers which is supposed to be the basis of a regional integration process. Africa remains the exceptional case on this point, to the extent that ineffective border controls links the issue of free movement of workers to the very process of state building. Thus, if free movement of workers is not always recognised de jure, it is nonetheless the de facto reality. See, eg Aderanti Adepoju, 'Fostering Free Movement of Persons in West Africa: Achievements, Constraints, and Prospects for Intraregional Migration' (2002) 40(2) *International Migration* 3. MERCOSUR has

and a significant increase in the number of trade agreements which include a social dimension having been concluded between countries from the South,[17] it seems sufficient to shed some tentative light on the situation to limit the comparison to these two experiences, especially since they share a federal dimension which has always proved to be a challenge for ILO standard-setting.

While the comparison confirms that the strategies/approaches followed by these key sponsors of social clauses start from fairly different institutional, political and practical premises, it also shows that they produce results which are not fundamentally different when it comes to the place they grant to international labour standards.

As we shall see next, this can be explained by the equally-applicable constraints of reciprocity, which tends to align each country's 'social clauses' to a common denominator which more often than not ends up being the application of national law.

A. 'Loyalty' to the ILO in US and EU Strategies

The naïve explanation for the scarcity of references to international labour standards in the social clauses of existing agreements would be that it simply reflects the sponsor's poor record of ratification.

The explanation seems to a large extent valid in the US case, where the use of the logic of the Commerce Clause and the Treaty Power to promote a level playing field, rather than ILO objectives and standards as such, is not inconsistent with the restraint shown in the spare use of these powers to implement ILO Conventions *within* the federal system. The situation in the European Union would at first seem to explode the usefulness of this naïve explanation: yet Europe's excellent ratification record[18] reflects the decisions of individual states, rather than a purposeful strategy on the part of the European Union as such.[19] While the Union's initial

followed the European approach, allowing almost total freedom of movement between member countries (International Organization for Migration, *Supplemental Materials* (International Dialogue on Migration Intersessional Workshop on Free Movement of Persons in Regional Integration Processes, Brussels, 18–19 June 2007) 15). ASEAN has seen a trend of migration freedom only for the most skilled workers (Trebilcock, *Labour and Employment Implications* (above) 31).

[17] Franz C Ebert and Anne Posthuma, 'Labour Provisions in Trade Agreements: Current Trends and Prospects' (Research Conference on Key Lessons from the Crisis and Way Forward, Geneva, February 2011), available at www.ilo.org/inst/events/WCMS_192387/lang--en/index.htm, 15–18.

[18] Every EU Member State has ratified all eight Conventions concerning fundamental rights at work.

[19] Unlike the situation in the United States, the ratification of international labour Conventions in the European Union continues to lie within the jurisdiction of the individual Member States in accordance with the ILO Constitution. It is intriguing in this regard that, by contrast to the US situation, where federal jurisdiction is hampered by the concern not to invade individual state jurisdiction, EU Member States find themselves in the opposite situation where they face the possibility of being thwarted in their willingness to ratify and implement ILO Conventions by claims from the European Commission that the decision to ratify is one properly taken at the EU level as a result of the extension of its external competence, parallel to its internal competence under the relevant jurisprudence of the ECJ. This claim has more or less fizzled out since the ECJ's 'nebulous' 1993 advisory opinion in which the Court, instead of accepting the Commission's claim that the decision to ratify Convention No 170

ambition, contrary to the US strategy, was probably to project the EU social model as much as possible beyond the Union's borders, this ambition seems to have been diluted by the logic of enlargement and the pressure exerted by the orthodoxy of global trade liberalisation

(i) A US Strategy Less Concerned with ILO Standards than with Undistorted Competition

The limited place occupied by ILO instruments and procedures in the US strategy of including a social dimension in its bi- or multilateral trade agreements should not come as too much as a surprise. Rather, it is completely consistent with the status generally accorded to ILO Conventions in US law, and more specifically with what Senator Hatch once described as the country's 'dismal' ratification record.[20] Indeed, even in the rare event when ratification has been forthcoming, its application has come predicated on obligations being consistent with federal and state law.

This 'dismal' situation has traditionally been justified by reference to the constraints of US federalism, and more specifically by the concern of federal authorities not to upset the 'federal balance' by legislating on matters that are by tradition left to the individual states. This excuse does not, however, come without some striking ironies (if not contradictions) from the viewpoint of the present analysis. First, the restraint which marked the US approach as soon as it joined the ILO in 1934 seemed less than totally consistent with the expansion of federal legislation in social and labour matters during the New Deal, justified by reference to the Commerce Clause as re-interpreted by the Supreme Court.[21] In fact, the US failure

on Chemicals at Work fell within the exclusive competence of the Community, simply advised the parties to work together (ILO, *Advisory Opinion of the Court of Justice of the European Communities on Ratification of The Chemicals Convention* (Governing Body, 256th Session, May 1993). On this subject see Ailish Johnston, 'EU-ILO Relations: Between Regional and Global Governance' in Jan Orbie and Lisa Tortell (eds), *The European Union and the Social Dimension of Globalization: How the EU Influences the World* (London, Routledge, 2009) 84. Note that the Commission has very recently authorised Member States to ratify the recent and popular Convention (No 202) on Domestic Workers – when some of them had already decided to do so!

[20] Orrin G Hatch, 'Ratify international labour Conventions', *Christian Science Monitor*, 10 December 1985, 27. Among other reasons, the need to respect and safeguard 'federal equilibrium' continues to be invoked to justify legislating on the basis of either the Commerce Clause or the Treaty Power to ratify ILO Conventions, including the fundamental Conventions.

[21] Depending on the shifting temperament of the Supreme Court and the overall political context, the Commerce Clause was used either, according to the 'dormant theory', to prevent states in the United States from adopting social legislation which might impact on current or future exercise of federal jurisdiction or, quite to the contrary, to prevent the federal government from enacting legislation that entered into the social competence of the individual states. It finally permitted the intrusion of federal jurisdiction into the regulation of certain key social issues, including freedom of association and racial discrimination. For a detailed though rather old comparative analysis of the Commerce power, see Alexander Smith, *The Commerce Power in Canada and the United States* (Toronto, Butterworths, 1963). Specifically, Congress has jurisdiction to regulate commerce among the Federated States and the Indian tribes, as well as with foreign states. The concept is given scope wide enough to cover any situation where trade is 'affected' by an external situation or practice, which serves to justify, inter alia, their willingness to apply countermeasures against workers' rights violations (Laurence Dubin, *La protection des normes sociales dans les échanges internationaux* (Presses Universitaires d'Aix-Marseille, 2003) 55 ff).

to ratify ILO Conventions after its admission (despite a clear case laid out by David Riesman for doing so)[22] led unitary states to complain that they were put at a comparative disadvantage vis-à-vis federal states.[23]

The second paradox is that the unwillingness of the United States to use either the Commerce Clause, or its Treaty Power,[24] to overcome internal resistance to the ratification of ILO Conventions did not prevent it from using both when it sought to impose on other countries compliance with internationally recognised workers' rights during the completion of the Uruguay Round that led to the Marrakech Treaty establishing the WTO.

The last paradox, pointed out by Charnovitz, is that this negative attitude towards labour rights instruments stands in stark contrast with the country's 'unabashed ardor for intellectual property conventions'.[25] It is hard not to attribute this difference in treatment to the influence of strategic self-interest, and by a particular concern to preserve and expand its particular competitive advantages in international trade.

(ii) A Strategy that Tends to Privilege the Fight Against Competitive Erosion of Social Legislation Through 'Ratchet Clauses'

Despite these paradoxes, the US treatment of ILO standards seems nevertheless perfectly consistent with a strategy that is less interested in promoting ILO objectives of social progress than in combating distortions in competition.

The external policy of the United States is legally framed by the Omnibus Foreign Trade and Competitiveness Act (OTCA) of 1988, empowering US

There is a certain analogy here with the situation in the European Union. According to Tonia Novitz, the current situation seems to have ILO standards selected and promoted by the European Union only insofar as they might advance the common market: 'What one can see emerging in the EU is the use of labour standards to serve an internal market agenda by setting fair terms of competition, promoting freedom of contract and enhancing labour market productivity' (Tonia Novitz, 'In Search of a Coherent Social Policy: EU Import and Export of ILO Labour Standards?' in Jan Orbie and Lisa Tortell (eds), *The European Union and the Social Dimension of Globalization: How the EU Influences the World* (London, Routledge 2009) 39). This confirms the relevance of the analysis provided by Jean-Pierre Faugère (Jean-Pierre Faugère, 'La régulation sociale dans la construction européenne' in Pierre de Senarclens (ed), *Maîtriser la mondialisation: la régulation sociale internationale* (Presses de Sciences-Po, 2000) 217), discussed below.

[22] David Riesman, 'The Constitution of the United States and International Labor Legislation' (1941) 44(2) *International Labour Review* 123.

[23] Indeed, this is what led the ILO Delegation on Constitutional Questions to adopt a reform to Art 19(7) in 1946 which was intended to increase the ILO's capacity to put pressure on federal states to ratify and implement ILO Conventions. The Delegation on Constitutional Questions was itself established by the ILC in 1945 to adapt the ILO Constitution to the new institutional context of the post-war period. See ILO, *Report II(1): Constitutional Issues: Reports of the Conference Delegation on Constitutional Questions* (ILC, 29th Session, Montreal, 19 September– 9 October 1946) paras 48 and 60.

[24] On the restraint shown by the federal government in the use of 'treaty power', see Peter J Spiro, 'Resurrecting Missouri v. Holland' (2008) 73 *Missouri Law Review* 1029; Curtis A Bradley, 'The Treaty Power and American Federalism' (1998) 97 *Michigan Law Review* 390; Curtis A Bradley, 'The Treaty Power and American Federalism, Part II' (2000) 99 *Michigan Law Review* 98.

[25] Steve Charnovitz, 'Editorial Comments: The ILO Convention on Freedom of Association and its Future in the United States' (2008) 102(1) *American Journal of International Law* 90, 95.

authorities generally and the Office of the United States Trade Representative (USTR) specifically to defend the interests of the United States against so-called 'unreasonable' trade practices.[26] This legislative framework empowers the competent authorities to take action of any kind, including through unilateral measures that can (in theory) work either by stick[27] or by carrot,[28] but also through bilateral or multilateral agreements negotiated by the USTR.

Reflective of the perspective intended by these provisions, one finds, among the 15 principal trade objectives established by the OTCA, a goal for US negotiators during the Uruguay Round to seek adoption 'as a principle of the GATT, that the denial of worker rights should not be a means for a country or its industries to gain competitive advantage in international trade'.[29]

Within this over-all framework, the nature and content of social clauses so far negotiated has unsurprisingly evolved in line with the priorities resulting from the complex political dynamics of the United States Congress, and the contradictory claims and demands (sometimes cutting across employers' and workers' interests) of the various sectors of the economy, depending on their negative or positive exposition to international trade which has varied over time. Box 9.1 gives a summary of the initial content and the progressive evolution of the social clauses under successive administrations, and the modulating pressure brought to bear by public opinion.

Box 9.1 Social clauses in recent US trade agreements

The North American Agreement on Labour Cooperation (NAALC)[a] was the first international agreement linking labour provisions to economic integration as per the provisions of the OTCA.[b] Annexed to NAFTA[c] and concluded in 1993 (one year before the Marrakesh Accords), the agreement was negotiated by the administration under the OTCA's 'fast track authority' and thus approved by Congress without changes and after only limited debate.[d] While it deals with labour issues, its scope is quite limited: its stated objectives[e] make no

[26] Such practices include, under s 2411(d)(iii), any acts, policies or practices '[which] constitute a persistent pattern of conduct that (I) denies workers the right of association; (II) denies workers the right to organize and bargain collectively; (III) permits any form of forced or compulsory labour; (IV) fails to provide a minimum age for the employment of children; (V) fails to provide standards for minimum wages, hours of work, and occupational safety and health of workers' (19 USC s 2411). The Omnibus Trade and Competitiveness Act (OTCA) of 1988, inter alia, amended s 301 of the Trade Act of 1974 to make the systematic violation of internationally recognizsd workers' rights an unfair trade practice.

[27] The potential 'chilling effect' these provisions can exert on other WTO members were put 'under surveillance' in the dispute settlement system of the WTO by the Panel in *US – Section 301 Trade Act* (*United States – Sections 301–310 of the Trade Act of 1974,* WTO Panel Report (27 January 2000) WT/DS152/R). As we discussed above, the AFL-CIO unsuccessfully petitioned the USTR to apply s 301 against China because of its 'alleged' violations of the rights listed in the text.

[28] Particularly in the form of preferential access to US markets under the Generalised System of Preferences, discussed in more detail below.

[29] See Dubin, *La protection des normes sociales* (n 21) 85, n 248. The language still exists in slightly amended form in 19 USC s 2901(b)(14).

explicit reference to ILO standards, and economic sanction provisions desired by the United States were significantly watered down as a result of opposition from Canada and Mexico, who were distrustful of disguised protectionism.[f] Unlike subsequent agreements which provided explicit 'ratchet clauses' (detailed below), the agreement provides no enforceable protection against manipulations that would lower existing legislative protections to seek competitive advantage.[g] The current Mexican debate on a bill restricting freedom of association illustrates the profound limitations of this approach.[h]

Despite the expiration of 'fast track authority' in 1994 (the refusal to renew resulted in part from the hostility of a Republican-led Congress to the inclusion of labour rights clauses in trade agreements), the Clinton administration managed to sign a free trade agreement with Jordan that was the first to directly integrate labour provisions into the core text, rather than relegating them to a separate schedule.[i] Social clauses were thereby subjected to the same dispute settlement system as the other obligations in the agreement.[j] The agreement also refers to the ILO, though still foregoing substantive reference to ILO standards, asking each party to 'strive to ensure' that it does not suspend or otherwise derogate from applicable national laws or from 'internationally recognised workers' rights' in order to promote competitiveness.[k] No doubt, this agreement represents an improvement over the NAALC, although one could easily side with Marley Weiss, who suggests that labour obligations in the Jordan Agreement are still 'too thin and watery to do the job',[l] in particular because the parties agreed not to resort to sanctions in matters relating to the social dimension.[m]

It was not until 6 August 2002 that President Bush signed the Trade Act of 2002, setting out a set of principles to consider in future trade agreements,[n] focused on preventing the competitive weakening of protective standards, notably through the consolidation of pre-existing legislation[o] rather than any improvement in line with ILO standards, particularly those identified in the 1998 Declaration. A significant number of bilateral free trade agreements were concluded under this framework.[p] Even before 'fast track authority' expired in July 2007, however, a newly-elected Democratic Congressional majority pushed the Bush administration to modify agreements it had already completed with Panama, South Korea, Colombia and Peru, making Congressional approval subject to certain environmental and workers' rights protections.[q]

[a] North American Agreement on Labour Cooperation (signed 17 December 1992, entered into force I January 1994).

[b] Franz C Ebert and Anne Posthuma, *Labour Standards and Development Finance Institutions: A Review of Current Policies and Activities*, International Institute of Labour Studies, Discussion Paper 204 (2010) 9.

[c] The North American Free Trade Agreement entered into force on 1 January 1994, creating a free-trade zone among the United States, Canada and Mexico.

[d] Bob Hepple, *Labour Laws and Global Trade* (Oxford, Hart Publishing, 2005) 114.

[e] Namely, a high level of social protection for fundamental principles and rights at work, protection of basic working conditions in line with US provisions, minimum guarantees for migrant workers – the effective implementation of laws in these areas. Notably, the agreement also urges each party to ensure 'that its labor laws and regulations provide for high labor standards' and 'continue to strive to improve those standards in that light' (Art 2) (Franz C Ebert and Anne Posthuma, 'Labour Provisions in Trade Agreements: Current Trends and Prospects' (Research Conference on Key Lessons from the Crisis and Way Forward, Geneva, February 2011) 9).

[f] Robert Finbow, *The Limits of Regionalism: NAFTA's Labour Accord* (Burlington, Ashgate, 2006) 61.

[g] Laurence Dubin, *La protection des normes sociales dans les échanges internationaux* (Presses Universitaires d'Aix-Marseille, 2003) 271–72.

[h] See International Trade Union Confederation, *Mexico: Labour Legislation Reform Without Consultation* (Press Release, 6 April 2011).

[i] Bob Hepple, *Labour Laws and Global Trade* (Oxford, Hart Publishing, 2005) 116.

[j] As put by Christine Kaufmann, the United States–Jordan Agreement is a good example of a treaty bringing the social clause in 'by the back door', simply bypassing the logic of the WTO. Note that this approach elicited responses from the United States Chamber of Commerce who had advocated for the withdrawal or abandonment of such provisions (Christine Kaufmann, *Globalisation and Labour Rights: The Conflict Between Core Labour Rights and International Economic Law* (Oxford, Oxford University Press, 2007) 193).

[k] Bob Hepple, *Labour Laws and Global Trade* (Oxford, Hart Publishing, 2005) 117.

[l] Marley Weiss, 'Two Steps Forward, One Step Back – Or Vice Versa: Labor Rights Under Free Trade Agreements from NAFTA, Through Jordan, via Chile, to Latin America, and Beyond' (2003) 37(3) *University of San Francisco Law Review* 689, 718.

[m] Mary Jane Bolle, *Jordan-US Free Trade Agreement: Labor Issues*, Congressional Research Service Report (27 May 2003) RS20968, 3.

[n] In particular: (a) prevent non-compliance by the parties with their labour laws 'through a sustained or recurring course of action or inaction in a manner affecting trade'; (c) strengthen the ability of trading partners to promote respect for core labour standards; and (g) ensure that policies and practices of parties to trade agreements with the United States 'do not arbitrarily discriminate against US exports or serve as disguised barriers to trade' (Bob Hepple, *Labour Laws and Global Trade* (Oxford, Hart Publishing, 2005) 115).

[o] The formula contained in the post-NAALC agreements signed by the United States and in a number of agreements signed by the European Union prohibits 'encouragement of trade or investment through weakening of labour law'. See Franz C Ebert and Anne Posthuma, 'Labour Provisions in Trade Agreements: Current Trends and Prospects' (Research Conference on Key Lessons from the Crisis and Way Forward, Geneva, February 2011) 9–10.

[p] Including with Chile (in 2004), Singapore (in 2004), Australia (in 2005), Morocco (in 2006), Bahrain (in 2006), and Central America and the Dominican Republic (the CAFTA, in 2006) and Oman (in 2009) (ibid 9–10).

[q] See United States Trade Representative, Bipartisan Agreement on Trade Policy (May 2007), available at www.ustr.gov/trade-agreements/free-trade-agreements/peru-tpa.

Recent agreements (re)negotiated pursuant to the compromise reached under the pressure of a Democratic Congressional majority in 2007 contain the most demanding protection of fundamental rights so far, and go beyond the mere implementation of national legislation. The United States-Peru Agreement which came into force in 2009,[30] and agreements with Panama, Colombia and South Korea finalised by President Obama in 2011,[31] go beyond the application of national law, requiring the parties to 'adopt and maintain' protections for the fundamental rights listed in the 1998 Declaration, and opening the dispute resolution mechanism to infringements of the labour provisions in the agreement.[32] In the case of Colombia, final agreement was also subject to the effective implementation of an 'action plan' to strengthen its social legislation and address violence against trade unionists, matched to a series of specific deadlines.[33]

The emphasis thus placed on fundamental workers' rights is perfectly consistent with the logic according to which these rights are the 'rules of the game' that should allow the workers concerned to get their fair share of the benefits accrued to the country under the Agreement[34] and thus prevent efforts to gain an unjustified competitive advantage. The question which remains to be addressed, however, is the extent to which these more progressive clauses are implemented in a way that is capable of making a real difference.

B. European Strategy Fluctuating Between the Projection of its 'ILO Inspired' Social Model Outside and its Dilution in the Global Market?

As already noted, the ILO's early interest in European integration was inspired by the conviction that its success could help ILO objectives by providing a model which explicitly combined social progress and inter-state solidarity, in particular through the free movement of workers across the borders. The fact that Europe's model could for decades boast of combining an unparalleled ratification rate of ILO Conventions with respectable economic dynamism and prosperity made it a sort of showcase for what the ILO hoped to stand for.

That view was certainly shared in Brussels, allowing Jacques Delors to proclaim the European Union the 'laboratory of globalisation'.[35] Hardly 10 years ago, the Commissioner for Employment and Social Policy could still boast that the Union

[30] See Peru Trade Promotion Agreement, ibid.

[31] The agreements were signed into law by President Obama in October 2011 (United States Trade Representative, *Statement by US Trade Representative Ron Kirk on Presidential Signature of Trade Legislation* (Press Release, 10 October 2011). The United States-South Korea Agreement came into force on 15 March 2012 (United States Trade Representative, *Jobs on the Way: US-Korea Trade Agreement Enters into Force* (Press Release, 15 March 2011).

[32] Ebert and Posthuma, 'Labour Provisions' (n 17) 8–9.

[33] United States Trade Representative, Colombian Action Plan Related to Labor Rights (7 April 2011).

[34] Don Wells, '"Best Practice" in the Regulation of International Labor Standards: Lessons of the US-Cambodia Textile Agreement' (2006) 27(3) *Comparative Labor Law and Policy Journal* 358.

[35] President Jacques Delors, 'The European Community and the New World Order' (Address to the Royal Institute of International Affairs, London, 7 September 1992).

was 'emerging as a new world model of development'.[36] This brave statement has unfortunately not met with corresponding results.

First, the way in which this ambition translated itself within the European Union was not always felicitous from the viewpoint of the organisation's efforts to project its own standards onto its Members. Social progress may sometimes have been a casualty of the European Commission's ambition to project itself as a major international actor. The European Commission's claims to external competence paradoxically interfered with the ratification process of individual Members – without showing parallel interest regarding the way Members fulfilled the obligations they already had under ratified Conventions.[37] But this ambition also manifested itself through a tendency to project EU legislation and relevant Directives into draft ILO instruments, without necessarily paying too much attention to the relevance such standards may have had in terms of social progress at the universal level.[38] While it is a natural tendency for each Member to do the same, the practice had a much more massive effect (which would, however, need to be documented) on the legislative process when applied collectively by the European Union and its Member States.

Secondly, the fact is that despite this stated ambition and an excellent record of ratification (especially for core Conventions), the result of the EU strategy as regards the social dimension of its trade agreements does not differ in any striking way from that of the United States, even if the most recent agreements contain more frequent references to ILO Conventions.

It may be tempting to explain this situation by the progressive dilution of the initial ambition to project its social model outside into the orthodoxy of global liberalisation[39] and the realities of enlargement;[40] or in other words, by a shift in the respective importance accorded to social and trade considerations, both within and outside the Union, that ultimately brings Europe closer to the US strategy.

A certain coincidence has indeed been noted by some observers between the pace of enlargement and a shift in European trade and development policy starting

[36] Anna Diamantopoulou, 'Making Europe Work for People' (Address at 10th European Trade Union Confederation Statutory Congress, Prague, 26 May 2003).

[37] Indeed, Tonia Novitz has gone so far as to call the difference between the internal and external treatment of ILO instruments a 'double standard' that unfortunately puts in question the legitimacy of the European Union's use of ILO Conventions in its external relations. Tonia Novitz, 'The European Union and International Labour Standards: The Dynamics of the Dialogue between the EU and the ILO' in Philip Alston (ed), *Labour Rights as Human Rights* (Oxford, Oxford University Press, 2005).

[38] Tonia Novitz went so far as to describe the European Union's resulting approach to ILO standards as 'bland' (ibid 238).

[39] This trend may usefully be placed against the background of Faugère's analyis (Faugère, *La régulation sociale* (n 21) which distinguished between three liberal conceptions of Social Europe. The first would focus on economic development, treating Social Europe as a simple byproduct of a successful European economy. The second would consider Social Europe as a component of the realisation of economic Europe, with labour mobility necessary for the realisation of a unified labour market. According to this view, the specific purpose of Social Europe lies in ensuring the effective freedom of movement of labour. Under the third view, the assumption that national social regulations are impediments to growth would see Social Europe as putting labour regulations systems in competition, thereby eliminating the most counterproductive.

[40] See Jacques Sapir, *La démondialisation* (Paris, Seuil, 2011).

in the late 1990s. Up to that point, trade policy was as much as anything seen as connected to international development goals, and had therefore made room for a certain amount of solidarity (obviously not totally devoid of commercial motives) with former European colonies (particularly the countries of Africa, the Caribbean and the Pacific (ACP)). This latter group had preferential access to European markets without any demand for reciprocity. The European Union justified the abandonment of this joint development strategy by invoking the constraints of WTO rules and standards, gradually replacing these concessions with a network of much stricter agreements. Without a doubt, the prior arrangements had themselves been widely criticised, particularly by developing countries who did not receive the same benefits. Some analysts, however, have suggested that reference to these criticisms was only a pretext: the Union had previously been granted a 'waiver' by the WTO to continue the APC regime, and there is no evidence that it would not have been able to extract an extension. As Richard Gibb neatly summarises the problem: 'the WTO is at the centre of these post-Lomé negotiations because the EU has placed it there'.[41]

From this perspective, as much as the European Union's much-touted profession of support for the decent work strategy may have given the impression of an everlasting honeymoon,[42] a closer examination reveals a less idyllic picture.[43] Under the guise of support for the ILO and in accordance with a strategy designed to encourage the endogenous development of international labour standards via trade,[44] some analyses raise suspicions that the Union is masking its renunciation of a goal – projecting a model of 'upward harmonisation' beyond its borders – that it no longer has either the will or the ability to move forward, even among its own newest Member States.[45]

[41] Richard Gibb, 'Post-Lomé: The European Union and the South' (2000) 21(3) *Third World Quarterly* 457, 478.

[42] *cf* European Commission, *Report on the EU Contribution to the Promotion of Decent Work in the World* (2 July 2008) 34, where the Commission states, 'the EU contribution to decent work throughout the world is part of its efforts to strengthen the social dimension of globalization both in the EU and outside' (ibid 4) and also rightly points out that 'ratification and application of the related Conventions by the Member States add value to the EU's drive for more and better jobs' (ibid 31).

[43] On the European Union's support for decent work, see ibid in which, in the lyricism of bureaucratic rigour, it 'reaffirms its commitment to promoting the internationally-agreed decent work agenda', specifying that 'one objective is to strengthen sustainable development in our bilateral trade relations through new cooperative provisions on labour standards and environmental protection. In this context, decent work issues are taken up systematically in all ongoing bilateral Free Trade Agreements and Partnership Cooperation Agreements (PCA) negotiated with a view to including chapters on trade and sustainable development in all agreements'.

[44] As summarised in a document prepared under the direction of Jean-Marc Siroën, 'The objective of promoting decent work and sustainable development is no longer to deal with the negative effects of opening up trade, but rather at supporting or boosting the endogenous development of labour standards resulting from the part played by trade in development' (Jean-Marc Siroën and others, *The Use, Scope and Effectiveness of Labour and Social Aspects and Sustainable Development Provisions in Bilateral and Regional Free Trade Agreements*, Final Report of the European Commission (2008) 12).

[45] See, eg Maarten Keune, 'EU Enlargement and Social Standards: Exporting the European Social Model' in Jan Orbie and Lisa Tortell (eds), *The European Union and the Social Dimension of Globalization: How the EU Influences the World* (London, Routledge 2009) 45, 58–59.

Similar doubts or suspicions have been voiced as regards the impact of enlargement on the original ambition of an 'upward harmonisation' within the European Union itself, as a result of a well-known evolution of the jurisprudence of the European Court of Justice (ECJ),[46] most notably reflected in *Viking* and *Laval*,[47] which has prompted an endless flow of critical comments. Among the first, Alain Supiot argued that this jurisprudence, rooted in wealth differentials and welfare issues between the new additions from Eastern Europe and older Member States, introduced a kind of 'market communism'[48] insofar as it seemed to place the fundamental freedoms of the common market above state compliance with fundamental rights at work, even when such compliance is imposed by the international obligations individual states may have assumed by ratifying relevant ILO Conventions (especially Conventions Nos 87 and 98 on freedom of association and collective bargaining).

The reality, however, is more nuanced.[49] The ECJ was quite careful to balance one interest – free movement for people and services within the Union – against the protection of freedom of association and the right to collectively bargain. The fact remains, however, that the very act of balancing the freedoms inherent in the single market against the fundamental social rights derived from the ratification of relevant Conventions is tantamount to diluting the Member States' obligations as a matter of general international law[50] into the requirements of the 'four freedoms'. In a recent case confronting this tension, the ILO Committee of Experts

[46] A position strongly contrasting with the bold reversal by the European Court of Human Rights in favour of collective bargaining and the right to strike, perhaps most famously in *Demir and Baykara v Turkey* [2008] ECHR 1345. See Franz C Ebert and Martin Oelz, *Bridging the Gap Between Labour Rights and Human Rights: The Role of ILO Regional Human Rights Law in Short*, IILS Discussion Paper DP/212/2012 (2012) 9–11.

[47] Case C-438/05 *Viking (The International Transport Workers' Federation and The Finnish Seamen's Union)* [2007] ECR I-10779; Case C-341/05 *Laval un Partneri Ltd v Svenska Byggnadsarbetareförbundet and others* [2007] ECR I-11767. This jurisprudence was recently taken up in Case C-271/08 concerning public contracts in Germany. Despite 'equal ranking for fundamental rights and fundamental freedoms' (or perhaps, translated differently from the original German, their 'equal status') (Case C-271/08 *European Commission v Federal Republic of Germany* [2010] ECR I-07091, Opinion of AG Trsienjak, paras 183–99), the Grand Chamber of the ECJ reiterated that the 'terms of collective agreements are not excluded from the scope of the provisions on freedom of movement for persons' and held specifically that the 'exercise of a fundamental right such as the right to bargain collectively may be subject to certain restrictions' and even where the right is guaranteed by a state's Constitution, 'that right must be exercised in accordance with European Union Law' (Case C-271/08 *European Commission v Federal Republic of Germany* [2010] ECR I-07091 paras 42–43).

[48] Alain Supiot, 'Voilà l'économie communiste de marché', *Le Monde* (Paris), 25 January 2008.

[49] For a detailed discussion of this jurisprudence, see Marie-Ange Moreau, 'The Evolution of European Social Integration under Globalization' in Adelle Blackett and Christian Lévesque (eds), *Social Regionalism in the Global Economy* (London, Routledge, 2011) 229–33, where the author concludes that the 'ECJ has left little space for social actors to take effective coordinated action to resist a deterioration of labour conditions through allowing firms to take with them "the least regulatory regime of the member states with which they have a connection"' (ibid 233).

[50] This kind of balancing will likely have to continue for the foreseeable future, since, for obvious reasons, the question of the relationship between social rights and fundamental economic freedoms has not been decided. On this subject, see Monika Schalter, 'Reconciliation between Fundamental Social Rights and Economic Freedoms' (Conference on Fundamental Social Rights and the Posting of Workers in the Framework of the Single Market, Brussels, June 2011).

coyly reframed its reading of this larger issue in a manner that tried to address the problem, but in a way that sidestepped this core concern.[51] It is unfortunately not certain that international labour law will emerge as a winner in this unequal dialogue, unless the European Court of Human Rights can come to its rescue as a result of its own jurisprudence and the adhesion of the Union to the European Convention on Human Rights.[52]

While this 'rebalancing' of social and trade considerations certainly brings the EU approach closer to the US strategy, it would be a mistake to consider it as a decisive factor in explaining the scope and content of the 'social clauses' actually concluded.

Rather, in both the EU and the US cases, these clauses are above all ultimately a reflection of the constraints of reciprocity. As we shall see, the European Union has in fact tried to use ILO standards whenever they were compatible with the constraints of reciprocity (the most advanced examples being agreements with the CARIFORUM countries and South Korea)[53] and whenever these constraints did not apply.[54]

[51] In 2010, the ILO's Committee of Experts on the Application of Conventions and Recommendations addressed an injunction that had been brought against employees of British Airways, prohibiting them from striking so as to prevent the establishment of BA subsidiaries in other EU states. In its arguments, the United Kingdom tried to justify the injunction by taking shelter behind this ECJ case law. The Committee found that the injunction 'created a situation where the rights under the Convention cannot be exercised' (ILO, *Report III(1A): Report of the Committee of Experts on the Application of Conventions and Recommendations* (ILC, 99th Session, Geneva, 2–8 June 2010) 209). The Committee nonetheless founded its decision almost totally in terms of the potentially dire consequences for the union of exercising its rights, being careful not to rule on the underlying cause, that is to say, on the contradiction between Community law as interpreted by the Court and the international law obligations of Community Member States arising from their adherence to relevant ILO Conventions. As for the Conference Committee on the Application of Standards, it chose not to select the case for tripartite review, a totally understandable decision given the technical legal issues raised, but one which nonetheless leaves the problem completely unresolved.

[52] The 'titanic battle of the juristocrats' forecast by some commentators (Keith D Ewing and John Hendy, 'The Dramatic Implications of *Demir and Baykara*' (2010) 39(1) *Industrial Law Journal* 42) following the *Demir and Baykarav v Turkey* decision (n 63) taken by the Grand Chamber of the European Court of Human Rights in November 2008 may never come to pass. While this decision, followed by the less flamboyant *Enerji Yapi-Yol* decision (*Enerji Yapi-Yol Sen v Turkey* App No 68959/01 (ECtHR, 21 April 2009)) have provoked a flurry of speculations, it is interesting to note that Judge Raimondi has in a recent analysis struck a more cautious note. In an article to be published in the *Melanges en l'honneur de Yves Berger*, he draws attention to the fact that the Grand Chamber did not actually rule that the right to strike was to be considered as an essential element of freedom of association, but only an important one; he suggests that the Court might find some subsequent occasion to clarify the issue. What does already seem clear is that a resolution is unlikely to come from the executive. The document *Towards a Single Market Act: For a Highly Competitive Social Market Economy* presented by the European Commission to the European Parliament in 27 October 2010 unfortunately fails to deliver on the promise of its title and is certainly unlikely to advance European jurisprudence (COM(2010)608 final). The controversy raised by the *Viking* and *Laval* jurisprudence did subsequently lead the Commission, in May 2012, to submit a proposed Regulation (COM(2012)130), attached to a long memorandum whose long-term impact would be unclear if the whole project did not already appear to be still-born.

[53] Ebert and Posthuma, 'Labour Provisions' (n 17) 13–15.

[54] See Ebert and Posthuma, 'Labour Provisions' (n 17) 9–14 (Tables 3 and 5). Partially on this basis, Ailish Johnston emphasises the mutual benefits of the relationship between the ILO and the European Union since the 1950s (Johnston, 'EU-ILO Relations' (n 19) 81). Quite contrary to this position is Tonia

C. Constraints of Reciprocity and their Impact on the Scope/ Content of Decentralised Social Clauses

Whatever the underlying strategies developed by their sponsors, a conclusion seems to emerge from the mass of available information with almost mechanical rigour, that the requirements of reciprocity imposed by trade agreements tend to pull down the strength of the 'social clauses' introduced therein. It seems axiomatic in this regard (though the EU case provides an awkward fit) that an individual country can hardly be so hypocritical as to demand standards from another country it would be unwilling to accept for itself.[55] But then, the enthusiasm for imposing whatever standards are domestically acceptable tends to be dulled in practice by the promise of the economic benefits to accrue from reciprocal market access – often from a country which will inevitably want to pull minimum standards in an agreement down to its own level. This point is just as true for the scope of the 'social clauses' in these agreements as it is for the level of the normative references in ILO instruments, as one can verify by examining the counterexample provided by Europe's Generalised System of Preferences (GSP).

(i) Normative Content Often Determined by Trading Partner Sensitivities

In both bilateral and universal negotiations (and perhaps even more so in the former case), a country's willingness to include 'social clauses' in an agreement must ultimately cede some ground to the overall concern not to alienate the negotiating partner.

Thus, if some sort of reference to fundamental rights is consistently found in agreements made by the United States, the level and content of the resulting coverage is far from systematic. Very significantly, in accordance with section 301 of the OTCA, non-discrimination was left almost totally by the wayside until 2006. One needs to refer to the political-cultural inclinations of potential trading partners to reconcile the notable absence of anti-discrimination protections from American GSP conditions,[56] with the subject's inconsistent inclusion in the cohort of

Novitz, who sees the EU appropriation of ILO standards as entailing a real risk of their gradual erosion (Novitz, 'In Search' (n 21) 38–41).

[55] Steve Charnovitz put a sharp point on this aspect when he admitted from his own experience 'the indelicacy of asking other governments to guarantee the right to organize and bargain collectively when the United States itself has not ratified the applicable ILO Conventions' (Charnovitz, 'Editorial Comments' (n 25) 95).

[56] Jeffrey Vogt and Lance Compa explain that discrimination protections were originally excluded from the US GSP scheme because '[s]ome officials in the administration feared souring relations with allied oil-producing states where discrimination against women and non-Muslims is prevalent' (Lance Compa and Jeffrey Vogt, 'Labor Rights in the Generalized System of Preferences: A 20 Years Review' (2001) 22(2–3) *Comparative Labor Law and Policy Journal* 119, 203). The appearance of this incomplete list of US-defined 'internationally recognised workers' rights' in the GSP provisions led to their subsequent inclusion in the OTCA (ibid 205).

agreements negotiated between 1994 and 2006.[57] On the other hand, if references to fundamental rights in US agreements are not exhaustive, nor are they exclusive. Thus, US agreements have often included references to occupational health, minimum wages and maximum working hours pursuant to section 301's conception of 'internationally recognised workers' rights'.[58]

It is true that the bilateral US agreements negotiated since 1998 have seen a surge of *general* references to the Declaration on Fundamental Principles and Rights at Work.[59] Yet as much as this undoubtedly reflects the growing authority the category attracts, this practice should be greeted with neither complacency nor naiveté. Such references are in some sense used to circumvent the difficulty of formulating specific obligations in terms of fundamental rights, since by hypothesis the Declaration is intended to bind all ILO members. If referring to the Declaration helps cover fundamental rights whose explicit recall is likely to offend a finicky partner, it also avoids setting an explicit level of protection, as would a reference to the relevant Conventions and the jurisprudence under them. In this regard, even if the agreements finalised in the last four years go so far as to require 'maintenance in statutes and regulations' of the complete (and explicitly enumerated) list of fundamental rights,[60] at best this new practice reinforces the 'self-referential' standard which is a common feature of all the agreements they have negotiated in the last 20 years.

(ii) A Frequently Self-Referential Level of Protection

There is one standard of worker protection which no country would normally dismiss as too high: the level already set in its own legislation! It is therefore hardly surprising that solutions based on precisely this standard have been so popular. An approach based on reference to each country's existing laws has long been included in agreements concluded by the United States. This is a more radical version of not demanding from the other party anything that the country would not do itself; after all, a trading partner can hardly object to an obligation to respect its own laws. This solution further offers the twin advantages of, first of all, vindicating the principle that each country should be free to determine its own level of social

[57] In her analysis of the United States-Jordan Agreement, Kaufman finds it strange that '[i]n contrast to the NAALC, this agreement noticeably leaves out non-discrimination in employment' (Christine Kaufmann, *Globalisation and Labour Rights: The Conflict Between Core Labour Rights and International Economic Law* (Oxford, Oxford University Press, 2007) 192). Yet, given that the framework which existed (and continues to exist) under the OTCA does not include anti-discrimination principles, it is the *inclusion* of anti-discrimination protections in the NAALC which needs to be explained, and indeed, can only be explained with reference to Canadian (or Mexican) negotiating interests.

[58] Again, however, NAALC provisions covering the rights of migrant workers cannot be explained without reference to trading partner interests.

[59] Agreements with Chile, Singapore, Australia, Morocco, Bahrain, Oman and the CAFTA-DR each recognise the 'principles' in the Declaration along with the US-defined list of 'internationally recognised labour rights'. See Ebert and Posthuma, 'Labour Provisions' (n 17) 9–10 (Table 3).

[60] It is also worth noting that the language in these agreements flows only from the 2006 Bipartisan Trade Deal; the list of rights in the OTCA still excludes anti-discrimination, meaning even this minimally concrete level of reference remains highly dependent on domestic political battles.

protection, but also as a result forecloses on any suspicion of protectionism or cultural imperialism that 'social clauses' so often provoke. This goes some way toward explaining why such clauses have since 2008 found their way into agreements signed by the European Union as well.

While the effective implementation of a country's own legislated standards might seem almost tautological for states respecting the rule of law, there are at least two reasons why the benefits of such provisions should not be underestimated.[61]

First, as pointed out by Bob Hepple with regard to the NAALC, such provisions can 'change the culture of law enforcement'.[62] In the case of many agreements concluded within the Americas, it seems that this cultural change has gone hand in hand with real, practical changes, backed up by an influx of significant technical cooperation aimed in particular at strengthening the administration of justice relating to labour issues.[63] It might even be suggested that, more than the dispute resolution mechanisms which most easily attract attention from lawyers, the value of these social clauses is actually located in this latter dimension.

Secondly, such clauses offer a convenient low-water mark against which to measure any competitive erosion of working conditions. And that is why the reference to national legislation is supplemented by (or, in the case of recent EU-negotiated agreements, inextricably linked to)[64] non-regression clauses exercising a 'ratchet effect' on existing law. Such mechanisms were evidently designed by developed countries to prevent any attempt at competitive erosion of labour rights and social protection on the part of their less-developed trading partners. Perhaps unexpectedly, however, such clauses might also have a 'boomerang effect' for those who first devised them: neither Europe nor the United States seem to have taken into account the symmetrical commitment they were undertaking not to weaken their own social protections. Indeed, insofar as it is easy to imagine that this legislation is more advanced, no doubt they may be exposed to greater temptation to put in place some 'flexibility' in response to exacerbated international competition.[65] Their signature on clauses that prohibit any competitive decrease in social protection, or that impose an improved protection for workers, also represents an

[61] The weakness of trade unions, labour administrations and labour inspectors go a long way to explaining, in combination with a weak court system, the severe limits on the real impact of existing legislation in, for example, Mexican maquiladoras. Indeed, while that situation explains the priority given to the effective implementation of national legislation starting with the NAALC, given the decline in trade unions and labour administrations since the mid-1990s, similar factors are relevant even in developed countries.

[62] Bob Hepple, 'The WTO as a Mechanism for Labour Regulation' in Brian Bercusson and Cynthia Estlund, *Regulating Labour in the Wake of Globalisation: New Challenges, New Institutions* (Oxford, Hart Publishing, 2008) 166.

[63] Ebert and Posthuma, 'Labour Provisions' (n 17) 26–28.

[64] ILO and IILS, *World of Work Report 2009* (n 14) 73. The formula was first implemented in the CARIFORUM agreement, and is also found in the agreements concluded with the Republic of Korea and provisionally in force since July 2011 (Ebert and Posthuma, 'Labour Provisions' (n 17) 14–15).

[65] The attempted introduction of the 'Contrat nouvelle embauche' in France offers a vivid illustration of this temptation, at least to the extent that the legislation in question was found under the ILO complaints procedure to imply a decline relative to France's international obligations.

obstacle to reducing their own standards of protection. Moreover, as suggested by a team of authors which included the ILO's Marion Jansen, those provisions should provide them all the more encouragement not to 'backslide' given the ample resources they have at their disposal compared to developing countries.[66] It also seems relevant here to consider the relative value of this kind of decentralised ratchet clause when compared to the potential of Article XXIII of GATT to operate as a kind of *universal* ratchet clause, as elaborated at the end of the previous chapter.

(iii) ILO Instruments Referenced Rarely (At Best)

It goes without saying (again) that from the ILO's perspective, social clauses that reflect its instruments, and those referring to fundamental Conventions in particular, are far preferable to general references to Declarations that have neither the same binding force nor the same level of precision.

Such references are exceptional in agreements signed by the United States, for the reason already noted that, of the fundamental Conventions, they have ratified only Conventions Nos 105 and 182.[67] Instead, as mentioned above, references have generally been limited to the 1998 Declaration. On the other hand, explicit references to the fundamental Conventions can be found in some (especially newer) agreements signed by the European Union, sometimes side by side with a reference to the 1998 Declaration. There are, however, large fluctuations. Thus, the agreements with the Palestinian Authority, Morocco, Israel, Algeria and Cameroon contain only vague provisions on cooperation in labour matters, while the Accession Treaties with new applicants for EU membership are much more restrictive.[68] However, even the recently signed (and most demanding) agreements do not go so far as to mandate that the parties ratify and implement these Conventions.[69] More vaguely, they aim either to ensure the implementation of core standards, enforced only by possible non-trade sanctions (European Union-CARIFORUM) or to 'realise and promote ILO Fundamental Conventions' (European Union-Republic of Korea).[70]

(iv) A Telling Counterexample: Unilateral Preferences

Such reciprocity considerations are largely, if not completely, absent from unilateral arrangements. As a consequence, countries offering preferential access to their

[66] Christian Häberli, Marion Jansen and José-Antonio Monteiro, *References to Domestic Labour Market Regulation in Regional Trade Agreements*, NCCR Trade Regulation Working Paper No 2011/35 (2011).

[67] It is no coincidence that the only reference to fundamental Conventions that is found in the agreements made since 2004 (Chile, Australia, Morocco, Bahrain, Oman, CAFTA and Peru) is to Convention No 182 (ILO and IILS, *World of Work Report 2009* (n 14) 69, Table 3.2).

[68] ILO and IILS, *World of Work Report 2009* (n 14) 73, Table 3.6.

[69] Perhaps this approach has been avoided because it would inevitably raise the question of potential application of ILO procedures to verify compliance. This consequence probably explains why universal ratification of the relevant Conventions has also been ruled out as the way to promote the social foundation of the European Union.

[70] ILO and IILS, *World of Work Report 2009* (n 14) 73, Table 3.6.

own markets as a form of development aid have a much greater margin of discretion regarding the choice of conditions attached to this privilege.[71] Given the objections which have been levelled against such 'conditionality' in light of WTO rules,[72] reference to ILO standards and procedures provide a veneer of multilateral respectability, thereby reducing the political cost of a policy already seen as having little economic downside. It is therefore not surprising that the European system of unilateral incentives has relied more and more on ILO instruments and supervisory procedures. The United States' situation, on the other hand, offers a rather remarkable departure: the United States-Cambodia Textile Agreement, a kind of 'boutique' project with an atypical, and very significant, role for the ILO.

(a) Case of the European GSP

The European Union's Generalised System of Preferences (GSP) provides developing countries with a suspension from the Union's common *ad valorem* tariffs for a particularised list of products. In 1995, those GSP benefits were tied to fundamental rights at work (with the exception of the prohibition on forced labour): the extension of benefits required national legislation that conformed with ILO standards in each area, though ratification of the relevant Conventions was not required. No doubt influenced by the passage of the 1998 Declaration, the fundamental Conventions and ILO procedures were subsequently given increased importance both in granting and in withdrawing GSP privileges.[73]

Similarly, the granting of GSP+ 'special incentives'[74] for 'sustainable development and good governance' had previously been predicated on national legislation incorporating the substance of standards laid out in the eight fundamental Conventions. Under Article 8 of Regulation 732/2008,[75] which takes over and expands the previous regulation, the programme now requires the country to have ratified *and* to effectively apply the Conventions listed in an Annex, including the eight core ILO Conventions.

With regard to punitive measures, withdrawal or suspension of privileges in the original GSP system originally fell totally within the jurisdiction of European

[71] Such preferential access is empowered by the 'enabling clause', which provides the basis for the Generalised Systems of Preferences (GSP) in favour of developing countries. See GATT, *Differential and More Favourable Treatment, Reciprocity and Fuller Participation of Developing Countries* (1979) GATT BISD 26S/210.

[72] To the extent that some authors see the introduction of conditionality as a perversion of the goals of equity and solidarity which originally inspired the adoption of the enabling clause (see, eg Frieder Roessler, 'Domestic Policy Objectives and the Multilateral Trade Order: Lessons from the Past' in Anne O Krueger (ed), *The WTO as an International Organization* (Chicago, IL, University of Chicago Press, 1998) 218–20).

[73] Jan Orbie and Lisa Tortell, 'The New GSP+ Beneficiaries: Ticking the Box or Truly Consistent with ILO Findings?' (2009) 14 *European Foreign Affairs Review* 663, 666.

[74] This incentive system has existed since 1998 and became the current GSP+ with the 2005 reform (ibid).

[75] Council Regulation (EC) 732/2008 of 22 July 2008 applying a scheme of generalised tariff preferences for the period from 1 January 2009 to 31 December 2011 and amending Regulations (EC) 552/97, 1933/2006 and Commission Regulations (EC) 1100/2006 and (EC) 964/2007 [2008] OJ L211/1, 4.

authorities and did not require a finding of a violation through ILO procedures.[76] Today, penalties depend on a finding of a violation within the ILO, undoubtedly to the benefit of the perceived objectivity and legitimacy of the GSP conditions.[77] According to Article 15(1)(a) of the Regulation, temporary withdrawal of GSP or GSP+ benefits can be based on various factors including, first, 'the serious and systematic violation of principles laid down in the Conventions listed in Part A of Annex III, on the basis of the conclusions of the relevant monitoring bodies'. At first sight, this formulation appears perfectly consistent with the ILO's exclusive jurisdiction to establish violation of its own Conventions.[78] Starting in 2007, the European Union moved beyond rhetoric to suspend GSP benefits to Belarus based on their systematic violation of freedom of association and the right to collective bargaining, and with explicit reference to ILO core Conventions (in this case Conventions Nos 87 and 98).[79] There is, on the other hand, some concern that the weight and cost of the relevant ILO procedures, and the fact that control over whether it gets triggered at all falls to the ILO Governing Body, might lead the Union, acting under the pressure of public opinion, to act on a more expeditious though legally more dubious basis,[80] rather than waiting for the uncertain establishment of a Commission of Inquiry under Article 26 of the ILO Constitution.[81]

[76] This was not without problems in legal terms. Indeed, from a strict perspective of international law, the only authority competent to establish a violation of obligations resulting from the ratification of an ILO Convention is the ILO itself. Without suggesting that it would have to wait for Art 33 to be activated, it would at the very least seem that some sort of findings by a Commission of Inquiry set up under the complaints procedure (findings not successfully challenged at the ICJ) would be a necessary precondition for taking such action.

[77] Jan Orbie and Lisa Tortell, 'The New GSP+ Beneficiaries: Ticking the Box or Truly Consistent with ILO Findings?' (2009) 14 *European Foreign Affairs Review* 663, 671.

[78] However, to put the scope of these references to ILO procedures in greater perspective: EU organs retain broad discretion in this regard, given the vagueness of 'serious and systematic violations' and of references to the 'principles' laid down in the Conventions. Thus, in practice, a finding of a violation by the ILO does *not* automatically lead to the withdrawal of GSP or GSP+ benefits. In fact, several countries found in violation of ILO Conventions (Colombia, Guatemala and Georgia) continue to benefit from the programme (Novitz, 'In Search' (n 21) 34–35). Despite these various limitations, Orbie and Tortell consider the application of sanctions by the EU GSP to be consistent with the ILO's hierarchy of sanctions: 'There is a clear consistency between the application of GSP sanctions by the EU and the hierarchy of ILO condemnation' (Orbie and Tortell, 'The New GSP+' (n 77) 675 ff). By their conclusion, it was the formal and unambiguous condemnation by the ILO (especially in the case where an inquiry has been conducted) which led to clear sanctions against both Myanmar and Belarus, even if the same situations may have had broader foreign relations ramifications within the European Union.

[79] The suspension procedure was originally launched in 2003. Orbie and De Ville have suggested that the delay in the decision actually to implement sanctions against Belarus (the European Commission originally recommended withdrawal in August 2005) resulted from cynical political calculations which put the legitimacy of the social GSP clause into question. Jan Orbie and Ferdi de Ville, 'Core Labour Standards in the GSP Regime of the European Union: Overshadowed by Other Considerations' in Tonia Novitz and Colin Fenwick (eds), *Human Rights at Work: Perspectives on Law and Regulation* (Oxford, Hart Publishing, 2010) 504–5.

[80] That is, they might be tempted to rely solely on an observation of the Committee of Experts or the Committee on Freedom of Association, or possibly the publication of a decision made on completion of the Art 24 Representation procedure.

[81] Which raises the interesting question of whether it should be contemplated that fully respecting international law may require allowing the European Union itself to take the initiative to undertake the Representation procedure (but if it was given this power, what about the (considerable) costs inherent in establishing a Commission of Inquiry?).

Overall, while the EU GSP scheme may raise some eyebrows from WTO observers[82] it appears not only to be consistent with ILO objectives and standards, but also to provide substantial reinforcement to the ratification and implementation of ILO instruments. Under the reformed GSP, many countries have been led to ratify one or more of the fundamental Conventions in return for being granted increased market access (including Bolivia, Venezuela, Mongolia and El Salvador).[83] It is true that the record is more mixed regarding the effective implementation of these Conventions, a concern that is supposed to be an inherent part of GSP+ conditionality. With rare exceptions (children's rights in El Salvador and improvements in legislation and reporting frequency in Sri Lanka), inclusion in this system does not seem to meaningfully improve the application of fundamental ILO standards in recipient countries.[84] In many cases, GSP and GSP+ beneficiaries continue to be regularly rebuked at the ILO, including a number of lucky winners selected for GSP+ in 2009–2011.[85]

On the other hand, the February 2010 decision to temporarily withdraw Sri Lanka's GSP+ benefits for failing to implement the International Covenant on Civil and Political Rights, the Convention Against Torture and the Convention on the Rights of the Child demonstrates that the European Union is ready to play 'hardball' with GSP+ beneficiaries who fail to meet their end of the bargain.[86] It remains to be seen whether this conclusion will apply as strongly to workers' rights, which, despite an equivalent status, might be said to earn less attention in international public opinion.

(b) Case of the United States-Cambodia Textile Agreement

The United States' GSP programme predates the 1998 Declaration by almost 15 years, and it is not totally surprising that its implications for the ILO are much less direct. Benefits are tied not to the application of ILO standards, but to compliance with the previously-referenced 'internationally recognised workers' rights'.[87] The

[82] Franz C Ebert, 'Between Political Goodwill and WTO-Law: Human Rights Conditionality in the Community's New Scheme of Generalised Tariff Preferences (GSP)' (2009) *ZERP-Arbeitspapier* 8/2009.

[83] Orbie and Tortell, 'The New GSP+' (n 77) 672–73.

[84] Weifeng Zhou and Ludo Cuyvers, 'Linking International Trade and Labour Standards: The Effectiveness of Sanctions Under The European Union's GSP' (2011) 45(1) *Journal of World Trade* 63.

[85] Commission Decision 2008/938/EC of 9 December 2008 on the list of the beneficiary countries which qualify for the special incentive arrangement for sustainable development and good governance, provided for in Council Regulation (EC) 732/2008 applying a scheme of generalised tariff preferences for the period from 1 January 2009 to 31 December 2011 [2008] OJ L334/90, 90–91.

[86] See Implementing Regulation (EU) 143/2010 of the Council of 15 February 2010 temporarily withdrawing the special incentive arrangement for sustainable development and good governance provided for under Regulation (EC) 732/2008 with respect to the Democratic Socialist Republic of Sri Lanka [2010] OJ L45/1, 1–2.

[87] Originally established under the Trade Act of 1974, the renewal of the US GSP scheme in 1984 included an amendment, driven by pressure from human rights and workers' rights activists, introducing conditions based on compliance with certain standards to protect workers. For reasons more political than legal, the law omits one category of fundamental rights: the prohibition against any form of discrimination. This omission was likely due to President Reagan's desire not to antagonise oil-producing countries by putting into question their laws and practices relating to women and

withdrawal of preferences is determined through an internal procedure which leaves considerable room for political expediency, a fact formally recognised by American courts.[88]

On the other hand, the ILO, or more accurately the International Labour Office,[89] was given a remarkable role in certain trade benefits granted to Cambodia, a country that was not at the time a WTO member and had not previously been a GSP beneficiary. With an agreement signed in January 1999 and renewed every three years, the United States pledged to expand Cambodia's textiles and garments quota to 14 per cent, provided that the conditions of work in the industry respected both national legislation and 'internationally recognised workers' rights'. The quota was subsequently expanded to 18 per cent in 2001, subject to the requirement for Cambodia to establish a programme to improve working conditions and respect for human rights through existing labour laws. The entire project is complemented by activities to strengthen the capacity of the state and the role of associations of employers and workers.[90] What is perhaps most remarkable about this system is the place given to the ILO, which not only provides logistical support[91] but also lends the whole endeavour the organisation's moral endorsement and legal sign-off.[92]

In practical terms, the project seems to have truly helped a country which could seriously benefit from additional business. The reputation of the ILO-sponsored programme mobilised textile importers in US markets, who saw a clear

non-Muslims. On the other hand, a category not covered by the 1998 Declaration did make its way into the list of conditions: the defence of so-called 'acceptable conditions of work' including the existence of a minimum wage, limits on working time, and provisions to ensure health and safety at work. Besides an annual general review, the GSP scheme provides a process allowing any interested person to submit a request to the USTR to review a beneficiary country's alleged non-compliance with its commitments. After giving an opportunity for the requesting party to present its arguments, the Commission may decide to maintain or suspend benefits (Bob Hepple, *Labour Laws and Global Trade* (Oxford, Hart Publishing, 2005) 194–97).

[88] The pressure from oil interests, for example, seems to have led to the decision to place Indonesia and Malaysia under 'supervision' rather than suspending their benefits (Compa and Vogt, 'Labor Rights' (n 56) 222–28; Julien Burda, 'Le droit international économique et les droits sociaux fondamentaux: pour un dimension sociale de la libéralisation des échanges' (unpublished manuscript on file with author, 2009) 340).

[89] The agreement's implications for the ILO and its officials were never put before the organisation's deliberative bodies.

[90] ILO and IILS, *World of Work Report 2009* (n 14) 81, Box 3.1.

[91] This resulted in a primarily US-funded technical assistance programme being entrusted to the ILO, in turn given the task of overseeing Cambodian textile factories and improving the capacity of government, employers and workers to collaborate on improved working conditions. Participation in the supervision programme was the precondition to being granted an export licence. The results of this supervision, exercised at enterprise level by ILO-appointed staff, are published online (Sandra Polaski, *Harnessing Global Forces to Create Decent Work in Cambodia*, IILS/Better Work Research Series 119 (2009).

[92] Indeed, the situation raises an obvious question: given that the basic logic of the agreement would seem repugnant to a majority of governments, how could it ever have received a seal of approval without causing waves in the ILO's decision-making bodies? One answer is that they were never asked for their opinion, but part of the explanation has to be that the relative calm surrounding the arrival of the new Director-General, who no one suspected of colluding on the social clause issue, created poor conditions to start a fight.

commercial interest in the social dimensions of their purchasing, and thereby increased the attractiveness of 'Made in Cambodia' fashions.[93]

The reality of improvements in Cambodian firms was perhaps more open to debate. Those who had been involved in the programme for the US administration touted its results, claiming that it was 'arguably the best investment the United States has ever made in promoting international labour rights'.[94] This positive assessment was repeated far and wide by various commentaries affirming the significant improvements which had been seen in employment, wage levels, respect for working conditions and association rights.[95] It is not universally shared, however, and one cannot turn a blind eye to dissident facts and views.[96] The most radical criticism, coming from a political scientist, is that the project is typical of an approach that 'atomises problem solving' and is fundamentally disempowering to the ability of unions to mobilise workers on more fundamental issues, including reform of labour laws, anti-corruption and greater social justice.[97] While, as pointed out by Adler and Woolcock, the negative impact of the project may be exaggerated,[98] the question of the 'atomisation' of social progress through this kind of initiative does have wider ramifications which will be considered in Part IV and in the Conclusion.

[93] Polaski, *Harnessing Global Forces* (n 91) 1.

[94] Sandra Polaski, 'Protecting Labor Rights Through Trade Agreements: An Analytical Guide' (2004) 10(13) *Journal of International Law and Policy* 13, 25. From 1999 to 2002, Polaski was the US Secretary of State's special representative for international labour affairs.

[95] See, eg Doug Miller, 'Business as Usual? Governing the Supply Chain in Clothing: Post MFA Phase-Out: The Case of Cambodia' (2009) 1(1) *International Journal of Labour Research* 9; Wells, 'Best Practice' (n 34); Polaski, *Harnessing Global Forces* (n 91); Kevin Kolben, 'Trade, Monitoring, and the ILO: Working to Improve Conditions in Cambodia's Garment Factories' (2004) 7 *Yale Human Rights and Development Law Journal* 79, 101. See also Kevin Banks, 'Trade, Labor and International Governance: An Inquiry into the Potential Effectiveness of the New International Labor Law' (2011) 32(1) *Berkeley Journal of Employment and Labor Law* 45, 106–13, who uses the Agreement to argue for the superiority of a model of 'Leveraged Deliberative Cooperation' for improving labour rights, over models based on either 'sunshine or moral suasion' or 'adjudication and sanctions-based constitutionalism'.

[96] For instance the investigation published by *Harper's Magazine* which was conducted by a journalist posing as a potential purchaser who gained 'unfiltered' access to the enterprises concerned but which unfortunately does not seem to have been discussed with ILO officials in charge of the programme. It offers a more nuanced view and puts in question what is described as an 'extra coat of whitewash' offered by the ILO's *Better Factories Cambodia* monitoring programme (which in 2004 was expanded into a broader 'Better Work' programme). By the author's estimation, it is 'quickly evident to any visitor that the ILO is an advocate for the apparel companies that fund its work and pay for its reports, which are kept strictly confidential'. According to his interviews, local officials are most interested in the programme's ability 'to build confidence among our stakeholders, because the industry is so important to Cambodia and the lives of its people'. Ken Silverstein, 'Shopping for sweat: the human cost of a two-dollar T-shirt', *Harper's Magazine* (New York), January 2010.

[97] Caroline Hughes, 'Transnational Networks, International Organizations and Political Participation in Cambodia: Human Rights, Labour Rights and Common Rights' (2007) 14(5) *Democratization* 834.

[98] Daniel Adler and Michael Woolcock, 'Justice without the Rule of Law? The Challenge of Rights-based Industrial Relations in Contemporary Cambodia' in Tonia Novitz and Colin Fenwick (eds), *Human Rights at Work: Perspectives on Law and Regulation* (Oxford, Hart Publishing, 2010) 544 and 552.

II. A Limited 'Enforcement' Blessing for Workers

What should be taken from the above is that the social dimension of trade agreements, even when limited to the lowest common denominator of simply applying each country's law, can still lead to measurable progress, so long as it is accompanied by effective monitoring that would supplement the often less-than-absolute guarantees offered by national enforcement mechanisms and jurisdictions. Three preliminary conclusions might be gleaned from this broad review.

A. Inherent Limitations of Sanctions

First off, the possibility of sanctions is quickly revealed to provide no more of a panacea than they are at the universal level. While negative consequences are attached to terms in many agreements, they can usually be put in place only subject to a complex set of conditions[99] in multilateral[100] as much as in bilateral agreements.[101] This may explain why none of the 'social clauses' contained in these agreements have ever actually led to the removal of trade advantages or other penalties.[102]

Perhaps equally significant are the cases where sanctions *have* been applied for social reasons, in the form of suspended or withdrawn preferences previously granted *unilaterally* by the United States[103] or the European Union[104] under their respective GSPs. On the other hand, the effectiveness of these sanctions remains in serious doubt.[105]

(i) Practical Effectiveness Remains Unproven

While it is recognised that a system can theoretically be effective even in the absence of sanctions, it is difficult not to be struck by how varied their effectiveness seems to have been in practice. No doubt, that diversity is primarily a result of (not always explicit) differences in the evaluation criteria being applied.

[99] Indeed, in many US cases, their application is specifically limited to violations impacting on trade, while excluding what matter most to the collective defence of rights, that is to say, freedom of association, collective bargaining and the right to strike (NAFTA and bilateral agreements with Chile, Singapore, Morocco, Australia, etc) (ILO and IILS, *World of Work Report 2009* (n 14) Tables 3.1, 3.2 and 3.3).

[100] According to the NAALC Agreement, for example, monetary compensation is provided only in the event of systematic failure, and can be awarded only at the end of the applicable procedure to ensure the effective application of its technical labour standards in the (three) areas specified.

[101] ILO and IILS, *World of Work Report 2009* (n 14) 69, Table 3.2.

[102] ibid 78–79.

[103] In 13 out 57 petitions examined (ibid 79, Table 3.11).

[104] Specifically, Belarus and Myanmar. The fact is that the suspension or withdrawal of preferences no more resolved the situation in Myanmar than did the 'activation' of Art 33, although the threat did seem to register some progress in the case of Belarus.

[105] Yaraslau Kryvoi, 'Why European Union Trade Sanctions Do Not Work' (2008) 12(2) *Minnesota Journal of International Law* 209. See also Zhou and Cuyvers, 'Linking International Trade' (n 84).

The NAALC provides an example in which relevant clauses allow for the system to be monitored with the assistance of civil society. Yet, the *World of Work Report 2009* notes that, of the 37 petitions submitted under the Agreement, none have proceeded beyond the stage of 'consultations'. On the basis of various sources, the Report estimates that evidence of contributions to significant improvements are limited: there are only a handful of examples with concrete results.[106] The widespread disappointment with the operation of NAALC procedures in practice[107] has meant that, for some activists, the most remarkable merit of the regime is ultimately that it helped increase cross-border solidarity between workers![108]

A number of commentators have suggested, however, that these provisions have to be given some credit as a result of the pressure that has been generated by the publicity the petition system has brought to alleged violations.

Authors who have expressed scepticism about the coherence of social clauses in trade agreements do at the same time recognise their 'procedural value', especially insofar as they make it possible for social actors to act at the supranational level to help ensure the visibility of violations.[109] While such provisions are rarer in the bilateral setting,[110] it would seem that in some cases, they have nevertheless helped

[106] ILO and IILS, *World of Work Report 2009* (n 14) 78–79. More than half resulted in 'cooperative activities', working groups or seminars, but these were sometimes boycotted as irrelevant by the unions or NGOs involved. For some of those most interested in the social dimensions of trade integration, the results from NAALC complaints have been so disappointing and insubstantial that they 'decided no longer to engage with the procedures in their scholarly texts'. Blackett and Lévesque, *Social Regionalism* (n 4) 5.

[107] As put by Graciela Bensusán, 'the scepticism generated by the faulty functioning of the NAALC . . . rapidly dampened what few expectations there had been that the region would have an instrument able to halt the deterioration in job quality' (Graciela Bensusán, 'Labour Reform from the Regional Perspective: Experiences in the Americas' in Adelle Blackett and Christian Lévesque (eds), *Social Regionalism in the Global Economy* (London, Routledge, 2011) 208).

[108] Hepple, *Labour Laws* (n 87) 120 and 128, relying on Lance Compa, 'The North American Free Trade Agreement and the North American Agreement on Labour Cooperation' in Roger Blainpain (ed), *International Encylopedia for Labour Law and Industrial Relations* (Deventer, Kluwer, 1998).

[109] Although the intervention of the NAO when thus seized is limited to the possibility of cooperating with the authorities of the country concerned and, if need be, to recommending to state authorities that there be consultations on the case with the impugned state, the publicity given to these communications can exercise considerable pressure on the defaulting party (Marie-Ange Moreau, *Normes sociales, droit du travail et mondialisation: confrontation and mutations* (Paris, Dalloz, 2006) 205–6).

[110] Even in the best-case scenario (for example, the well-received United States-Jordan Agreement), bilateral agreements merely provide each party with the right to challenge a breach of its partner's obligation to protect the rights of its own workers. Allegations can then be transmitted to a neutral panel for determination. More recent agreements restrict access to cases where there is actually a violation of the partner's own pre-existing national labour law (Cleopatra Doumbia-Henry and Eric Gravel, 'Free Trade Agreements and Labour Rights: Recent Developments' (2006) 145(3) *International Labour Review* 185, 192). Conversely, however, Marley Weiss seems to be concerned that the opportunity for interested parties to raise issues has resulted in collective rights being better protected than individual rights (including those of children or victims of accidents), because the latter have no appointed representatives (Marley Weiss, 'Two Steps Forward, One Step Back – Or Vice Versa: Labor Rights Under Free Trade Agreements from NAFTA, Through Jordan, via Chile, to Latin America, and Beyond' (2003) 37(3) *University of San Francisco Law Review* 689, 748–49). Finally, this type of system leaves open the difficult question of when the actions of an individual firm also constitute a failure by the state to enforce its own legislation (Dubin, *La protection des normes sociales* (n 21) 267–70).

leverage 'transnational pressure' into improvements in the enforcement of national legislation.[111]

In the final account, the considerable and rapidly growing literature committed to the subject provides a rather mixed picture,[112] one which Christine Kaufmann goes so far as to describe as a 'broken promise'.[113] It may well be, as suggested by Ebert and Posthuma, that the value of these social clauses, abetted by cooperation and 'capacity building' programmes (notably applied in the CAFTA-DR case to strengthen infrastructure for the administration of national labour legislation) could be greater than the contribution made by the deterrent aspects under the agreements.[114]

(ii) What Value Added (or Removed) for ILO Supervisory Mechanisms?

The troubling question which has to be raised at the close of this overview, and which has not been otherwise addressed in the literature, is whether the system does not in some respects represent a risk of regression in comparison to ILO standards and procedures.

To understand the nature of this concern, note that in a number of cases, especially in Latin America, the national law referred to in these agreements is also the legislative implementation of international labour legislation. The well-known case No 9601, submitted under the NAALC in 1997 by Human Rights Watch and other NGOs, alleging that a Mexican *maquiladora* was subjecting potential female employees to a pregnancy test, provides a vivid and effective illustration. Mexico is also bound by Convention No 111; yet, if the National Administrative Office (NAO) of the United States charged with addressing the case did refer to the jurisprudence of the Committee of Experts, those references had no clear impact on its conclusions about the compliance of the practices in question with national law (keeping in mind that the determinative issue was Mexico's compliance with its own legislation).[115]

[111] Michael Piore and Andrew Schrank provide the example of noticeable improvement to labour rights in some Central America countries,'where [fundamental reforms] are a product of transnational pressures emanating from the campaign for a US-Central America Free Trade Agreement' (see Michael Piore and Andrew Schrank, 'Trading Up? An Embryonic Model for Easing the Human Costs of Free Markets' (2006) 31(5) *Boston Review* 11. See also Michael Piore and Andrew Schrank,'Toward Managed Flexibility: The Revival of Labor Inspection in the Latin World' (2008) 147(1) *International Labour Review* 1, 3).

[112] See, eg the recent article from Kevin Banks ('Trade, Labor and International Governance' (n 95)) who argues that the dispute-resolution model in these agreements is too episodic and ill-informed, concluding his rather comprehensive analysis by expressing grave doubts about the ability of the model in these preferential agreements to support substantial improvements in even the most basic rights protection.

[113] Kaufmann, *Globalisation and Labour Rights* (n 57) 191. Meanwhile, Julien Burda, who in his thesis thought he saw the emergence of social justice through international economic law, for his part considers these experiments 'cause for profound disappointment' (Burda, 'Le droit international économique' (n 88) 375 ff).

[114] Ebert and Posthuma,'Labour Standards' (n 17) 26–29.

[115] Dubin, *La protection des normes sociales* (n 21) 274.

The case suggests that ILO representation or complaint procedures would, if not more directly, at least much more reliably (given their tripartite dimension) verify the extent to which national legislation giving effect to ratified Conventions is effectively implemented. Moreover, this case shows just how important it would be, in order to correctly assess the contribution these agreements make to respect for fundamental rights, to systematically identify where national laws overlap and diverge with obligations taken on through the ILO, and with those taken on under these agreements.[116] Some more research on the subject would seem to be called for under the follow-up to the 2008 Declaration.

III. Conclusion: Is there More to the Phenomenon than Meets the Eye?

Two key conclusions can be drawn from the above analysis.

The first addresses the salience of 'decentralisation' for the ILO. What the findings above confirm is that the development of social clauses in preferential trade agreements represents a 'second best' solution that is as much of a mixed blessing for the ILO as it has been described to be for the WTO.

Obviously, the question of most immediate interest from the ILO perspective is whether the phenomenon creates an incentive or a disincentive to ratify Conventions and apply ILO procedures. If the answer is clear in the case of EU GSP+, the image is much murkier for preferential agreements; at the very least it deserves further empirical study before it can be understood as a net benefit.

Indeed, insofar as these clauses allow countries to obtain tangible benefits in return for relatively light commitments (like a promise to apply existing national legislation), the obligations attaching to the ratification of ILO Conventions can be perceived in contrast as more stringent, and from an economic standpoint, less rewarding. Although references to the 1998 Declaration have been made with increasing frequency (by itself a very encouraging trend), it is impossible without further study to say how far these references have pushed in the direction of the Declaration's underlying aims (that is, toward verifiable efforts in terms of legislation and practice to respect, promote and realise fundamental principles and rights at work), and to what degree, to the contrary, they have earned participating

[116] Doumbia-Henry and Gravel, 'Free Trade Agreements' (n 110) 193. The authors note, in connection with the incentive to comply with ILO standards, that when a country has ratified its Conventions, the ILO provides effective mechanisms to ensure that they are actually observed, but without analysing in how many cases the national legislation referred to is in fact is the transposition of ratified ILO Conventions. A similar question arises with regard to the many references found to the 1998 Declaration in agreements subsequent to its adoption, particularly in agreements to which the United States is a party. It does not seem, in this regard, that these references are subject to any form of monitoring. In some manner, they seem a bit of a retreat compared to the 1998 Declaration itself, given that the latter has at the very least led to a significant number of ratifications of the core Conventions.

countries the advantages stipulated in the agreements, while sparing them the need to ratify the relevant Conventions.

Which leads precisely to the second set of concerns, starting with a simple question: is the prize worth the fight? The answer is not easy. First of all, in the end the effect of the phenomenon remains rather uncertain. This conclusion holds for the overall improvement in the condition of workers. If one considers the very selective and inconsistent support afforded as a result of the need to take into account trading partner sensitivities, it seems even more the case from the point of view of the effective implementation of the 'rules of the game', ie fundamental rights. More than that, the preferences used to encourage action may inevitably be subject to diminishing returns. Indeed, the average level of tariffs levied globally is already relatively low.[117] The value of compensation provided in the form of preferential market access is thus likely to fall victim to further erosion – unless, of course, protectionist pressures, as yet kept within reasonable limits since the outbreak of the financial crisis, run out of control.[118]

A second question following from the first is the degree to which the 'advances' promised in these social clauses serve primarily as symbolic pledges to public opinion and especially to workers sceptical of the benefits of trade liberalisation,[119] rather than truly altering the course of events.[120] If the inventiveness of social actors has fortunately been able to thwart these cynical calculations and nonetheless succeeded in giving the agreements practical and positive consequences not totally foreseen by the negotiators, it is worth keeping in mind the risk that a large amount of energy is being expended on efforts that might bear more fruit if they were exercised at the universal level.

This brings us to the last and even more radical question: if decentralised, ad hoc social clauses do not provide a satisfactory alternative to an (impossible) universal solution, might this alternative be sought in the direction of larger and more homogenous blocks sharing at least common rules of the game, if not a common social project? This alternative, long advocated by a group of economists that

[117] If some people, including Bob Hepple, believe that these benefits are substantial, we would like to be able to measure more precisely how far they have contributed to concrete improvements. See WTO, *World Trade Report 2011: The WTO and Preferential Trade Agreements: From Co-existence to Coherence* (2011), in which Pascal Lamy states in the Preface that the fall in tariffs has reduced the attractiveness of preferential agreements, at least for these reasons (ibid 3).

[118] One might well argue that by putting everyone in the same boat, the gradual erosion of rights could strengthen a country's interest to deepen the comparative advantage of its relatively lower labour costs. The viability of this thesis can already be checked against the realities of the European Union. If the lure of EU membership remains very attractive, not least because of the access it provides to the European common market, it is clear that applicants during each of the different rounds of expansion demonstrated no particular enthusiasm of paying for the privilege with major social reforms of their own.

[119] That is, the question is to what degree these social clauses provide '"aspirational standards" rather than actual commitments' (Doumbia-Henry and Gravel, 'Free Trade Agreements' (n 110) 197).

[120] This criticism is most easily levelled against the US conditions for the adoption of the NAALC as well as those that informed the Bipartisan Trade Promotion Authority Act of 2002. Significant in this regard is the controversy surrounding job losses attributable to NAFTA. This dispute over numbers tends to drift toward the evaluation of the even larger number of jobs which might have been destroyed without the Agreement.

includes Nobel Prize winner Maurice Allais, seemed like a nostalgic fantasy until recently. President Obama's reactivation of the old project of a trans-Atlantic free trade zone may give it a new lease on life. Even if it is unlikely to include a common vision of the social model to be pursued in that area, it may willy-nilly raise the question of making the common 'rules of the game' binding among the countries concerned. This obviously raises the question of the role the ILO could or should play in such a key policy debate.

Finally, in comparing the conclusions that emerge here with those from the preceding chapter, one cannot help feeling overwhelmed by the complexity of the problems, as much on the universal level as in the decentralised approach, that are raised by a hypothetical linking of open markets for goods, services and capital with measures to promote fundamental workers' rights as the basic 'rules of the game'. Might it not be simpler, smarter and ultimately more effective to promote these rules through the free choice of consumers in markets rather than trying to make access to these markets depend on compliance with those rules? That is precisely the question that we consider in the next Part by examining the feasibility of an international labelling system aimed at providing consumers with information that allows them to act effectively on their 'social preferences'.

Part IV
The 'Market for Social Justice' to the Rescue of the ILO's Persuasive Capacities?*

Introduction

What the last three Parts should have ably illustrated is that globalisation has forced the ILO to once again take up 'the social regulation of international economic integration'. Yet at the same time, the organisation has had to confront the apparent inadequacy of its persuasive methods to achieve that task.

As we have seen, the challenges posed by today's globalised realities, and global competition, have led many to conclude that only binding solutions can effectively establish a 'level playing field' of social norms. It was precisely that conviction which led to the ideas explored in the previous two chapters of making the dismantling of trade barriers subject to compliance with (internationally recognised) fundamental labour rights.

While such a solution would rest on solid logical and ethical grounds, the explorations in Part III confirmed that it remains a political and practical non-starter. Indeed, it should have become clear by now that universal, mandatory regulation, irrespective of its likely benefits and downsides, would require a universal consensus which ironically can only be achieved through persuasion. Thus, the current stalemate on the social clause does not categorically end the debate. Rather, it points to the need for a form of persuasion sufficiently powerful to overcome the refusal by a number of states to accept the 'social' rules of the game as binding on them. The object of this Part is to explore the hypothesis that such persuasion is more likely to come from the emerging market for social justice, than from the prospect and promises of better or free access to foreign markets.

I. The Paradox of 'Coercive Persuasion'

It is easy to fall prey to the type error that imagines the difference between the ILO's so-called voluntary methods and the binding social clause-type solutions as a matter of the former (and not the latter) requiring prior acceptance from the participating parties. Not so: the difference lies instead in the nature and extent of

* The author wishes to express his gratitude to Konstantinos Papadakis of the International Labour Office for his comments and suggestions on this Part.

the compensation offered for accepting the relevant standards and solutions as binding.

Thus, the so-called binding solution of a social clause can be understood as the supply of concrete and immediate compensation in the form of free (or at least preferential) access to the market of the trading partner, in return for accepting a comprehensive set of social provisos (through a 'single undertaking'). If the social clause is likely to remain a non-starter, it is simply because, in contrast to what happened with the TRIPS Agreement (and perhaps in part *because* of that precedent),[1] the compensation on offer is still considered inadequate by too many states to reach the degree of consensus that would be necessary to implement it.

On the ILO side, the compensation for the acceptance of obligations flowing from the ratification of individual Conventions is political, moral and (only incidentally) legal: first off, ratifying an agreement earns an individual government the potential benefit of pleasing domestic workers,[2] satisfying public opinion[3] or supporting some other internal political objectives;[4] secondly, there is the moral influence and credibility a state may earn vis-à-vis other members,[5] and the possible domino effect which would be the ideal result; and finally, ratification of a Convention offers the legal right under Article 26 of the ILO Constitution to challenge the manner in which another Member is meeting its obligations under the same Convention.[6]

The ILO has also had a long history of trying to convince Members of the *economic* benefits they might draw from accepting the constraints of ILO Conventions.

[1] To the extent that developing countries realised early on that they had bound themselves to obey the rules of a rather one-sided market.

[2] Such support is not always assured, especially insofar as the social partners, and especially employers, need not necessarily support a Convention at the national level, even when they have voted for it in Geneva.

[3] Francis Maupain, 'Persuasion et contrainte aux fins de la mise en œuvre des normes et objectifs de l'OIT' in George Politakis (ed), *Les normes internationales du travail: un patrimoine pour l'avenir. Mélanges en l'honneur de Nicolas Valticos* (Geneva, ILO, 2004) 695–96.

[4] Note, on the other hand, that ratifying a Convention can make no autonomous contribution to internal *policy* objectives, because any legal changes connected to a Convention's particular objectives can be implemented whether or not the Convention is itself ratified.

[5] The search for a certain 'social respectability' in the international system in the face of allegations of 'social dumping' cannot be totally outside the thoughts of the decision-makers behind the recent spate of ratifications seen in certain Asian countries – ratifications for the most part targeting fundamental conventions or, in the case of China, the so-called 'governance' conventions.

[6] It is interesting to note here that the benefits of ratification were originally intended to include the commercial interest of equalising competitive conditions: under the assumption of widespread ratification, the idea was that as a result of accepting the obligations under a Convention, Art 26 would thereby provide a ratifying government with a right to review how *other* governments were fulfilling their own obligations. But this benefit in principle has become almost a virtual one in practice, given the most significant players refuse to participate in the game. The real problem in this context is the inability to exercise authority over countries that do *not* ratify. However, this lacuna was filled, at least as applied to the marine industry, with the passage of Convention No 147 and especially the Maritime Labour Convention of 2006, which gave port states which had ratified the Convention the power to inspect and regulate ships even from non-ratifying flag states, and consequently provided a strong incentive to ratify (Maupain, 'Persuasion et contrainte' (n 3) 706).

Taking this approach is a somewhat fraught proposition as it can indirectly, when applied to fundamental rights, undermine their status.[7] Moreover, if we judge the trend of ratifications, especially for those instruments not implementing fundamental rights, it also seems clear that Members have not found these arguments particularly convincing – and there are in fact a few good reasons for their reticence to take the economic claim at face value.

First of all, the empirical data remains somewhat inconclusive.[8] The 1996 OECD study, which proved so useful to the ILO in the run-up to the 1998 Declaration, was intended only to show the weakness of the evidence for a negative correlation between compliance with ILO standards and a state's competitive position.[9] Even leaving aside the methodological criticisms levelled against the study when it was released, it is a big step from the absence of a negative correlation to concluding that these rights have a positive economic impact.[10] For instance, if it seems easy enough to prove the common-sense view that child labour, or at least child exploitation, is liable to destroy a country's future by creating an obstacle to 'human capital' development, it is more difficult to make a similar demonstration for other fundamental rights.[11] One does not need to go that far into the past to find those willing to argue that slavery ensured the prosperity of the southern slave states in the United States, representing a real advantage in the economic rivalry with their northern cousins. And, as was already taken from World Bank orthodoxy (with the *Doing Business* report providing the clearest demonstration), the economic

[7] *cf* Kerry Rittich, 'Rights, Risk, and Reward: Governance Norms in the International Order and the Problem of Precarious Work,' in Judy Fudge and Rosemary J Owens (eds), *Precarious Work, Women, and the New Economy: The Challenge to Legal Norms* (Oxford, Hart Publishing, 2006) 43. She particularly stresses the risk of instrumentalising labour protections in the name of growth. See also Guy Davidov, 'Comment on Alan Hyde: The Perils of Economic Justifications for International Labor Standards' (2009) 3(2) *Law and Ethics of Human Rights* art 3.

[8] Indeed, several studies have attempted to measure the relationship between the application of core labour standards and competitiveness, with rather contradictory findings. At an ILO conference of 25 May 2005, Christoph Scherrer identified three generations of empirical studies, supporting three different results. Studies in the 1990s, including that conducted by the OECD, showed no correlation between trade and standards; a second wave in the early 2000s found a positive correlation between GDP growth and rising ratification rates, yet without being able to demonstrate a causal relationship. Finally, recent studies (including, eg Matthias Busse, 'On the Determinants of Core Labour Standards: The Case of Developing Countries' (2004) 83(2) *Economic Letters* 211) examining the dynamic which prevailed from the 1970s until the 2000s in fact discovered a negative correlation, while others point to differences between regions (David Kucera and Ritash Sarna, How Do Trade Union Rights Affect Trade Competitiveness?, International Labour Organization Policy Integration Department, Statistical Development and Analysis Group Working Paper No 39 (2004). At the aforementioned conference, Scherrer meanwhile pointed out that an institutionalist approach could take into account factors more complex than the rate of ratification and GDP alone.

[9] See Organization for Economic Cooperation and Development, *Trade, Employment and Labour Standards: A Study of Core Workers' Rights and International Trade* (1996).

[10] For criticisms, see, eg Steve Charnovitz, 'Trade, Employment and Labour Standards: The OECD Study and Recent Developments in the Trade and Labour Standards Debate' (1997) 11(1) *Temple International and Comparative Law Journal* 131.

[11] Indeed, Davidov, 'Comment on Alan Hyde' (n 7) has suggested that even a prohibition on child labour is not an obvious economic case for developing countries.

impact of freedom of association, collective bargaining and related practices still seems quite open to debate.[12]

The second reason is that, even if there were conclusive evidence that compliance had no influence on a state's competitive position (or even that it had a positive impact), this would not necessarily be enough to convince a country to ratify. There is a simple explanation for this gap: even if there were irrefutable proof that respect for fundamental human and workers rights contributes to economic competitiveness, that might suffice to push states into adapting laws and practice in line with those rights, but would not necessarily persuade them to accept the lock-in or 'ratcheting' effect that would come with ratifying the relevant Conventions.[13] The third and perhaps most decisive reason is that the gains in terms of economic efficiency and greater social cohesion are likely to be reaped much more in the long term than in the present day. For governments that have to reckon with the immediacy of present problems and the political pressure for quick results, the promise of a reward with a delayed maturity date can provide only a limited incentive.[14] This suggests that, to be truly persuasive, it would be best if the expected rewards could come immediately on the heels of practical compliance with the 'rules of the game'. But what might such compensation look like, if neither free access to foreign markets, nor moral heft, nor domestic political credit have shown themselves sufficient to secure universal and effective compliance?

The answer to that question is that, ironically, the solution might come from the very phenomenon in which the 'prisoner's dilemma' finds its origins, ie from the existence of a global and interdependent market which extends competition beyond borders. If the universal extension of market forces puts states into a prisoner's dilemma, it may only be *through those market forces* and more specifically on the basis of the emerging 'market for social justice' that states may find the necessary incentives to overcome that dilemma.

II. The Market for Social Justice: A Persuasive Force to be Leveraged by States?

The widespread outbreak of corporate social responsibility (CSR) (understood here as brand strategies and company management practices that attempt to

[12] A document submitted to the 101st session of the ILC addresses some of the recent research on this subject (ILO, *Report VI: Fundamental Principles and Rights at Work: From Commitment to Action* (International Labour Conference, 101st Session, Geneva, 30 May–14 June 2012) paras 23–29).

[13] Especially in light of influential advice about country-level investment that is ambivalent at best about countries that do protect these rights, countries may not only want to avoid the legal liabilities connected to ratification, but might, theoretically, worry that ratification would harm their reputation with investors!

[14] This 'short-termism' is in this respect a *general* phenomenon that also contributed greatly to the 2008 financial crisis (see Tommaso Padoa-Schioppa, 'La crise en perspective: rester tranquille a un coût' (2009) 125 *Commentaire* 9).

integrate ethical standards of conduct that exceed strict legal requirements under national law) is a phenomenon which has attracted considerable attention.[15]

The object of this Part is neither to add to the enormous body of literature which has already tried to tackle the abstract question of what contribution the phenomenon has actually made to the promotion of workers' rights.[16] As important as this inquiry may be, it would take us too far away from the focus of this book. The object of the Part is rather, first, to understand the market logic of the phenomenon, but with a view to then assessing its possible relevance to the specific subject of this book: ie the ILO's capacity to persuade states to fulfil their commitment to the organisation's objectives, notwithstanding the constraints and inhibitions inherent to economic inter-dependence.

What the CSR phenomenon demonstrates is that socially and environmentally responsible behaviour can have a direct pay-off for firms, not so much because good corporate citizenship necessarily entails direct economic benefit, but because it enables them to improve their corporate image, and thereby win the loyalty of consumers.[17] It seems obvious in this respect that the explosion[18] of codes of conduct, labels and other manifestations of commitment to CSR practices[19] is not a unilateral and spontaneous phenomenon exclusively inspired by philanthropic considerations. It comes to meet a growing demand from consumers who are increasingly ready and willing to 'lift the veil' on visible, physical products' characteristics to consider their origin and production methods.

In other words, the CSR phenomenon is evidence that there is a 'market for social responsibility and social progress' which is sufficiently dynamic (and economically rewarding) to persuade firms to commit themselves to environmentally and socially responsible behaviour. Among many other initiatives, the UN 'Global Compact' provides an illustration of just how widespread, powerful and attractive this market has become at the international level.[20]

[15] See, eg the more than 800-page long collective volume edited by Isabelle Daugareilh in 2010 (below, n 19) whose English translation is under way.

[16] Though much turns on the degree to which the need for 'social responsibility' is cast as a need for greater regulation, Keith Ewing has put the obvious case for social responsibility somewhat polemically: 'if the still näive need any convincing about corporate social responsibility, take a look at the global financial crisis, caused by the corporate social irresponsibility of some of the biggest corporations in the world, now compounding their irresponsibility by insisting on paying their executives massive bonuses at the public's expense, after having been bailed out by taxpayers in what amounts to the biggest welfare scheme in history' (see Keith D Ewing, 'Foreword' in Tonia Novitz and Colin Fenwick (eds), *Human Rights at Work: Perspectives on Law and Regulation* (Oxford, Hart Publishing, 2010) xiii).

[17] And as will become clear, this is not to be cynical or disparage the sincerity of the motives they are so quick to flaunt. It suffices to convince ourselves to compare the pejorative image that has traditionally stuck to the concept of 'paternalism' (which could just as easily be deployed to respond to sincere motives) to that enjoyed by CSR and the incredible number of seminars, essays, treatises and conferences which have lavished attention on the subject.

[18] Anne Peeters, 'La responsabilité sociale des entreprises' (March 2004) 1828 *Courrier hebdomadaire du CRISP* 1.

[19] See, generally, Isabelle Daugareilh (ed), *La responsabilité sociale de l'entreprise transnationale et la globalisation de l'économie* (Brussels, Bruylant, 2010).

[20] For a broad collection of perspectives on the Global Compact, see Andreas Rasche and Georg Kell (eds), *The United Nations Global Compact: Achievements, Trends and Challenges* (Cambridge, Cambridge University Press, 2010).

The question to be examined here is whether there is anything, in principle or in practice, that would prevent states from seeking (and receiving) a similar reward from that market for *their* commitment to fundamental workers' rights.

To try and answer this question three aspects must be considered.

The first question, dealt with in Chapter 10, is to address the issue of *why* states can or should get involved in that market. As we shall see, the answer is that it is not only in their interests but also in the interest of the market and its equilibrium.

The second matter is *how* such information might be made available to consumers. In practice, the phenomenon in question is more-or-less transnational: consumers interested in 'ethical' purchasing are by no means limited to one set of countries, and their demand is almost by definition origin-neutral. Thus, any formula which left each state to deal exclusively with its own consumers would likely be inefficient at best and, as will be seen, actually counterproductive in most cases. In other words, the information supplied should have a correspondingly transnational character, best attached to some sort of multilateral framework negotiated between participating countries.

Ancillary to the design of an appropriate framework is a third issue of *what* information needs be made available to consumers to satisfy their interests. Should it be limited to informing them about the most fundamental aspects of workers' rights or might it be more general, referring to (and even creating) a 'decent work' (or even 'social justice') standard of some kind? These two related issues are dealt with in Chapter 11.

10

A Lopsided 'Market for Social Justice' Calling for Public Involvement

Without ignoring the possibility that the 2008 crisis may have temporarily eroded consumer empathy for those at the other end of their supply chains, the general economic trend has been one of a gradually expanding cohort of consumers anxious to inform their consumption at least in part with reference to its social or environmental impacts.[1] This change in behaviour is part of a broader social trend, reflected in company behaviour, social movements and legal reforms, that validates expanding consumer expectations about the amount of production-process information they will have access to when they are making their purchases.[2] Yet, as it turns out, the legitimacy of the corresponding legal reforms based on these trends are not as self-evident as it may seem at first glance.[3]

Given the resistance to information overkill, what is the best case for meeting consumer expectations on such issues? After all, as legitimate as a consumer's curiosity about production conditions may be, it should be clear that curiosity alone is an insufficient justification to actually establishing an information system to guide their demand.

The first argument is that a consumer's desire to know, in fact, proceeds from the will to act or put pressure to modify those conditions.[4] As a result, consumers

[1] We have already mentioned the WTO Appellate Body jurisprudence recognising the legitimacy of accounting for consumer perceptions in deciding the 'likeness' of physically similar products. This practice has been eloquently defended by Douglas Kysar, who has pointed out that 'just as money is purely fungible to social beings, consumer products – even when physically indistinguishable – are not perfect substitutes to the extent that they are produced using different processes about which consumers have strong feelings' (Douglas Kysar, 'Preferences for Processes: The Process/Product Distinction and the Regulation of Consumer Choice' (2004) 118 *Harvard Law Review* 525, 532).

[2] For a popular take on the positive possibilities of this trend, see James Livingston, *Against Thrift: Why Consumer Culture is Good for the Economy, the Environment, and Your Soul* (New York, Basic Books, 2011).

[3] Some believe that the state should in fact limit itself to intervening (if it must) only to ensure products can be compared based on objective characteristics, and that the outbreak of considerations related to production methods having no impact on the consumption of the product is simply irrelevant to the proper functioning of the market. As Kysar describes it, '[b]roadly speaking, policy makers and litigants in a number of critical subject areas have argued in favour of a conceptual demarcation between production processes and the goods that result from them' (Kysar, 'Preferences for Processes' (n 22) 530).

[4] For Kysar, 'Private consumption takes on a self-consciously political dimension: consumer behaviour is directed not merely at satisfying personal needs or desires but at shaping the way in which goods are produced' (ibid 531).

who want to change things are strongly influenced by a sense of the concrete impact their purchase will have.[5] It has thus been argued that, in making a purchase, the consumer exercises a moral choice – or at least sends a message – which in the end is not radically different from the ballot which he casts as a citizen.[6]

A second element, less frequently observed but equally important for our purposes, is that the consumer is not only (in principle) a citizen, but also in most cases a worker, or a former worker, or even (as a result of corporate social responsibility (CSR)), an employer. The rise of this 'consumer-actor' opens the possibility of a totally separate foundation for transnational solidarity.[7] The exercise of such solidarity was previously understood to be possible only on the basis of collective action, through trade unions for whom that solidarity was a core value.[8] As a result of consumer interests and demand, it seems possible for this solidarity to express itself on an *individual* basis, and in a context that, for better or for worse, seems destined to become increasingly individualistic. Thus, according to Kysar '[p]rocess preferences can be expected to capture the displaced moral and political sentiments of individuals who have been encouraged to regard the market as a more sure route to self expression and efficacious activity than traditional public channels'.[9]

It seems all the more legitimate that the 'consumer-actor' would take up the baton previously carried by collective solidarity given that the energy of collective action has been drained in two ways: the rise of individualism has undermined the power of collective values, and the material power of collective action has been cut down by the loss of union influence.[10]

Letting consumers take over this role has raised a fair share of doubts. Numerous criticisms have been levelled on the basis of the deficiencies that inevitably

[5] Indeed, Carmen Valor notes: 'When consumers believe that their purchase decision may make a difference, they are more likely to buy responsibly' (Carmen Valor, 'Can Consumers Buy Responsibly? Analysis and Solutions for Market Failures' (2008) 31 *Journal of Consumer Policy* 315, 317).

[6] In response to Mark Sagoff's efforts to draw a hard line between the sphere of the citizen and the jurisdiction of the consumer, Kysar has argued that such distinctions are increasingly difficult 'as citizens come to view government and the political process in primarily market terms' and where 'voting becomes simply another self-conscious manifestation of market preferences' (Kysar, 'Preferences for Processes' (n 1) 528).

[7] It is interesting to note that according to the latest papal encyclical, 'Hence the consumer has a specific social responsibility, which goes hand-in-hand with the social responsibility of the enterprise. Consumers should be continually educated regarding their daily role, which can be exercised with respect for moral principles without diminishing the intrinsic economic rationality of the act of purchasing' (Benedict XVI, *Caritas in veritate [Charity in Truth*] (2009) para 66).

[8] The view was epitomised by Wendell Berry's claim that '[t]he global economy institutionalizes a global ignorance, in which producers and consumers cannot know or care about one another, and in which the histories of all products will be lost' (Wendell Berry, 'The Whole Horse' in Normann Wirzba (ed), *The Art of the Commonplace: The Agrarian Essays of Wendell Berry* (Berkeley, CA, Counterpoint Press, 2002) 244.

[9] Kysar, 'Preferences for Processes' (n 1) 534.

[10] This reality provides all the more support to the case for providing 'process information' since, as we shall see, individual motivation empowered in this way need not be exercised at the expense of collective action. In fact, it may actually strengthen collective action, by reinforcing respect for the rules of the game among which protection for collective fundamental rights figures so prominently.

undermine consumer rationality, whether inherently cognitive, or tied to limits on the information available to them. It is true that consumer preferences are idiosyncratic in every meaning of the word, and that each individual's preferences fluctuate over time. And there is in addition a well-documented gap between expressed intentions on 'ethical purchasing' and actual behaviour. [11]

The fact remains, however, that the underlying preferences do have an impact, and one that can be measured in hard currency. Various surveys[12] have confirmed that a significant percentage of consumers are willing to pay a substantial premium to satisfy those preferences.[13] More forcefully, it is not clear why rational, consistent, prioritised desires should be a precondition for consumers to express themselves through their purchases, any more than the lack of such idealised rationality stands in the way of individuals acting as citizens.

In the end, the 'legitimacy' of people exercising political action as consumers rather than citizens is somewhat moot. What matters more for our purposes is that, rational or not, real or imaginary, those preferences have managed to impose themselves on the business strategy of many large companies. Their response to these preferences makes an integral contribution to their brand image, which risks paying a high price for misconduct.[14]

The harder question, then, is how the existence of this demand can contribute to states' efforts and provide the 'compensation' they need to liberate themselves from the prisoner's dilemma. The answer to this question is that they need each other: states can supply the information relating to applicable legislation which consumers need to optimise the impact of their purchasing decisions on social progress; consumers, through their informed purchasing decisions, can provide

[11] Leading to what Emma Boulstridge and Marilyn Carrigan label the 'attitude-behaviour gap' (Emma Boulstridge and Marilyn Carrigan, 'Do Consumers Really Care about Corporate Responsibility? Highlighting the Attitude–Behaviour Gap' (2000) 4(4) *Journal of Communication Management* 355. A list of studies documenting these behavioural shortcomings can be found in Valor, 'Can Consumers Buy Responsibly?' (n 5) 316. This leads, for example, to critiques of labelling genetically modified foods from academics who question consumer limited capacity to assess the degree to which any promised environmental, health and safety benefits will be realised (Karen Goldman, 'Labeling of Genetically Modified Foods: Legal and Scientific Issues' (2000) 12(3) *Georgetown International Environmental Law Review* 717, 722).

[12] See, eg Justine Burns, James Heintz and Robert Pollin, 'Global Apparel Production and Sweatshop Labour: Can Raising Retail Prices Finance Living Wages?' (2004) 28(2) *Cambridge Journal of Economics* 153; Michael Hiscox and Nicholas Smyth, 'Is There Consumer Demand for Improved Labor Standards? Evidence from Field Experiments in Social Labeling' (unpublished manuscript, 2011), available at www.people.fas.harvard.edu/~hiscox/ethicalsupplychains.html.

[13] The work of Elliot and Freeman specifically aimed at measuring the differential that consumers were willing to pay when purchasing goods made under 'ethical' conditions (Kimberly Elliott and Richard Freeman, *Can Labor Standards Improve Under Globalization?* (Washington, DC, Institute for International Economics, 2003).

[14] Judging by how quickly large brands have rushed to remedy injuries caused by the discovery and dissemination of information about production methods contrary to codes, objectives or labels, it may be that the less rational and more emotional these preferences are, the more influential they may actually be. It is unclear what justification there could be in subjecting companies to the effect (or even manipulation) of this influence, while refraining from applying the same influence to encourage states to respect social rules of the game which they have already collectively committed to.

the necessary incentives for the states to overcome the fear that steps they take to promote workers' rights could undermine their competitive advantage.

I. Consumer Preferences to the Rescue of Failing State Resolve

Given the discussions in the preceding chapters, there is little need to expand on a state's inability to do this work on its own. It will suffice to touch on three points. First, the findings in Part III show that there is little hope to escape from the prisoner's dilemma through a universal regime imposing minimum workers' rights protections under threat of trade sanctions. However, this finding may well entail negative consequences for the long-term sustainability of the universal trade regime: if it seems that trade cannot be effectively reconciled with social protection, then there is a real possibility of the politics of trade protectionism gaining ground in its place.[15] Despite the small lapses seen in some parts of the world in the last five years, it may still seem unlikely that states acting individually would repeat the errors of the inter-war period. As envisaged at the end of Part III, that does not completely rule out, however, the possibility of a refragmentation of global trade into more homogeneous trade blocs that share commitments on monetary policy, and environmental and social protection, which has been advocated by a few economists,[16] but would presumably be a far cry from President Obama's recent initiative in favour of a trans-Atlantic trade deal.[17]

Secondly, there is still a long way to go to achieve satisfactory levels of global respect for fundamental rights. While the 1998 Declaration was able to significantly raise ratification rates of the fundamental Conventions, the picture is less bright if light is shone instead on the proportion of the global working population benefitting from legal protection of their rights.[18]

Thirdly, if the job of meeting the global demand for socially responsible products was left solely to private initiative, there is a real risk that it would contribute even further to disempowering states, many of which are already too quick at shrinking their responsibilities in the face of the social constraints of globalisation. In this respect, the development of CSR seems to involve a self-fulfilling rhetoric: state weakness justifies the proliferation of these initiatives, but this development

[15] Kevin Banks, 'Trade, Labor and International Governance: An Inquiry into the Potential Effectiveness of the New International Labor Law' (2011) 32(1) *Berkeley Journal of Employment and Labour Law* 45, 68.

[16] For example, see Jacques Sapir, *La démondialisation* (Paris, Seuil, 2011).

[17] Obama expressed his desire to enter into a 'Transatlantic Trade and Investment Partnership' in his February 2013 State of the Union address (see Nicholas Kulish and Jackie Calmes, 'Obama Bid for Europe Trade Pact Stirs Hope', *New York Times* (New York), 14 February 2013).

[18] ILO, *Report VI: Fundamental Principles and Rights at Work: From Commitment to Action* (International Labour Conference, 101st Session, Geneva, 30 May–14 June 2012) 18, Table 2.3.

in turn maintains and perpetuates their institutional weakness, and could even lead to their power being delegitimised[19] in favour of various forms of private regulation.[20]

But the only way to promote authentic, lasting social progress is to ensure that states have both the ability and desire to guarantee it. This point was strongly emphasised in the preparations leading up to the adoption of the 2008 Declaration and is indeed reflected in the text itself.[21]

II. Public Supply of Information to Overcome Market Failure

Consumer demand for 'socially responsible products' has so far been met almost exclusively by private initiatives,[22] in the form of codes of conduct and a diversity of measures intended to inform (and reassure) consumers about the social or environmental conditions under which their potential purchases were produced. In fact, a flourishing industry has sprung up, offering an ever-growing army of consultants a stable niche of 'decent work' in crafting strategies to help companies avoid the lost market share and defunct business relationships that feature in stories obligingly provided by the 'industry' itself. [23]

It is also true, as noted around the same time in an ILO document, that a fine line separates 'market ethics' from an 'ethics market'.[24] And, as pointed out by Guy

[19] Susan Strange, 'L'échec des Etats face à la mondialisation' (December 2011) 308 *Esprit* 62.

[20] See Pascal Van Griethuysen, 'La RSE: nouvelle régulation du capitalisme ou interprétation capitaliste de la régulation ?' in Isabelle Daugareilh (ed), *La responsabilité sociale de l'entreprise transnationale et la globalisation de l'économie* (Brussels, Bruylant, 2010) 113, who underlines that CSR can indeed contribute to the further weakening of the state. Perhaps paradoxically, the attempt to apply direct liability to non-state entities in international law may suffer from a similar logic. John Ruggie had good reason to warn against attempts at the United Nations to submit businesses to direct human rights obligations (John G Ruggie, 'Business and Human Rights: The Evolving International Agenda' (2007) 101(4) *American Journal of International Law* 819). According to him, '[i]mposing on corporations the same range of duties as states for all rights they may affect conflates the two spheres and renders effective rule making itself highly problematic' (ibid 827). Specifically, although the aim would be to offset the capacity limitations of state action in globalisation, 'doing so can itself have adverse effects on governance capacities' (ibid 838).

[21] 'Members have a key responsibility to contribute, through their social and economic policy, to the realization of a global and integrated strategy for the implementation of the strategic objectives, which encompass the Decent Work Agenda' (ILO Declaration on Social Justice for a Fair Globalization (adopted 10 June 2008) para II.B).

[22] There are exceptions, including the Belgian label described below.

[23] As Naomi Roht-Arriaza predicted years ago: 'stories of lost contracts and dropped suppliers abound, fanned no doubt by an environmental consultant industry seeking a new market niche' (Naomi Roht-Arriaza, 'Soft Law in a Hybrid Organization: The International Organization for Standardization' in Dinah Shelton, *Commitment and Compliance: The Role of Non-Binding Norms in the International Legal System* (Oxford, Oxford University Press, 2000) 277.

[24] ILO, *Overview of Global Developments and Office Activities Concerning Codes of Conduct, Social Labelling and Other Private Sector Initiatives Addressing Labour Issues* (Governing Body, 273rd Session, Geneva, 27 October–6 November 1998) para 124. More recently, Robert Reich has used the ecological

Ryder, former Secretary-General of the International Trade Union Confederation (ITUC) (and since elected as ILO Director-General), there is a real risk that the practice could become a kind of 'Potemkin village'.[25] What matters most here, however, is not whether these initiatives follow exclusively (or at all) from altruistic motivations, or from a shared ideological commitment to social progress. The only relevant question is what practical impact they are likely to have on achieving ILO objectives. Contrary to Einstein, who claimed to prefer silent vice to ostentatious virtue, the logic of CSR shows that there can be real value in giving ethics a prominent headline, even when the underlying motives are not so pure.

In this regard, it appears that, (i) the current collection of initiatives cannot consistently or reliably guide consumer choices toward the promotion of social objectives as elaborated in ILO normative instruments; (ii) it seems unlikely that their shortcomings can either correct themselves spontaneously, or be overcome through the establishment of a common harmonised framework; (iii) even if they could be, such changes could not cure a 'genetic' handicap in their capacity to contribute to social progress, inasmuch as by their very nature they tend to deepen the divide between national workers on the basis of their relationship to international trade.

A. Inconsistencies, Gaps and Uncertainties in Existing Information

It seems useful here to briefly sum up at least three well-known and widely documented defects that stand in the way of initiatives of this sort providing a consistent and reliable point of reference to consumers who are enthusiastic about using their purchasing decisions to promote social progress.

(i) A Confusing Proliferation of Options

The rush by companies to join the CSR bandwagon may be laudable, but it has also left consumers immersed in confusion about what particular companies are doing – or even what they claim to be doing.[26] Though they are designed to facilitate consumer choice by providing an accessible 'shorthand' for the information

disaster caused by an oil-spill in Alaska to extensively and fiercely critique just how little concern large companies show for their codes of conduct, once the commitments cease to coincide with their essential interests (Robert B Reich, *Supercapitalism: The Transformation of Business, Democracy and Everyday Life* (New York, Knopf, 2007) 196–97).

[25] Guy Ryder, 'The Promise of the United Nations Global Compact: A Trade Union Perspective on the Labour Principles' in Andreas Rasche and Georg Kell (eds), *The United Nations Global Compact: Achievements, Trends and Challenges* (Cambridge, Cambridge University Press, 2010) 57.

[26] As recalled by Valor: 'Consumers can buy responsibly if they have information about corporate impact on social welfare. However, consumers report having difficulties in finding this information' (Valor, 'Can Consumers Buy Responsibly?' (n 5) 318). See also Patrick De Pelsmacker and others, 'Consumer Preferences for the Marketing of Ethically Labelled Coffee' (2005) 22(5) *International Marketing Review* 512, 515.

consumers are interested in,[27] it is not clear that labels have done a good job of ending that confusion. As reiterated in the ILO document referred to above,[28] there is the reasonable worry that the 'mass of labels of all origins, natures and motivations'[29] replaces a deficit of information with a surfeit of it. Experience appears to have largely vindicated that view. Indeed, the volume and diversity of existing labels (about 240 in Europe alone)[30] has had the result of reducing their overall impact. This inflation has negative influences on all levels: on readability, comparability, credibility of the supervisory mechanisms and contribution to consumer confidence.[31]

(ii) *Selectivity and Heterogeneity of Normative Content*

The choice of normative standard referenced in social responsibility initiatives is largely a function of each company's individual marketing policies, and the image it hopes to reflect to the public. But this quickly leads to the phenomenon mocked by Professor Supiot as 'self-service normativity'.[32]

By way of the document prepared by the International Labour Office (on request) for the November 1998 meeting of the Governing Body, the ILO tried to specifically address this aspect of the problem. After going through 215 operational or model codes accessible for analysis at the time, the report highlighted

[27] Caswell and Mojduszka have usefully broken down the product attributes consumers use in making their purchasing decisions into 'search attributes' that can be determined prior to purchase, 'experience attributes' that can be determined only after the purchase, and 'credence attributes' that can be (or must be) determined without relation to the purchase (Julie A Caswell and Eliza M Mojduszka, 'Using Informational Labeling to Influence the Market for Quality in Food Products' (1996) 78(5) *American Journal of Agricultural Economics* 1248, 2149). See also Maria L Loureiro, Jill J McCluskey and Ron C Mittelhammer, 'Will Consumers Pay a Premium for Eco-Labeled Apples?' (2002) 36 *Journal of Consumer Affairs* 203. In this language from the marketing literature, labels could in theory convert credence attributes into search attributes (see, eg De Pelsmacker and others, 'Consumer Preferences' (n 26) 515).

[28] ILO, *Overview of Global Developments* (n 24).

[29] ILO, *The ILO, Standard Setting and Globalization: Report of the Director-General* (ILC, 85th Session, Geneva, June 1997). The term from the French version of the Director-General's report ('maquis') certainly gives a more evocative picture of the problem.

[30] See De Pelsmacker and others, 'Consumer Preferences' (n 26) 515.

[31] Valor, 'Can Consumers Buy Responsibly?' (n 5) 321. See also Mario F Teisl, Brian Roe and Alan S Levy, 'Eco-certification: Why it May Not be a Field of Dreams' (1999) 81 *American Journal of Agricultural Economics* 1066. In their study, the authors (as described in De Pelsmacker and others, 'Consumer Preferences' (n 26) 515) 'concluded that eco-labels do not provide an objective basis for company marketing claims, that these claims are often vague, unverifiable, and misleading, and that the proliferation of eco-labelling increases consumer confusion and erodes consumer confidence in environmental labelling'. Therefore, the difficulties in assessing consumer labels come not from a lack, but from a proliferation of information. Kenneth Cukier has said that confirmation, clarification and verification of the accuracy of a label takes time (Kenneth Cukier, 'Data, data everywhere, a special report on managing information', *The Economist* (London), 27 February 2010). Unfortunately, the more time it takes to understand the ethical attributes a label stands for, the less likely the consumer is to purchase the 'ethical product' (Deirdre Shaw and Ian Clarke, 'Belief Formation in Ethical Consumer Groups: An Exploratory Study' (1999) 17(2) *Marketing Intelligence and Planning* 109).

[32] Alain Supiot, 'Du nouveau au self-service normatif: La responsabilité sociale des entreprises' in Albert Arsequel and others, *Etudes offertes à Jean Pélissier: Analyse juridique et valeurs en droit social* (Paris, Dalloz, 2004) 541.

both the selective nature of the rights they chose to protect, and the complete lack of uniformity in their definition. The limited place accorded to freedom of association and collective bargaining was particularly problematic, in view of the special significance of these rights.[33] Equally significant was the finding that, in the vast majority of cases, the content of these rights was often 'self-referential', ie there was a claim to protect the principle, but without any reference to either national or international standards as regards its specific content. It is clear that a commitment not to use child labour does not have the same significance when a child is understood to be any person under 12 years of age, as it does when 'child' includes anyone under the age of majority. The measures examined admittedly included some examples which made reference to national standards, and, though even more rarely, to international standards.[34] Yet, if they do not refer to national legislation, the provisions relating to wages or health and safety protections are of necessity expressed in quite general terms (including references to 'equity' or to satisfying basic needs).[35]

It must be recognised that the emergence of new types of initiatives that imply greater involvement of civil society and unions, and particularly, the so-called 'International Framework Agreements' (IFAs) negotiated between multinationals and global union federations,[36] have brought some significant improvement in the situation from that point of view. As noted by Marie-Ange Moreau, the participation of social partners or representatives from civil society in the development and implementation of these initiatives has contributed to harmonisation of content, and is correlated in particular with a higher frequency of references to ILO standards.[37] Moreover, the disregard so often seen in other codes of conduct for freedom of association and collective bargaining is replaced by an approach which

[33] It is probably no accident that freedom of association and collective bargaining were absent from the vast majority of these codes (75%), though forced labour was also, surprisingly, addressed only in 25% of cases. Wage levels, quite understandably, were mentioned more frequently (40% of cases), as well as child labour (45%), non-discrimination (66%), health and safety (75%). See ILO, *Overview of Global Developments* (n 24) paras 46–59.

[34] Examples were even found where provisions clearly contradicted international standards, with some particular cases suggesting that freedom of association activities were unnecessary given the quality of the working conditions offered by the company!

[35] In cases that appear to be relatively rare, there was a contrasting approach that focused very sharply on particular aspects of safety policy ('emergency exits and training for employees for emergency evacuation, healthful and safe facilities and conditions, well-ventilated and well-lit facilities, adequate medical assistance in case of emergencies, education and training for designated employees in first aid and health'). See ILO, *Overview of Global Developments* (n 24) para 58, relying on International Council of Toy Industries, Code of Business Practices (2001), available at www.icti-care.org/resources/codeofbusinesspractices.html.

[36] It is interesting to note that these IFAs give (albeit somewhat delayed!) substance to the vision that inspired the creation of the ILO industrial committees in the 1970s, intended to 'sponsor the development of machinery for the negotiation between representatives of employers and workers of agreements of an international character' (ILO, *Report I: Future Policy, Program and Status of the ILO* (International Labour Conference, 26th Session, Philadelphia, 20 April–12 May 1944) 76).

[37] Marie-Ange Moreau, *Normes sociales, droit du travail et mondialisation: confrontation and mutations* (Paris, Dalloz, 2006) 181.

puts those issues front and centre.[38] However, even leaving aside the particular challenges of making their implementation effective,[39] the number of beneficiaries of IFAs remains quite limited (an estimated 6 million workers under approximately 80 agreements);[40] as an example, they therefore suggest that there may be a trade-off between an increased interest from civil society and a certain version of the 'dual economy' concern explored below.

(iii) And a Persistent Credibility Gap

Limitations on the reliability of the systems put in place to monitor self-proclaimed codes of conduct were also discussed in the 1998 International Labour Office document. It seems there has since been little progress on this front.[41]

Many initiatives are not only self-defined, they are in most cases also self-checked and self-certified.[42] This way of doing things has been justified by the need to protect confidential and proprietary data, and to embed codes of conduct into corporate culture, but these explanations are obviously insufficient to dispel doubts about the seriousness of their application. Without an arms-length evaluation, it is difficult for consumers to know how much credit they can give to the assurances on offer about production conditions. This is why many voices, including from workers' organisations,[43] have argued that the first step toward greater credibility lies in assigning auditing responsibilities to third parties, particularly to audit firms which would gradually gain real social expertise.

The problem is that doing so is in many cases unrealistic. Such systems are obviously very expensive; even if part of the cost can be defrayed by increased prices for consumers, this still leaves it out of reach for most companies. Even large companies have apparently on occasion been deterred by the magnitude of these costs.[44]

Moreover, even where this method is possible, it will not suffice to ensure absolute reliability in the implementation of the underlying commitments. First, even if they are legally independent of the company in question, lingering doubts will remain if auditing firms still depend for their income on the maintenance of a

[38] Konstantinos Papadakis (ed), *Shaping Global Industrial Relations: The Impact of International Framework Agreements* (London, Palgrave Macmillan, 2011) 2.

[39] ibid 12.

[40] ibid 5.

[41] On this subject, see Daugareilh's introduction to her edited collection (Isabelle Daugareilh, *La responsabilité sociale de l'entreprise transnationale et la globalisation de l'économie* (Brussels, Bruylant, 2010)), speaking of a series of 'mascarades qui en dit long sur l'inconsistance des contrôles organisés par le donneur d'ordre international ou la société mère'.

[42] *cf* Alan C Neal, 'Corporate Social Responsibility: Governance Gain or Laissez-faire Figleaf' (2008) 29(4) *Comparative Labor Law and Policy Journal* 459.

[43] See, eg Patrick Itschert, 'Multinationales, RSE et dialogue social-pour un renforcement mutuel' in Isabelle Daugareilh (ed), *La responsabilité sociale de l'entreprise transnationale et la globalisation de l'économie* (Brussels, Bruylant, 2010) 191.

[44] Naomi Roht-Arriaza cites the case of the company Procter & Gamble eliminating a system of third party certification under the ISO as a result of prohibitive costs involved (Roht-Arriaza, 'Soft Law' (n 23) 276).

good relationship with their clients[45] – doubts with some parallel to those levied against the rating agencies following the 2008 financial crisis. Secondly, even when the commitments are implemented in good faith and at great cost, realistic and effective implementation of these initiatives along the entire production chain is extremely difficult. No company is immune from the discovery of contravening practices, which damages consumer confidence and permanently tarnishes a brand's image, a set of circumstances perhaps most memorably experienced by Nike.[46]

B. That Seem Unlikely to be Corrected by Self-Regulation or External Harmonisation

Apart from confusion that arises from information presented to the consumer in 'bad faith', which might fall under the relevant national legislation relating to anti-competitive or unfair trade practices,[47] it would not seem that neither deliberate self-regulation or a process of Darwinian survival of the fittest is likely to spontaneously dissipate the confusion arising from the above state of affairs.[48]

This being so, the question of an international regulation or harmonization of CSR initiatives becomes inevitable.[49] So far, however, the results appear rather inconclusive.

Thanks to its mandate and tripartite structure, the ILO would seem ideally equipped for that purpose. It might conceivably offer a 'model code' to help align content and methods of implementation; that model could even take the form of a Protocol to the Tripartite Declaration on Multinational Enterprises,[50] providing

[45] See Gay Seidman, *Beyond the Boycott: Labor Rights, Human Rights and Transnational Activism* (New York, Russell Sage Foundation, 2007) 7.

[46] Neal, 'Corporate Social Responsibility' (n 42) 460.

[47] The way this issue is currently tackled, of course, varies greatly according to each state's courts and legal system. It is interesting to note in passing that to avoid the consequences arising from this characterisation, companies relying on codes in the United States have tried to protect their claims, no matter the truth of their content, in terms of freedom of expression! Another approach that has received particular attention in this regard is whether these codes of conduct could, despite their declaratory character, have certain binding legal consequences for the employees concerned before the competent national tribunals. See Moreau, *Normes sociales* (n 37) 325–26, citing Lance Compa's claim that '[t]aking action under a corporate code of conduct might be an effective way to take advantage of a company's public promise to respect workers' rights' (Lance Compa, 'Pursuing International Labour Rights in US Courts: New Uses for Old Tools' (2002) 57(1) *Industrial Relations* 48, 69).

[48] Indeed, the recent battles over the meaning and ownership of the 'fair trade' label (particularly as it relates to coffee) suggests a future of continued normative fragmentation, doubts about authenticity and consumer confusion. See Scott Sherman, 'The brawl over fair trade coffee', *The Nation* (New York), 10 September 2012.

[49] See Michel Dispersyn, 'La regulation juridique internationale de la RSE: un scénario possible?' in Isabelle Daugareilh (ed), *La responsabilité sociale de l'entreprise transnationale et la globalisation de l'économie* (Brussels, Bruylant, 2010), which considers various projects and proposals based on the review of practices and the expectations of enterprises.

[50] ILO, Tripartite Declaration of Principles concerning Multinational Enterprises and Social Policy (adopted 1977) as amended at the 279th Session (November 2000) and 295th Session (March 2006) of the Governing Body.

companies an opportunity to make a voluntary undertaking to implement all or part of the guidelines contained in the document and, as far as necessary, to provide a verification or 'peer review' mechanism to those who wish to 'go all in', with all the implied credibility such a step would earn. It might thereby help to harmonise these initiatives with its own objectives, offering an authoritative system of implementation and verification capable of providing relevant and credible guidance to consumers.

Such possibilities were actually outlined in the wake of the 'Overview' conducted by the Office in 1998[51] and in subsequent documents.[52] However, they raised sensitive political issues, within the Employers group in particular. To the extent that initiatives of this type could lead to a direct relationship between the ILO and multinational companies, they were regarded with some suspicion by the International Organization of Employers (IOE), which sees itself as an indispensable intermediary between the ILO and national employers organisations, a role it has settled into over the decades.[53] That explains why the only concrete step eventually seen was the creation of a 'help desk' intended to provide information on standards and ILO principles to companies wishing to develop CSR initiatives.[54] While the 2008 Declaration raised this issue again, it is not clear how much momentum it will be able to provide in the end.[55]

It should be no surprise that the vacuum left by the ILO's inaction inexorably led others (including Kofi Annan with the Global Compact) to heed the call. It was the ILO's substantive absence from the field that provided the impetus for the ISO's (International Organization for Standardization) work on the subject.[56]

[51] ILO, *Overview of Global Developments* (n 24).

[52] The possibility to adopt a protocol to the MNE Declaration that would open the possibility for interested multinationals to voluntarily subject themselves to a social audit was mentioned in the report: ILO, *Report V: Strengthening the Capacity of the ILO to Assist its Members' Efforts to Promote its Objectives in the Context of Globalization* (International Labour Conference, 96th Session, Geneva, 30 May–15 June 2007) 42, para 131.

[53] See International Organization of Employers, *IOE Position on the Final Draft International Standard (FDIS) of the ISO 26000 Guidance on Social Responsibility* (10 September 2010).

[54] See Marieke Louis, 'The ILO's Helpdesk for Business on International Labour Standards: Using the NICT to Bring Multinational Enterprises Back in the Tripartite Regulation Game' (53rd Conference of the International Studies Association, San Diego, April 2011).

[55] The 2008 Declaration referred in its Preamble to the extension of the tripartite dialogue 'within and across borders', which evidently aims at the possibility of international collective bargaining which could support, among other outcomes, the adoption of 'global compacts'. But much more specific in this regard is Part IIA (v), requiring the organisation to review its institutional practices, in order to develop new partnerships with non-state entities, including multinational enterprises to 'enlist their support in any appropriate way, and otherwise promote the ILO strategic objectives'. Notable in this regard is the subsequent sentence, which aims to assuage any concerns like those mentioned above. The preparatory work on the Declaration even considered the possibility of these entities funding some programmes. There is good reason to worry that the highly sensitive nature of the subject and the lack of real structure to ensure follow-up by the Office means that paths leading in this direction are quickly becoming overgrown, if not impassable. See Francis Maupain, 'New Foundation or New Façade? The ILO and the 2008 Declaration on Social Justice for a Fair Globalization' (2009) 20(3) *European Journal of International Law* 823.

[56] See Janelle M Diller, 'Private Standardization in Public International Law Making' (2011) 33(3) *Michigan Journal of International Law* 491, in particular 499–503 concerning the ILO and other IGOs involvement in the process.

Though mediated by an ILO 'counter capture' operation aimed at ensuring there was no impact on its competence or recognised expertise, the ISO has since finalised and adopted a standard on social and environmental responsibility, ISO 26 000.[57] The resulting text undeniably contains some conceptual innovations and intriguing practices.[58] Yet, the standard cannot provide a consistent and reliable benchmark to consumers. Such a role for the resulting 'standard' is prevented first of all by its content, which, while including international labour Conventions among the numerous international instruments it references, still settles on an approach based on the elaboration of general principles to be applied, rather than providing detailed standards to be followed. Moreover, unlike previous texts produced by the ISO, this standard ('une norme de plus' as put by Isabelle Daugareilh)[59] is not intended to be subject to certification (even if there are good odds that certification firms will not take too long to push into the market opportunities opened up by the standard's conclusion).[60] From the perspective of interest here, it is also particularly significant (as it directly affects the question) that the United States was one of the few countries to have voted against adoption, justifying their refusal on the grounds, inter alia, that social responsibility falls within state competence alone.

C. And Innately Linked to a Dual Economy that it Helps Perpetuate

Even if it were possible to help existing initiatives evolve in the right direction, the result would leave in place an apparently innate defect, namely, that the information provided concerns only the conditions of production within an individual firm (or at best within its production chain), and has nothing to say about the conditions applying to the rest of the workers in the country of production, in either law or practice.

This concerning feature, shared by both existing initiatives and most popular proposals, has attracted significantly less attention than other shortcomings. Yet it may be the most significant from an ILO perspective. Indeed, if corporate social responsibility can in some way compensate for the structural inadequacy of state regulations facing the realities of internationally fragmented production, it cannot be called upon to substitute for them, at least until the disappearance of the

[57] Isabelle Daugareilh, 'L'ISO à l'assaut du social: risques et limites d'un exercice de normalisation sociale' in Isabelle Daugareilh (ed), *La responsabilité sociale de l'entreprise transnationale et la globalisation de l'économie* (Brussels, Bruylant 2010) 582–86.

[58] Including both the 'sphere of influence' within which firms are expected to apply social responsibility principles (a concept first proposed by the ILO), and the idea that responsibility requires exercising 'due diligence'.

[59] Daugareilh, 'L'ISO' (n 57).

[60] cp, eg Antoine Reverchon, 'Interview with Michel Capron: La comptabilité vire au vert', *Le Monde* (Paris), 29 September 2010. See also the IOE Position (n 53), which specifically criticises the ISO 26000 standard for being treated, despite all the promises to the contrary, as a basis for certification by some national affiliates in search of new 'business'.

territorial dimension which currently remains a conceptual underpinning of the ideas of 'social progress' and social justice.

This conclusion has much in common with equivalent findings pointed to at the end of the discussion of 'transplanting' workers' rights into the universal trade regime (at least to the degree that such a transplant was framed as an extrapolation of the idea of dumping). By any reasonable assumption, CSR commitments regarding working conditions are limited to workers employed by the multinational enterprises making those commitments, along with their subsidiaries (presumably), and their subcontractors (possibly).[61] Now, recognising that the actual fate of these workers does not always line up with the image advertised in a code of conduct, their conditions are nonetheless in almost all cases still better than workers who are not working for export. As already noted more than 10 years ago in the ILO document addressing some of these issues, lending aid to CSR initiatives could therefore have the disadvantage of perpetuating a two-track or two-speed system.[62]

The risk, in other words, is that any gain in 'horizontal' equity is accompanied by a deepening gap between workers who have access to this social windfall and those who do not,[63] to the particular detriment of workers in local production and the informal sector. Once again, this inequity is one likely to weigh most heavily on the already vulnerable; and in particular on children, who may paradoxically have more to lose than to gain from commitments made within the framework of codes of conduct.[64]

It is precisely this risk that led the ILO to develop projects to assist in the education of children removed from production lines. In one example, from 1997 to 2004, the ILO worked with Sialkot, a company manufacturing soccer balls, and with the government of Pakistan on a programme with the lofty goal of 'remov[ing] children from soccer ball production while protecting the welfare of child stitchers and their families'.[65]

This solution, however, begs a simple but troubling question. If the willingness of companies to demonstrate good corporate citizenship and contribute to social progress in their host country beyond their immediate circle of activities and legal

[61] There is an interesting parallel here with the UN Guiding Principles on Business and Human Rights (Human Rights Council, Resolution on Human Rights and Transnational Corporations and Other Business Enterprises, Res 17/4 (6 July 2011)). Though the 'sphere of influence' concept (n 58) that appeared in an earlier draft was abandoned, the document still speaks in terms of the responsibility of companies to 'seek to prevent or mitigate adverse human rights impacts that are directly linked to their operations' (ibid para 13).

[62] For instance, cases where children were removed from production lines in anticipation of newly-introduced codes or labels has, in the absence of any accompanying rehabilitation measure, resulted in these children (and sometimes their parents) being placed in even greater distress, pushing them in some cases into begging or prostitution. ILO, *Overview of Global Developments* (n 24) paras 65, 129.

[63] To the extent that the workers of the companies involved benefit from improvements tied not to the national context, but to a single company's ability to deliver consistent improvements conforming to whatever idea of equity external consumers happen to have.

[64] ILO, *Overview of Global Developments* (n 24) para 129.

[65] International Textile, Garment and Leather Workers Federation, 'Government of Pakistan: The Sialkot Initiative' (ILO Tripartite Workshop, Islamabad, 21–22 February 2007).

requirements is certainly laudable, why could it not take the simpler form of 'good fiscal citizenship'? This would imply that they would not go out of their way – (sometimes by playing one country against the other) to benefit from preferential tax regimes, or from practising 'tax optimisation' (to use the more recent and polite OECD terminology). Such an approach could be at least as convincing for companies to show their determination to contribute to global social progress (including the elimination of child labour) beyond their immediate circle of activities more effectively, and certainly more convincingly than through ad hoc projects. It is striking that, apart from their somewhat tautological commitment to respect the laws of the countries where the firms operate, codes of conduct and similar social responsibility initiatives keep silent on the theme of fiscal citizenship.

To provide a summary and a conclusion:

(i) Social progress cannot be 'atomised' into a mere juxtaposition of fragmentary improvements in working conditions across a collection of individual companies, no matter how valuable those improvements may be. Rather, social justice implies that all workers, whether or not they are coupled to the engine of international trade, and whether or not they work in the organised (formal) sector, can benefit from improvements in their rights and working conditions according to their country's capacities. This means that social progress cannot flow solely out of initiatives from individual companies. It also depends on the existence of relevant laws of general application, and on their effective, universal implementation within a country.

(ii) Making consumer pressure a successful spur to genuine social progress is therefore only possible if interested consumers are provided with a way to impact on the lives of all workers, on the basis of information about the broadly-applicable laws determining working conditions in the country of origin.

With those insights, the next important question is *how*? Given the transnational nature of demand, it would be absurd to imagine that each state could be responsible for informing its own consumers about the conditions prevailing in each country of origin. Indeed, the demand can only be met by a transnational information regime, which in turn implies the existence of a multilateral agreement.

11

Meeting Transnational Demand with a Transnational Supply: A Jointly Established Labelling System

Insofar as the goal is social progress, what follows from the above analysis is that consumers interested in using their purchases to improve working conditions (or at least in avoiding the chance that their purchasing habits would contribute to a race to the bottom) need to be provided with relevant information about the working conditions prevailing in the country of origin.[1]

The appropriate mechanism for providing such information seems relatively clear: it is the formula of a social label.[2] Lopez-Hurtado has suggested (incorrectly as we shall see!) that because they are based on providing information and responding to consumer preferences, labels necessarily represent an exclusive *alternative* 'to public funding or regulation to provide financial incentives to the improvement of social and labour conditions'.[3] What a label does is simply offer a shorthand for the most salient information on social (or environmental) production conditions. Of course, the state can have a number of roles in providing and regulating that information; what is most relevant about the labelling solution is that the information provided allows interested consumers to exercise informed preferences, confident that their choices are likely to have a real correspondence with working conditions.

The label formula thus seems the appropriate way to inform consumers about the salient aspects of the working conditions under which a good or service was produced, by reference to applicable legislation in the country of origin. But it cannot discharge this function without proper legal support.

[1] 'Country of origin' should be understood within the meaning of the World Trade Organization Agreement on Rules of Origin, Art 3 ('either the country where the good has been wholly obtained or, when more than one country is concerned in the production of the good, the country where the last substantial transformation has been carried out'). It does not apply in principle to intermediate products used to manufacture the final product. Using this version implies some limitations on the initiative, but those limitations are not unique to this situation; moreover, it is conceivable that those limitations might be superseded once an agreement of this kind was actually put in place.

[2] For an extensive review of social labels and their relationship with trade law, see Carlos Lopez-Hurtado, 'Social Labelling and WTO Law' (2002) 5(3) *Journal of International Economic Law* 719.

[3] ibid 720.

Some intricate questions must be addressed in this respect. The first question is who is to provide the label? For reasons we will consider at some length below, it seems clear that the state of origin has to be the one that takes on the labelling responsibilities, rather than the importing state; but conversely, it is equally clear that the label will only attract consumer attention and exercise normative relevance if it is recognised as valid within the destination country; these two factors together require that the labels must be mutually recognised through a multilateral system of some sort.

I. From the Difficulties of 'Labelled at Destination' to the Possibilities of 'Labelled at the Origin'

The idea of establishing a state-supported system of social labels informing consumers about the labour standards applied during the creation of goods and services is hardly a novel proposition. Numerous studies and proposals have been developed over the years to allow the granting of a 'social label' that would provide a guarantee that the product or service being offered had been manufactured in accordance with certain predetermined standards of workers' rights. Some have even gone as far as proposing the internationalisation of the idea. The least which can be said of these initiatives is that they have yet to gain traction either nationally or internationally.

The idea of an agreement on a global social label was included in the 1997 annual report of the Director-General among a broad collection of proposals to address the role of standard-setting in the era of globalisation.[4] Though the proposal in the report did not specify whether destination countries or countries of origin would be responsible for granting the label, the idea nonetheless raised a wave of criticism inspired not only by procedural concerns (there was a sense that a proposal of this sort should have seen prior consultation), but also by strictly economic and political resistance (the proposal was seen by some to constitute a new form of disguised protectionism).[5] Despite this setback, the idea still had reverberations, not least among them being the legislation introduced a few years later in Belgium.[6]

[4] ILO, *The ILO, Standard Setting and Globalization: Report of the Director-General* (ILC, 85th Session, Geneva, June 1997) 27–32. The proposal actually appeared earlier, in the Director-General's report on the eve of the ILO's 75th anniversary: see ILO, *Defending Values, Promoting Change: Report of the Director-General* (ILC, 81st Session, Geneva, 7–24 June 1994) 65.

[5] The full transcript of the views expressed can be found in the Record of the discussions at the 85th Session of the ILC. For a summary of the respective positions, see Lucio Baccaro, 'Orchestration for the "Social Partners" Only: Internal Constraints on the ILO' in Kenneth Abbott and others (eds), *International Organizations as Orchestrators*, unpublished paper

[6] *cf* Pieter Leenknegt, *Social Labelling Legislation: At the Crossroads of Global Trade and Labour* (Lausanne, EDIS, 2007).

The Belgian initiative was specifically intended to address consumer confusion which had been exacerbated by the proliferation of private schemes on offer providing information about production conditions. Though it promised substantive clarity, the scheme encountered procedural difficulties, on two fronts:

(i) As a matter of legal principle, the legislation was the subject of a communication to the WTO, asking the appropriate committee to determine whether it was consistent with the provisions of the TBT Agreement. The resulting discussion admittedly drew no clear conclusions; but no subsequent action was taken against it.[7]
(ii) In practice, the system's social effectiveness appears to have been severely hampered by the combined difficulties of using the mechanism in practice, and specifically by the overall complexity of demonstrating compliance compared to the relative size of the target market.[8]

These experiments lead to a clear conclusion that if the consumer needs to be guided by a credible and reliable label, it simply will not do for that label to be granted by the importing country. To serve a sufficiently large market and fend off possible objections about legality under the universal trade regime, it needs to be awarded by the country of origin.

Even though attributed by the exporting country, there is a potential residual claim that the label could have a detrimental impact on like (but unlabelled) products from other countries in the importing market. To prevent it, it must be made absolutely clear that in no circumstances can the label become a precondition of market access, whether in the country of origin or in the country where the product is ultimately to be consumed. For the system to be compatible with the obligations attaching to WTO membership, it must furthermore be totally non-discriminatory and completely open to new members.[9] The Belgian label, insofar as it was designed to provide the consumer with information sufficient to distinguish between 'like' products without implying a more favourable treatment for domestic products, was prima facie consistent with this condition.

Strict legal compliance with WTO rules, however, would likely not be enough to defuse the potential torrent of objections, and baseline mistrust for the scheme that was demonstrated by the controversy it inspired at the ILC in 1997. The fact that such a label would not require destination countries to apply prima facie judgement about the practices of its trading partners, but would rather rely on a

[7] See ibid and discussions at the Expert Meeting on Trade Policy and Application of International Labour Standards, *The Belgian Social Label and Dutch Proposal to Ban Child Labour Imports: Effectiveness and Legality According to ILO and WTO Criteria* (The Graduate Institute, Centre for Trade and Economic Integration, Geneva, 26–27 February 2009), available at http://graduateinstitute.ch/ctei/forthcoming_events/trade_labour.html.

[8] ibid. See also the note submitted by the Belgian delegation at the above seminar.

[9] It might even be suggested, given the inclusion of 'improvement of standards of living' and 'sustainable development' among WTO objectives, that a system granting a 'decent work' label based on a multilateral framework (possibly even making reference to ILO standards), would be able to invoke the presumption of consistency with the trade regime in accordance with Art 2:5 of the WTO Agreement on Technical Barriers to Trade (entered into force 1 January 1995) ('TBT Agreement').

baseline assumption that each country had the competence to label products originating within its own borders, will certainly cut short many of the anxieties about 'protectionism' (and their 'paternalist' variations) that have sometimes been faced by labelling proposals of this sort.

II. Need for a Multilateral System of Mutual Recognition and Impartial Verification

The whole scheme, of course, turns on the answer to the naïve question of why an importing country would have any interest in accepting or recognising the validity of a label, issued by another country, that claimed production had complied with legislation according with certain requirements of social justice.

The answer is twofold. The first interest involved (already seen in the Belgian case) is a desire in developed countries to encourage other countries to bring their legislation and practice into line with standards universally considered to be fundamental. This motivation is perfectly in line with the ILO Constitution, and fits well with aspects of the 2008 Declaration.[10] However, there is another and much more practical reason for members to be interested in the scheme envisioned here: countries accepting such labelled products for sale would simultaneously be the country of origin for another set of products or services benefiting from recognition of such a label. In other words, countries would have an incentive to integrate themselves into the system for reasons of reciprocity.

This implies, of course, that an individual country's label must be applied pursuant to a *system of mutual recognition.* As its name indicates, an agreement establishing such a system would require that whenever a party to the agreement affixed a 'label' or some other form of certificate to its products or services, it would have to be automatically recognised as valid (subject to a duty of reciprocity) by all the other parties to the agreement.

An effective and even-handed system requires two conditions: first, it would need to be based on a freely negotiated agreement, and secondly, it would have to provide a mandatory and universal verification system.

[10] The 2008 Declaration explicitly suggests, among the responsibilities Members can pursue to achieve the ILO's strategic objectives, the 'provision on a bilateral, regional or multilateral basis, insofar as their resources permit, of appropriate support to other Members' efforts to give effect to the principles and objectives referred to in this Declaration' (ILO Declaration on Social Justice for a Fair Globalization (adopted 10 June 2008) II B vii).

A. Freely Negotiated Content

The content and purpose of the label must first of all be freely negotiated and approved through a process of mutual agreement among any interested parties.[11] This freedom, however, comes with an obvious legal limitation: the agreement would have to be compatible with the pre-existing legal commitments already undertaken by the participating states. This principle would be particularly salient as applied to compliance with obligations flowing from membership in international organisations and particularly, of course, membership in the ILO and the WTO.

On the WTO side, it would be a question of ensuring compatibility between the resulting scheme and multilateral trade disciplines, especially the principle requiring non-discrimination (national treatment and most-favoured-nation) against all other WTO members. The Technical Barriers to Trade (TBT) Agreement may create a 'space' for technical regulations and other voluntary standards, as long as they are not more restrictive than necessary to achieve legitimate objectives. In this case, the agreement would set up a label based on internationally recognised standards, as part of a text approved by the ILO (as per section IIA(iv) of the 2008 Declaration).[12] It also has two features that should shield it from accusations of protectionism or arbitrariness: first, the application of the label by the country of origin would make it nigh on impossible to accuse the destination country of playing favourites; secondly, the fact that the label or its absence does not in any way determine market access among the countries bound by the agreement, but simply allows consumers of those countries to distinguish between available products with similar characteristics.[13]

On the ILO side, it would also avoid any contradiction between the stipulations of the label and a country's obligations under ratified Conventions.[14] This condition would in principle be automatically satisfied if the agreement were to take the form of an ILO Convention. However, it would be perfectly legitimate and

[11] This point will be taken up further below.

[12] As previously noted, to qualify for a rebuttable presumption of compatibility with Art 2.2 of the TBT Agreement (n 9) (a presumption itself raised in Art 2.5), an 'international standard' would have to be created by an international body open to 'at least all' WTO members. In *United States – Measures Concerning the Importation, Marketing and Sale of Tuna and Tuna Products*, WTO Appellate Body Report (12 June 2012) WT/DS381/AB/R, para 359, the WTO Appellate Body read these provisions so that they would apply in a very narrow number of cases, or possibly no cases at all. This reading, however, impacts only on the allocation of the burden of proof, not on the actual test to be applied. It remains that reliance on an internationally negotiated regime presumptively open to all countries would lend significant weight to claims of necessity, validity of objective, and legitimacy of the regulatory distinctions used to implement the scheme.

[13] As discussed at the end of Chapter 8, these three features – origin-neutrality in the policy itself, reference to an international standard, and empowerment of consumer choice rather than prohibition on otherwise 'like' products – each weigh in favour of compatibility with the TBT Agreement. Given that a scheme might have to be compliant both with the TBT Agreement and with the GATT itself, these three factors could also help prove the lack of 'less favourable treatment' under Art III:4 and, if it came to it, validity under Art XX.

[14] With the understanding that the requirements of the label may be higher.

reasonably feasible for the text establishing the labelling system to take the form of an open multilateral agreement independently negotiated among interested parties. The relevant parameters for the choice between the two are discussed below.

B. With a Mandatory Mutual Verification Process

For the labelling scheme actually to be effective, the labels would have to constitute more than just a product-level 'flag of convenience'. This means that the automatic and mandatory recognition guaranteed to the country of origin's label would have to be counterbalanced by the offer of an adequate guarantee to destination countries that the label they were recognising was not a 'label of convenience' but a label awarded strictly under the agreed-to conditions. The agreement would therefore have to include a system to effectively resolve disputes arising in a destination country (or even within the country of origin) regarding the conformity of the granted label with the conditions stipulated in the agreement itself. The scheme would thus have to provide for a multilateral verification system that could take various forms which could be quickly mobilised on the basis of any duly motivated complaint, which would then have to be subject to an objective and adversarial process and could include as appropriate on-the-spot investigation. The precise structure and conditions of verification would, of course, be set by the agreement itself (including a possible tripartite dimension), which would oblige the country of origin to cooperate and to be bound by the result. The effectiveness of such a mechanism for the promotion of rights at work would, of course, compare quite favourably with litigation under the ILO's constitutional procedures (as a simple example of the advantages, consider that a Commission of Inquiry established under Article 26 cannot investigate within a country under examination until and unless it has received that country's consent).

Finally, to be effective, the agreement would also have to specify the consequences that would attach to substantiated violations of the agreement. Such consequences could range from a formal notice, to a suspension of rights, and possibly to the full withdrawal of recognition by the other partners. The important thing would be to ensure that the resulting penalties were sufficient to maintain consumer confidence in the meaning and reliability of the label, but the specifics would, of course, be the result of negotiations between the participants.

C. Which Could Take the Form of an International Labour Convention or a Multilateral Agreement Open to all Interested Members of the ILO and the WTO

For the reasons discussed above, the proposed agreement would have to be open to absolutely any country which was willing to use consumer information to promote better working conditions, while respecting existing obligations to international organisations. However, these conditions do not prejudice the choice of how such an agreement might eventually take shape. While it could take the form of an ILO Convention, it could also be a stand-alone, multilateral treaty.

At first glance, using the ILO framework and proceeding by way of an international labour Convention, in particular, would seem to be the most appropriate approach to developing such a system. There are at least two reasons why. It would, first of all, automatically give the instrument a tripartite foundation. It would, however, also provide all countries an equal voice on the agreement and its eventual content, even those that did not plan to immediately commit to the scheme. It should be noted that, as clearly shown by the Maritime Labour Convention, taking this option would still leave open a pair of possible innovations: (i) setting substantial obligations by reference to international labour Conventions without necessarily entailing an obligation to ratify those Conventions;[15] (ii) endowing the instrument with a sui generis, self-contained inspection and dispute resolution mechanism like those just mentioned.

Despite (or perhaps because of) these benefits, it would be understandable if the ILO route was seen as too slow or unpredictable. A free-standing multilateral agreement negotiated only by the interested participants could be more expeditious, except that: (i) the negotiations should ensure appropriate participation by the social partners, allowing them to make as meaningful a contribution as they might at an ILO conference; and (ii) the resulting instrument should remain open to any interested partner who is already a member of both the WTO and the ILO. Ironically, it may be that launching such a multilateral initiative outside the ILO might be the best way to get the organisation itself to become involved.

III. To Guarantee What? Effective Application by Each Party of Legislation Satisfying Agreed International Labour Standards

What information would the scheme actually provide to the consumer (apart from the background knowledge that the label itself can be trusted)? While a final answer to that question would ultimately reflect the compromises that would emerge from negotiations between the relevant stakeholders, clarity on three issues would seem indispensable to any feasible scenario: the nature of the workers' rights addressed in the legislation of participating countries (whether limited to fundamental rights or otherwise); the level or standard of protection provided (whether it corresponds to the level set out in international labour Conventions or otherwise); and finally, the scope of the guarantee, ie whether the legislation in

[15] See George Politakis, 'Deconstructing Flexibility in International Labour Conventions' in George Politakis (ed), *Les normes internationales du travail: un patrimoine pour l'avenir. Mélanges en l'honneur de Nicolas Valticos* (Geneva, ILO, 2004) 489.

question is guaranteed only for the product or service bearing the label, or across all production in the country of origin. Each of these aspects is discussed below.

A. Which Rights to be Covered: Fundamental Rights or Other Aspects of Decent Work?

It is clear that no label could offer guarantees on *every* aspect of the working conditions prevailing during the production process: it would be impracticable and ultimately meaningless to consumers. Instead, it makes sense for it to target aspects of work that are either intrinsically recognised and/or seen by the consumer as having special significance.

When it comes to choosing the normative scope of the guarantee, fundamental rights at work are without a doubt the obvious candidates, given they have been explicitly recognised since the 1998 Declaration as having the 'special significance' of being the *sine qua non* of progressive realisation of other workers' rights.[16]

This does not mean that the scheme must necessarily be limited to fundamental rights. It is well-known (and was in part laid out above) that private initiatives, while often overlooking certain fundamental rights, also often contain other commitments, in terms of wages or other issues significant to global 'consumer-workers'. It would therefore be quite open to participating countries to settle on a wider coverage through a 'decent work' label that could then, at last, give to the concept an authoritative meaning and content.[17]

B. What Level of Protection? National Law that Meets the Standards in the Relevant Conventions (Whether Ratified or Not)

In the abstract, it would be conceivable to determine the level of protection for the rights covered by the agreement by reference to an international Convention, according to national standards alone, or even according to some sui generis set of norms.

As was briefly mentioned above, the reference to international labour Conventions seems a natural fit in the context of a system that would per hypothesis be multilateral. But there are two reasons why making the ratification of international Conventions a prerequisite could doom the agreement to significantly reduced participation, or even stop it from getting off the ground at all. First of all, it would in principle limit participation to states that had already ratified the relevant instruments. Moreover, if the goal was compliance with those Conventions,

[16] See above, Chapter 7.

[17] As discussed in Part I, the significance (if not the definition) and status of the concept, considered by many to be too 'soft' to ever have concrete value, was clarified to some degree by the 2008 Declaration. However, its attachment to an instrument settled by international agreement would confer on it an unquestionable, operative legal content.

this limitation would also mean that the verification procedures as implemented (see above) would have to depend on the ILO's constitutional supervision machinery, namely, the structures provided by the Complaint procedure and its follow-up under Articles 26–33.

The question obviously deserves more expansive consideration than it is possible to provide here. Without going into detail, one conceivable alternative would be a sort of 'hybrid', which would require the application of national legislation 'substantially equivalent' to the protections specified in ILO instruments. Proceeding in this way would circumvent the very difficult problem of potential interpretation disputes. The potential implementation of the 'substantial equivalence' doctrine for ILO instruments has actually been considered on numerous occasions and in various forms since 1946,[18] and resurfaced with particular salience for our purposes in the context of the recent Maritime Labour Convention.[19]

Clearly, however, such a solution could be convincing only to the extent that the 'equivalence' between national legislation and the requirements established in existing Conventions was subject to independent, objective verification, in accordance with the system established to verify the effective implementation of the legislation in question to the actual production of the labelled good or service. As discussed above, such verification could be ensured by a dispute settlement scheme concerning the authenticity of the label, implying in turn the possibility of mandatory on-site inspections; it would thus presumably be a question of an *ex post facto* process initiated on the basis of complaints from interested parties. This is, however, without prejudice to the possibility of supervising equivalence between existing legislation and the requirements of the agreement *a priori*. One thing at least seems clear: the two forms of supervision should at least be coordinated by an independent registry under the control of the parties to the agreement.

[18] The idea of a certificate of 'substantial equivalence' had its first mention in the report of the 1946 Conference Delegation on Constitutional Questions. In connection with a suggestion (which seems to have come from the United States) to authorise ratification even when national legislation 'though not fulfilling in detail the requirements of the Convention concerned, had been found by an appropriate organ of the ILO to be substantially equivalent to the requirements of the Convention from the standpoint of the level of social protection afforded by it'. The delegation report, while pointing to constitutional difficulties with the proposal, dangled the alternative which could be provided by the amended Art 19 to recognise at the international level those cases where 'legislation, while not conforming in detail with the requirements of the Convention, is of an equal or higher level from the standpoint of the social protection which it affords' (ILO, *Report II(1): Constitutional Issues: Reports of the Conference Delegation on Constitutional Questions* (ILC, 29th Session, Montreal, 19 September–9 October 1946) paras 57–58). The idea returned in the Director-General's report to the 70th Session of the ILC (ILO, *Report of the Director-General* (ILC, 70th Session, Geneva, 6–26 June 1984) 22–23).

[19] The concept of 'substantial equivalence' is used in the Maritime Labour Convention in Art VI para 3. See Politakis, 'Deconstructing Flexibility' (n 15) 489. See, generally, Moira McConnell, Dominick Devlin and Cleopatra Doumbia-Henry, *The Maritime Labour Convention, 2006: A Legal Primer Year to Emerging International Regime* (Boston, Martinus Nijhoff, 2011).

C. What Scope of Protection? Broad, Effective Application of Relevant National Law

It has been established that the label must guarantee that: (i) existing legislation satisfies the conditions applicable to the production of the good or service; and (ii) the application of this legislation is effective and can be verified. The question then becomes whether this condition applies only to the product bearing the label or must be of general application within the country of origin.

Prioritising broad interest and the widest possible membership, and specifically seeking sufficient flexibility to attract countries at unequal levels of development, would tend to support the first option. Indeed, organising the scheme in this way would reflect realistic differences between country capacities and, above all, facilitate a wider, if gradually implemented uptake of the scheme.

This would allow each country (preferably subject to prior tripartite consultations) to limit the application of the label only to those products or services where it felt confident it could ensure standards were being effectively implemented. Of course, the scope of application could be broadened at a later time. Combining a requirement for a uniformity of production standards with discretion for each party to vary the application of the label according to its ability to certify effective implementation in a given industry or sector would reconcile two goals: first, promoting progress for all, including those not directly tied into international trade; and secondly, providing enough flexibility to accommodate the diverse and evolving realities of each sector. Thus, a state could initially adhere to the requirements within a narrow band of the economy, but would have the ability to expand the selection of labelled products step by step with its expanding capacity to implement the applicable standards in different sectors or industries.

IV. In Conclusion: Is there a Market for a Market-based Approach to Social Justice?

The technical feasibility of a social labelling scheme of the type just described is a condition but certainly not a guarantee of its political acceptability and viability. The last and most difficult question to be considered is thus whether such a scheme is doomed to remain in the realm of legal fiction, or has some chance of one day becoming a reality. The answer depends to a large extent on the evolution of the public's perceptions about globalisation, and its sensitivity about human and workers rights violations. The possible expansion of social movements generally, and resistance to globalisation specifically, may weigh heavily on these developments. The potential for a sufficient synergy of interests is left to those with more expertise in political questions, addressed here only to summarise the reasons that

ILO stakeholders themselves might have an interest in supporting this sort of scheme.

A. Among Workers and their Organisations

Support should be expected to come first and foremost from workers and their organisations. As noted on several occasions, globalisation has placed them on the defensive; and as much as they may nurse hopes of regaining a position of influence by way of international collective bargaining, the realisation of that prospect remains a distant mirage. For the vast majority of workers, this approach offers no real alternative to strong, enforceable guarantees in state-level legislation that empowers them to obtain fair compensation for their particular contribution to society's prosperity. The introduction of a labelling system like the one described here should in this regard provide an attractive method to help put those laws in place.

One cannot, however, ignore the cognitive dissonance that might be entailed for workers in supporting a scheme that seems to pursue the trade union's goals only by embracing an individualistic philosophy symbolically at odds with the principles of collective action and solidarity underlying the trade union movement since its origins. Unions, however, must be attentive to the practical reality that placing these individual preferences in the service of fundamental rights would paradoxically allow this scheme to expropriate pervading individualism to the benefit of collective action itself. Indeed, no matter how it may feel in principle to rely on individualism, that makes using it seem no less compelling.[20]

A similar objection can be drawn from the consideration that when they are acting in the market as consumers, most workers lack sufficient means to allow them to choose products that are likely to be more expensive. Might the establishment of a social label therefore seem to lay some of the blame on them, or even confirm the cynical view that immediate economic considerations always take precedence over long-term solidarity? The answer to this objection is simple: the effectiveness of the device depends not on the actual behaviour (or feelings) of workers who would be the primary beneficiaries, but on how companies (or states) perceive the aggregate response that consumers will have to information regarding conditions of production in the company or the state of origin, with or without a coordinated campaign of criticism.[21] And experience has amply demonstrated that even the anticipation of a consumer response is enough to have a powerful persuasive effect.

[20] And all the more so given that the character of such a choice does not exclude the exercise of collective action (but may in fact strengthen it through the reinforcement it gives to respect for rules which include someprominent human rights groups).

[21] It would be very much in the role of national and international unions to attract the attention of consumers in general about the meaning of such a label.

B. Among Firms

This leads directly to the question of whether *businesses* would have any interest in such a proposal, given the substantial number that have already accepted at least some form of corporate social responsibility (CSR). The answer has to start with the reality that CSR remains primarily the province of large companies with access to considerable resources. While the cost may be partially passed on to consumers, and partially recovered by the market gains theoretically associated with the label, the costs of CSR commitments must largely be borne by the company (especially when those commitments are first made), leaving them permanently out of reach for many small and medium-sized companies, not to mention whole sectors teetering on the edge of economic uncertainty.[22] To this may be added, the existing CSR system is unfair to companies acting in good faith and strictly abiding by national law, but who do so without any benefit to their brand image or market position, because they happen not to fall into a network or sector covered by an existing CSR scheme. Thus, for the vast majority of companies, the scheme would provide the possibility to be indirectly rewarded through the label without having to undergo a disproportionate cost burden.

C. On the Part of States

It is clear that, beyond workers and firms, the potential future of the social label formula, once matured, will be decisively decided by whether or not it can captivate a critical mass of states (if not all of them). Though the scheme could function well enough even with a limited number of members, the point of such a system is after all to promote better working conditions more effectively than current tools, which means that functional effectiveness depends on the participation of a large number of countries.

Depending on its design, however, the scheme should be embraced almost immediately by the vast majority of ILO Members (133) which have already ratified all eight fundamental Conventions. At the moment, these countries primarily derive a moral (and reputational) benefit from these commitments; with the implementation of the labelling scheme, that benefit would be much more tangible. Moreover, were a 'functional equivalence' formula selected, the circle of

[22] This creates a kind of financial discrimination against those who seek not only to respect the law but to develop good social practices, but are prevented from receiving equivalent benefit to consumers. It is very significant in this context that the International Organization of Employers (IOE), which represents employers in the ILO, but includes national employers dominated by medium-sized firms, came out against the ISO 26000 initiative. It considered that the complexity of the guidelines showed they had been created with large enterprises in mind, which 'affects the applicability of the guidance to the smaller or medium-sized organisations, which will find that huge sections of the text is either beyond their capacity or simply not practical for smaller organisations' (International Organization of Employers, *IOE Position on the Final Draft International Standard (FDIS) of the ISO 26000 Guidance on Social Responsibility* (10 September 2010).

eligible states could easily expand beyond this group of 133. But of course, they would have to agree to submit to the jurisdiction of a dispute settlement system capable of ensuring the accuracy and reliability of the label as particularised in the eventual agreement.

D. And for the ILO Itself

Finally, we must ask what the interest of such a system would be for the ILO itself. The ILO might first of all be interested in using this kind of scheme to modernise the image of its normative system, in the wake of the adoption of the Maritime Labour Convention which effectively demonstrated the great potential ILO traditional normative tools have when applied in far-from-stereotypical ways. Beyond the reputational benefits of innovation, however, the ILO obviously has a deeper, existential interest in the effective implementation of workers' rights, and in the realisation of fundamental rights in particular. The establishment of a system of social labels connecting these rights to the market mechanism and to consumers could no doubt constitute a considerable value-added from this perspective.

Finally, it is important to remember that each individual is not only a consumer but also, in principle, a citizen (ideally engaged in questions of public concern) and in most cases also a worker, a former worker, or quite possibly an employer – in this final case, no doubt concerned about the conditions under which competitor's offerings are being produced. The fact that the said consumer/citizen/worker is disposed to guide his or her purchases with reference to the social impact of their production conditions would express a new form of cross-border solidarity which the ILO would have every reason to promote. This would be all the more necessary since, as already noted, the twin engines of traditional solidarity seem to be failing with the rise of individualism, and the erosion of unions' influence.

This apparent confluence of interests, however, begs an obvious question: why does the ILO seem to have turned its back on the subject since 1997? It is interesting that this question has been addressed most pointedly by an outsider, Lucio Baccaro, who tried to explain the fate of the 1997 labelling idea by contrast with the adoption of the Worst Forms of Child Labour Convention (No 182) two years later.[23] Baccaro's explanation turns on the prevalence of a 'corporatist' model of tripartism at the ILO, which leaves the social partners extremely suspicious of any form of opening to civil society in this case consumers – and that can be overcome in his view only by a concerted coalition of Northern and Southern countries. Without prejudice to the validity of either the comparison[24] or the analysis, this conclusion tends to confirm that interested governments, in the North and South

[23] Baccaro, 'Orchestration for the "Social Partners" Only' (n 5).

[24] To some degree, his comparison overlooks the fact that the label proposal was one of the many (very tentative) ideas contained in the Director-General's policy report at the ILC; this report and the ideas contained therein has nothing to do, legally and politically speaking, with formal draft proposals for a new ILO instrument before the ILC which already reflect a succession of discussions and compromises.

both, might well be inspired to initiate the scheme outside the ILO under an appropriate 'orchestrator'. As already suggested, this might ultimately be the best way to get the ILO involved in what may be the only plausible solution to make the 'rules of the game' really and quickly effective.

Conclusion: Reinventing the ILO?

It has sometimes been said that if the ILO did not exist it would have to be invented – though doing so would probably be impossible today. One need only look to the difficulties which have dogged proposals for systemic UN reform, changes almost everyone accepts are necessary in the face of the twenty-first century's realities and today's rebalanced political equilibriums, to be convinced that, short of a cataclysm similar to the ones the founders faced a century ago, there is little chance of finding a catalyst that could drive the search in 2019 for institutional solutions as bold as those they imagined in 1919. Even if one is not obliged to share his conclusions, Robert Cox is definitely on to something when he claims that the new multilateralism 'will not be born from constitutional amendments to existing multilateral institutions but rather from a reconstitution of civil societies and political authorities on a global scale building a system of global governance from the bottom up'.[1]

This is far from dire news for the ILO. While the organisation's greatest merit is that it already exists, what has hopefully become clearer through the foregoing pages is that thanks to an ingenious constitutional framework it also has the capacity to reinvent itself from the inside to meet the expectations of its founders and become a more effective social regulator of the global economy.

Key elements of that transformation are already in place. There is no doubt, however, that none of the particular avenues sketched out above and recapitulated below can occur without acute resolve and a clear sense of purpose informed by the whole cohort of current challenges to humanity's survival, environmental risks not least among them.

I. Three Necessary and Feasible Aspects of an Institutional Reinvention

In the light of the foregoing chapters, it appears that the ILO's credibility and effectiveness will ultimately depend on its capacity to make a more imaginative and efficient use of the persuasive tools at its disposal as it meets three major challenges.

[1] Robert Cox, *The New Realism: Perspectives on Multilateralism and World Order* (Basingstoke, Palgrave Macmillan, 1997) xxvii.

A. Ensuring the Universal and Effective Diffusion of the 'Rules of the Game'

It would be hard to overstate the importance of the contribution that the ILO made to global governance when it crystallised a consensus around fundamental principles and rights at work as the basic 'rules' supporting a fair distribution of the benefits and costs of growth. Yet it can hardly be said that the job is done, considering that the proportion of the world's population benefitting from a guarantee for the fundamental rights of a collective nature still falls short of 50 per cent.[2]

Indeed, confidence in the ILO's capacity to perform the two functions at the core of its *raison d'être* will be lacking as long as this unsatisfactory state of affairs persists. First of all, its efforts to disseminate (and preserve) its tripartite model of pluralist social progress cannot but suffer from the competition with a seemingly more efficient 'market Leninism' model. On the other hand, its ability to efficiently reconcile the constraints of economic interdependence with a fair distribution of its benefits and costs will be put seriously into question as long as the majority of working people are deprived (to use the 1998 Declaration terms) of their right to 'claim freely and on the basis of equality of opportunity their fair share of the wealth which they have helped to generate'.

We have seen in Part III that the 'quick fix' of grafting these fundamental rights onto universal trade disciplines is unlikely to come about very quickly at all. Obviously, one cannot rule out the possibility that new crises in the global economy, and any attendant retreat into protectionism, might fuel global trade tensions that spark off renewed debate on the formalisation of the 'link'; for now, however, such a formal grafting remains both politically unlikely and potentially counterproductive in terms of the level of protection that would ultimately be offered under such a scheme. The gradual implementation of a 'slow fix', involving a progressively expanding recognition of these rules and their special status and significance through the jurisprudence of the WTO Appellate Body may be a more plausible hypothesis, but one that remains only a long-term possibility – by no means a present certainty. The ILO should certainly keep itself ready to lend a hand in clarifying certain issues if and when such advice becomes needed, but there seems no way for it to be a proactive participant in such efforts.

Thus, for the time being, it seems clear that for all practical purpose solutions must involve, if not come from, the ILO itself. In principle, the situation in states which have not ratified the relevant Conventions is supposed to be addressed through the follow-up to the 1998 Declaration, and more specifically through the

[2] According to the recurrent report discussed by the ILC in 2012 (ILO, *Report VI: Fundamental Principles and Rights at Work: From Commitment to Action* (International Labour Conference, 101st Session, Geneva, 30 May–14 June 2012), as discussed above.

'annual review' to which they are subject.[3] With their increasingly routine and repetitive character, however, annual reviews are likely to prove inadequate for the challenge.

This unsatisfactory state of affairs may at the same time represent an exceptional opportunity for the ILO to make a more imaginative deployment of its persuasion capacities. After all, it is well-understood that the lion's share of the situation largely comes (if we may say so) from the four mammoths of the global economy, each of which enjoys a non-elected seat on the ILO's Governing Body, and two of which, at least, are vying for global leadership.[4] While the potential non-observance of the 'rules' by such influential players certainly accentuates the ILO's serious credibility problems, the rivalry between them may also spur each country to be proactive in showing their commitment to the 'rules' with or without ratification; it could thus help extract their cooperation in an in-depth factual study of their respective situations, perhaps even tied to an offer of objective advice on the critical steps, if any, needed to achieve a situation of non-violation, if not full compliance.

As extravagant as such a scenario may seem, it is a rather modest version of what was already done over 50 years ago in a context of infinitely greater tension, and without the benefit of the 1998 Declaration.

At the height of the Cold War, the Director-General (then David Morse) decided on the basis of a report from the Committee on Freedom of Employers and Workers Organisations,[5] to put a tendentious proposal before the Governing Body, with a view to conducting an inquiry into the factual situation regarding freedom of association in each Member. He was able to extract, from a very restive and divided Governing Body, a mandate to carry out fact-finding missions in all countries willing to host them.[6] Perhaps more importantly, the rivalry between the

[3] The mechanism set up to address freedom of association complaints may at first glance seem more 'progressive' in this regard than this type of recurrent examination. But the complaints procedure has its limits, especially the degree to which the state can place strong deterrents on complainants who are thinking about making a submission. The fact that the state can legally prevent the formation of an independent trade union may not totally prevent the filing of an admissible complaint to the Committee on Freedom of Association, but the control it exerts, whether through a central party or through other forms of social supervision, may be a strong deterrent vis-à-vis those who intend to submit such a complaint from within such a state. This explains why the number of complaints brought before the Committee on Freedom of Association against a particular country is a completely unreliable indicator of the existence or absence of freedom of association protections in that country. Thus, numerous countries that can hardly be accused of systematically violating freedom of association rights are 'regulars' before the Committee, while China has only rarely been the subject of a complaint, given the high personal costs such proceedings can have for the complainants. (On this issue, see Karen Curtis, 'Democracy, Freedom of Association and the ILO' in George Politakis (ed), *Les normes internationales du travail: un patrimoine pour l'avenir. Mélanges en l'honneur de Nicolas Valticos* (ILO, 2004) 100.) The act of reviewing the situation in *all* states which have not ratified should push against this limitation, offering the opportunity to review the status of legislation and its possible shortcomings, be they problems of compatibility of legislation or difficulties in putting that legislation effectively into practice.

[4] Namely: the United States, China, Russia and Brazil, which between them count for nearly 30% of the global population and nearly 40% of global GDP.

[5] The so-called 'McNair Committee' named after its chair, a former President of the ICJ.

[6] The Members were divided between those fearful of a 'relativist' drift in the meaning of freedom of association, and those who were distrustful of possible encroachments on their sovereign right to

two super-powers of the time ultimately proved sufficiently powerful to convince both to simultaneously (in fact on the very same day!) give their agreement to participate.

It would be an exaggeration to call the experience a resounding success in every respect: officially, the immensity of the task and its attendant cost[7] led to its suspension in 1963.[8] The present moment would, however, seem to provide an auspicious context to give the experience another chance: the group of countries which have not ratified the two Conventions has considerably shrunk (largely as a result of the 1998 Declaration) but still includes, as previously noted, the biggest players.[9] The competition for global influence is just as likely to stimulate their willy-nilly cooperation in the present context as it did in 1957. It seems clear at the same time that such cooperation cannot be expected unless it is perfectly clear that the object of the exercise is not to pass judgement on their situation; it would be to establish the facts and, as may be agreed, to identify the steps that could be taken to eliminate possible incompatibilities and move progressively to a situation of 'substantial equivalence'.

Should the ILO prove unable, despite its solemn pledge in 1998, to push further towards the effective implementation of these rules of the game, the vast majority of countries who have agreed to play by these rules could hardly be blamed for looking elsewhere for solutions to restore the balance. Among the possibilities, of course, is the appeal to consumer arbitrage through a shared social label (a solution which would not only leave the search for a binding solution relatively dubious, but also render it somewhat superfluous).

B. Creative Redeployment of its Normative Tools to Promote a Dynamic Relation Between Globalisation and Social Progress

While the 'rules of the game' are necessary to ensure those concerned can claim their fair share of the benefits accruing from economic interdependence, it has to be recognised that these rules are not sufficient to ensure that dynamic link. They are not designed to provide Members with the guidance they need to choose and

ignore freedom of association. The purpose of these studies was, in the words of the International Labour Office paper prepared to discuss the continuation of these studies, not 'to say whether freedom of association existed or not. The question was . . . rather, a question of ascertaining what was the extent of freedom of association, by what conditions it was affected and in what circumstances it was exercised' (ILO, *Minutes: Review of the Freedom of Association Survey* (Governing Body, 14th Session, Geneva, March 1963) Annex XIV).

[7] The other non-official but important reason was the fear that this process could involve interference in the supervisory procedures for countries that had ratified.

[8] See Jean de Givry, *Droits de l'homme, travail et syndicats* (Paris, Editions Universitaires, 1989) 115–24.

[9] Consider, as evidence of the project's feasibility, the response of the United States to the proposals put forward by the Director-General to overcome the challenge that globalisation represented to the ILO's objectives; not only did a government representative reiterate a proposal to review all ILO Members for their adherence to core labour standards, but it was very clear that 'the United States would agree to go first'. See ILO, *Provisional Record* (ILC, 85th Session, Geneva, June 1997) 127.

implement the combination of policies they should apply to take advantage of the opportunities offered by globalisation, including education and training to prepare for anticipated changes and develop relevant capabilities, social protection systems to facilitate the necessary adjustment, and labour market regulation designed to ensure an equitable redistribution of the benefits of growth and the costs of adjustment.[10]

To have an impact, such guidance has to be provided within an appropriate institutional framework. And, to become the more effective 'regulator' of globalisation it was expected to be, the ILO needs to develop a new type of normative instrument which, instead of defining the *product* Members are expected to deliver with respect to each specific objective, would provide a framework and guidance for the dynamic[11] *process* of translating the benefits of increased prosperity into social progress (and vice versa) – though this is not to suggest that the traditional normative technique[12] would lose any of its relevance in dealing with certain subjects.[13] Achieving this dynamic focus could be done through a new type of self-contained 'Social Policy' or Coherence instrument, including a sui generis follow-up to include a voluntary peer review system for interested states to draw the lessons of each other's experiences.

C. Promoting Greater Coherence Among Sister Organisations

Each of the book's four Parts has touched on the key contribution the ILO can make to the coherent pursuit of the economic and social objectives conferred upon the universal organisations with corresponding mandates. In this regard, the ILO has the comparative advantage of being able to invite the relevant organisations to the table, without having to extract a promise of reciprocity.

Clearly, however, it will have little chance of attracting top officials from these organisations unless the topic on the table is a project of sufficient mutual interest. Such interest might be drummed up if the ILO planned to put its normative tools

[10] In line with the 2008 Declaration, the specific mix of measures would be left to each country to define on a tripartite basis, taking into account relevant ILO standards.

[11] As already envisaged in the report, 'Globalization is a dynamic phenomenon. While due respect must at all times be paid to fundamental principles and rights at work, the requirements of social justice in such a context are also dynamic. The real issue for the ILO is thus not so much to define a static level playing field as to maintain a dynamic of progress by permanently encouraging and accompanying the efforts of all its Members with all the means at its disposal' (ILO, *Report V: Strengthening the Capacity of the ILO to Assist its Members' Efforts to Promote its Objectives in the Context of Globalization* (International Labour Conference, 96th Session, Geneva, 30 May–15 June 2007) para 9).

[12] This technique also needs to be revisited with a view to consolidating its normative 'products', ie the multitude of existing instruments addressing specific aspects of ILO strategic objectives, into a small number of framework instruments, as already envisaged in the 1997 Director-General's report, and convincingly accomplished with respect to maritime Conventions with the adoption of the Maritime Labour Convention in 2006.

[13] The approach has limited but not inconsequential value, most recently demonstrated by the standards on domestic workers completed by the ILC in 2011, which almost immediately saw their impact on, inter alia, migrant domestic workers in Persian Gulf countries.

at the disposal of the entire cohort of peer organisations to jointly develop, and jointly implement, a framework enabling states to ensure greater policy coherence, perhaps of the type just discussed above. It may well be in this respect that, as desirable as it may for the ILO to develop its own autonomous research capacity in all the areas covered by its mandate, its future may more realistically lie in systematically submitting the research and activities of other organisations to a critical tripartite discussion at the ILC,[14] as in fact contemplated by the Declaration of Philadelphia.

II. Which Requires Mobilising All Actors and Drawing on its Full Array of Transformative Powers

It is equally clear, however, that none of these possibilities can be developed without active engagement from all ILO's major players. Indeed, each of these prospects is likely to remain a tantalising mirage unless it can earn the support of the organisation's key stakeholders. The terrain will necessarily run between two markers: internally, it will touch on the reform of the ILO's working methods to reactivate interest from constituents; externally, it will be a matter of restoring the capacity of the ILO's traditional subjects, namely states themselves.

A. An Internal Reinvention?

First and foremost, successfully canvassing the support of those with the power to make change happen is a matter of defining a vision, and attractively framing the institutional reforms necessary to put that vision into action. In accordance with the constitutionally-structured practice that strongly differentiates the organisation's institutional identity from its peer organisations, the impetus for that vision can only come from the Office and its Director-General. At the same time, the Director-General's commitment to reform will be for naught unless it is shared by the tripartite constituency of the Governing Body and the International Labour Conference, a reality that brings us back to the ILO's capacity to represent the real economy (as opposed to the 'paper market' of the financial world).[15] Indeed, this capacity may still be the ILO's greatest potential asset. It is tripartism alone which gives gravitas and clout to the organisation's presence and advice, not least at forums like the G20. It is tripartism, as well, which could help rebuild a common vision for the future between employers and workers, based on tying increasing

[14] Which would, on the other hand, require centralised, focused research and analytical capacities touching the full cohort of relevant subjects.

[15] A division reminiscent of Albert Thomas' exclamation evoking some of his initiatives over the years: 'une grande idée a été lancée: celle d'une économie du travail substituée à l'économie de profit' (Albert Thomas, 'Justice sociale et paix universelle', *Revue de Paris* (Paris), 15 March 1924) 18).

global demand to expanding production through a more equitable and sustainable dynamic redistribution of the fruits of growth, including from an environmental viewpoint. And, last but not least, it is tripartism that could help put the seal on a new normative 'compact' between workers and employers and thereby fill a void which has proven so detrimental since the end of the Cold War.

At the same time, the ILO's claim to represent the real economy needs to be backed up by the tripartite 'bench strength' of the ILC and the Governing Body. In other words, it requires real decision-makers from business, worker and government circles to make a priority of adequate representation at the ILO, attending themselves where necessary. The parade of Heads of State and other VIPs at the ILC plenary has undoubtedly contributed to the organisation's visibility in recent years, but it also gives an inaccurate picture of the situation that prevails at more technical meetings at the ILC or in the Governing Body. How the level of representation in these meetings compares to yesteryear would certainly be a fascinating subject for political scientists; an anecdotal assessment suggests that it has passed its halcyon days, when the ILO's activities were considered sufficiently important to more than occasionally justify attendance from the elected leadership of each group.[16]

Beyond the strength of representation, this objective puts into play a multitude of factors. Some are practical (eg those relating to the agenda, the duration of sessions, and the functioning of the Governing Body and the International Labour Conference).[17] Others are more fundamental: this is the case in particular with regard to the ability of national organisations to represent the realities of work in all their diversity, as much for those providing the work (including multinationals),[18] as for those who depend on the work provided (not to mention those who have to create work for themselves). This is an important concern, especially insofar as the representatives from industrial, salaried and subordinate work at the centre of the founders' vision are no longer a majority, and face blurred boundaries caused particularly by the expansion of informal and precarious work.[19]

The ILO's vast potential to exercise its capacity more effectively sketched out in this book can only be realised if the constituents are both determined to explore

[16] The latest exception is provided by Marc Blondel, who has, on an ongoing and effective basis, taken part in the work of the ILO Governing Body, first as a member of the Workers group, then as their spokesman in the Programme and Budget Committee. It is unfortunate that no empirical studies have yet captured an accurate picture of how the level and quality of representation in the groups have evolved within the Conference and Governing Body. We eagerly await the research outcomes of any scholar who happens to become interested in the subject.

[17] Of course, the pertinence of the subjects and the more or less conventional debates in the representative bodies dictate the level of representation and the presence of important decision-makers, as much as vice versa.

[18] On the management side, it is important to realise in this regard that the focus in the ILO's system of representation on national employer organisations provides no clear access point for multinational companies except through the filter of these national organisations, grouped together into the International Organization of Employers (IOE). Of course, this reality might not necessarily be a handicap in terms of representing the real economy!

[19] *cf* Alain Supiot (ed), *Beyond Employment: Changes in Work and the Future of Labour Law in Europe* (Paris, Flammarion, 1999).

them, and if they are sufficiently representative; for better or worse, each of these conditions of course somewhat determining the other. Without anticipating too much of a debate that ultimately calls for a separate study, it should be noted at the very least that the challenge arises primarily at the level of national organisations. As interpreted by the PCIJ, the ILO's constitutional framework in fact leaves a wide margin of discretion to national authorities to designate those who are to represent the particular (and diverse) 'masses'[20] of workers concerned.[21]

B. That Calls for the Reconfiguration of its Relationship with States

Strengthening the ILO's persuasive capabilities is obviously not an end in itself. What good is it to persuade your audience if it no longer has the capacity to act effectively? After all, the ILO's orientation is grounded in the Westphalian paradigm that previously tied the market and the state together; if the state lacks the institutional capacity to stay above the quickly rising swells of social change in the era of financial globalisation, does that leave the ILO anchored to a sinking paradigm?[22] Is the ILO not particularly weighed down by a Constitution that interfaces imperfectly with a situation of regional integration, and the broad powers possessed by competing supra-state actors?

Confronted with this turbulence, it would be easy for the ILO to yield to either of two temptations: to passively sit by as state capacities take on water, or to try catch the wave of 'social responsibility' and surf in whatever direction it leads. Either course of action would be a mistake.

[20] 'Masses' is the term found in the French version of the decision; the English uses the decidedly more confusing language of 'classes' of workers, bringing shades of (apparently unintended) Marxist sociology to questions of worker diversity.

[21] The PCIJ in its (first ever) Opinion recalled that the goal was for governments to designate representatives, 'choosing persons who, having regard to the particular circumstances, will be able to represent at the Conference the views of the working classes concerned' (*Designation of the Workers' Delegate for the Netherlands at the Third Session of the International Labour Conference* [1922] PCIJ Rep Series B No 1, reproduced in (1922) 6(7) *ILO Official Bulletin* 292, 300). This reference to 'the working classes concerned', coupled with the fact that the Constitution specifically considers the case where there is no representative organisation, could open up opportunities for governments to include, after consultation with the existing organisations, representatives of classes concerned in national tripartite delegations.

[22] Long before the recent financial crisis, Susan Strange estimated that the system was unable to save capitalism given that 'les intitutions nationales et internationales qui devraient réguler le marché financier sont de moins en moins capables de suivre les évolutions technologiques toujours plus rapides du secteur privé, ce qui pourrait avoir des conséquences dramatiques pour l'économie mondiale' ['national and international institutions which ought to regulate the financial market are less and less able to follow the always swifter technological developments of the private sector, which could lead to dramatic consequences for the global economy', trans] (Susan Strange, 'L'échec des Etats face à la mondialisation' (December 2011) 308 *Esprit* 62, 64). From a much more philosophical perspective, William Scheuerman has argued that the speed of social change threatens the responsive capacities of the traditional social-democratic governance models (William Scheuerman, *Liberal Democracy and the Social Acceleration of Time* (Baltimore, MD, Johns Hopkins University Press, 2004).

Despite glaring disparities and asymmetries in the capacity of individual states, and the obvious humbling of many of those which quite recently seemed rather sure of themselves, there are number of reasons why it may be a bit premature to extol the historical inevitability of state decline.

First, analysis has to be alert to the fact that lamentations about state powerlessness can act to some degree as self-fulfilling prophecy whose realisation is obligingly anticipated by all those who have deliberately shirked their responsibilities in social policy under the alleged constraints of globalisation.[23] The rise of high-profile cross-border social movements has by now made it clear to all governments that sinking legitimacy is likely to be the price to pay for their reluctance or failure or to meet their social responsibilities.[24]

Secondly, current trends actually seem to flow in the opposite direction. In the face of a globalisation that has been cast as a rising tide lapping at the shores of state power, the countries that seem best prepared to rise above are those with strong states, whether authoritarian like China,[25] democratic and developed like the Scandinavian countries, or emerging democratic powers like Brazil.[26]

Last and perhaps more forcefully, the ILO has little choice in the matter: from an institutional perspective, its fate is irrevocably bound up with the fortunes of the state. It would be absurd, if not suicidal, to play along with those who lament the death of state powers only because they have an interest in rushing to bury it; so far, no one has been able to show how the ILO's goals can be meaningfully pursued through a 'deterritorialisation' of social justice.[27] Thus, ensuring its own credibility may ultimately be tied to the continued legitimacy of its Members as the primary caretakers of social progress. The ILO has no choice but to face the problem head-on.

Which leads to a harder question: does the ILO have the means to pursue such an ambition? While rightly pointing to the ILO's responsibility to strengthen the institutional capacity of its Members, the 2008 Declaration only makes a passing reference to the mobilisation of its technical cooperation and expertise,[28] a framing of the necessary work that seems a bit inadequate to the task. We have seen that

[23] See Pierre de Senarclens, *Mondialisation, souveraineté et théories des relations internationales* (Paris, Armand Colin, 1998).

[24] As pointed out by Susan Strange (though she is hardly alone in this claim), state power has traditionally been linked 'to the control the State has exercised over the national economy and the fiscal resources it could draw on to pursue economic and social redistribution' (Strange, 'L'échec' (n 22) 63).

[25] China's relative weathering of the financial crisis in particular led some to go as far as predicting that the emergence of state capitalism actually threatens the survival of the market economy! (Ian Bremmer, *The End of the Free Market: Who Wins the War Between States and Corporations?* (New York, Portfolio, 2010)).

[26] The key may lie in the fact that, within states as between them, '[g]lobalization must be planned, and planned carefully', as put by Prime Minister Mahathir bin Mohamed from the rostrum of the ILC in a speech which was received like a bombshell at the time, but which seems remarkably prescient in retrospect (ILO, *Provisional Record* (ILC, 91st Session, 11th Sitting, Geneva, 3–19 June 2003) 4).

[27] Michel Hansenne expressed his scepticism about such a prospect when he described 'a global civil society . . . answerable only to the laws of economic rationality' (ILO, *The ILO, Standard Setting and Globalization: Report of the Director-General* (ILC, 85th Session, Geneva, June 1997) 6.

[28] In s IIA(ii).

the range of possibilities is much wider than this modest reference might suggest. The real challenge is whether this larger potential can be integrated into a coherent strategy. In light of previous developments, such a strategy could develop in three interdependent directions.

(i) Giving the State a Hand Up

The first would be to place the institutional capacity of its Members more clearly and prominently at the core of its various means of action, in particular:

- by defining, as required by the 2008 Declaration, a coherent doctrine of technical cooperation that would give priority to strengthening the institutional capacity of the Members that need it most, with the active support and participation of social partners;
- by placing greater emphasis on the rule of law and the fight against corruption in its normative activities. The role and mobilisation of workers' and employers' organisations at the national and international level can, of course, strengthen the visibility and credibility of any such action. The ILO has done a lot to assist and encourage Members to build up their administrative infrastructure, and their labour administrations and labour inspectorates in particular. There is, however, one missing aspect which could make a big difference: the independence of the judiciary;[29]
- by launching a kind of counter-capture strategy vis-à-vis multinational corporations which would mobilise their expressed commitment to 'social responsibility' in favour of ILO activities aimed at the institutional reconstruction and empowerment of states. As rightly noted by John Ruggie, the global business community may become increasingly interested 'to channel some of the pressure it faces into the construction of at least minimally effective public sectors'.[30] While it is doubtful that the ILO can persuade corporations to provide such assistance by (for example) deliberately seeking additional tax liability, it would be well within the organisation's prerogative under the 'new partnerships' envisioned in the 2008 Declaration[31] to seek their contribution to programmes to finance the administrative and judicial infrastructure necessary to ensure the rule of law and fair administration of justice;
- by developing a sharper understanding, and defining a clearer strategy towards regional integration and similar arrangements in which Members agree to pool

[29] For workers' and employers' organisations, this issue has particular salience when it comes to the adjudication of individual and collective labour disputes, but its implications stretch much beyond that context. It is true that the ILO has developed various activities aimed at judges (especially at its Turin training centre), but it may be time to consider some appropriate form of normative action. This gap is probably even more surprising given that the activities to support national judiciaries have not only proven very popular but have also had a definite impact.

[30] John Gerald Ruggie, *Taking Embedded Liberalism Global: The Corporate Connection*, New York University International Law and Justice Working Paper 2003/2 (2003) 27.

[31] Under s IIA (v).

their efforts and commitments towards ILO objectives as envisioned by the 2008 Declaration.

(ii) Seriously Tackling Corporate Social Responsibility

The second direction would be to define a coherent policy concerning corporate social responsibility and its relation to the state's own responsibilities.

The fact that the ILO's fate is genetically linked to the state's own fortunes does not mean that the ILO can turn a blind eye to the rise of corporate social responsibility, or ignore the associated privatisation of international labour standards. Quite the opposite; the ILO must attempt to define a coherent policy, lest this phenomenon should develop to the detriment of state capacities to discharge its own social responsibility and, to use Ruggie's provocative image, 'gnaw away at its governance monopoly from the inside'.[32] It is regrettable in this respect that attempts made by the Director-General and the International Labour Office as early as 1998 to encourage the Governing Body to define such a doctrine on a tripartite basis stalled in the face of employer reservations and the indifference of most governments.[33] This had two consequences: within the ILO, it meant that what (rare) initiatives actually came to fruition in the area developed largely 'below the radar', without a preliminary tripartite discussion or a formal endorsement from the Governing Body. This was the case, for example, with the 'Help Desk' for multinationals[34] and the 'Better Work' project.[35]

Outside the ILO, the space left empty by ILO inaction was swiftly occupied by external initiatives, from Kofi Annan's Global Compact[36] to the effort to put together the ISO 26000 social responsibility standard.

Under these circumstances, the ILO should not necessarily try to compete at all costs in the relatively crowded market of corporate social responsibility. Rather, it should try to build upon its own institutional comparative advantage; it could, for instance, offer interested multinationals a (purely voluntary) opportunity to undergo audit on a tripartite basis, using its own Declaration of Principles on Multinational Corporations as a benchmark. Such a possibility could be offered either on some agreed-upon ad hoc basis, or within the framework of a negotiated protocol that could be added to the tripartite declaration itself.

[32] Ruggie, *Taking Embedded Liberalism Global* (n 30) 13.

[33] ILO, *Overview of Global Developments and Office Activities Concerning Codes of Conduct, Social Labelling and Other Private Sector Initiatives Addressing Labour Issues* (Governing Body, 273rd Session, Geneva, 27 October–6 November 1998).

[34] See Marieke Louis, *The ILO's Helpdesk for Business on International Labour Standards: Using the NICT to Bring Multinational Enterprises Back in the Tripartite Regulation Game* (53rd Conference of the International Studies Association, San Diego, April 2011).

[35] The Better Work programme, a joint project of the ILO Social Dialogue sector and the World Bank's IFC, grew out of the Better Factories programme discussed at the end of Part III. There is a great deal of information on their website, www.betterwork.org.

[36] Which is not a code of conduct but a partnership to promote certain UN principles, including Fundamental Principles and Rights at Work which work, inter alia, through a 'learning forum'. Ruggie, *Taking Embedded Liberalism Global* (n 30) 20–21.

(iii) Mediating Models of Tripartism

The third dimension would be to restore the ILO's strategic role in regulating the competition between alternative conceptions of the state's intended role in the framework of tripartism.

If the 'corporatist' European social model and its associated vision of labour law has been the key reference for tripartism within the ILO since its inception, it is now clear that this model has been displaced from a hegemonic position and faces competition from two opposite directions.

First, even if would be an exaggeration to talk in terms of the 'fundamental incommensurability' Michael Piore sees between the 'Franco-Latin' model of labour market regulation and that of the United States,[37] there is a persistent difference of approach across the Atlantic, relating to the specific role of the state and legislation.[38] This difference traces back to the very foundation of the ILO, and the contributions of Samuel Gompers.[39] While the New Deal radically modified perspectives regarding the role of the state (despite the initial reticence of the American Federation of Labour) after the Second World War the suspicion persisted among both American business and labour[40] that the ILO and its standards (especially in the field of social security) were too complacent about state intervention in the economy and could, without sufficient prudence being exercised, even pave the way to a Soviet-type regime.[41] While this obsession subsided with globalisation, the support for projects that choose to improve the lot of workers through engagements along the production chain (such as the UN Global Compact or the ILO's Better Work programme) rather than through legislation, may be the most recent

[37] Michael J Piore, 'Flexible Bureaucracies in Labor Market Regulation' in Guy Davidov and Brian A Langille (eds), *The Idea of Labour Law* (Oxford, Oxford University Press, 2011) 405.

[38] Of course, a great deal of energy has been expended comparing the model in the United Kingdom to the Wagner Act model that prevails in the United States and Canada. Emphasising the relationship of the social partners with the state, however, shows British 'voluntarism' and North American 'pluralism' have more common features than divergences.

[39] See Samuel McCune Lindsay, 'The Problem of American Cooperation' in James Shotwell (ed), *The Origins of the International Labor Organization* vol 1 (New York, Columbia University Press, 1934), in which the author underlines 'the distrust of reliance which has generally characterized and underpinned the actions of workers and employers alike' (ibid 331) in the United States, and according to whom the source of such distrust was founded in a reticence to call on the state's coercive powers unless absolutely necessary. From the start, the US social partners, and Gompers himself, expressed unease with tripartism as understood and promoted by its European protagonists. They instead saw the role of the (federal) state and its legislation as ideally limited to establishing a framework which would exonerate social partners from the prohibition of conspiracy under the Clayton Act (the origin of the 'Labour is not a commodity' slogan), thereby leaving the social partners free to develop on a mainly bipartite basis (ibid 332–33).

[40] According to Bob Cox, the convergence of business and labour visions of US policy abroad was so great that he once dared to describe the AFL CIO as 'the soldier of American capitalism' (Robert W Cox, 'Labor and Hegemony' (1977) 31(3) *International Organization* 385, 397).

[41] The indictment of the 'erosion of tripartism' by Kissinger was as much inspired by Georges Meany as by the American Chamber of Commerce; and it directed against state encroachments on the autonomy of the groups' intervention. The sad irony is that with the end of the Cold War, the erosion of tripartism has been followed by the accelerated erosion of EU influence in the United States, and its virtual exclusion from global policy-making.

incarnation of this attitude of suspicion toward the state and its legislation as the spearhead of social progress.

In the opposite direction lies the more radical challenge from the Chinese social model. It may seem strange to even frame Chinese labour relations as a 'model' for tripartism given how many would argue that China's labour policy represents the very negation of the concept. Three simple facts, however, must be kept in mind. First, the labour situation in China is not only complex, but changing just as rapidly as its economy and society. Secondly, whether tripartite or not, the Chinese system subjects the traditional tripartite model and its credibility to intense competition as a result of its apparent capacity for economic growth. Thirdly, the role of the so-called Party-State bears only passing resemblance to what it was in the Soviet model: indeed, it explicitly leaves a certain 'space' or autonomy to social partners at the decentralised (enterprise) level (so that there are 1.8 million local unions). In fact, a kind of paradox lies in the fact that autonomy seems to hold more value for employers, who are less subject to the directives of the Party-State than the official union (ACFTU), which under its Charter is supposed to be 'a bridge and bond linking the Party and the masses' much in the same way as unions did in the former Soviet Union.[42]

It seems clear, however, that to maintain its efficacy, the Chinese model needs to develop an industrial relations system that is commensurate with worker levels of education, sophistication and access to information. Yet, the process is threatened by the Tocquevillian malediction thrown on any authoritarian state, which by engaging in reforms inevitably opens the gate to what may become an uncontrollable flood. No wonder then that the 'factory of the world' is peering with interest at the ILO's toolkit of comparative knowledge and experience of world systems. This competition between the different systems, along with the stubborn challenge that persistent informality poses to all three, should be excellent news for the ILO. Together, they might recreate the conditions under which the organisation can recover the strategic roles it had as a major actor and arbitrator but also an important stake during the Cold War.

The bad news, however, is that the European Union, which about 10 years ago was proudly proclaiming that '[t]he European Union is emerging as a new world model of development'[43] seems to be turning its back on this model which, as we have seen, is diluting with enlargement, and seen by many Member States to be connected to European sluggishness. As a consequence, there seem to be no strategic vision regarding the role and use of the ILO in this confrontation. This state of affairs is surely not irreversible, though the change is admittedly unlikely to arise spontaneously from EU institutions, whose representatives in ILO

[42] See Zhining Ma, 'Industrial Relations in China: A Review Based on a Six-party Model' (2011) 150(1–2) *International Labour Review* 145, according to whom, '[i]t remains a puzzle why – in a country nominally "led by the working class" – the breakthrough in reform for freedom of association has come not from the association of workers/employees, but from the association of employers/capitalists' (ibid 154).

[43] Anna Diamantopoulou, 'Making Europe Work for People' (Address at the 10th European Trade Union Confederation Statutory Congress, Prague, 26 May 2003).

decision-making (in most cases) lack the necessary authority and competence to develop such strategic vision. It is more likely to come from the interest prompted in wider intellectual, government and civil society circles by the coincidence between the ongoing crisis of the European social model and the upcoming celebration of the ILO's 100th anniversary.

III. And Widening the Horizon of Social Justice

The reference to 'social justice' in the ILO's Constitution has led to a great deal of ink being spilled, including very early on in the writings of Albert Thomas.[44] As we have seen, the concept has had mixed fortunes during the organisation's first century: it was on the lips of every side during the Cold War, became overshadowed with the beginnings of globalisation, and made a surprising (and perhaps prescient) comeback in the 2008 Declaration.

It would not be totally out of place, however, to level the same questions directed at the references to employment or standards of living in the IMF and WTO Charters: is the reference ultimately an essentially symbolic, decorative feature whose absence would more than anything undermine only the rhetorical harmony of the Preamble? Just as employment is regarded by some as an axiomatic byproduct of a well-run economy, is social justice not just the axiomatic result of free and organised confrontation of the interests held by the various stakeholders?

A sufficiently serious answer to those questions will take another book. Suffice it to note at this point that the growing inequality associated with financial globalisation has given the concept renewed relevance. As a consequence, however, it places new expectations on the ILO.

Meeting those expectations head-on will in turn expand the conceptual horizon, perhaps even developing two dimensions which have hitherto been relatively neglected in the ILO's conceptual foundations: the transnational and the inter-generational.

A. The Question of Transnational Justice

Questions related to inter-state equality and inequality are not explicitly addressed in the ILO Constitution. The reference to social justice appears as a commitment

[44] In an article entitled 'Justice sociale et paix universelle' that appeared in the *Revue de Paris* of 15 March 1924 where he said very significantly that 'ce n'est point parce que l'injustice sociale provoque directement le mécontentement intérieur, c'est parce qu'elle créée sur les marchés du monde de redoutables rivalités, génératrices de conflits, qu'elle compromet la paix' ['it is not the fact that social injustice directly causes domestic discontentment, it is because it creates on world markets some fierce rivalries, generating conflicts, that it compromises peace', trans]. As noted in the Introduction, the ILO's peace-keeping role according to him consisted in 'substituer une émulation loyale et humaine à la concurrence déloyale fondée sur une exploitation des forces ouvrières. (Thomas, 'Justice sociale' (n 15) 8).

individually assumed by acceding Members, who are in turn supposed to individually implement it, taking into account ILO objectives, giving effect to the ILO instruments which elaborate these objectives where possible, and thereby remedying economic rivalries and conflicts at their source.

The merits of this approach can certainly be critiqued on the doctrinal level. It is notable that Rawls, who became interested in this inter-state dimension of social justice only late in his own writing, used arguments based on cultural pluralism and the impossibility of creating completely reciprocal relationships between societies with different principles of organisation to come to conclusions that bear some similarity to the approach generally taken to the ILO Constitution.[45]

This position has unsurprisingly been the subject of various criticisms. Charles Beitz, for one, has challenged the underlying principle. According to him, all that is required to establish a question of distributive justice within any political space are common institutions responsible for distributing harms and benefits. According to Beitz, this condition already exists in view of the transnational interdependence brought about by existing global institutions.[46] One can, of course, argue that, in legal terms, it would be somewhat unwarranted to draw a similar conclusion as long as the competent organisation's mandate (ie the ILO) seems postulated on the idea that distributive justice is a matter for each individual Member alone.

From a more mundane point of view, the argument nevertheless sheds an interesting light on ongoing discussions.

It is indisputable that globalisation is not spontaneously generated. As already stated in the final report of the World Commission on the Social Dimension of Globalization, it is instead a phenomenon constituted in part by certain rules and institutions, including multilateral trade disciplines. But it is also clear that these rules and that regime have led to a redistribution of wealth between the heretofore developed countries and a number of emerging or emergent countries. Indeed, the resulting redistribution may have been more substantial than was generated by all the claims made and efforts deployed on behalf of the 'right to development' (including the United Nations' two so-called 'development decades').

If one agrees that inter-state redistribution, operated thanks to access to other markets, must be accepted as a requirement of social justice among states, it becomes difficult not to accept what seems to be a logical corollary: the reciprocal right to a form of 'oversight', if not over actual redistribution, at least on the existence and respect by the other country for fundamental rights at work, which (again quoting from the 1998 Declaration) enable those concerned to claim 'their fair share of the wealth which they have helped to generate' and therefore represent a necessary condition for such redistribution to take place.

[45] John Rawls, *The Law of Peoples* (Cambridge, MA, Harvard University Press, 1999).

[46] His criticism was laid out in a book written well before John Rawls approached the question of international justice: Charles Beitz, *Political Theory and International Relations* (Princeton, NJ, Princeton University Press, 1979).

B. The Question of Intergenerational Justice

The ILO and its constituents cannot be indifferent to questions arising with more and more frequency in debates at the national level. Given the complexity of the subject, it is impossible to address it more than superficially, but there are two very preliminary points which can be made in this respect. The first is that the issue clearly illustrates the limits of a merely procedural view of social justice as the byproduct of the reconciliation between the legitimate interests of workers and employers through their freely chosen representatives; by definition, future generations can have no 'freely chosen' representatives. The second is that, in pretty much every case, the question of justice for future generations puts in question environmental protection and, by definition 'sustainability' issues.

Without pushing these issues any further, they already force the realisation that strengthening the ILO's institutional capacity also involves finding an appropriate way to fit tripartism together with a trio of objectives: social, economic and environmental. The prospect of doing so, on the other hand, may seem both far-off and hard to pin down. To understand how easy it is to define practical consequences for such concerns, without suggesting that their realisation is imminent, one need only imagine the possibilities and challenges of eventually establishing, within a tripartite framework, an inter-state system of mutually recognised social and environmental labels following the model laid out in Part IV.

One conclusion unequivocally emerges from all this: a massive project lays before the organisation, but only so long as it does more than survive, and also remains true to itself, showing how effectively it can implement the essential functions it was originally assigned.

The celebration of its 100th anniversary may provide the impulse that is unlikely to come from the outside. It is a fact that the impulse for change and for institutional reform in particular has historically come from outside the ILO or from external circumstances.[47] Judging by the stalled Doha Round, the pieties which came out of Rio+20 and the diminishing attention paid to UN reform in comparison to the excitement which bubbled up around ideas like the proposed establishment of a Council for Economic and Social Security, it is hard to see where such an external impulse could come from.

The celebration of its centenary provides the ILO with a convenient and indeed institutionally more satisfactory alternative. It would offer a unique opportunity to address a bevy of issues which are the key to a successful entry into its second century of existence and to do so serenely, with clarity, and in close consultation with its officials and its constituents, as well as all its peer organisations.

[47] It is well known, for instance, that the adoption of the OECD Guidelines for Multinational Enterprises led the ILO Governing Body to adopt the 1976 Tripartite Declaration on Multinational Enterprises, an entirely original and sui generis instrument. And we had ample opportunity in preceding chapters to measure the special debt the ILO has to the WTO, which on two occasions (Singapore in 1996 and Seattle in 1999) became a real, albeit unwilling, ally in the institutional innovations introduced in the 1998 and 2008 Declarations.

Of course, all this must be organised. Again, the rich practice under the ILO Constitution will no doubt provide useful precedents.[48]

The question to be asked is much like that already posed by Jenks on the occasion of the ILO's 50th anniversary: 'This epilogue is but a prologue. How will our successors 50 years from now, judge what we will then have done during our second half century?'[49]

[48] Recall here that in anticipation of the report submitted to the ILC, the ILO's 75th anniversary occasioned an extensive consultation of staff about the vision they had of the future of the ILO and the reforms necessary to achieve it. Such consultation, provided it is conducted under conditions that protect freedom of expression and transparency of agents, seem even more justified in view of the centenary.

[49] Speech of Wilfred Jenks reproduced in ILO, *Social Policy in a Changing World: The ILO Response: Selected Speeches by Wilfred Jenks* (Geneva, ILO, 1976) 263.

BIBLIOGRAPHY

Books, articles etc

Adepoju, A, 'Fostering Free Movement of Persons in West Africa: Achievements, Constraints, and Prospects for Intraregional Migration' (2002) 40(2) *International Migration* 3

Adler, D and Woolcock, M, 'Justice Without the Rule of Law? The Challenge of Rights-based Industrial Relations in Contemporary Cambodia' in T Novitz and C Fenwick (eds), *Human Rights at Work: Perspectives on Law and Regulation* (Oxford, Hart Publishing, 2010) 529–54

Agusti-Panareda, J, 'La Banque Mondiale' in JM Thouvenin and A Trebilcock (eds), *Droit international social* (Brussels, Bruylant, 2013)

Aidt, T and Tzannatos, Z, *Unions and Collective Bargaining: Economic Effects in a Global Environment* (Washington, World Bank, 2002)

Alcock, A, *The History of the International Labour Organization* (New York, Macmillan, 1971)

Alston, P, 'Making Space for New Human Rights: The Case of the Right to Development' (1988) 1 *Harvard Human Rights Yearbook* 3

——'Labor Rights Provisions in US Trade Law: Aggressive Unilateralism?' (1993) 15(1) *Human Rights Quarterly* 1

——'"Core Labour Standards" and the Transformation of the International Labour Rights Regime' (2004) 15(3) *European Journal of International Law* 457

——'Facing Up to the Complexities of the ILO's Core Labour Standards Agenda' (2005) 16(3) *European Journal of International Law* 467

Alvarez, J, *International Organizations as Law Makers* (Oxford, Oxford University Press, 2005)

Arthur, O, Prime Minister of Barbados, 'Address at the Opening of the CSME Unit Office' (Central Bank of Barbados, Bridgetown, 14 October 2002)

Arup, C, *The New World Trade Organization Agreements: Globalizing Law Through Services and Intellectual Property* (Cambridge, Cambridge University Press, 2000)

Attali, J, *Demain, qui gouvernera le monde ?* (Paris, Fayard, 2011)

Auer, P, 'The Internationalization of Employment: A Challenge to Fair Globalization?' (2006) 145 *International Labour Review* 119

Badie, B, *La diplomatie de connivence: Les dérives oligarchiques du système international* (Paris, La Découverte, 2011)

Baccaro, L, 'Orchestration for the "Social Partners" Only: Internal Constraints on the ILO'; unpublished manuscript; Université de Genève

Banks, K, 'Trade, Labor and International Governance: An Inquiry into the Potential Effectiveness of the New International Labor Law' (2011) 32(1) *Berkeley Journal of Employment and Labor Law* 45

Barber, B, 'TUC Response to DFID Multilateral Aid Review and the ILO' (Trades Union Congress, 9 May 2011)

Barroux, R, 'Le G20 fait de l'emploi des jeunes et de la mise en place d'un socle de protection sociale une priorité', *Le Monde* (Paris), 5 November 2011

Barry, C and Reddy, SG, 'International Trade and Labour Standards: A Proposal for Linkage' (2006) 39 *Cornell International Law Journal* 545

Bartels, L, 'Social Issues: Labour, Environment and Human Rights' in S Lester and B Mercurio, *Bilateral and Regional Agreements: Commentary, Analysis and Case Studies* (Cambridge, Cambridge University Press, 2009) 342–66

Baverez, N, 'L'Europe à l'âge de l'histoire universelle' (2011) 135 *Commentaire* 640

Bedjaoui, M, *Pour un nouvel ordre économique international: Nouveaux défis au droit international* (Paris, UNESCO, 1979)

Beigbeder, Y, 'The United States' Withdrawal from the International Labor Organization' (1979) 34 *Industrial Relations* 226

Beitz, C, *Political Theory and International Relations* (Princeton, NJ, Princeton University Press, 1979)

Bello, W, *Deglobalization: Ideas for a New World Economy*, 2nd edn (New York, Zed Books, 2004)

Benedict XVI, *Caritas in veritate [Charity in Truth]* (2009)

Bensusán, G, 'Labour Reform from the Regional Perspective: Experiences in the Americas' in A Blackett and C Lévesque (eds), *Social Regionalism in the Global Economy* (London, Routledge, 2011) 207–24

Bentolila, S and Saint-Paul, G, 'Explaining Movements in the Labor Share' (2003) 3(1) *BE Journal of Macroeconomics* 9

Benvenisti, E and Downs, GW, 'The Empire's New Clothes: Political Economy and the Fragmentation of International Law' (2007) 60(2) *Stanford Law Review* 595

Bernhard, M, 'The Leadership Secrets of Bismarck and Imperial Germany, and Competitive Authoritarianism' (2011) 90(6) *Foreign Affairs* 150

Berry, W, 'The Whole Horse' in N Wirzba (ed), *The Art of the Commonplace: The Agrarian Essays of Wendell Berry* (Berkeley, CA, Counterpoint Press, 2002) 236–48

Bertrand, M, *L'ONU* (Paris, La Découverte, 2006)

Bezou, C, *La clause sociale: la négociation internationale menée par l'OIT* (Paris, ESKA, 2008)

Bhagwati, JN, *Free Trade Today* (Princeton, NJ, Princeton University Press, 2002)

Blackett, A and Lévesque, C, 'Introduction: Social Regionalism in the Global Economy' in A Blackett and C Lévesque (eds), *Social Regionalism in the Global Economy* (London, Routledge, 2011) 1–30

Blanchard, F, *L'organisation internationale du travail: De la guerre froide à un nouvel ordre mondial* (Paris, Seuil, 2004)

Bleicher, S, 'UN v. IBRD: A Dilemma of Functionalism' (1970) 24 *International Organization* 31

Boulstridge, E and Carrigan, M, 'Do Consumers Really Care about Corporate Responsibility? Highlighting the Attitude–Behaviour Gap' (2000) 4(4) *Journal of Communication Management* 355

Bradlow, D, 'The World Bank, the IMF and Human Rights' (1996) 6 *Transnational Law and Contemporary Problems* 47

Bradlow, D and Schlemmer-Schulte, S, 'The World Bank's New Inspection Panel: A Constructive Step in the Transformation of the International Legal Order' (1998) 54(2) *Heidelberg Journal of International Law* 353

Bradsher, K, 'Signs of changes taking hold in electronics factories in China', *The New York Times* (New York), 26 December 2012

Bremmer, I, *The End of the Free Market: Who Wins the War Between States and Corporations?* (New York, Portfolio, 2010)

Brett, B, 'Letters to the Editor: Social clause delayed, but not dead', *Financial Times* (London), 10 May 1995 Boisson de Chazournes, L, 'Banque mondiale et développement social: les termes d'un partenariat' in P de Senarclens (ed), *Maîtriser la mondialisation: la régulation sociale internationale* (Paris, Presses de Sciences-Po, 2000)

Boisson de Chazournes, L and Mbengue, MM, 'À propos du soutien mutuel – les relations entre le protocole de Cartagena et les accords de l'OMC' (2007) 4 *Revue Générale de Droit International Public* 829

Bolle, MJ, *Jordan-US Free Trade Agreement: Labor Issues*, Congressional Research Service Report RS20968 (27 May 2003)

Bonnechère, M, 'L'optique du travail décent' (February 2007) *The Right Worker* 57

Boutin, C, *De la mondialisation à l'universalisation: une ambition sociale*, Rapport intermédiaire au Président de la République (Paris, La Documentation française, 2010)

Boyle, AE and Chinkin, CM, *The Making of International Law* (Oxford, Oxford University Press, 2007)

Bradley, CA, 'The Treaty Power and American Federalism' (1998) 97 *Michigan Law Review* 390

——'The Treaty Power and American Federalism, Part II' (2000) 99 *Michigan Law Review* 98

Brown, A and Stern, R, 'What are the Issues in Using Trade Agreements to Improve International Labour Standards?' (2008) 7(2) *World Trade Review* 331

Burda, J, 'Le droit international économique et les droits sociaux fondamentaux: pour un dimension sociale de la libéralisation des échanges' (unpublished manuscript on file with author, 2009)

Burns, J, Heintz, J and Pollin, R, 'Global Apparel Production and Sweatshop Labour: Can Raising Retail Prices Finance Living Wages?' (2004) 28(2) *Cambridge Journal of Economics* 153

Busse, M, 'On the Determinants of Core Labour Standards: The Case of Developing Countries' (2004) 83(2) *Economic Letters* 211

Caswell, JA and Mojduszka, EM, 'Using Informational Labeling to Influence the Market for Quality in Food Products' (1996) 78(5) *American Journal of Agricultural Economics* 1248

Centre d'études sur l'intégration et la mondialisation (CEIM), 'Lien commerce-emploi: les organisations internationales se prononcent' (December 2010) 1(2) *Chronique Humaniser le commerce* 3

Charnovitz, S, 'The Influence of International Labour Standards on the World Trading System: A Historical Overview' (1987) 126(5) *International Labour Review* 565

——'Promoting Higher Labor Standards,' (1995) 18(3) *Washington Quarterly* 167

——'Trade, Employment and Labour Standards: The OECD Study and Recent Developments in the Trade and Labour Standards Debate' (1997) 11(1) *Temple International and Comparative Law Journal* 131

——'The Neglected Employment Dimension of the World Trade Organization' in VA Leary and D Warner (eds), *Social Issues, Globalisation and International Institutions: Labour Rights and the EU, ILO, OECD and WTO* (Leiden, Martinus Nijhoff Publishers, 2006) 136

——'Editorial Comments: The ILO Convention on Freedom of Association and its Future in the United States' (2008) 102(1) *American Journal of International Law* 90

Charnovitz, S, Earley, J and Howse, R, *An Examination of Social Standards in Biofuels Sustainability Criteria* (International Food and Agricultural Trade Policy Council, Poznan, 9 December 2008)

Chavagneux, C, 'L'instabilité du monde: inégalités, finance, environnement', *Esprit* (Paris), December 2011

Ciorciari, JD, 'The Lawful Scope of Human Rights Criteria in the World Bank Credit Decisions' (2000) 33 *Cornell International Law Journal* 331

Cissé-Niang, A, 'L'interdiction internationale du travail des enfants vue d'Afrique' (2002) 1095 *Semaine Sociale Lamy* 9

Cohen, D, *La prospérité du vice* (Paris, Albin Michel, 2009)

Cohen, E, *La tentation hexagonale: la souveraineté à l'épreuve de la mondialisation* (Paris, Fayard, 1996)

Collins, H, 'Theories of Rights and Justifications for Labour Law' in G Davidov and BA Langille (eds), *The Idea of Labour Law* (Oxford, Oxford University Press, 2011)

Compa, L, 'The North American Free Trade Agreement and the North American Agreement on Labour Cooperation' in R Blainpain (ed), *International Encylopedia for Labour Law and Industrial Relations* (The Hague, Kluwer Law International, 1998)

—— 'Pursuing International Labour Rights in US Courts: New Uses for Old Tools' (2002) 57(1) *Industrial Relations* 48

——'Workers' Freedom of Association in the United States: The Gap between Ideals and Practice' in JA Gross (ed), *Workers' Rights as Human Rights* (Ithaca, NY, Cornell University Press, 2006)

Compa, L and Vogt, J, 'Labor Rights in the Generalized System of Preferences: A 20 Years Review' (2001) 22(2–3) *Comparative Labor Law and Policy Journal* 119

Cordova, E, 'Some Reflections on the Overproduction of International Labour Standards' (1993) 14 *Comparative Labor Law and Policy Journal* 138

Cox, R, 'Labor and Hegemony' (1977) 31(03) *International Organization* 385

—— *The New Realism: Perspectives on Multilateralism and World Order* (London, Palgrave Macmillan, 1997)

Craig, JDR and Lynk, M (eds), *Globalization and the Future of Labour Law* (Cambridge, Cambridge University Press, 2006)

Cukier, K, 'Data, data everywhere, a special report on managing information', *The Economist* (London), 27 February 2010

Curtis, K, 'Democracy, Freedom of Association and the ILO' in G Politakis (ed), *Les normes internationales du travail: un patrimoine pour l'avenir. Mélanges en l'honneur de Nicolas Valticos* (Geneva, International Labour Organization, 2004) 89–106

Dañino, R, 'The Legal Aspects of the World Bank's Work on Human Rights' (Lecture at New York University School of Law, New York, 1 March 2004)

Daugareilh, I, 'L'ISO à l'assaut du social: risques et limites d'un exercice de normalisation sociale' in I Daugareilh (ed), *La responsabilité sociale de l'entreprise transnationale et la globalisation de l'économie* (Brussels, Bruylant, 2010) 563–87

Daugareilh, I (ed), *La responsabilité sociale de l'entreprise transnationale et la globalisation de l'économie* (Brussels, Bruylant, 2010)

Davidov, G, 'Comment on Alan Hyde: The Perils of Economic Justifications for International Labor Standards' (2009) 3(2) *Law and Ethics of Human Rights* Article 3

De Givry, J, *Droits de l'homme, travail et syndicats* (Paris, Editions Universitaires, 1989)

De Pelsmacker, P and others, 'Consumer Preferences for the Marketing of Ethically Labelled Coffee' (2005) 22(5) *International Marketing Review* 512

Deakin, S, 'Social Rights in a Globalized Economy' in P Alston (ed), *Labour Rights as Human Rights* (Oxford, Oxford University Press, 2005) 25–60

Decorzant, Y, 'Répondre à la demande sociale et à la demande du marché: les prémisses de la régulation économique dans les années 1920' in A Aglan, O Feiertag and D Kévonian (eds), *Albert Thomas, société mondiale et internationalisme* (Paris, Les Cahiers Irice, 2008)

Delors, J, 'The European Community and the New World Order' (Address to the Royal Institute of International Affairs, London, 7 September 1992)

Diamantopoulou, A, 'Making Europe Work for People' (Address at 10th European Trade Union Confederation Statutory Congress, Prague, 26 May 2003)

DiCaprio, A, 'Are Labor Provisions Protectionist? Evidence from Nine Labor-Augmented U.S. Trade Arrangements' (2004) 26(1) *Comparative Labor Law and Policy Journal* 1

Diller, JM, 'Private Standardization in Public International Law Making' (2011) 33(3) *Michigan Journal of International Law* 491

Dispersyn, M, 'La regulation juridique internationale de la RSE: un scénario possible?' in I Daugareilh (ed), *La responsabilité sociale de l'entreprise transnationale et la globalisation de l'économie* (Brussels, Bruylant, 2010) 515

Doumbia-Henry, C and Gravel, E, 'Free Trade Agreements and Labour Rights: Recent Developments' (2006) 145(3) *International Labour Review* 185

Drouin, R-C and Duplessis, I, 'La régulation internationale du travail de 1998 à 2008: un Eldorado normatif ou un désert interprétatif' (2009) 14(2) *Lex Electronica* 18

Drzewicki, K, 'Freedom of Association in One-Party Systems' (1990) *Nordic Journal of Human Rights* 28

Dubin, L, *La protection des normes sociales dans les échanges internationaux* (Aix en Provence, Presses Universitaires d'Aix-Marseille, 2003)

Dupuy, R-J (ed), *Manuel sur les organisations internationales* (Leiden, Martinus Nijhoff Publishers, 1998)

Ebert, FC, 'Between Political Goodwill and WTO-Law: Human Rights Conditionality in the Community's New Scheme of Generalised Tariff Preferences (GSP)' (2009) ZERP-Arbeitspapier 8/2009

Ebert, FC and Oelz, M, *Bridging the Gap Between Labour Rights and Human Rights: The Role of ILO Regional Human Rights Law in Short*, IILS Discussion Paper DP/212/2012 (2012)

Ebert, FC and Posthuma, A, *Labour Standards and Development Finance Institutions: A Review of Current Policies and Activities*, International Institute of Labour Studies Discussion Paper 204 (2010)

——'Aligning Private Sector Investment and Labour Standards? The Case of Policies of the Development Finance Institutions' (Research Conference on Key Lessons from the Crisis and Way Forward, Geneva, February 2011)

——*Labour Provisions in Trade Agreements: Current Trends and Prospects*, International Labour Organization and International Institute of Labour Studies Discussion Paper 205 (2011)

Einhorn, J, 'The World Bank Mission Creep' (2001) 80(5) *Foreign Affairs* 22

Elliott, K and Freeman, R, *Can Labor Standards Improve Under Globalization?* (Washington, DC, Institute for International Economics, 2003)

Emmerij, L, Jolly, R and Weiss, TG, *Ahead of the Curve? UN Ideas and Global Challenges* (Bloomington, IN, Indiana University Press, 2001)

Ewing, KD, 'Foreword' in T Novitz and C Fenwick (eds), *Human Rights at Work: Perspectives on Law and Regulation* (Oxford, Hart Publishing, 2010)

Ewing, KD and Hendy, J, 'The Dramatic Implications of Demir and Baykara' (2010) 39(1) *Industrial Law Journal* 42

Fairise, N, 'L'exception de moralité publique dans les accords de l'OMC et son application dans le différend canado-européen sur la chasse au phoque' (Master's thesis, Université de Montréal, 2010)

Faugère, J-P, 'La régulation sociale dans la construction européenne' in P de Senarclens (ed), *Maîtriser la mondialisation: la régulation sociale internationale* (Paris, Presses de Sciences-Po, 2000) 217

Faujas, A, 'Le très libéral FMI vire-t-il social démocrate?', *Le Monde* (Paris), 15 September 2010

—— 'Pascal Lamy: "La démondialisation est un concept réactionnaire" ', *Le Monde* (Paris), 30 June 2011

Feiertag, O, 'Réguler la mondialisation: Albert Thomas, les débuts du BIT et la crise économique mondiale de 1920–1923' in A Aglan, O Feiertag and D Kévonian (eds), *Albert Thomas, société mondiale et internationalisme* (Paris, Les Cahiers Irice, 2008)

Fiorentino, RV, Verdeja, L and Toqueboeuf, C, *The Changing Landscape of Regional Trade Agreements: 2006 Update*, WTO Trade Policies Review Division, Regional Trade Agreements Section, Discussion Paper 12 (2006)

Finbow, R, *The Limits of Regionalism: NAFTA's Labour Accord* (Burlington, Ashgate, 2006)

Fischer, G, 'Les rapports entre l'Organisation internationale du travail et la Cour permanente de justice internationale' (DPhil thesis, University of Geneva, 1946)

Foroobar, R, 'The truth about the US poverty crisis', *Time* (New York), 26 September 2011

Frachon, A and Vernet, D, 'Le grand malentendu' (2012) 35(140) *Commentaire* 1189

Fudge, J, 'The New Discourse of Labor Rights: From Social to Fundamental Rights?' (2007) 29 *Comparative Labor Law and Policy Journal* 29

Ghebali, V-Y, *The International Labor Organization* (Geneva, Georg, 1987)

Gibb, R, 'Post-Lomé: The European Union and the South' (2000) 21(3) *Third World Quarterly* 457

Goldin, A, 'Extending Social Security Coverage: The Normative Route' (2006), 27(2), Social Protection and Decent Work: New Prospects For International Labor Standards, *Comparative Labor Law & Policy Journal*, 257–72

Goldman, K, 'Labeling of Genetically Modified Foods: Legal and Scientific Issues' (2000) 12(3) *Georgetown International Environmental Law Review* 717

Gravel, E, Kohiyama, T and Tsotroudi, K, 'The Role of International Labour Standards in Rebalancing Globalization: A Legal Perspective' in International Labour Organization (ed), *The Global Crisis, Causes, Responses and Challenges* (Geneva, International Labour Organization, 2011) 209–22

Grossmann, H and Koopman, G, 'Social Standards in International Trade: A New Protectionist Wave?' in H Sander and A Inotai (eds), *World Trade After the Uruguay Round: Prospects and Policy Options for the Twenty-first Century* (London, Routledge, 1996) 115–33

Guérin, D, *Albert Thomas au BIT 1920–1932: De l'internationalisme à l'Europe* (Geneva, Europa, 1996)

Guerreau, M, *Une nouvelle institution du droit des gens: l'Organisation permanente du travail* (Paris, Rousseau, 1923)

Guzman, AT, 'Trade, Labor, Legitimacy' (2003) 91 *California Labor Review* 885

Haas, EB, *Beyond the Nation-State: Functionalism and International Organization* (Stanford, CA, Stanford University Press, 1964)

—— *Beyond the Nation-State: Functionalism and International Organization* (Colchester, ECPR Press, 2008)

Haas, P, 'Epistemic Communities and International Policy Organization' (1992) 46(1) *International Organization* 1

Häberli, C, Jansen, M and Monteiro, J-A, *References to Domestic Labour Market Regulation in Regional Trade Agreements*, NCCR Trade Regulation Working Paper 2011/35 (2011)

Haji, R, *Normes du travail, commerce et développement*, Centre d'études sur l'intégration et la mondialisation Research Paper 10-01 (2010)

Hansenne, M, *Un garde-fou pour la mondialisation: Le BIT dans l'après-guerre froide* (Geneva, Zoe, 1999)

Hassner, P, 'Rousseau et les relations internationales' (2012) 140 *Commentaire* 1089

Hatch OG, 'Ratify International Labour Conventions', *Christian Science Monitor*, 10 December 1985, 27

Hepple, B, *Labour Laws and Global Trade* (Oxford, Hart Publishing, 2005)

—— 'The WTO as a Mechanism for Labour Regulation' in B Bercusson and C Estlund (eds), *Regulating Labour in the Wake of Globalisation: New Challenges, New Institutions* (Oxford, Hart Publishing, 2008) 161–78

Hiscox, M and Smyth, N, 'Is there Consumer Demand for Improved Labor Standards? Evidence from Field Experiments in Social Labeling' (unpublished manuscript, 2011)

Hoffmann, S and Fidler, DP (eds), *Rousseau on International Relations* (Oxford, Clarendon Press, 1991)

Horsey, R, *Ending Forced Labour in Myanmar: Engaging a Pariah Regime* (London, Routledge, 2011)

Horta, K, 'Rhetoric and Reality: Human Rights and the World Bank' (2002) 15 *Harvard Human Rights Law Journal* 227

Howse, R, 'The World Trade Organization and the Protection of Workers' Rights' (1999) 3 *Journal of Small and Emerging Business Law* 131

Howse, R and Genser, J, 'Are EU Trade Sanctions on Burma Compatible with WTO Law?' (2008) 29(2) *Michigan Journal of International Law* 165

Howse, R and Langille, J, 'Permitting Pluralism: The Seal Products Dispute and Why the WTO Should Accept Trade Restrictions Justified by Noninstrumental Moral Values' (2012) 27(2) *Yale Journal of International Law* 367

Hughes, C, 'Transnational Networks, International Organizations and Political Participation in Cambodia: Human Rights, Labour Rights and Common Rights' (2007) 14(5) *Democratization* 834

Hughes, S and Haworth, N, 'A Shift in the Centre of Gravity: The ILO Under Harold Butler and John G. Winant' in J van Daele and others, *ILO Histories: Essays on the International Labour Organization and Its Impact on the World During the Twentieth Century* (Bern, Peter Lang, 2010) 301

Hull, C and Berding, AHT, *The Memoirs of Cordell Hull* (New York, Macmillan, 1948)

International Labour Organization, *Social Policy in a Changing World: The ILO Response: Selected Speeches by Wilfred Jenks* (Geneva, International Labour Organization, 1976)

—— *World Employment Report 1998–99: Employability in the Global Economy: How Training Matters* (Geneva, ILO, 1998)

—— *Improving the Impact of International Labour Standards through Technical Cooperation: A Practice Guide* (Geneva, ILO Department, 2008) – *Global Employment Trends 2013: Recovering from a Second Jobs Dip* (2013)

International Labour Organization and International Institute for Labour Studies, *World of Work Report 2008: Income Inequalities in the Age of Financial Globalization* (Geneva, International Labour Organization, 2008)
—— *World of Work Report 2009: The Global Jobs Crisis* (Geneva, International Labour Organization, 2010)
—— *Making Recovery Sustainable: Lessons from Country Innovations* (Geneva, International Labour Organization, 2011)
—— *World of Work Report 2011: Making Markets Work for Jobs* (Geneva, International Labour Organization, 2011)
International Labour Organization and World Trade Organization, *Globalization and Informal Jobs in Developing Countries* (Geneva, World Trade Organization, 2009)
International Monetary Fund, *World Economic Outlook: Advancing Structural Reforms* (Washington, DC, International Monetary Fund, 2004)
—— *World Economic Outlook October 2007: Globalization and Inequality* (Washington, DC, International Monetary Fund, 2007)
—— *World Economic Outlook 2012: Coping with High Debt and Sluggish Growth* (Washington, DC, International Monetary Fund, 2012)
International Organization for Migration, *Supplemental Materials* (International Dialogue on Migration Intersessional Workshop on Free Movement of Persons in Regional Integration Processes, Brussels, 18–19 June 2007)
International Textile, Garment and Leather Workers Federation, 'Government of Pakistan: The Sialkot Initiative' (ILO Tripartite Workshop, Islamabad, 21–22 February 2007)
International Trade Union Confederation, *Doing Business 2010: World Bank Discourages Extension of Social Protection* (Press Release, 9 September 2009)
—— *ILO-IMF Conference on Employment: Concrete Action Must Follow Announcement of Good Intentions* (Press Release, 14 September 2010)
—— *ITUC Calls on World Bank to Complete Overhaul of "Doing Business"* (Press Release, 5 November 2010)
—— *Mexico: Labour Legislation Reform Without Consultation* (Press Release, 6 April 2011)
Itschert, P, 'Multinationales, RSE et dialogue social-pour un renforcement mutuel' in I Daugareilh (ed), *La responsabilité sociale de l'entreprise transnationale et la globalisation de l'économie* (Brussels, Bruylant, 2010) 191
Javillier, J-C, 'The Employer and the Worker, the Need for a Comparative and International Perspective' in BA Langille and G Davidov (eds), *Boundaries and Frontiers of Labour Law* (Oxford, Hart Publishing, 2006) 355
Jayadev, A, 'Capital Account Openness and the Labour Share of Income' (2007) 31(3) *Cambridge Journal of Economics* 423
Jenkins, H, Lee, E and Rodgers, G, *The Quest for a Fair Globalization Three Years On: Assessing the Impact of the World Commission on the Social Dimension of Globalization* (Geneva, International Labour Organization and International Institute for Labour Studies, 2007)
Jenks, W, *L'OIT en temps de guerre* (Brochure Edited by the Canadian Department of Labour on the Occasion of the ILO's 50th Anniversary, 1969)
—— 'Universality and Ideology in the ILO' (Address at the Institute of International Studies, Geneva, 27 October 1969) reproduced in (1970) 1 *Annals of International Studies* 45
—— 'ILO Standards: Are They Obsolete, Premature, Marginal or Important' in ILO, *Social Policy in a Changing World: The ILO Response: Selected Speeches by Wilfred Jenks* (Geneva, International Labour Organization, 1976)

Johnston, A, 'EU-ILO Relations: Between Regional and Global Governance' in J Orbie and L Tortell (eds), *The European Union and the Social Dimension of Globalization: How the EU Influences the World* (London, Routledge, 2009) 81–97

Karbowski, J, 'Grocery Store Activism: A WTO Compliant Means to Incentivize Social Responsibility' (2008) 43(2) *Virginia Journal of International Law* 760

Kaufmann, C, *Globalisation and Labour Rights: The Conflict Between Core Labour Rights and International Economic Law* (Oxford, Oxford University Press, 2007)

Keune, M, 'EU Enlargement and Social Standards: Exporting the European Social Model' in J Orbie and L Tortell (eds), *The European Union and the Social Dimension of Globalization: How the EU Influences the World* (London, Routledge, 2009) 45–61

Kingsbury, B and Casini, L, 'Global Administrative Law Dimensions of International Organization Law' (2009) 6(2) *International Organizations Law Review* 319

Kolben, K, 'Trade, Monitoring, and the ILO: Working to Improve Conditions in Cambodia's Garment Factories' (2004) 7 *Yale Human Rights and Development Law Journal* 79

Koskenniemi, M and International Law Commission, *Fragmentation of International Law: Difficulties Arising from the Diversification and Expansion of International Law*, Report of the Study Group of the International Law Commission, A/CN.4/L.682 (13 April 2006)

Kristof, N, 'China sees "Market-Leninism" as way to future', *New York Times* (New York), 6 September 1993

——'Dreaming of sweatshops', *International Herald Tribune* (Paris), 5 January 2009

Kryvoi, Y, 'Why European Union Trade Sanctions Do Not Work' (2008) 12(2) *Minnesota Journal of International Law* 209

——'The World Bank and the ILO: Two Visions of Employment Regulation' in R Blanpain and C Grant (eds), *Fixed-Term Employment Contracts: A Comparative Study* (Bruges, Vanden Broele Publishers, 2009) 47–58

Kucera, D and Sarna, R, *How Do Trade Union Rights Affect Trade Competitiveness?*, International Labour Organization Policy Integration Department, Statistical Development and Analysis Group Working Paper No 39 (2004)

Kuijper, PJ, *Conflicting Rules and Clashing Courts: The Case of Environmental Agreements, Free Trade Agreements and the WTO*, International Centre for Trade and Sustainable Development Issue Paper No 10 (September 2010)

Kulish, N and Calmes, J, 'Obama bid for Europe trade pact stirs hope', *New York Times* (New York), 14 February 2013

Kysar, D, 'Preferences for Processes: The Process / Product Distinction and the Regulation of Consumer Choice' (2004) 118 *Harvard Law Review* 525

La Hovary, C, *Les droits fondamentaux au travail* (Paris, Presses Universitaires de France, 2009)

Lamy, P, 'The WTO Needs Your Scrutiny' (Steering Committee of the Parliamentary Conference on WTO, IPU Headquarters, 22–23 September 2005)

——'Quels leviers de régulation mondiale pour le social' (Roundtable of L'Observatoire Social International, Paris, 12 April 2010)

——'Lamy Says Trade Pacts Pose New Challenge to the Multilateral Trading System' (Launch of the *World Trade Report 2011*, 20 July 2011)

Langille, BA, 'The ILO and the New Economy: Recent Developments' (1999) 15(3) *International Journal of Comparative Labour Law and Industrial Relations* 229

——'Core Labour Rights: The True Story (Reply to Alston)' (2005) 16(3) *European Journal of International Law* 409

Langille, BA, 'The ILO is Not a State, Its Members are Not Firms' in G Politakis (ed), *Protecting Labour Rights as Human Rights: Present and Future of International Supervision* (Geneva, International Labour Organization, 2007) 247–56

——'Imagining Post-"Geneva Consensus" Labor Law for Post-"Washington Consensus" Development' (2010) 31 *Comparative Labor Law and Policy Journal* 523

Lee, E, 'Employment and Poverty Reduction' in G Rodgers and others, *The ILO and the Quest for Social Justice* (Geneva, International Labour Organization, 2009)

Leenknegt, P, *Social Labelling Legislation: At the Crossroads of Global Trade and Labour* (Lausanne, EDIS, 2007)

Lemoine, J, 'International Trade Regimes in Retrospect' in MA Boisard, E Chossudovsky and J Lemoine (eds), *Diplomatie multilatérale: système des Nations Unies à Genève: guide de travail* (The Hague, Kluwer Law International, 1998)

Livingston, J, *Against Thrift: Why Consumer Culture is Good for the Economy, the Environment, and Your Soul* (New York, Basic Books, 2011)

Lopez-Hurtado, C, 'Social Labelling and WTO Law' (2002) 5(3) *Journal of International Economic Law* 719

Lorenz, EC, *Defining Global Justice: The History of US International Labor Standards Policy* (Notre Dame, IN, University of Notre Dame Press, 2001)

Louis, M, 'Intégrer les marges', *La Vie des Idées* (Paris), 9 December 2010

——'The ILO's Helpdesk for Business on International Labour Standards: Using the NICT to Bring Multinational Enterprises Back in the Tripartite Regulation Game' (53rd Conference of the International Studies Association, San Diego, April 2011)

——*L'organisation internationale du travail et le travail décent: Un agenda social pour le multilatéralisme* (Paris, L'Harmattan, 2011)

Loureiro, ML, McCluskey, JJ and Mittelhammer, RC, 'Will Consumers Pay a Premium for Eco-Labeled Apples?' (2002) 36 *Journal of Consumer Affairs* 203

Luff, D, *Le droit de l'Organisation Mondiale du Commerce: Analyse critique* (Brussels, Bruylant, 2004)

Ma, Z, 'Industrial Relations in China: A Review Based on a Six-party Model' (2011) 150 (1–2) *International Labour Review* 145

Mainwaring, J, *The International Labour Organization: A Canadian View* (Ottawa, Canadian Government Publishing Centre, 1986)

Majid, N, 'The Working Poor in Developing Countries' (2001) 140(3) *International Labour Review* 271

Maljean-Dubois, S, 'Le spectre de l'isolation clinique: quelle articulation entre les règles de l'OMC et les autres instruments et principes internationaux' (Taiwan University National Conference, Taipei, 12 November 2007)

Marceau, G, 'WTO Dispute Settlement and Human Rights' (2002) 13 *European Journal of International Law* 756

——'Trade and Labour' in D Bethlehem and others (eds), *The Oxford Handbook of International Trade Law* (Oxford, Oxford University Press, 2009) 540–70

Marceau, G and Wyatt, J, 'The WTO's Efforts to Balance Economic Development and Environmental Protection: A Short Review of Appellate Body Jurisprudence' (2013) 1(1) *Latin American Journal of International Trade Law* 291

Maskus, KE, *Regulatory Standards in the WTO*, Peterson Institute for International Economics Working Paper 00-1 (2000)

——'Regulatory Standards in the WTO: Comparing Intellectual Property Rights with Competition Policy, Environmental Protection, and Core Labor Standards' (2002) 1(2) *World Trade Review* 135

Massiah, G, *Grandeur et décadence de l'ajustement structurel: Les programmes d'ajustement structurel et le développement* (Association internationale de techniciens, experts et chercheurs (AITEC), 2000)

Maul, D, *Human Rights, Development and Decolonization: The International Labour Organization, 1940–70* (Geneva, International Labour Organization, 2012)

Maupain, F, 'Fédéralisme et Conventions internationales du travail' (1987) 126(6) *International Labour Review* 701

——'La réforme de l'Organisation internationale du Travail' (1987) 33(33) *Annuaire français de droit international* 478

——'Particularismes institutionnels et vocation universelle: les défis croisés des relations CEE-OIT' (1990) 1190(1) *Revue générale de droit international public* 50

——'La succession à l'OIT' in G Burdeau and B Stern (eds), *Dissolution, continuation et succession en Europe de l'Est: succession d'États et relations économiques internationales* (Paris, Montchrestien, 1994)

——'L'OIT, la justice sociale et la mondialisation' (1999) 278 *Recueil des Cours de l'Académie de Droit International* 331

——'The Settlement of Disputes Within the International Labour Organization' (1999) 2(2) *Journal of International Economic Law* 273

——'International Labour Organization Recommendations and Similar Instruments' in D Shelton, *Commitment and Compliance: The Role of Non-Binding Norms in the International Legal System* (Oxford, Oxford University Press, 2000) 372

——'Mondialisation de l'économie et universalité de la protection des droits des travailleurs' in Institut René Cassin (ed), *Commerce mondial et protection des droits de l'homme: les droits de l'homme à l'épreuve de la globalisation des échanges économiques* (Brussels, Bruylant, 2001)

——'Le renouveau du débat normatif à l'OIT de la fin de la guerre froide à la mondialisation' (2001) *Bulletin de droit comparé du travail et de la sécurité sociale* 3

——'Persuasion et contrainte aux fins de la mise en œuvre des normes et objectifs de l'OIT' in G Politakis (ed), *Les normes internationales du travail: un patrimoine pour l'avenir. Mélanges en l'honneur de Nicolas Valticos* (Geneva, International Labour Organization, 2004) 687–709

——'Is the ILO Effective in Upholding Workers Right? Reflections on the Myanmar Experience' in P Alston (ed), *Labour Rights as Human Rights* (Oxford, Oxford University Press, 2005) 85

——'Revitalization Not Retreat: The Real Potential of the 1998 ILO Declaration for the Universal Protection of Workers' Rights' (2005) 16(3) *European Journal of International Law* 439

——'La "valeur ajoutée" de la Déclaration relative aux principes et droits fondamentaux au travail pour la cohérence et l'efficacité de l'action normative de l'OIT' in I Daugareilh (ed), *Mondialisation, travail et droits fondamentaux* (Brussels, Bruylant, 2005) 1

——'New Foundation or New Façade? The ILO and the 2008 Declaration on Social Justice for a Fair Globalization' (2009) 20(3) *European Journal of International Law* 823

——'Une Rolls Royce en mal de révision ? L'efficacité du système de supervision de l'OIT à l'approche de son centenaire' (2010) 3 *Revue générale de droit public* 465

Maupain, F, *L'OIT à l'épreuve* de la mondialisation financière, peut-on réguler sans contraindre? (Geneva, International Labour Organization, 2012)

Maurin, E, *La peur du déclassement: Une sociologie des récessions* (Paris, Seuil, 2009)

McConnell, M, Devlin, D and Doumbia-Henry, C, *The Maritime Labour Convention, 2006: A Legal Primer to an Emerging International Regime* (Leiden, Martinus Nijhoff Publishers, 2011)

McCune Lindsay, S, 'The Problem of American Cooperation' in J Shotwell (ed), *The Origins of the International Labor Organization* (Columbia, OH, Columbia University Press, 1934) vol 1, 331

McRae, D, 'The Place of the WTO in the International System' in D Bethlehem and others (eds), *The Oxford Handbook of International Trade Law* (Oxford, Oxford University Press, 2009) 54

Merrien, F-X, 'Nouveau régime économique international et devenir des États Providence' in P de Senarclens (ed), *Maîtriser la mondialisation: la régulation sociale internationale* (Paris, Presses de Sciences-Po, 2000) 77

Mestrum, F, 'La pauvreté multidimensionnelle: La dynamique sémantique dans le discours de la Banque mondiale' (2008) 88 *Mots* 2

Mickelson, K, 'Rhetoric and Rage: Third World Voices in International Legal Discourse' (1997–1998) 16(2) *Wisconsin International Law Journal* 353

Miller, D, 'Business as Usual? Governing the Supply Chain in Clothing: Post MFA Phase-Out: The Case of Cambodia' (2009) 1(1) *International Journal of Labour Research* 9

Montesquieu, C-L de Secondat, *The Spirit of Laws* (trans T Nugent, London, G Bell & Sons, 1914)

Moreau, M-A, *Normes sociales, droit du travail et mondialisation: confrontation and mutations* (Paris, Dalloz, 2006)

—— 'The Evolution of European Social Integration under Globalization' in A Blackett and C Lévesque (eds), *Social Regionalism in the Global Economy* (London, Routledge, 2011) 225

Morse, DA, *The Origin and Evolution of the I.L.O. and its Role in the World Community* (Ithaca, NY, Cornell University, 1969)

Moyers, B, 'Shades of Howard Zinn: It's OK if It's Impossible', *Common Dreams*, 2 November 2010

Myrdal, H-G, 'Social clause issue "practically dead"', *Financial Times* (London), 4 May 1995

Neal, AC, 'Corporate Social Responsibility: Governance Gain or Laissez-faire Figleaf' (2008) 29(4) *Comparative Labor Law and Policy Journal* 459

Novitz, T, 'The European Union and International Labour Standards: The Dynamics of the Dialogue Between the EU and the ILO' in P Alston (ed), *Labour Rights as Human Rights* (Oxford, Oxford University Press, 2005) 214

—— 'In Search of a Coherent Social Policy: EU Import and Export of ILO Labour Standards?' in J Orbie and L Tortell (eds), *The European Union and the Social Dimension of Globalization: How the EU Influences the World* (London, Routledge, 2009) 27

O'Brien, R, 'Organizational Politics, Multilateral Economic Organizations and Social Policy' (2002) 2(2) *Global Social Policy* 141

Orbie, J and Tortell, L, 'The New GSP+ Beneficiaries: Ticking the Box or Truly Consistent with ILO Findings?' (2009) 14 *European Foreign Affairs Review* 663

Orbie, J and Ville, F de, 'Core Labour Standards in the GSP Regime of the European Union: Overshadowed by Other Considerations' in T Novitz and C Fenwick (eds), *Human Rights at Work: Perspectives on Law and Regulation* (Oxford, Hart Publishing, 2010) 487

Organization for Economic Cooperation and Development, *OECD Jobs Study: Evidence and Explanations* (Paris, OECD, 1994) – *OECD Jobs Strategy: Pushing Ahead with the Strategy* (1996)

—— *Trade, Employment and Labour Standards: A Study of Core Workers' Rights and International Trade* (1996)

—— *International Trade and Core Labour Standards* (2000)

—— *Boosting Jobs and Incomes: Policy Lessons from Reassessing the OECD Jobs Strategy* (2006)

Organization for Economic Cooperation and Development and International Labour Organization, World Bank and World Trade Organization, *Seizing the Benefits of Trade for Employment and Growth: Final Report* (G20 Summit, Seoul, 11–12 November 2010)

Padoa-Schioppa, T, 'La crise en perspective: rester tranquille a un coût' (2009) 125 *Commentaire* 9

Palacio, A, 'The Way Forward: Human Rights and the World Bank' (Washington, DC, World Bank, 2006)

Papadakis, K (ed), *Shaping Global Industrial Relations: The Impact of International Framework Agreements* (London, Palgrave Macmillan, 2011)

Peeters, A, 'La responsabilité sociale des entreprises' (March 2004) 1828 *Courrier hebdomadaire du CRISP* 1

Peters, J, 'The Rise of Finance and the Decline of Organized Labour in the Advanced Capitalist Countries' (2011) 16(1) *New Political Economy* 73

Piore, MJ, 'Flexible Bureaucracies in Labor Market Regulation' in G Davidov and BA Langille (eds), *The Idea of Labour Law* (Oxford, Oxford University Press, 2011) 385

Piore, MJ and Schrank, A, 'Trading Up? An Embryonic Model for Easing the Human Costs of Free Markets' (2006) 31(5) *Boston Review* 11

—— 'Toward Managed Flexibility: The Revival of Labor Inspection in the Latin World' (2008) 147(1) *International Labour Review* 1

Polaski, S, 'Protecting Labor Rights Through Trade Agreements: An Analytical Guide' (2004) 10(13) *Journal of International Law and Policy* 13

—— *Harnessing Global Forces to Create Decent Work in Cambodia*, International Institute of Labour Studies/Better Work Research Series 119 (2009)

Politakis, G, 'Deconstructing Flexibility in International Labour Conventions' in G Politakis (ed), *Les normes internationales du travail: un patrimoine pour l'avenir. Mélanges en l'honneur de Nicolas Valticos* (Geneva, International Labour Organization 2004) 463

Rainey, S, 'Britons are "lazy" and "addicted to benefits", China claims', *The Telegraph* (London), 20 October 2011

Rajan, R, *Fault Lines: How Hidden Fractures Still Threaten the World Economy* (Princeton, NJ, Princeton University Press, 2010)

Rampell, C, 'US jobless stay silent despite bleak prospects', *International Herald Tribune* (Paris), 11 July 2011

Rasche, A and Kell, G (eds), *The United Nations Global Compact: Achievements, Trends and Challenges* (Cambridge, Cambridge University Press, 2010)

Rawls, J, *The Law of Peoples* (Cambridge, MA, Harvard University Press, 1999)

Rehn, O, 'Austerity is working: Europe must stay the course', *Financial Times* (London), 11 December 2012

Reich, RB, *Supercapitalism: The Transformation of Business, Democracy and Everyday Life* (New York, Knopf, 2007)

Reverchon, A, 'Interview with Michel Capron: La comptabilité vire au vert', *Le Monde* (Paris), 29 September 2010

Riesman, D, 'The Constitution of the United States and International Labor Legislation' (1941) 44(2) *International Labour Review* 123

Rittich, K, 'Core Labour Rights and Labor Market Flexibility: Two Paths Entwined?' in International Bureau of the Permanent Court of Arbitration (ed), *Labor Law Beyond Borders: ADR and the Internationalization of Labor Dispute Settlement* (The Hague, Kluwer Law International, 2003) 157

——'Rights, Risk, and Reward: Governance Norms in the International Order and the Problem of Precarious Work' in J Fudge and RJ Owens (eds), *Precarious Work, Women, and the New Economy: The Challenge to Legal Norms* (Oxford, Hart Publishing, 2006) 31

——'Global Labour Policy as Social Policy' (2008) 14(2) *Canadian Labour and Employment Law Journal* 272

Rodrik, D, *The Globalization Paradox: Democracy and the Future of the World Economy* (New York, WW Norton & Company, 2011)

Roessler, F, 'Domestic Policy Objectives and the Multilateral Trade Order: Lessons from the Past' in AO Krueger (ed), *The WTO as an International Organization* (Chicago, IL, University of Chicago Press, 1998) 213

Roht-Arriaza, N, 'Soft Law in a Hybrid Organization: The International Organization for Standardization' in D Shelton, *Commitment and Compliance: The Role of Non-Binding Norms in the International Legal System* (Oxford, Oxford University Press, 2000) 263

Rousseau, J-J, *The Social Contract* (trans GDH Cole, Dover, Mineola, 2003)

Ruggie, JG, 'International Regimes, Transactions, and Change: Embedded Liberalism in the Postwar Economic Order' (1982) 36(2) *International Organization* 379

—— *Taking Embedded Liberalism Global: The Corporate Connection*, New York University International Law and Justice Working Paper 2003/2 (2003)

——'Business and Human Rights: The Evolving International Agenda' (2007) 101(4) *American Journal of International Law* 819

Ryder, G, 'The Promise of the United Nations Global Compact: A Trade Union Perspective on the Labour Principles' in A Rasche and G Kell (eds), *The United Nations Global Compact: Achievements, Trends and Challenges* (Cambridge, Cambridge University Press, 2010) 44

Saith, A, 'Reflections: Louis Emmerij' (2005) 36(6) *Development and Change* 1163

Samet, AJ, 'Doha and Global Labor Standards: The Agenda Item that Wasn't' (2003) 37(3) *International Lawyer* 757

Samson, K, 'The Protection of Economic and Social Rights Within the Framework of the International Labour Organization' in F Matscher, *Implementation of Economic and Social Rights: National, International and Comparative Aspects* (Kehl Am Rhein, Engel Verlag, 1991) 123

Santos, A, 'Labor Flexibility, Legal Reform and Economic Development' (2009) 50 *Virginia Journal of International Law* 43

Sapir, J, *La démondialisation* (Paris, Seuil, 2011)

Sarfaty, G, 'Why Culture Matters in International Institutions: The Marginality of Human Rights at the World Bank' (2009) 103 *American Journal of International Law* 647

Sarkozy, N, President of the French Republic, 'Address to the International Labour Conference, 15 June 2009' reproduced in ILO, *Provisional Record* (ILC, 98th Session, 11th Sitting, Geneva, 15 June 2009) 11A/20

——'Speech delivered to the 40th World Economic Forum' (40th World Economic Forum, Davos, 27 January 2010)

Scelle, G, *L'Organisation internationale du travail et le BIT* (Paris, Editions M Rivière, 1930)

Schalter, M, 'Reconciliation Between Fundamental Social Rights and Economic Freedoms' (Conference on Fundamental Social Rights and the Posting of Workers in the Framework of the Single Market, Brussels, June 2011)

Scheuerman, W, *Liberal Democracy and the Social Acceleration of Time* (Baltimore, MD, Johns Hopkins University Press, 2004)

Seidman, G, *Beyond the Boycott: Labor Rights, Human Rights and Transnational Activism* (New York, Russell Sage Foundation, 2007)

Sen, A, *Development as Freedom* (New York, Knopf, 1999)

—— *The Idea of Justice* (Cambridge, MA, Belknap Press, 2009)

Senarclens, P de, *Mondialisation, souveraineté et théories des relations internationales* (Paris, Armand Colin, 1998)

Servais, J-M, 'Flexibility and Rigidity in International Labour Standards' (1986) 125(2) *International Labour Review* 193

Shaw, D and Clarke, I, 'Belief Formation in Ethical Consumer Groups: An Exploratory Study' (1999) 17(2) *Marketing Intelligence and Planning* 109

Sherman, S, 'The brawl over fair trade coffee', *The Nation* (New York), 10 September 2012

Shihata, I, *The World Bank in a Changing World* (Leiden, Martinus Nijhoff Publishers, 1998) vol 2

Shotwell, JT, *The Origins of the International Labour Organization* (New York, Columbia University Press, 1934) vol 1

Siroën, J-M and others, *The Use, Scope and Effectiveness of Labour and Social Aspects and Sustainable Development Provisions in Bilateral and Regional Free Trade Agreements*, Final Report of the European Commission (2008)

Silverstein, K, 'Shopping for sweat: the human cost of a two-dollar T-shirt', *Harper's Magazine* (New York), January 2010

Smith, A, *The Commerce Power in Canada and the United States* (Toronto, Butterworths, 1963)

Social Protection Floor Advisory Group, *Social Protection Floor for a Fair and Inclusive Globalization* (Geneva, International Labour Organization, 2011)

Sohn, LB, 'The Contribution of the International Labour Organization to the Concept of Economic, Social and Cultural Rights' in R-J Dupuy and L-A Sicilianos (eds), *Mélanges en l'honneur de Nicolas Valticos: droit et justice* (Paris, Pedone, 1999) 595

Spiro, PJ, 'Resurrecting Missouri v. Holland' (2008) 73 *Missouri Law Review* 1029

Standing, G, 'The ILO: An Agency for Globalization?' (2008) 39 *Development and Change* 355

Strange, S, 'L'échec des Etats face à la mondialisation' (December 2011) 308 *Esprit* 62

Supiot, A (ed), *Beyond Employment: Changes in Work and the Future of Labour Law in Europe* (Paris, Flammarion, 1999)

——'Du nouveau au self-service normatif: La responsabilité sociale des entreprises' in A Arsequel and others, *Etudes offertes à Jean Pélissier: Analyse juridique et valeurs en droit social* (Paris, Dalloz, 2004) 541

——'La place de la sécurité sociale dans le système des normes internationales du travail' in A Supiot (ed), *Protection sociale et travail décent: Nouvelles perspectives pour les normes internationales du travail* (Supplement No 1272, *Semaine Sociale Lamy*, 2006) 7

——'Voilà l'économie communiste de marché', *Le Monde* (Paris), 25 January 2008

Supiot, A *L'esprit de Philadelphie: La justice sociale face au marché total* (Paris, Seuil, 2010)
Taylor, R, 'WTO urged to stress labour standards', *Financial Times* (London), 9 March 1995
Teisl, MF, Roe, B and Levy, AS, 'Eco-certification: Why it May Not be a Field of Dreams' (1999) 81 *American Journal of Agricultural Economics* 1066
Thomas, A, 'The International Labour Organization: Its Origins, Development and Future' (1921) 1 *International Labour Review* 5
—— 'Justice sociale et paix universelle', *Revue de Paris* (Paris), 15 March 1924
—— *International Social Policy* (Geneva, International Labour Organization, 1948)
Torres, R, *Towards a Socially Sustainable Global Economy: An Analysis of the Social Pillars of Globalization*, Studies on the Social Dimensions of Globalization, Geneva, International Labour Organization (2001)
Tortell, L, Delarue, R and Kenner, J, 'The EU and the ILO Maritime Labour Convention: "In our Common Interest and in the Interest of the World"' in J Orbie and L Tortell (eds), *The European Union and the Social Dimension of Globalization: How the EU Influences the World* (London, Routledge, 2009)
Trebilcock, A (ed), *Labour and Employment Implications of the ASEAN Free Trade Agreements* (Geneva, International Labour Organization, 2005)
Trebilcock, MJ and Howse, R, *The Regulation of International Trade*, 3rd edn (London, Routledge, 2005)
Trubek, DM, Mosher, J and Rothstein, JS, 'Transnationalism in the Regulation of Labor Relations: International Regimes and Transnational Advocacy Networks' (2000) 25 *Law and Social Inquiry* 1187
Tsogas, G, 'Labour Standards in International Trade Agreements: An Assessment of the Arguments' (1999) 10(2) *International Journal of Human Resources Management* 351
United Nations Development Programme, *Human Development Report 2010: The Real Wealth of Nations: Pathways to Human Development* (New York, UNDP, 2010)
—— *Sustainability and Equity: A Better Future for All* (New York, UNDP, 2011)
United States Trade Representative, *Statement from USTR Spokesman Regarding China Labor Petition* (Press Release, 21 July 2006)
—— *Bipartisan Agreement on Trade Policy* (May 2007)
—— *Jobs on the Way: U.S.-Korea Trade Agreement Enters into Force* (Press Release, 15 March 2011)
—— *Colombian Action Plan Related to Labor Rights* (7 April 2011)
—— *Statement by U.S. Trade Representative Ron Kirk on Presidential Signature of Trade Legislation* (Press Release, 10 October 2011)
Valor, C, 'Can Consumers Buy Responsibly? Analysis and Solutions for Market Failures' (2008) 31 *Journal of Consumer Policy* 315
Valticos, N, 'La Charte sociale européenne: sa structure, son contenu, le contrôle de son application' (September–October 1963) 26 *Droit social* 466
—— *Droit international du travail*, 2nd edn (Paris, Dalloz, 1983)
—— 'The Nature and Scope of the Legal Ratification of International Labour Conventions' in Y Dinstein (ed), *International Law at a Time of Perplexity: Essays in Honour of Shabtai Rosenne* (Dodrecht, Martinus Nijhoff, 1989) 987
Van Daele, J and others, *ILO Histories: Essays on the International Labour Organization and Its Impact on the World During the Twentieth Century* (Bern, Peter Lang, 2010)
Van Griethuysen, P, 'La RSE: nouvelle régulation du capitalisme ou interprétation capitaliste de la régulation?' in I Daugareilh (ed), *La responsabilité sociale de l'entreprise transnationale et la globalisation de l'économie* (Brussels, Bruylant, 2010) 113

Van Roozendaal, G, 'Social Challenges to Trade: Trade Unions and the Debate on International Labour Standards' (DPhil thesis, University of Amsterdam, 2001)

Vosko, L, *Managing the Margins: Gender, Citizenship, and the International Regulation of Precarious Employment* (Oxford, Oxford University Press, 2010)

Weiss, F, 'Coherence in International Law and Organization' (Presentation to the International Labour Organization, Geneva, 27 November 2011)

Weiss, M, 'Two Steps Forward, One Step Back – Or Vice Versa: Labor Rights Under Free Trade Agreements from NAFTA, Through Jordan, via Chile, to Latin America, and Beyond' (2003) 37(3) *University of San Francisco Law Review* 689

Wells, D, '"Best Practice" in the Regulation of International Labor Standards: Lessons of the US-Cambodia Textile Agreement' (2006) 27(3) *Comparative Labor Law and Policy Journal* 358

Wolf, M, 'Growth requires painful choices, not platitudes', *Financial Times* (London), 2 March 2004

Wolfehnson, J, 'The Other Crisis' (Speech to the Board of Governors of the International Monetary Fund, 6 October 1998)

World Bank, *Core Labor Standards and the World Bank* (2000)

—— *Development and Human Rights: The Role of the World Bank* (1998)

—— *Human Rights Indicators in Development: An Introduction* (2010)

—— *MILES: A Multi-Sector Approach to Foster Job Creation, Poverty Reduction and Growth* (4 October 2007)

—— *World Development Report 1995: Workers in an Integrating World* (New York, Oxford University Press, 1995)

—— *World Development Report 2013: Jobs* (Washington, DC, World Bank, 2013)World Bank and International Finance Corporation, *Doing Business 2011: Making a Difference for Entrepreneurs* (Washington, DC, World Bank, 2011)

—— *Doing Business 2013: Smarter Regulations for Small and Medium-Size Enterprises* (Washington, DC, World Bank, 2013)

World Commission on the Social Dimension of Globalization, *A Fair Globalization: Creating Opportunities for All* (Geneva, International Labour Organization, 2004)

—— *World Trade Report 2011: The WTO and Preferential Trade Agreements: From Co-existence to Coherence* (2011)

World Commission on the Social Dimension of Globalization and International Labour Organization, *Trade and Employment: Challenges for Policy Research* (2007)

World Trade Organization, *Singapore WTO Ministerial 1996: Ministerial Declaration* (13 December 1996)

Zhou, Weifeng and Cuyvers, L, 'Linking International Trade and Labour Standards: The Effectiveness of Sanctions under the European Union's GSP' (2011) 45(1) *Journal of World Trade* 63

Zhou, Weihuan, '*US – Clove Cigarettes* and *US – Tuna II (Mexico)*: Implications for the Role of Regulatory Purpose under Article III:4 of the GATT' (2012) 15(4) *Journal of International Economic Law* 1075

Zoellick, RB, World Bank Group President, 'Speech at the International Labour Organization' (International Labour Organization, Geneva, 17 March 2008)

Zumbansen, P, 'The Parallel Worlds of Corporate Governance and Labor Law' (2006) 13 *Indiana Journal of Global Legal Studies* 261

International materials

European Commission, Proposal for a Council Regulation on the exercise of the right to take collective action within the context of the freedom of establishment and the freedom to provide services, COM(2012)130

—— *Report on the EU Contribution to the Promotion of Decent Work in the World* (2 July 2008)

—— *Towards a Single Market Act: For a Highly Competitive Social Market Economy* COM (2010) 608 final

Expert Meeting on Trade Policy and Application of International Labour Standards, *The Belgian Social Label and Dutch Proposal to Ban Child Labour Imports: Effectiveness and Legality According to ILO and WTO Criteria* (Graduate Institute, Centre for Trade and Economic Integration, Geneva, 26–27 February 2009)

G8, *G8 Leaders Declaration: Responsible Leadership for a Sustainable Future* (G8 Summit, L'Aquila, 8 July 2009)

G20, *G20 Leaders Statement* (G20 Summit, Pittsburg, 24–25 September 2009)

—— *Labour and Employment Ministers' Conclusions* (G20 Meeting, Paris, 26–27 September 2011)

—— *Cannes Summit Final Declaration: Building Our Common Future: Renewed Collective Action for the Benefit of All* (G20 Summit, Cannes, 4 November 2011)

—— *Labour and Employment Ministers' Conclusions* (G20 Meeting, Guadalajara, 17–18 May 2012)

—— *G20 Leaders Declaration* (G20 Meeting, Los Cabos, 18–19 June 2012)

—— *The Los Cabos Growth and Jobs Action Plan* (19 June 2012)

GATT, *Report on the Accession of Japan* (Special Committee on Agenda and Intersessional Business, GATT doc L/76, 13 February 1953)

—— *Worker Rights* (Preparatory Committee, GATT doc PrepCom(86)W/43, 25 June 1986)

—— *Differential and More Favourable Treatment, Reciprocity and Fuller Participation of Developing Countries* (GATT BISD 26S/210, 1979)

—— Communication of the United States Concerning the Relationship between International Human Rights Workers and International Trade (GATT doc C/M/2/12, 6 August 1987)

International Organization of Employers, *IOE Position on the Final Draft International Standard (FDIS) of the ISO 26000 Guidance on Social Responsibility* (10 September 2010)

United Nations, *Programme of Action of the World Summit for Social Development* (World Summit for Social Development, Copenhagen, 6–12 March 1995)

—— *Report of the World Summit on Social Development* (19 April 1995) A/CONF.166/9

—— *Economic Uncertainty, Fiscal Austerity Not Excuses for Doing Less, But Reasons to Do More, Secretary-General Says, in Message for Poverty Eradication Day* (Press Release, 12 October 2010) SG/SM/13176, DEV/2839, OBV/922

INDEX